FrontPage 2003

THE MISSING MANUAL

*The book that
should have been
in the box*

D1416219

Other resources from O'Reilly

Related titles
Creating Web Sites: The Missing Manual

Web Design in a Nutshell, Second Edition

HTML and XHTML: The Definitive Guide, Fifth Edition

Learning Web Design, Second Edition

HTML Pocket Reference, Second Edition

Dreamweaver MX 2004: The Missing Manual

oreilly.com
oreilly.com is more than a complete catalog of O'Reilly books. You'll also find links to news, events, articles, weblogs, sample chapters, and code examples.

oreillynet.com is the essential portal for developers interested in open and emerging technologies, including new platforms, programming languages, and operating systems.

Conferences
O'Reilly brings diverse innovators together to nurture the ideas that spark revolutionary industries. We specialize in documenting the latest tools and systems, translating the innovator's knowledge into useful skills for those in the trenches. Visit *conferences.oreilly.com* for our upcoming events.

Safari Bookshelf (*safari.oreilly.com*) is the premier online reference library for programmers and IT professionals. Conduct searches across more than 1,000 books. Subscribers can zero in on answers to time-critical questions in a matter of seconds. Read the books on your Bookshelf from cover to cover or simply flip to the page you need. Try it today with a free trial.

FrontPage 2003
THE MISSING MANUAL

Jessica Mantaro

POGUE PRESS™
O'REILLY®

Beijing · Cambridge · Farnham · Köln · Paris · Sebastopol · Taipei · Tokyo

FrontPage 2003: The Missing Manual
by Jessica Mantaro

Published by O'Reilly Media, Inc., 1005 Gravenstein Highway North, Sebastopol, CA 95472.

O'Reilly books may be purchased for educational, business, or sales promotional use. Online editions are also available for most titles (*safari.oreilly.com*). For more information, contact our corporate/institutional sales department: (800) 998-9938 or *corporate@oreilly.com*.

Editor:	Peter Meyers
Production Editor:	Mary Brady
Cover Designer:	Ellie Volckhausen
Interior Designer:	David Futato

Printing History:

August 2005:	First Edition.

 This book uses RepKover,™ a durable and flexible lay-flat binding.

ISBN: 0-596-00950-X

[M]

Table of Contents

Part Three: Building and Managing a Web Site

Part Four: Forms and Databases

Part Five: FrontPage and Microsoft Office 2003

Part Six: Appendix

The Missing Credits

About the Author

 Jessica Mantaro is an experienced technical writer who has also worked as an instructor, training professionals to use Microsoft FrontPage. She is now a freelance writer living in New England. Prior to all that, she spent time in New York's art world, where she toiled to boost technical savvy among the old-fashioned and inexperienced.

About the Creative Team

Peter Meyers (editor) works as an editor at O'Reilly Media on the Missing Manual series. He lives with his wife and cat in New York City. Email: *peter.meyers@gmail. com*.

Linley Dolby (copy editor) spent several years in the production department at O'Reilly before moving to Martha's Vineyard to pursue a freelance career. She now helps whip technical books into shape for several companies, including O'Reilly and Pogue Press. Email: *linley@gremlinley.com*.

Chris Leeds (technical reviewer) is a long-time digital photographer and Web enthusiast. He's a Microsoft MVP, and a member of both the International Webmaster's Association and the HTML Writer's Guild. Chris has recently released a software product that allows Webmasters to easily create Web sites that can be edited and managed with just a browser. See *http://ContentSeed.com/*.

Kathleen Anderson (technical reviewer) started using FrontPage in 1997 and thinks the next version can't possibly be any better the last, but it always is. She is known in some circles as the "Database Wizard Queen" and in others as the "Accessibility Diva." You can reach Kathleen by email at *spiderwebwoman@mvps.org*.

Rose Cassano (cover illustration) has worked as an independent designer and illustrator for 20 years. Assignments have ranged from the nonprofit sector to corporate clientele. She lives in beautiful Southern Oregon, grateful for the miracles of modern technology that make working there a reality. Email: *cassano@highstream. net*. Web: *www.rosecassano.com*.

Acknowledgements

Heaps of gratitude to Peter Meyers, whose edits and guidance have improved this book enormously. Additional credit goes to Kathleen Anderson and Chris Leeds for sharing their expertise so generously. Thanks too to my agent, Lynn Palmer, to Sarah Milstein, and to Gus for his steadfast companionship throughout this project. A lifetime of appreciation goes to my mom and dad for making everything possible. Special thanks to Dani for making it a joy.

The Missing Manual Series

Missing Manuals are witty, superbly written guides to computer products that don't come with printed manuals (which is just about all of them). Each book features a handcrafted index; cross-references to specific page numbers (not just "see Chapter 14"); and RepKover, a detached-spine binding that lets the book lie perfectly flat without the assistance of weights or cinder blocks.

Recent and upcoming titles include:

Creating Web Sites: The Missing Manual by Matthew MacDonald

Dreamweaver MX 2004: The Missing Manual by David Sawyer McFarland

Windows XP Home Edition: The Missing Manual by David Pogue

Windows XP Pro: The Missing Manual by David Pogue, Craig Zacker, and

Linda Zacker

Google: The Missing Manual by Sarah Milstein and Rael Dornfest

eBay: The Missing Manual by Nancy Conner

Home Networking: The Missing Manual by Scott Lowe

Excel: The Missing Manual by Matthew MacDonald

Windows 2000 Pro: The Missing Manual by Sharon Crawford

Photoshop Elements 3: The Missing Manual by Barbara Brundage

QuickBooks 2005: The Missing Manual by Bonnie Biafore

Introduction

These days, almost everybody's got a Web site—from your local sewing circle to the world's largest corporations. So, why not you? Maybe you're finally ready to put up that family Web site or get your shop online. Or perhaps it's just time the world knew more about your pet llama collection. Whatever the reason, FrontPage 2003 has everything you need to join the crowd. The program is ready to help a little, or a lot—whichever you please.

If you're the kind of person who likes everything done lickety-split, with a minimum of technical fussing, FrontPage is your dream come true. Answer a few questions, and FrontPage will create your entire Web site for you. (Really.) If you're not ready to cede quite that much control, you can ask the program to handle only those jobs you don't care to do yourself. For example, FrontPage can help the design-challenged add an eye-pleasingly coordinated set of colors, fonts, and buttons throughout your site.

On the other hand, maybe you're a do-it-yourself type with very specific ideas about what should go into your site and how everything should look. If that's the case, FrontPage's cookie-cutter solutions probably aren't flexible enough to suit you. In fact, the program's reputation for automating everything may even disturb you a bit. Don't worry. You can bypass the canned options and create a completely custom site. The latest release of FrontPage includes new features that make it easy to create a site from scratch. In short: if you're a Web purist, the program is now better than ever at getting out of your way.

The main goal of this book is to lay out all your options clearly. Once you know what FrontPage 2003 has to offer, you can decide which tools are right for you.

What FrontPage Does

In the early days of the Web, anyone who

wanted to create a site had to know *HTML,* the programming language of the Web. While HTML (short for Hypertext Markup Language) is relatively simple, learning it can still take a fair amount of time.

Some companies like Microsoft saw an opportunity to make Web site creation easier and more intuitive. FrontPage provides lots of guidance and assistance to both beginning and advanced Web authors. Simple menus and toolbars let you create complex page elements with one click of the mouse. For example, instead of needing to write out a line of HTML to insert a picture, FrontPage lets you do this with just a click of a toolbar button. Behind the scenes, the program takes your commands and converts them into HTML. Even someone who's never heard of HTML can create an entire Web site. FrontPage handles the dirty work.

FrontPage also helps you picture what your Web pages are going to look like while you're creating them. As you insert pictures and text, they appear in FrontPage more or less as they'll eventually display in a Web browser. You may hear people refer to FrontPage as a *WYSIWYG* (pronounced wizzy-wig) editing program. WYSIWYG stands for "What You See Is What You Get." In other words, FrontPage shows you what you're creating as you work, which isn't possible if you're writing out HTML code like people did back in the dark ages of the last millennium.

Of all the things FrontPage brings to the table, this visual working mode is really the core benefit. But by no means is that the whole story. FrontPage offers many other powerful and time-saving tools, including:

- **Site management.** As a site gets bigger, keeping track of hyperlinks, image files, and outdated pages can turn into a logistical nightmare. FrontPage helps you tame the monster you created. The program's tracking tools and reports do things like find broken links and help reorganize your files. You're bound to use these site management tools again and again.

- **Site publishing.** Of course, you can create, edit, and manage a Web site with FrontPage, but at some point, you're going to need to get it off your computer and out onto the Web. That's where FrontPage's publishing feature comes in, which lets you upload your site to a live Web server. The key benefit? You won't need to buy separate software for this purpose.

- **Templates and wizards.** FrontPage has, for better or for worse, just about automated the creation of pages and sites. In some instances, the program creates an entire Web site at the click of a button, and all you have to do is slug in the text and images you want to use. While the results aren't going to win any design awards, the program has helped even total greenhorns get started quickly.

- **Collaboration tools.** Often, multiple people work on the same Web site. How do you avoid confusion over who's working on what? FrontPage provides tools that track tasks and unfinished pages. Sometimes, as the number of content contributors increases, so do a site's unexpected errors. To help you avoid slip-ups, the program includes additional collaboration aids, like dynamic page templates, which allow you to protect certain areas of a page from a careless colleague.

- **Integration with Microsoft Office.** You may need to move files or portions of files from other Microsoft Office programs into FrontPage. As you might expect, the program handles this easily, which is especially helpful if you're collaborating with coworkers who are using Microsoft Word or Excel.

What's New in FrontPage 2003

When you tell your geek friends that you're using FrontPage to create your Web site, you're likely to get disparaging looks, if not outright howls at your Web naiveté. The truth is, FrontPage has a tarnished reputation with most Web professionals. Older versions of the program spat out messy and overloaded HTML code, which meant that pages would take a long time to load in most Web browsers or not even load at all. Also, up until now, a FrontPage author couldn't collaborate on a site with people who used other Web development tools, such as Macromedia's Dreamweaver. Microsoft has been listening to the complaints and has actually addressed a lot of old shortcomings in the new version. The 2003 release introduces an HTML cleanup tool that helps alleviate the bloated code problem, and FrontPage is now on speaking terms with other Web editors.

Here are some of the new features you'll find in FrontPage 2003:

- **HTML Split view** lets you see the visual layout of a page (Design view) alongside its HTML code (Code view). Viewing both sides of the page simultaneously like this is a great way to learn HTML. Plus, whenever you highlight an element in Design view, FrontPage highlights the corresponding HTML code.

- **HTML Cleanup** is a new and most welcome addition to the program. The Optimize HTML feature clears out extraneous code created by the program. The result? Faster page downloads.

- **Quick Tag Selector** displays HTML tags that are active while you're working in Design view. This handy toolbar saves you the trouble of switching to Code view and having to search through heaps of HTML. Use it to select and edit HTML tags with a simple click.

- **XML** (Extensible Markup Language) is a coding language that's a lot like HTML except it holds data instead of Web page content. In a way, XML is like an all-text database, which makes it very flexible—no special software necessary. Not surprisingly, its popularity is growing fast. FrontPage now recognizes XML as a data source. (As long as you have the right software on your Web server, that is—see Chapter 13.)

- **Macromedia Flash** is now better integrated into FrontPage, which lets you drag Flash movies directly onto your Web page.

- **Find and Replace** can help you find items within HTML and also do more complex searches based not only on specific text, but even patterns of text.

- **Expanded publishing options** include the ability to publish via FTP and Web-DAV. (Turn to page 255 if you can't wait to find out what these are.) Previously, FrontPage publishing worked well only with Microsoft-compatible Web servers. Thanks to improved FTP options and the addition of WebDAV, a FrontPage-authored site can now venture out of Microsoft-land and live on any Web server. (As long as the site is plain vanilla with no special FrontPage functionality—but more on that later.) A side benefit is that FrontPage now works more smoothly with other editors such as Macromedia's Dreamweaver.

- **Browser compatibility tools** now include the ability to design your pages for specific browsers and preview them at different screen resolutions.

- **Layout tables** can help you structure and design your page. Microsoft created this feature as an improvement on the traditional HTML table. Unlike their predecessors, these new tables give you pixel-precise control over page layout.

- **Dynamic Web Templates** feature editable as well as noneditable regions. In other words, you can limit the damage a colleague might do by granting rights to edit only certain sections of a page.

- **Themes** are prepackaged visual element collections—like color, font, and page background—that let you automatically standardize the look of a site. FrontPage now applies themes using CSS (Cascading Style Sheets). You'll read all about CSS in Chapter 7. For the moment, all you need to know is that CSS helps pages download faster and look better.

- **Accessibility Checker** is a new feature that lets you make sure that visitors of all abilities—including the visually impaired—can read and use your Web site. The Worldwide Web Consortium (W3C) sets the accessibility standards that FrontPage's checker uses. Since it's difficult to check pages produced by FrontPage in the W3C's online code validator, this is an especially welcome addition to the program. You can read all about this tool in Chapter 12.

HTML 101

FrontPage is about to work miracles for you, but what's going on behind the curtain doesn't have to remain a complete mystery. In fact, even if you don't plan on writing one iota of HTML, familiarity with the language's basics can help you understand why FrontPage behaves the way it does. What follows is an ultra-fast HTML primer. It's quite a bit less than you'd actually need to write your own Web pages by hand, but it'll get you started if you need to take a peek at some of the HTML that FrontPage generates.

A Web page is nothing more than a simple text file containing HTML. When a Web browser summons an HTML file, it transforms this HTML into the kind of Web pages you're used to looking at online. You could actually create your entire site using only Notepad, Windows's bare-bones text editor.

Inside every HTML document you'll find two kinds of information: the actual *content* that appears in a Web browser ("Ike's Trip to Patagonia" and everything he has to say about it, for example) and some strange-looking fragments of text enclosed in brackets (< >) that are called HTML *tags*. These tags tell browsers how to display your content: how big it should be, how it should be formatted, and so on. Tags are easy to pick out. Just look for the brackets (< >) in this sample HTML page:

```
<html>

<head>
<title>Sample HTML Document</title>
</head>

<body>
<p>
This is sample text on a sample page.
Text can be <b>bold</b> or <i>italic</i> or plain.
</p>
</body>

</html>
```

Here's a breakdown of what's happening in that mini Web page:

- The <html> tag tells the browser what kind of document it has encountered.

- The <head> tags contain basic information about the page. For example, the document title appears here. (The text of the title appears between its own <title> tags so a browser can find and display it.) If this were a more complex page, the head might also include some style information or even a script that animates text or pictures.

- The <body> tags surround the star of the show: the content of your page. Everything between these tags is what viewers will see in their browsers.

- <p> indicates the beginning of a paragraph and </p> the end of the paragraph.

A tag actually consists of two parts: an opening tag and a closing tag. The closing tag is identical to the opening tag except that it contains a forward slash (/). When a browser comes across an opening tag, like the <b> bold tag in the example above, it applies the tag to everything that follows until the closing tag appears. In other words, tags enclose all the content they affect. So, all text between the opening <b> bold tag and the closing </b> bold tag will appear as bolded text. As you can see in the code just shown, each tag has an accompanying closing tag somewhere. The closing tag can be one character away or miles down the page. For instance, the closing </html> tag doesn't appear until the end of the document. That's because everything between the <html> tags is HTML. There are a few tags that don't require a closing tag, but they're the exception to the rule.

If you want to see more examples of HTML, just hop online. You can view the HTML code of any page on the Web. Depending on what browser you're using, select View → Source or View → Page Source, and a separate window opens displaying the page's HTML code.

About This Book

After buying FrontPage, you shook the box to find the manual...but only a flimsy pamphlet fell out onto the floor. Alas, Microsoft doesn't offer much in the way of operating instructions. They expect you to consult the program's online Help file, which can provide useful instructions on some topics, but leaves out a lot of important information. For example, the Help file tells you how to autostretch a table column, but not what autostretch means or why you might want to do it.

This book is the manual that should have been in the box. The chapters that follow put features in context and discuss their merits frankly and clearly. Wherever possible, explanations provide shortcuts, workarounds, and plain common sense. Try to find *that* in a Help file.

Note: This book periodically recommends *other* books, covering topics that are too specialized or tangential for a manual about FrontPage. Careful readers may notice that not every one of these titles is published by Missing Manual–parent, O'Reilly Media. While we're happy to mention other Missing Manuals and books in the O'Reilly family, if there's a great book out there that doesn't happen to be published by O'Reilly, we'll still let you know about it.

FrontPage 2003: The Missing Manual is meant for readers of all technical levels. If you don't have much Web experience, you'll want to consult sidebar topics titled "Up to Speed" that provide novices with some useful background information. Tech-savvy readers can check out more advanced sidebars called "Power Users' Clinic" for special tips and insights meant for you.

About the Outline

FrontPage 2003: The Missing Manual is divided into five parts, each containing several chapters:

• **Part 1, Creating a Basic Web Page,** begins with an explanation of all the stuff you see when you open FrontPage: basic menus, toolbars, panes, and view options. To introduce you to the program's workspace, you'll follow basic steps to create a sample Web site. Other chapters in this section teach you how to add page fundamentals, like text, images, and hyperlinks between pages.

- **Part 2, Improving Your Web Page,** is about polishing the apple—using advanced features of FrontPage to make your pages look better. See how tables can help you lay out a page. Learn to use Cascading Style Sheets to achieve the look you want. Toss in layers and FrontPage behaviors to bring action to your pages.

- **Part 3, Building and Managing a Web Site,** covers the creation, management, and publishing of your Web site. It shows you how to organize your site's files and keep on top of issues with FrontPage's built-in reporting tools. This section also deals with testing and collaboration features—like task tracking and document control—which help multiple authors work together on one site.

- **Part 4, Forms and Databases,** explains how to create forms for gathering data, how to display information from a database, and how your visitors can actually interact with a database.

- **Part 5, FrontPage and Microsoft Office 2003,** tells you how to get other products in the Microsoft Office Suite—Word, Excel, and PowerPoint—to play well with FrontPage.

About → These → Arrows

Throughout this book, and throughout the Missing Manual series, you'll find sentences like this one: "Select Insert → Picture → From File." That's shorthand for a much longer instruction that asks you to navigate through FrontPage menus like the one in Figure P-1. The long version would read: "On the FrontPage main set of menus, locate the Insert command and click it. Scroll down and hold your cursor over Picture to reveal a submenu. From the submenu that displays, select From File."

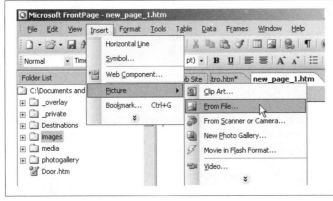

Figure P-1:
Arrows in the text lead you through nested menus like this.

The Very Basics

As you read this book, you'll encounter some basic terms that you need to know, if you don't know them already.

- **Clicking.** While learning FrontPage, your computer's mouse or trackpad will be getting a workout. You'll come across a few basic terms for handling this tool. To *click* is to hold your arrow cursor over an item, then press and release the button on the left. To *double-click* is to click the left button twice rapidly. To *drag* is to move the cursor while continuing to press the button. To *right-click* is to click the button on the right side of your device once.

- **Keyboard shortcuts.** Many a computer whiz can't bear to remove his hands from the keyboard. These individuals thrive on the speed they achieve when they don't have to waste precious time moving one hand over to the mouse. For them, and anyone else, this book contains keyboard shortcuts for menu items wherever possible. For instance, Ctrl+C is the keyboard shortcut for Copy in FrontPage. It means hold down the Ctrl key while pressing the C key.

- **Menu.** As in most other software programs, the FrontPage menu bar appears at the top of the program's main window. It looks like a horizontal list of words. These words are actually headings for groups of commands. To display and select commands, click on a heading. Then scroll down and click your selection. You can also drag down to an item and select it by releasing the mouse button.

About MissingManuals.com

At the *missingmanuals.com* Web site, you'll find articles, tips, and updates to the book. In fact, you're invited and encouraged to submit such corrections and updates yourself. In an effort to keep the book as up to date and accurate as possible, each time we print more copies of this book, we'll make any confirmed corrections you've suggested. We'll also note such changes on the Web site, so that you can mark important corrections into your own copy of the book, if you like. (Click the book's name, and then click the Errata link, to see the changes.)

In the meantime, we'd love to hear your own suggestions for new books in the Missing Manual line. There's a place for that on the Web site, too, as well as a place to sign up for free email notification of new titles in the series.

Safari Enabled

 When you see a Safari® Enabled icon on the cover of your favorite technology book that means the book is available online through the O'Reilly Network Safari Bookshelf.

Safari offers a solution that's better than e-books. It's a virtual library that lets you easily search thousands of top tech books, cut and paste code samples, download chapters, and find quick answers when you need the most accurate, current information. Try it for free at *http://safari.oreilly.com*.

Part One:
Creating a Basic
Web Page

1

Building a Basic Web Site

Many Web design graybeards consider their ability to write HTML code by hand a badge of honor. But for someone who's new to the Web, this approach is pretty over the top. Just because you'd like to post your party photos doesn't mean you want to become a programmer. Novices aren't the only ones who need a hand. Pretty much every Web developer has popped a page into a visual Web editor like FrontPage at some point.

People use FrontPage and similar programs because they make the creation of Web pages fast and easy. Advantages of using FrontPage include:

- **Hands-on editing.** Of all the benefits FrontPage offers, nothing beats its ability to let you see the changes to your Web page as you make them. While you're working, you pretty much see pages as visitors to your site eventually will. You add and edit visual elements—like images and hyperlink buttons—by clicking on them directly. When you move or resize an object, the results show immediately.

- **Speed.** Tasks that are extremely tedious when coding manually, like creating a table, are a snap in a program like FrontPage. In fact, many professionals who write their pages by hand often hop into programs like FrontPage just to add a table. In the process, they save themselves tons of typing.

- **Visual aids.** FrontPage provides diagrams to help manage even the abstract aspects of your site, like hierarchy and site navigation. An illustration can be a big help when you're having trouble organizing pages.

- **Guidance.** FrontPage menus and toolbars provide direction that's lacking in an all-text HTML world. For instance, even if you don't know exactly how to do something, like format a table border, you can most likely figure it out by searching through menus called Format or Table to find the right command.

This chapter introduces you to the FrontPage workspace. After a look around, you'll take a turn at the wheel, using FrontPage to create a simple Web site. Along the way, you'll get to know FrontPage's controls and windows and catch a glimpse of what the program makes possible.

The Main FrontPage Window

When you launch FrontPage, you see the basic program layout that you'll come to know well. This workspace is your control center for creating Web sites and pages.

The FrontPage 2003 editing window looks similar to that of other Microsoft products, so if you're familiar with programs like Word and Excel, you'll be at home in FrontPage. This familiar setup, pictured in Figure 1-1, features a menu along the top of the screen. Below that, toolbars feature shortcut buttons to menu commands.

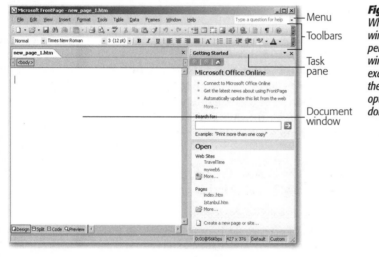

Figure 1-1:
When you first open FrontPage, a window like this appears. As you perform different tasks, the window's layout changes. For example, the task pane, shown on the right side, presents new options, based on what you're doing.

- The **menu** bar contains program commands. They follow the basic layout of Microsoft menus. (See Appendix A for a detailed explanation of every menu.)

- Two **toolbars**—Standard and Formatting—display the first time you open FrontPage. These two get top billing because they contain the most commonly used commands. Hold your cursor over a button to display its function. You'll probably want to keep these toolbars around, but if not, you can get rid of them. Select View → Toolbars to add or hide FrontPage toolbars.

- The screen is dominated by the **document window,** in which you'll do most of your work. This is your canvas, where you'll create and edit your Web pages. Buttons on the lower-left corner of the document window, pictured in

Figure 1-2, let you change the way this window shows your page. Your choices are described next.

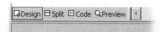

Figure 1-2:
These page view buttons let you look at your page in different formats.

FREQUENTLY ASKED QUESTION

Hidden Options

How can I turn off those mini-menus that don't show me all my menu options?

This feature is designed to save time, but can be frustrating. When you click on a menu heading, a list of basic choices appears, while the rest of the menu list is hidden. If you hold the menu open for a while, all the choices will eventually show up. Or you can click the double arrows at the bottom, as shown in the illustration, if you're impatient. Abbreviated menus are the standard setting in FrontPage, and they are sometimes called customized or personalized. If you leave them active, you'll notice that they display only your most recent selections. Until you're more familiar with the program, you will probably want to see all the options at

once. To do so, select Tools → Customize, click on the Options tab, and then turn on the Always Show Full Menus checkbox.

- **Design** view is where you'll be spending lots of time. Here you can edit in a display that mimics how pages appear in a browser.

- **Split** view shows HTML code in the top half of the window, and Design view shows code in the bottom half. Highlight an element in Design view, and FrontPage will highlight its code above. This view is an easy way to find a code snippet and also a great reference if you're learning HTML.

- **Code** view fills the window with the page's HTML code, which you're free to edit.

Tip: If all that code is too much for you, check out an additional "light" option. With the document window in Design view, select View → Reveal Tags. FrontPage peppers your page with yellow tag markers to give you a glimpse behind the scenes. To hide the tags, select View → Reveal Tags again.

- **Preview** is a page preview function, intended to display your page exactly as a browser would. Use this feature sparingly, as it's not necessarily 100% accurate. You're always better off previewing your pages in an actual browser anyway (more on that later). One advantage to this page preview option is that you can preview your page—including interactive features like hyper-links—more quickly than when using a browser. But beware—this function works in concert with your Microsoft browser. So it shows how your page appears in only Internet Explorer and not in other browsers like Netscape.

GEM IN THE ROUGH

Quick Tag Selector Toolbar

If you're interested in learning HTML, you'll love FrontPage's Quick Tag Selector toolbar, which helps you focus on which HTML tags FrontPage is using to create various parts of your page.

The toolbar, which appears just above the document window, displays small icons representing each tag surrounding wherever you've placed your cursor.

For example, the cursor in the illustration sits in a paragraph (next to the word "Gloves"), which is inside a table cell, which is inside a table. So, FrontPage displays tag icons for all these HTML elements in the toolbar.

If you hover over a tag in the toolbar (like the <p> paragraph tag, for instance), FrontPage projects a box over the Design view, outlining the area that the tag encompasses. If you're new to HTML, use the tag selector to help you identify which tags are at work behind the scenes to create what you're seeing in Design view.

Later, when you're formatting your pages, you'll find that the Tag Selector is also a great way to select elements, like a paragraph within a table, an image, or list item. When you click a tag in the toolbar, FrontPage selects the tag and all its contents. This ensures that you never leave out part of some text or select the wrong element by accident, which can sometimes happen when you're manipulating elements in Design view.

But that's not all. Each icon has a drop-down arrow to its right. If you click the arrow, FrontPage displays a menu that lets you select, edit, remove, or wrap the tag within another tag that you specify. If you want to make a quick edit to your HTML, the toolbar helps you do so with speedy pinpoint precision, saving you the need to slog through a whole page of code.

The Task Pane

Some commands are buried deep within submenus. It's a chore slogging through list after list to find and select the choice you want. Of course, FrontPage 2003 offers shortcuts like toolbar buttons and keystrokes. But the program includes another helpful feature that pops up now and then looking to assist you with a whole bunch of tasks. Not surprisingly, it's called the task pane.

The task pane displays on the right side of the screen (see Figure 1-1). The first time FrontPage opens, the Getting Started incarnation of the task pane appears.

This is just one of a number of separate task panes that display in this area. You can access other choices through the task pane menu, as shown in Figure 1-3.

Figure 1-3:
To see all the available task panes, click the down arrow on the right side of the task pane heading. The menu of available task panes displays. Choices within each of these task panes are usually shortcuts to various menu commands. Many panes include visual aids that can help you do things like preview a graphic or help you organize page elements.

As you use FrontPage, the task pane pays attention to what you're doing. When you carry out different functions, the pane changes automatically to offer selections that are appropriate to the task at hand. For example, if you select File → New, the task pane presents choices for creating a new page or a new Web site. If the pane takes up too much screen space, you can close it by clicking the x in the upper-right corner (of the task pane, not the overall FrontPage window). But you can't keep this feature down. The task pane opens again automatically if you select an activity that requires use of a task pane, like searching for clip art. And you'll definitely need the task pane if you ever want to do things like add layers or behaviors to a page. (You'll learn all about those features in Chapters 8 and 9.)

Creating a Simple Web Site

You've barely scratched the surface of what FrontPage has to offer. The menu and toolbar choices that you have yet to explore help you do things like create actual Web pages, so it's time to start moving around in the program a bit. Make your way through the simple steps below for creating a sample Web site. In the process, you'll learn more about the program's layout and get to check out some additional views and features. Complete coverage of all the skills you'll need to create the full-blown Web site of your dreams follows throughout the rest of this book.

Creating a New Web Site

Sure, you can create an individual Web page with no ties or connections to other pages, but Microsoft designed FrontPage to create and manage entire *sites*. The focus of the program is always on your Web site as a whole. As a result, the first thing you'll do when working in FrontPage is create a new Web site.

Note: In previous versions of FrontPage, Microsoft used the word "Web" to mean Web site. Because this term understandably created some confusion, Microsoft finally switched to the more appropriate "Web site." However, you'll still occasionally see the old moniker "Web" pop up from time to time.

---

1. **Launch FrontPage.**

   When the program first opens, a blank page appears. To avoid creating pages within an existing site, make sure you don't already have a Web site open by selecting File → Close Site. If the option is grayed out, you don't have a site open.

2. **Select File → New.**

   The New task pane displays on the right, presenting you with a bunch of choices for creating new sites or pages.

3. **Within the New task pane, beneath the New Web Site heading, click More Web Site Templates.**

   A selection of site templates appears. Most of these are Microsoft's automated templates that come with preset designs; they even include text and pictures. If you want to know more about a template, click once on it to read a description. For now, you'll create your own site from scratch without the help of a template.

4. **Click once to highlight the Empty Web Site option.**

   Next, FrontPage needs to know where to save the site. Usually, the location box is automatically set to your computer's My Webs folder (there's that old Microsoft-speak for "Web site" showing up). Saving in this folder is fine, though FrontPage isn't very creative with the site names it wants to use. Were you to save a few sample sites, you'd see the program name them *myweb1, myweb2,* and so on. Names like that make it hard later on to remember what's in the site. So, although what you're working on right now is just a sample Web site, you should go ahead and name it. For best results, don't include any spaces, capital letters, or special characters in the name, and keep it short. Later in this book, you'll find more detailed guidelines for naming Web sites and files.

Note: *Do not* create the site on the highest level (geeks call this the *root*) of your C:\ drive (meaning the location should never be something like *C:\mysite*). Always create the site in a folder that's at least a level or two away from plain C:\. This path could be something like *C:\misc\sites\mysite,* for instance—or better yet, just use the My Webs folder. If you create your site's folder directly on C:\ and not within an additional folder, you'll have problems later.

5. **Click in the Location box. At the end of the site name proposed by FrontPage, following the last back slash, change the name of your Web site to anything you want (Sample, Test, or whatever), and click OK.**

Your new empty Web site opens in FrontPage. The folder list is now visible on the left side of FrontPage's main window. The *folder list*, which (no surprise) shows the folders and files in your site, is the tool you'll use to keep your site organized. After all, you have to find your Web pages to edit them. Even though you haven't added a thing to this site yet, FrontPage has already placed two folders in the folder list, the *images* folder, used to hold your images, and the *_private* folder, used to hold files you wish to keep hidden from public view. You should sleep soundly knowing that FrontPage takes an active hand in managing your site. It creates and updates hidden files that your site needs to work correctly.

Adding Web Pages

A Web site is nothing without a page or two or 40. You can handle the creation of pages within your site in a few different ways. Some Web authors work from the outside in. In other words, they create a site's structure and then fill in the details on each page. Most people work from the inside out: they craft a Web site page by page, placing each page where it belongs in the pecking (or clicking) order until their site is complete.

For now, keep it simple. Create a page the old-fashioned way, in Design view.

1. **Create a new page.**

You can create a new page using one of the following methods: click the New Page icon on the toolbar, or press Ctrl+N on your keyboard, or select File → New and click New Page within the task pane.

The Layout Tables and Cells task pane may have automatically opened when you created the new page, as illustrated in Figure 1-4. If it didn't, open it now by selecting View → Task Pane. Then click the Task Pane drop-down menu and select Layout Tables and Cells.

2. Within the Layout Tables task pane, under the Table Layout section, click the third choice, "Corner, Header, Left, and Body," as illustrated in Figure 1-4.

FrontPage applies the layout to the page, dividing it into sections (which are really cells of the layout table). There are pros and cons to using layout tables, which you'll read about later. For now, proceed blithely on.

3. Close the task pane to increase your workspace.

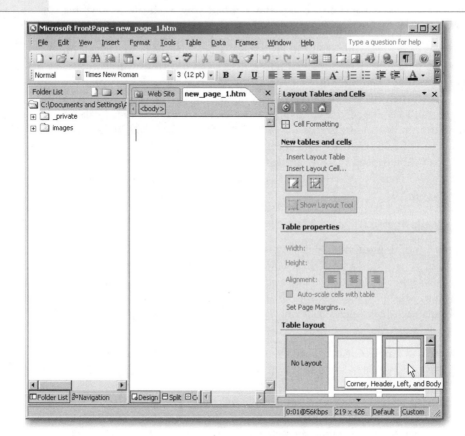

Figure 1-4:
FrontPage often automatically displays menus and dialog boxes it thinks you need. This particular task pane displays and previews options for adding tables that help you format a page.

Adding Content to Your Web Site

Whatever your site is about, one thing is always true: to get your message out there, you've got to get it onto your Web pages. Fortunately, FrontPage's features for adding text, pictures, and other elements are plentiful and easy to work with.

Adding Text

Even Web pages that consist mostly of pictures include a few words. For all the ins and outs of working with text in FrontPage, check out the next chapter. Meanwhile, the following steps give you a rudimentary start.

1. Click to place your cursor within the table cell on the top right of your new page and type a few words that will serve as the heading for your page.

2. Leaving your cursor on the line you just typed, click the Style drop-down menu on the formatting toolbar (where the current choice is Normal) and select Heading 1 from the list.

3. On the formatting toolbar, click the Center button.

   The text is now centered within that cell. If you weren't using a layout table, your text would be centered on the page.

4. Highlight all the text you just typed.

   To do this, drag your cursor across the entire line (just as though you were selecting text in Microsoft Word). Don't leave out any letters. The additional formatting you're going to apply is character-based, meaning it applies only to the characters you select.

5. On the formatting toolbar, click the drop-down arrow to the right of the Font Color button and select red.

6. Click to place your cursor in the cell on the lower right (just below the cell your heading's in).

   Your cursor should still be in the right side of the layout table. Perhaps you've seen Web pages that look similar to the format you're using? In the upper-left corner there's room for a logo. Below that on the left, a long narrow cell is a nice place to put a vertical menu bar with links to other parts of the site. On the right, you can enter general page content, as you're about to do.

7. Type a line of text and press Enter.

8. Type another line and press Enter.

You've now got yourself a simple Web page with some text on it. It's not going to win any awards, but it's a start.

Adding Hyperlinks

Hyperlinks are like glue. They bind the pages of your site to each other and also to the rest of the Web. If you forget to link to one of your site's pages, it could languish in oblivion, unread for ages. Actually, FrontPage can help you find these unlinked pages, but the point is that pages need hyperlinks if you want people to get to them.

You can add hyperlinks that open other pages or even initiate emails. Right now, you'll create another Web page in your site and link to it—all in one step.

1. Highlight a word or line of text on your page.

2. **Right-click and select Hyperlink.**

   The Insert Hyperlink dialog box opens (see Figure 1-5).

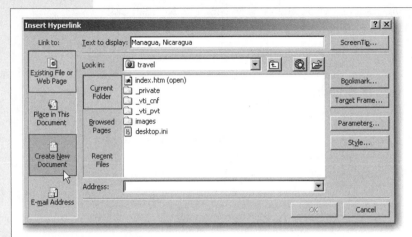

3. **Click once on the Create New Document link option on the left.**

   The dialog box presents some new options based on your selection. The "Text to display" box shows you the text on the page that will become your hyperlink. You can edit this text here or on the page itself.

4. **Within the Name field, type a name for your new page (again, don't include spaces, capital letters, or special characters) and click OK.**

   You've just created a new page within your Web site and linked to it at the same time. Your new page appears in the document window.

5. **At the top of your new page, type a heading, format it as Heading 1, center the text, and press Enter.**

   Did you forget how to do that already? Check out steps 2 through 5 in the previous section.

6. **Select Insert → Horizontal Line and press Enter again.**

   Once you're a FrontPage whiz, you'll probably use tables to lay out your pages (as you did in the previous section). But FrontPage gives you other elements you can use to organize a page, too. The horizontal line is an easy (if unrefined) way to break text into sections.

7. **If your cursor isn't centered on the page, click the Center button on the formatting toolbar.**

   Since you didn't lay this page out with a table, centering elements like headings and images is a quick way to make the page look better. (However, when it comes to longer paragraphs, left align looks more professional and is easier to read than centered text.)

Adding Images

Graphics can really spice up your page and help dazzle your visitors. Use images to share information (to show what your products look like) or provide guidance for what you want visitors to do (a picture of a house might be a link to your home page). Or they might just fulfill your decorative urges.

Whatever the reason, follow the steps below to add an image to your page. Later, when you create your own real site, you'll probably have your own original graphics. For now, just borrow from Microsoft's clip art collection.

1. **Select, Insert → Picture → Clip Art.**

   The Clip Art task pane displays on the right with a search box (see Figure 1-6). You don't need to search extensively. Don't even bother to type anything. Just click Go, and some pictures should display on the lower-right side of the task pane.

2. **Click any picture to select it.**

   The picture displays on your page.

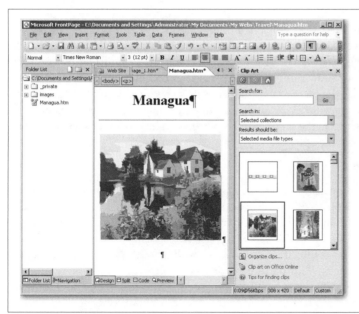

Figure 1-6:
Now that you have a couple of pages, the editing window includes more options. At the top of the document window, click the tabs to switch between open pages. An asterisk next to a page name indicates that the page contains unsaved material. (You'll learn how to save in a moment.) At left, within the folder list, your new page (Managua.htm, in this example) appears.

3. Close the task pane by clicking the x on the upper-right corner or selecting View → Task pane to turn it off.

Saving Your Work

Don't let your new miniature Web site go unsaved. Actually, you already saved the site itself when you created it. After that, you'll always be saving your site

content—like pages and images. Should you try to close a site by selecting File →
Close Site, FrontPage prompts you to save changes to individual pages one by one.
You've seen these kinds of prompts before when you've tried to close a program
that still has files open.

You're better off saving changes as you work. Saving frequently helps fend off the
danger of data loss (and nervous breakdown) due to a computer meltdown. If you
never lost work to a computer glitch, consider yourself one of the few and fortu-
nate. Caution aside, you'll find that saving your pages regularly eases site
maintenance.

Tip: If you have several pages open that contain unsaved changes, you can save them all at once by
selecting File → Save All. FrontPage saves everything that's open and unsaved.

Saving a Web Page

In the course of working on your site, FrontPage frequently prompts you to save
pages. Often that's because the program needs you to save in order to do things
that you've asked it to do, like preview your page in a browser.

Start now by saving the edits to your site's new page. The tab for your new page
still contains an asterisk, as illustrated in Figure 1-6, which tells you that the page
needs to be saved. Get rid of the asterisk with a simple click of the Save button on
the toolbar. Or select File → Save (Ctrl+S). When the Save dialog box appears,
FrontPage usually wants to name the page something like *new_page_3.htm*.
Rename it so that the file name actually means something to you within the context of your site. As with a Web site name, don't include any spaces, capital letters,
or special characters in the name, and keep it short. The process of saving this page
also takes care of some basic site maintenance, as you'll see.

1. **Save the page.**

   After you've named and saved the page, a Save Embedded Files dialog box displays. In the course of saving this page, FrontPage needs to know where it
   should save the image file you just incorporated in your site. (While pictures
   may look to you like they're part of a page, they actually exist behind the scenes
   as individual image files and *must* be saved within your site. Don't leave them in
   a random folder on your hard drive, or your Web server won't know where to
   find them later when you publish your site.) If you just click OK, FrontPage
   saves the image into whatever folder you're currently working in. As you create
   pages, the list of files associated with your site will grow quickly. It's important
   to organize these files intelligently. You'll get to site management later on in
   Chapter 10, but right now, put your best foot forward by saving this image file
   where it belongs: in the Images folder that FrontPage has automatically created
   within your site. But first, you've got to name the image properly.

2. **Click the Rename button and change the name to something fitting and descriptive.**

   As is, the image file name consists of some numbers and text that will mean nothing to you later on. Since you'll want to find the image easily in the future, rename it. Eventually you'll have a folder full of graphic files with names like *explodingeggplant.jpg* and *cleanuptools.gif*. You'll then be able to identify them without a hassle.

3. **Click the Change Folder button.**

4. **Click the Images folder and click OK.**

   The Save dialog box now shows the new location for the file. You can click OK, and—poof!—the asterisk on the page's tab disappears.

5. **Select File → Close to close the page.**

   The first page you created—which will be the site's home page—should be displayed in your document window. You now need to save it.

6. **Save the home page.**

   The Save As dialog box displays. Note that FrontPage has already entered a name for the file: *index.htm*. You should keep this name, as it tells the browser that this is the home page or first page the browser should open. FrontPage always designates the first page you create in a site as the home page. If you want, you can give the page a title, too (see Figure 1-7). (Chapter 10 covers everything you need to know about home pages, file names vs. titles, and site structure.)

7. **Within the Save As dialog box, make no changes and click Save.**

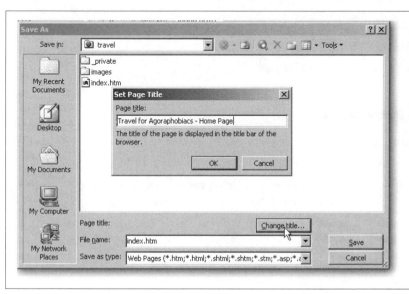

Figure 1-7:
If you click the Change Title button, you can give your page a title, too, which is different from its file name (like index.htm). Page title is for public display and appears to viewers in the title bar of their Web browser. (See Chapter 10.)

Viewing Your Site

Your new site has only two pages, but imagine that you've got 20 or 200. At that size, keeping track of all your files is a real challenge. How can you see what's going on?

FrontPage has got you covered. As you've already seen, the program provides different views for individual pages, so you can see and manage what's on your pages effectively. In much the same way, FrontPage's *site views* let you keep track of your entire site. You get a few different options. Use Folder view to group relevant files together so they'll be easy to find and edit. At a glance, Hyperlinks view assures you that your links lead to the right pages. Click and drag in Navigation view to rearrange the hierarchy or navigation of your site.

The next two sections show you all the different ways FrontPage lets you look at everything from individual pages to your entire site.

Exploring Page Views

You've read about FrontPage's different page views (page 5), but now that you have an actual Web page open in FrontPage, you can see them in action. Your document window has been set to Design view as you've been working. You'll probably spend most of your time there, but check out all your options, like Split view, pictured in Figure 1-8.

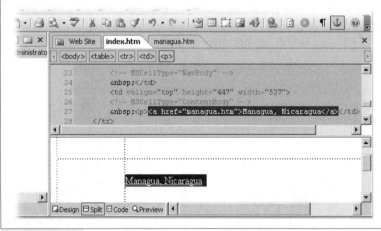

Figure 1-8:
In Split view, when you highlight text and elements in the Design pane, they appear highlighted in the Code pane, too. Use this feature to find a tag quickly or to learn HTML.

Explore some other page views by clicking the buttons on the bottom-left corner of the document window. For details on page view options, flip back to Figure 1-2.

Exploring Site Views

Managing an entire Web site means that you'll be handling lots of information. You've got to keep track of where things are, what files are linked to each other, and who's working on them.

You can handle it all with FrontPage's site view options. Not only do these views show you the details you need, they also give you a handy visual representation of your site. When you tackle abstract matters like site hierarchy and the flow of your hyperlinks, a diagram of page relationships is really helpful. You'll use site views to manage links, files, folders, and tasks.

Usually, you'll have a page active in the document window. Tell FrontPage that you'd like to get the big picture by clicking the Web Site tab at the top of the document window. A view of your site's folders appears in the document window. Also, the view buttons at the bottom-left corner of the document window change. They now reflect the following options to help examine your site:

- **Folders view** mirrors the display within the folder list on the left side of the FrontPage window. Though the information is the same, this view offers an expanded workspace, which is great for reorganizing folder structure or moving files around.

- **Remote Web Site view** is not relevant at the moment (you'll learn more about it in Chapter 13). The normal workflow for a Web site is to edit a copy of the site on your computer or network (the local site) and then upload it to a Web server (the remote site). Using this view, you can compare the two sites, publish only select files, and exclude files from being published.

- **Reports view** offers a variety of site tracking queries. For example, you can run a report that lets you know if your site contains unlinked pages that readers can't access, or check for pages that load too slowly.

- **Navigation view** provides a diagram of a site's hierarchy. It comes with one big drawback, however. You've got to create and manage this view manually. There are two cases in which you'd use this view: when you want to create a Web site structure *before* you create individual pages filled with content, or when you plan to use some of the features that need Navigation view to work, like FrontPage link bars (automated site navigation menus). Otherwise, you're better off using folders to handle issues of hierarchy.

- **Hyperlinks view**, illustrated in Figure 1-9, gives you a visual representation of the location and direction of your site's hyperlinks.

- **Tasks view** is your site's to-do list. You can enter notes about page edits or corrections. If you have a lot of people working on your site, use this view to delegate and track assignments.

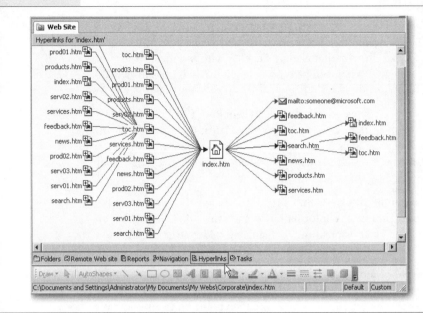

Figure 1-9:
Here's a Hyperlink view of the Corporate Web site, a template that comes with FrontPage. It shows how all pages are linked to each other. When you click the + on a page name, you reveal more hyperlinks.

Previewing Your Site

As you create your Web pages, keep in mind that there are a variety of operating systems and browsers out there, each with its own capabilities and quirks. Creating pages that look the way you want them to in browsers from different companies (and from different eras) is a challenge worthy of a United Nations interpreter.

Get used to the fact that you'll never have complete control over how your pages display in a browser. The browser takes fonts and other settings from a viewer's system, which may differ vastly from those you used to preview your site. Imagine, for example, that you create a beautiful page layout, only to discover that your Aunt Sophie has her old 640×480 monitor set to large fonts and your page turns to a jumble on her Windows 95 jalopy.

You probably won't have access to all the species of browsers that are out trawling the Web, but the latest release of FrontPage provides you with some additional preview options that can help. You can use these preview tools to avoid trouble and steer your site safely through most pitfalls.

Note: These preview tools work with whatever browsers are currently on your computer. So download and install as many different browsers as you can, including less common ones like Opera and Firefox. See Chapter 12 for details on getting your browsers to appear on FrontPage's list.

While the page Preview view gives you some idea of how your page will look, you should always preview using an actual Web browser. In fact, you should preview in *many* browsers, which FrontPage helps you do. Here's how:

1. **Confirm that *index.htm* is saved.**

   FrontPage won't let you preview your site in a browser until you've saved all changes.

2. **Click the Preview in Browser button.**

   This button is located on the Standard toolbar. It opens the page in your system's standard browser—the one that opens every time you go on the Internet. You can check the appearance of your page and test the hyperlinks and other interactive elements on your pages.

3. **Close the browser.**

4. **Select File → Preview in Browser to display the menu pictured in Figure 1-10.**

   This menu is where you pick from all the different browsers you've got loaded on your PC.

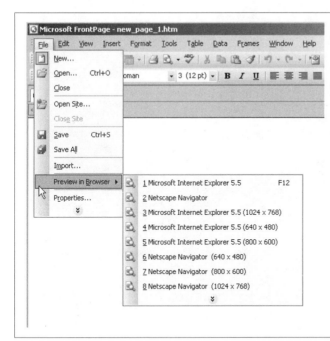

Figure 1-10:
FrontPage 2003 includes new options for previewing your work. Not only does the Preview in Browser menu offer whatever browsers you have loaded on your system, it lets you see what your page will look like at different screen sizes. A page that works on your 1024 × 768 screen may not work on a monitor set to 640 × 480.

5. **If you have multiple browsers, select one that you haven't used, or try a different screen resolution.**

You've done it! You've built a basic Web site and come to know some of FrontPage's editing options and controls. When it comes time to work on your own site, you'll constantly be using the skills you just sampled. You'll be creating pages, formatting text, adding images, and linking pages like crazy. The chapters that follow cover all of these procedures in detail.

Working with Text

Of course, your Web site is going to look great, but what's it going to say? In spite of all the fancy multimedia whirligigs out there—like digital video, audio, and Flash animations—text is still the lifeblood of the Web. Just ask your favorite search engine.

While FrontPage looks a lot like a word processing program, you'll soon find that you're not in Microsoft Word anymore. Sure, your cursor is plainly visible in the document window, typing is a breeze, and you can center text and italicize just like you always have. But something very different is going on behind the scenes. Your options for organizing text on the Web are more limited than they are in programs designed to produce printed pages.

The first thing you need to understand is that the choices you make in FrontPage don't always appear intact once your pages get out on the Web. Your viewer's Web browser ultimately determines the appearance of your Web pages. For example, if a visitor to your Web site doesn't have a special font you included on your page, her browser will replace it with another font. Because the browser's in charge, you never quite know how your text will display.

Sure, the browser is powerful—but so are you. There's a lot you can do to steer browsers in the right direction. This chapter covers everything you'll need to get your message down in writing. First, you'll learn to add and manipulate text. Then you'll move on to the finer points: making your words look great by using all the formatting tools FrontPage offers.

Adding Text

FrontPage makes adding text pretty straightforward. When you open a new blank page, your cursor sits at the top-left corner of the editing window. As you type, text moves from left to right, and when it's reached the right margin of the page, your words wrap automatically, continuing on the line below. Text aligns left and wraps like this within table cells, too. When you want to start a new paragraph, just press Enter. So far, so good.

Inserting Spaces

Where things get a bit tricky is when you start to insert spaces—either between paragraphs or between words. Most of the problems stem from the funky rules HTML has for dealing with spaces and the way FrontPage interprets those rules.

Spaces between paragraphs

You may already have noticed that when you type a line, press Enter, and type another line, the text appears double-spaced and there are no options to adjust it.

What's happening is that when you hit Enter, FrontPage creates a new paragraph. In HTML-ese, each paragraph is nestled between paragraph tags (<p>), which translates into a big honking double space between each paragraph. But what if you don't want that space? What if you want a garden-variety book-style single-space between each paragraph?

Enter the *line break*. A line break inserts a return *without* creating a new paragraph. To insert a line break hold down the Shift key when you press Enter or select Insert → Break → Normal line break (see Figure 2-1).

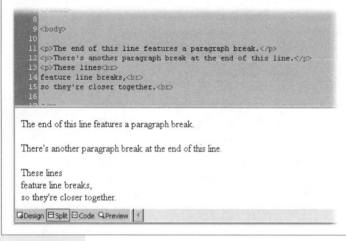

Figure 2-1:
To see how HTML differentiates paragraph and line breaks, write a few lines of text, separating them with a few breaks of each kind. Then highlight the text and click the Split view button on the lower-left corner of the document window. In the HTML code for the page, you'll see that wherever you entered a line break, FrontPage has inserted a <br> break tag instead of a </p> end paragraph tag.

Fortunately, you're not stuck choosing between these two relatively rudimentary tools. FrontPage gives you a lot more options for spacing text. For more details, see "Aligning and Spacing Paragraphs" on page 33.

Spaces between words

When you create spaces between your words, you'll encounter a similar bit of quirkiness. If all you want to do is Web-ify normal-looking sentences like the one you're reading right now—with a single space between each word—no problem. Type away blissfully in FrontPage, and your brilliant one-space-between-each-word prose will end up on Web browser screens everywhere. But where things get weird is when you want to insert *multiple* spaces between words. In the normal world of programs like Microsoft Word (or your typewriter, for that matter), each time you hit the Space bar, that's what you'd get on your page: a new space.

But HTML doesn't work like that. When a Web browser is presented with a page of HTML, the browser doesn't care how many spaces are between the words. So, the following:

```
<p>I've been working on the railroad.<p>
```

will display in a browser exactly the same way as:

```
<p>I've been     working    on the       railroad.<p>
```

The engineers at Microsoft decided that most people probably still want to have their Space bar work the way it always has, so FrontPage steps in and performs a little trick: it inserts a *nonbreaking space* whenever you hit a Space bar more than once. A nonbreaking space is a small string of characters in HTML code ( ) that tells a browser to display a space no matter what. Hit the Space bar nine times, and FrontPage plunks eight nonbreaking spaces into your underlying HTML. (The program doesn't know you're serious about making space until the second tap on your Space bar, so the first doesn't count.)

Tip: To see what nonbreaking spaces look like, set your document window to Split view. Find your cursor and type two spaces, or press Ctrl+Shift+Spacebar. In the top pane, you'll see the code for a nonbreaking space appear: .

Similarly, striking the Tab key in FrontPage inserts three nonbreaking spaces, letting you indent a paragraph or divide items on a horizontal menu.

Beware of holding down the Space bar, however. Doing so creates a string of nonbreaking spaces, sending adjacent text far off to the right, increasing the width of your page. This is because, true to their name, these spaces don't break away from one another or away from the words on either side of them—even at the end of a line. Lean on that Space bar too much and your Web site viewers are going to have to do an awful lot of horizontal scrolling to see what you've written.

The bottom line? *Don't* use lots of nonbreaking spaces to design or organize your page. The results will be unpredictable and disastrous, guaranteed. There are much better ways to lay out a page, which you'll learn about in the chapters that follow.

Adding Special Characters

At some point, you'll probably want to add a character that doesn't appear on your keyboard, like a £ (Pound sign) or © (copyright symbol). It's easy to insert symbols and other special characters. Just select Insert → Symbol, and the Symbol dialog box appears (see Figure 2-2). Search through it for the symbol or accented character that you want. Select the symbol and click Insert. Click Close when you're finished.

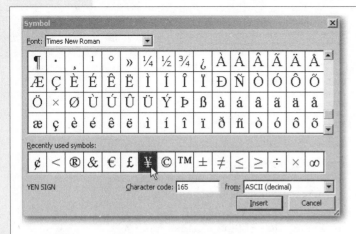

Figure 2-2:
To see additional symbol options, click the "from" drop-down list on the lower right and select Unicode (a more complex coding format that some symbols require).

Selecting and Moving Text

Once you get some text on your page, you'll want to edit it, and FrontPage gives you all the usual tools to cut, copy, and paste text. (If you'll be copying and pasting lots of content from other Microsoft Office programs, see Chapter 18 for more information.)

Before you can move or format text, first you've got to select it. Selecting or highlighting text tells FrontPage what text you want to modify. FrontPage gives you a variety of ways to select text:

• To select a word, double-click it.

• To select a paragraph, triple-click in it.

• To select any amount of text, drag your cursor over it.

- Use your keyboard to select any amount of text by pressing Shift and using the four arrow keys (left, right, up, down) to highlight the text you want.

- Press Ctrl+Shift and press your right or left arrow keys to select a word at a time.

WORKAROUND WORKSHOP

Symbols Display Incorrectly

Your symbol looks fine when you take a look at your site on your Windows computer, but on your friend's Mac, it displays incorrectly. Like a lot of other browser display problems you'll encounter throughout this book, this quirk stems from FrontPage's Microsoft-centric approach.

Depending on what the character is, FrontPage uses one of three different methods to insert it in your page's HTML code:

- Where possible, FrontPage inserts the character itself. This method applies to the most common symbols—those that appear when you first open the Symbol dialog box.

- The program inserts a numeric code, which you'll find on the bottom of the Symbol dialog box. FrontPage uses the numeric code for symbols beyond the basic set—those with a number code greater than 255. (Figure 2-2 shows the number code in the "Character code" box.)

- FrontPage inserts a *named entity*. Because some characters, such as the < (less-than sign) actually signify something within HTML code, telling a browser to display this character can be tricky. You can do it with a special set of characters that serve as a kind of HTML code word for the symbol: a named entity. For instance, the named entity for the less-than sign is <. Predictably, > is the named entity for the > (greater-than sign).

The first two methods work fine on any Windows computer because FrontPage speaks their language. But either one of these methods can cause problems for browsers on non-Microsoft operating systems. The third option saves the day. Any kind of browser can understand named entities. If you're having trouble getting a special character to display correctly, dive into your page's HTML code, locate the symbol, and replace it with the character's named entity. How do you know what the named entity is? Any good reference book or Web site on HTML will include a comprehensive list of named entities. Try searching the World Wide Web Consortium's site at *www.w3c.org* or consult O'Reilly's excellent *Webmaster in a Nutshell.*

Moving Text

Once you've selected text, you can easily cut, copy, and paste it using the corresponding commands on the Standard toolbar and within the Edit menu. These edit options work just like those in Microsoft Word and other programs. You're probably familiar with them, but you might not be aware of some additional ways to move text.

Drag and drop

You can drag and drop selected text to a new location. To move it, click once within the selected text and drag it to its new home. If you want to duplicate a passage instead of moving it, just hold down the Ctrl key while you drag.

Pasting options

When you're copying content between Web pages or *into* FrontPage from another program, the formatting can differ wildly between the original setting and the new or "destination" location. Will the new text look terribly out of place? Will you need to reset it all manually to match other text on your page? Or maybe you want to keep the original formatting. FrontPage gives you precise control over formatting and lets you decide what you want to do as soon as you're finished pasting. Whenever you paste text within Design view, the Paste Options icon pictured in Figure 2-3 appears.

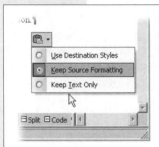

Figure 2-3:
Immediately after you paste text, the Paste Options icon displays just below the last paragraph mark. Click the icon to give FrontPage special pasting instructions.

Once you click the Paste Options icon, a menu appears offering a variety of formatting options for the new text. Depending on what kind of content you've pasted, some or all of the following choices may appear in the menu:

- **Use Destination Styles.** Pasted text takes on the formatting of the new document into which you pasted it.

- **Keep Source Formatting.** Pasted text retains the formatting it had in the source document (the one from which you cut or copied it).

- **Keep Text Only.** This option strips the text of all formatting. For example, a table would lose all its neat columns and rows and you'd be left with just the numbers and text that were inside the table.

Tip: When you're pasting content from another Microsoft Office program, like Word, the Keep Text Only selection is your best bet. If you use it, you can avoid polluting your page's code with all the gobbledygook that comes along with Word's formatting. FrontPage's Paste Special menu (explained next) offers similar pared-down pasting options.

Of course, you can also just ignore the Paste Options icon. If you do, FrontPage's standard setting is to keep source formatting.

If you want to paste text but exclude formatting like italics, underlining, or even font size specifications, the Keep Text Only option (explained above) does the job nicely. However, FrontPage offers you a few alternatives. Instead of selecting Edit → Paste, select Edit → Paste Special. You can choose to paste text in one of the following ways:

- **One formatted paragraph.** Pastes text in using a monospaced typewriter-like font (see page 35, later in this chapter). FrontPage replaces paragraph breaks with line breaks.

- **Formatted paragraphs.** Theoretically, this option is the same as the above, except it keeps paragraph breaks. But the paragraph breaks look just like line breaks, so there's really no difference between this and the previous option.

- **Normal paragraphs.** Pasted text takes on the document's Normal style (see page 35, later in this chapter). FrontPage substitutes paragraph and line breaks with spaces, creating one big paragraph.

- **Normal paragraphs with line breaks.** Same as the previous selection, but FrontPage replaces paragraph and line breaks with line breaks.

- **Do not convert.** Use this option to paste HTML code into Design view. Do so and FrontPage keeps tags out of site where they belong. Otherwise, the program would paste code directly onto the page as text, and you'd see the HTML right in a browser's window.

Formatting Characters

If you typed all your pages using only the simple formatting that FrontPage applies automatically, your readers' eyes may glaze over in boredom. Besides, you'll inevitably want to do things like emphasize specific words or characters within a paragraph. FrontPage gives you a ton of options to adorn your words and enhance your message.

You can really punch up the text on your page by playing around with font, size, italics, and text color. FrontPage dubs these selections "character formatting" options, because the program applies these changes character by character. But the fact is you can make *any* amount of text—be it a single character, a word, a sentence, or even multiple paragraphs—italicized, extra-large, pink, and so on.

Note: The instructions that follow tell you how to use FrontPage's basic text-formatting features. You do need to understand these options and how to use them in order to get the most out of FrontPage. However, Cascading Style Sheets (CSS) are a much more efficient and effective way to format your Web pages. You'll read all about CSS in Chapter 7.

Fonts

Using different fonts can do a lot to make your pages more appealing. You can use them to distinguish headings from text and to complement your content in subtle but meaningful ways. The list of fonts that come with FrontPage is long and varied. Maybe you've already taken a peek and are excited to use Papyrus font in your page on Egyptian crop yields. Are you sure you want to use that font? Yes, you say, you've thought out the design and think that your visitors will have no trouble deciphering the font. Fine, but what about their browsers? If a visitor doesn't have that Papyrus font loaded on his system, the browser will substitute another font, and suddenly your clever design idea looks terrible.

The best way to avoid unexpected results is to stick to the following basic fonts: Arial, Arial Black, Courier New, Comic Sans, Georgia, Impact, Times New Roman, Trebuchet, Verdana, Symbol, Webdings, and Wingdings. If you want to use type that's easy to read on a computer screen, try Georgia, Trebuchet, or Verdana. These three were created specifically for the Web.

Tip: If you must use an unusual font for some reason, try incorporating it within a graphic. For example, type your special font text and take a screenshot (Ctrl+PrtSc). Then you can paste the shot into a graphic-editing program, crop it, and save it as an image file. You should use this tactic only for short text snippets, of course. (See Chapter 4 to learn all about working with images in FrontPage.)

Applying a font is simple. First, select some text or place your cursor where you want to begin typing in your new font. Next, select a font from the Font drop-down list on the Formatting toolbar, or select Format → Font to open the Font dialog box, pictured in Figure 2-4.

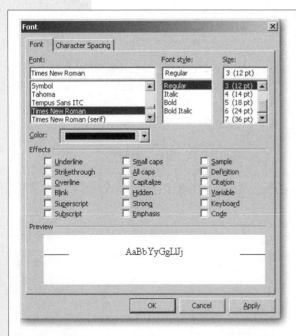

Figure 2-4:
The Font dialog box provides a preview pane and additional font effects on the bottom. Turn on an effect to preview its appearance within the dialog box. Some effects work only with browsers that support CSS. These include: Overline, Small caps, Capitalize, and Hidden.

Don't blink! Actually, go ahead, but not all browsers support blinking text. Don't worry. The consequences won't be serious. If a browser doesn't support an animated effect, it just ignores it.

Font Size

Just as site visitors may not have all your fonts on their systems, they also might set their browser to display fonts much larger or smaller than you intended. There's not much you can do about this, except design your page intelligently so that elements like headings, paragraphs, and menus are laid out in proportion to one another. When you do, even if a visitor sees everything at twice the size, she can still find her way around your site.

The font size list in Figure 2-4 contains two measurements for each selection. If you're an experienced word processor, you may be familiar with the point size measurement (12 pt, 14 pt, and so on). A point is equivalent to 1/72 of an inch. That's a very specific figure, but it won't be much help to a browser, which, as you've learned, doesn't necessarily display anything at a fixed size.

That's where the HTML font measurement comes in. The adjacent numbers within your font list (1, 2, 3, and so on) are "virtual" HTML font measurements. FrontPage's standard size for normal text is 3 (12 pt). Font sizes 1 through 7 are measured in terms relative to this standard size. Each increment represents a 20 percent difference. Therefore, size 2 is 20 percent smaller than 3, and size 4 is 20 percent larger. This is how HTML really measures fonts. In fact, FrontPage shows corresponding point measurements only to guide Web authors who are used to working with word processing programs. While font size 3 may look 12 point on your system, on another browser set to view large fonts, it might look more like 16 point.

Tip: If you want to see the difference, try changing the text size setting on your own browser. Open a Web page and select View → Text Size. Depending on what browser you're using, options on the submenu will differ, but they'll let you increase or decrease the text size.

You can change text size using the Font dialog box or the font size drop-down list on the Formatting toolbar. FrontPage also gives you a shortcut. Look down the Formatting toolbar to the right, and you'll see two buttons: Increase Font Size and Decrease Font Size. Use these buttons to increase or decrease the size of selected text by 20 percent each time you click them.

Text Color

Have you ever visited a Web page and found it illegible because the text color is hard to see against the background color? Text placed over a picture can cause similar problems. Put some thought into the colors you choose for your background and text. (You'll learn about setting your Web page's background color on page 77.) For best results, make you text contrast highly with the background. If you have really long passages of text, help your readers out by using dark text on a light background—a combo that makes for the easiest reading.

To set a text color, select some text and click the arrow to the right of the Color button on the Formatting toolbar. A small dialog box of standard colors displays (see Figure 2-5).

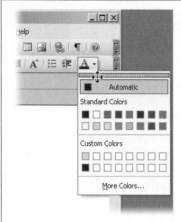

Figure 2-5:
If you're applying many colors, you can keep this dialog box active. Place your cursor over the bar at the top until it turns into a four-headed arrow, shown here. Then drag it off the toolbar.

You can select one of the standard colors that appear in the dialog box or click the More Colors option to display more choices (see Figure 2-6).

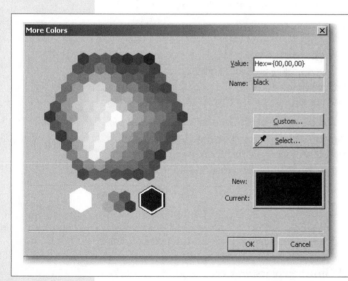

Figure 2-6:
Most of the choices under More Colors are Web-safe colors. This means that site visitors will definitely have these colors on their systems, and you can be certain that the page will look just as you want it to. You can click on any color, or, if you're Web savvy, feel free to enter the hexadecimal value in the box in the upper-right corner.

If you want to customize your colors even further, click the Custom button within the More Colors dialog box. But customize with caution. Unless you're absolutely sure that all your site visitors will have your exact operating system and browser (as in a corporate intranet, for example), it's a really bad idea to customize here. Any custom colors you create won't necessarily be *Web safe*. Web-safe colors are any of the 216 colors that exist on all computer systems. If a visitor doesn't have a color loaded on his system, the browser might substitute another color. Substitution with an unplanned color can result in dire consequences, like your text fading illegibly into a page's background color.

UP TO SPEED

Colors on the Web

Web-safe colors include six shades of red, six shades of green, and six shades of blue. Possible combinations of these hues add up to 216 Web-safe colors. These 216 colors make up what is called the *Web Palette* and render accurately on both Mac and Windows systems. In other words, *all* your visitors are sure to have these colors, and you can use them without worry.

HTML communicates color information by using hexadecimal values. A hex value is an alphanumeric string of six figures based on the shades of red, green, and blue available within the Web Palette. The first pair of characters designates the shade of red, the second pair indicates the shade of green, and the third indicates the shade of blue. There are 16 possible values for each figure in a pair: 0, 1, 2, 3, 4, 5, 6, 7, 8, 9, A, B, C, D, E, and F. For example, the hex value for fuchsia is: #FF00FF. The # sign indicates the start of a hexadecimal value.

Some hex values have corresponding names that are also recognized in HTML. Select one of these colors within the More Colors dialog box, and its name displays beneath its hex value in the upper-right corner. While FrontPage saves you the trouble of having to know and type in hex values, it's good to know what they are.

Since FrontPage is a program for making Web pages, you might think that the pretty hexagon in the More Colors dialog box would feature all 216 Web-safe colors, but it doesn't. If that's not frustrating enough, it turns out that a few of the colors in this dialog box aren't even Web safe. Not very helpful.

So how do you know if a color you've chosen is Web safe? Just look at the hexadecimal value listed in the upper-right corner of the More Colors dialog box. Hex values consist of three pairs of characters. If any pair is *not* 00, 33, 66, 99, CC, or FF, that means that the color isn't Web safe, as illustrated in Figure 2-7.

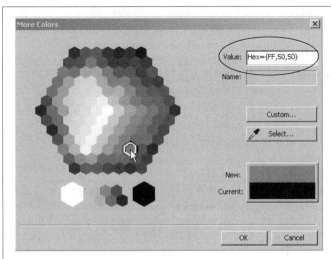

Figure 2-7:
The hex value for this color indicates that it's not Web safe. Two pairs within the hex value (50 and 50) deviate from the Web-safe formula outlined above. Thankfully, this color is an exception. Click on most of these colors, and you'll find that they're Web safe.

Match Colors to a Graphic

If you've added a graphic to a page (see page 58), you might want to color coordinate your page by matching the text color you're using to a color in the picture. Trying to make this match using the color selection tools you just learned about is pretty hard. You try one color and it's too dark. Then the next is too light. Fortunately, FrontPage gives you a handy tool that can take *any* color from a graphic and add it to your color palette:

1. **With your FrontPage Web page open, click the color button on the formatting bar and select More Colors.**

2. **Within the More Colors dialog box, click Select.**

   Your cursor changes into an eyedropper. As it passes over different colors within the graphic, each displays in the New section of the More Colors dialog box, and its hex value appears above.

3. **Click whatever color you want to use as your text color and then click OK.**

   The color you've chosen is now an active choice for text. Don't forget to check the hex value, if you want to make sure your new color is Web safe.

Tip: You can actually use your dropper to select *any* color that appears on your screen. Take the eyedropper for a spin around your desktop and see for yourself.

Formatting Paragraphs

Character formatting can pep up your prose, but FrontPage offers formatting control at an even higher level. Paragraph formatting expands your powers by letting you modify the way your text looks on an even broader scale.

A paragraph is just a collection of a bunch of characters, so what's the difference? Start at the basics. When you type a few words and press Enter, you create a paragraph. FrontPage's Design view indicates a paragraph break with a ¶ paragraph mark. (Click the ¶ Show All button on the Standard toolbar to reveal paragraph marks.) If you switch to Code view, you'll see that in the HTML, each paragraph is surrounded by a pair of <p> tags (the closing tag is a </p> tag). This means FrontPage applies certain formatting, like alignment, to entire paragraphs. Web designers often refer to this as *block-level formatting.* You've already learned how to apply other formatting, like italics or color, on a character level; that is, to a single character, word, or area of text. Paragraph formatting affects an entire block of text—everything between the <p> tags, for example.

Note: When you apply paragraph formatting, you don't need to select all the text you want to format. Just click once in the paragraph and then apply the new format.

FrontPage provides a variety of built-in paragraph styles such as headings and lists to help you organize your page. After you've applied one of these styles, you can format other attributes of any paragraph (like changing the alignment or the color), and you can also easily copy formatting from one paragraph to another.

BEHIND THE SCENES

Character and Paragraph Formatting

With FrontPage, you don't really need to know what's happening behind the scenes, but a quick look at the way HTML applies paragraph and character formatting may help you understand the difference between them. That can be helpful if you ever need to dive into your code and do some troubleshooting or fine-tuning. To get an idea of the difference between the two types of formatting, consider this paragraph:

```
<p align="center">This is a centered
paragraph.</p>
```

Align="center" is the formatting information for this line (which is actually a paragraph, as far as HTML is concerned). Because it resides *within* the <p> tag, a browser automatically applies center formatting to the *entire* paragraph.

On the other hand, if you look at how HTML applies *character* formatting, you can really see that it lives "closer to the text." That is, you apply character formatting to characters and words you want it to affect (rather than entire paragraphs). For example, look at this sentence:

```
Text can be <b>bold</b> or <i>italic</i>
or plain.
```

All text between the <b> bold tags will display in bold. The sentence would display in a browser like this: Text can be **bold** or *italic* or plain.

Basic knowledge of how HTML applies formatting can help you troubleshoot display problems within your site and better understand Cascading Style Sheets later.

Aligning and Spacing Paragraphs

FrontPage automatically sets text to align left (meaning that all lines sit flush against the left margin of the page). Inevitably, you'll want to use a different alignment for some paragraphs. Changing alignment to center, right-align, or justified (where the text aligns with both right and left margins) is very easy.

Note: Justified text can appear differently from browser to browser and even result in some strange occurrences—like words that repeat when displayed in a browser even though there's no duplicate in the underlying HTML. Don't use this alignment setting unless you know that all viewers have your exact browser make and version.

---

1. Click inside the paragraph you want to adjust.

2. On the Formatting toolbar, click the button for the alignment you want.

You can also set alignment using the Paragraph Properties dialog box (see Figure 2-8). To open it, select Format → Paragraph.

This dialog box lets you change spacing between individual paragraphs. But, if you want to space out paragraphs throughout an entire page, skip this dialog box.

You'll save loads of time by using either tables (which you'll learn about in Chapter 5) or Cascading Style Sheets (see Chapter 7).

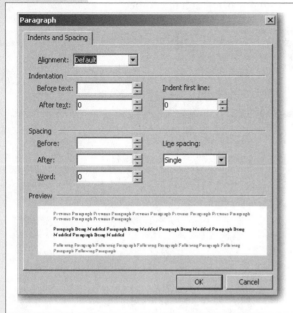

Figure 2-8:
Not only can you set paragraph alignment within Paragraph Properties, but you can fine-tune indentation and spacing between paragraphs. Settings here display in pixels. However, you can type in other units of measure, such as inches (.5 in) or centimeters (8 cm).

Built-in Paragraph Styles

You can create an endless number of custom paragraph styles, which you'll read about in Chapter 7. However, HTML contains some built-in styles, which appear on the FrontPage Style drop-down list for easy access (see Figure 2-9).

Figure 2-9:
FrontPage features these basic built-in styles. A paragraph mark to the left of a style designates it as a paragraph-level style. An underlined "a" (like the one beside Default Character Style) denotes a character style.

Normal text

For the bulk of your page content, you'll use Normal style. When you start a new blank page, the text is always set to Normal style. FrontPage defines "Normal" as size 3 (12 pt), Times New Roman text. But you're not stuck with that look. You can customize the attributes of the Normal style to match your overall design, as you'll see when you come to learn more about applying styles to pages and entire sites.

Formatted text

The Formatted text option within the Style drop-down list is FrontPage's name for what traditional Web developers call *preformatted text*. (In fact, if you look at the HTML code, you'll see that its tag is <pre>).

Here's a style for folks who miss their old typewriter. Formatted text looks and acts just like the type that your old Underwood used to plunk out. For instance, when you use Formatted style, the browser is able to see space and tab characters, eliminating the need to insert nonbreaking spaces. But the typewriter nostalgia doesn't end there. Formatted text is also a monospaced font, meaning that each character takes up exactly the same amount of space. Because each character is the same width, you can use the Space bar and Tab key to create columns that line up with one another—something that's impossible with any other font. For these reasons, many people use formatted text to display tabular data when inserting an actual table would be unsuitable.

Tables, of course, are a much better solution when you've got tabular data, and it's unlikely you'll use this old-fangled text style on a regular basis. But if you do find a use for the Formatted style, keep in mind that—just like on your grandfather's typewriter—the text doesn't wrap automatically. That means that unless you insert a paragraph or a line break, Formatted text will extend out and disappear beyond the browser window.

Address

Select Address style when you want to compress and italicize lines of text. Use this style for virtual or physical addresses and contact information.

HTML headings

Most of the text you read, whether it's in your newspaper, a corporate report, or even in this book, is organized and grouped beneath headings. HTML comes with a collection of six built-in heading styles, numbered from largest (Heading 1) to smallest (Heading 6). Figure 2-10 shows you what they look like.

If an author wants to create headings in a program like Microsoft Word, she might specify 16-point bold Arial font for one heading and 14-point Times New Roman for a subheading. In the early days of the Internet, you never knew what fonts a viewer had, so using fonts in this manner to organize a page was impossible. So how did our Web ancestors structure a page clearly? They used HTML headings as a workaround.

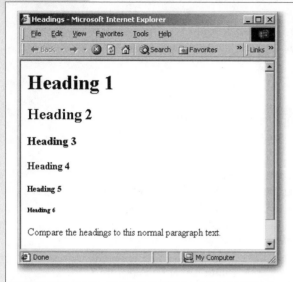

Figure 2-10:
The six HTML headings display in bold and are usually used as headlines. Headings decrease in size as the heading numbers get larger. Heading 6 is especially small, which makes it handy for copyright notices.

HTML headings provide basic structural guidelines to the browser without actually specifying a particular size. In other words, browsers understand certain rules, like Heading 1 is the largest, but it's up to the browser (or the person who's tweaking the browser's preferences) to decide what font to use when displaying a heading.

In spite of the explosion of sophisticated graphics on the Web, headings can still help you outline a page. They're very effective tools that designers often use to apply styles across a Web site. As you'll see in Chapter 7, Cascading Style Sheets, which can set formatting and display attributes for multiple pages, use headings to apply formatting to different paragraphs. For instance, a style sheet might specify that all of a site's Heading 2 paragraphs be bold, blue, and use Arial font.

Even if you're not that ambitious and just plan to use FrontPage's prepackaged graphic themes and Web site templates, you'll still see these headings throughout your pages, so you should know what they are and how to apply them.

You apply a heading style to a paragraph just as you would any other style.

1. **Click to place your cursor within the paragraph you want to turn into a heading.**

   Remember that a paragraph can consist of nothing more than a phrase—or even just a single word.

2. On the Formatting menu, locate the Style drop-down list and click the arrow to display the available styles (see Figure 2-9).

3. Choose the heading style you want.

Copy Formatting from One Paragraph to Another

Suppose you spent a lot of time formatting a paragraph to look just the way you want, but there are a ton of other paragraphs on the page that should match it. Don't worry—you don't have to do all that work over again for every paragraph. Copying paragraph formatting is fast and easy. The Format Painter on the toolbar makes it a breeze.

To copy formatting from one block of text to another:

1. **Click to place your cursor in the paragraph that has the style you want to copy.**

2. **Click the Format Painter button on the Standard toolbar in one of two ways:**

   • Click once if you're copying the style to only one paragraph.

   • Double-click if you're copying the style to multiple paragraphs.

   The Format Painter brush icon attaches to your cursor, indicating that it's active.

3. **Click in the paragraph to which you want to apply the style.**

   FrontPage copies the style to the destination paragraph. If you double-clicked in step 2, the Format Painter remains active so you can copy the style to additional paragraphs.

4. **Turn off the Format Painter by clicking the Format Painter button on the toolbar again.**

Removing Paragraph Formatting

If you want to strip a paragraph of all formatting, click to place your cursor in the paragraph and select Format → Remove Formatting or press Ctrl+Shift+Z.

Creating Lists

Lists are a common item on most Web pages. You might use a list to organize links to other spots within your site or just to organize information concisely so that it fits nicely within a browser window. Technically, a list is nothing more than a set of paragraphs that FrontPage groups together and bullets or numbers according to your instructions. You can choose from a variety of list types such as bulleted, numbered, and outline (see Figure 2-11), and then customize them to suit your needs.

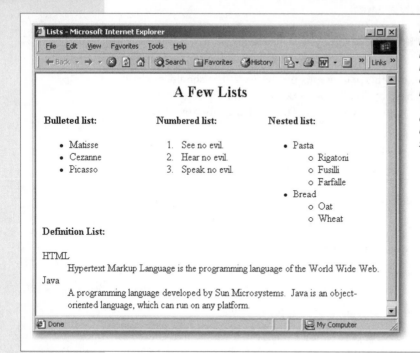

Figure 2-11:
HTML features these basic list formats. FrontPage does most of the work for you, adding bullets and numbering automatically. You can customize these lists a bit by choosing from different bullet and number styles.

Bulleted and Numbered Lists

You might think that bulleted and numbered lists are quite different from each other. For instance, numbered lists are, by definition, ordered, and bulleted lists aren't. However, they actually work the same way and therefore share a FrontPage dialog box.

To create a bulleted or numbered list:

1. **Within the document window, place your cursor where you want to insert the list.**

2. **Apply list formatting.**

   The fastest way to do this is to click either the Bullets or the Numbering button on the Formatting toolbar. These buttons automatically add the standard bullet or numbering styles. You can also choose Format → Bullets and Numbering, which gives you the chance to select alternate bullet or number styles. Later, you can always right-click within any list and select List Properties to change a list's appearance.

   The Style list on the Formatting toolbar also offers Bulleted and Numbered list styles. Selecting these styles is equivalent to clicking the Bullets or Numbering button on the toolbar.

3. **Type the first list item and press Enter.**

   Each line that follows inherits the list formatting, letting you type without interruption.

4. **To end the list, press Enter twice.**

If you have existing text that you want to turn into a list, it's just as easy. Select all the text that you want to appear in the list and pick the list style you want.

Picture bullets

FrontPage gives you the option of using an image file as a bullet point. Picture bullets are found throughout FrontPage's packaged themes and automated Web sites. You can also create your own small image file to use as a bullet style.

You can change any bulleted list into one that uses picture bullets:

1. **Click to place your cursor anywhere in the list.**

2. **Right-click and select List Properties from the pop-up menu.**

3. **Click the Picture Bullets tab.**

4. **Click Specify Picture, and then click the Browse button to find and select the image file you want to use.**

Note: If you haven't yet saved the image file in your Web site, you'll be prompted to do so when you save the page (page 14).

Outline Lists

Some lists are more complex than others. You may find that you need to break down an existing numbered or bulleted list even further, creating many levels and sublevels. This is what FrontPage calls an *outline style list*. HTML programmers and other Web-editing programs might refer to these lists as *nested* or *multi-level*. Once you've created a normal one-level list, you can turn it into an outline list and organize the list items any way you want.

Within an existing list, select the item(s) you want to move to a sublevel.

- To move items down a level, click the Increase Indent button on the Formatting toolbar twice.

- To move items up a level, click the Decrease Indent button.

- To align an item with bulleted text but remove its bullet, click the Increase Indent button once.

You can continue to move items farther up or down the hierarchy by clicking the Increase Indent and Decrease Indent buttons successive times.

If you want to change the bullet or numbering style for a group of items or sub-items, click to place your cursor anywhere in the list, right-click, select List Properties from the menu, and set your preference.

Collapsible lists

You can take any outline list and turn it into a *collapsible list* (Figure 2-12). A collapsible list lets you hide sublists under a so-called *parent item* so that the sublists display only when the parent is clicked.

To create a collapsible list:

1. **Create an outline list.**

2. **Place your cursor on one of the parent items in the list.**

3. **Right-click and select List Properties from the pop-up menu.**

4. **Turn on the Enable Collapsible Outlines checkbox.**

   Save and preview your list in a browser (page 18) to see how your collapsible list works.

Note: Use collapsible lists with caution. They work only in Internet Explorer. Also, even when they do work correctly, they suffer from another drawback: when you're looking at a collapsible list within a browser window, the parent items don't give any indication that they're clickable, as shown in Figure 2-12.

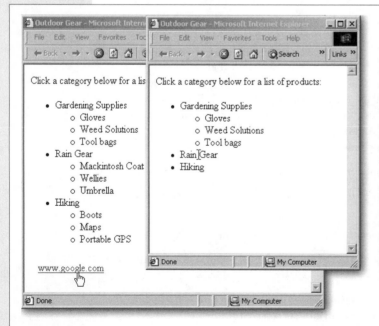

Figure 2-12:
Collapsible lists have potential but suffer from a serious display drawback. In the browser window on the right, two parent items are still collapsed. Running your cursor over the selection displays only an I-beam shaped edit cursor (which you can see within the "Rain Gear" heading). A visitor to your site will have a hard time understanding that he should click on "Rain Gear" to see the rest of the items in that list. Most people are used to seeing their cursor change from an arrow into the "press here" pointer shown over the Google hyperlink. This means that you should probably include some indication within your text or through nearby images that your list items are clickable.

Other Lists

FrontPage has some additional list options, which also appear within the List dialog box. The styles discussed below are less popular than those already covered, but you might find them handy.

Definition list

This format is designed for dictionary-style entries, in which one line for a word or phrase is set apart from its definition. If your site features a glossary, definition lists are a handy formatting tool.

You create definition lists using the Style list on the Formatting toolbar.

1. **Type a term, leaving your cursor on the same line as the term.**

2. **From the Style drop-down list, select Defined Term and then press Enter.**

3. **Type the term's definition.**

   Take another look up at the Style drop-down menu. FrontPage has set it to Definition for you. Press Enter when you're done writing your definition.

4. **Type the next term.**

   FrontPage automatically formats each line with the appropriate alternating style so you can keep typing continuously.

5. **When you're finished with the list, press Enter twice.**

   FrontPage returns you to Normal text style.

You can also apply definition list styles to existing text. Click in the appropriate paragraph and use the Style drop-down list to apply either the Defined Term or Definition style.

The definition can also appear on the same line as the term, but only if the term is very short. To get this format, turn on the Compact Layout checkbox within the List Property dialog box. If you don't see a change, your term is too long.

Menu and directory lists

The two least-used list styles are *Menu* and *Directory*. *Menu* lists are appropriate for one-line entries, and *directory* lists are used for very short one-line entries. A directory list is actually supposed to display as columns across the page. However, the style doesn't work in most browsers. Developers designed both these lists to display more compactly than a regular bulleted list. But unfortunately, you can't see any discernible difference between these selections and a regular list. So, you may as well just use a regular bulleted list.

Hyperlinks

In your travels around the World Wide Web, you've clicked on thousands of hyperlinks. Without hyperlinks, how would you move from page to page and site to site? How would you access your Google search results? The latest movie listings? Your *American Idol* contestant tracker? Hyperlinks make the Web possible.

Now that you're ready to create your own hyperlinks, you need to understand exactly what they are and how they work. FrontPage gives you an assortment of hyperlink types to add to your site, all of which you'll learn about in this chapter. You can link to pages or files within your site or anywhere out on the Web. You'll also learn how to send a viewer to a specific spot on a Web page and create a link that lets visitors send emails to your inbox.

Understanding Hyperlinks

Sure, you know what a hyperlink is. You've clicked them to check the weather at the beach, to learn about giant squid, and to find bobble head dolls on eBay. But do you really know exactly what's happening behind the scenes when you click on a link?

A *hyperlink* is an HTML command that tells a browser to display a specific Web page. A link can lead to another spot on the same Web page or across the world to a different Web site.

Sounds pretty simple. But since you're about to create hyperlinks, not just click them, you'll need to learn a bit more. For example, there are different kinds of hyperlinks: *absolute* and *relative*. FrontPage helps you manage each type, but you should know how they work.

Hyperlinks in HTML Code

A Hyperlink in HTML looks like this:

```
<a href="http://www.cnn.com/">Get news
now.</a>
```

A viewer sees only the text between the tags, of course. It appears as a hyperlink. In other words, the phrase "Get news now." is underlined or displayed in a different color, depending on how you've formatted the link's appearance.

When a cursor passes over the phrase, its arrow changes into a "click here" pointing hand.

What do the tags mean? The *a* at the beginning of the tag stands for anchor. An <a> tag marks the hot spot that links to another page or file. The *href* attribute (short for "hypertext reference") specifies the address of the page the link opens. The sample link above opens CNN's home page.

Absolute vs. Relative URLs

Say you've just published your new Web site. It looks great out there on the Web, but wait! Your links aren't working. Your images don't show up. What happened?

A lot of new Web authors run into problems like these because no one ever told them about the difference between absolute and relative URLs. This section tells you everything you need to know.

What's a URL?

The destination of a hyperlink is called a *URL* (Uniform Resource Locator). URLs don't just appear within a Web page's HTML code. You find URLs all over the place—even in magazine ads and on TV. A URL is simply an Internet address. For instance, the URL *http://www.eatyourveggies.com/greens/lettuce.html* brings one distinct page that's out on the Web into your browser's window.

URLs are divided up into different sections—all of which direct a browser to a particular page. Here's a look at how the above address breaks down:

- **http** stands for hypertext transfer protocol. A protocol is a set of communication rules that lets the browser know how to converse with the Web server. (Other protocols you might have seen are FTP [File Transfer Protocol] and email protocols like POP (Post Office Protocol) or IMAP (Internet Message Access Protocol).

- *www.eatyourveggies.com* specifies the domain, or Web server address, where the site is stored.

- **greens** is the name of a folder within that Web site.

- **lettuce.html** is the name of the actual Web page that opens in the browser.

Absolute URLs

The World Wide Web is a big place. A browser uses every part of a URL to find the particular page that a hyperlink is pointing to. For example, the combination of domain name, folder, and file name in the Web address listed above is precise and unique, much like a phone number that is connected to one particular household. In either case, the location is *absolute*. Just as there's no other house in the world that has your phone number, every absolute URL points to one specific Web page.

Relative URLS

On the other hand, when you link to another page inside your *own* Web site, things work differently. That's because a browser doesn't need as much information. If a browser is on your site's home page, it already has some of the address details that it needs. It knows the first two components of the Web address: the protocol it's using, and the Web server (or domain) it's on. So, if you direct the browser to another location within the same domain, it needs only to know how to get there from where it is. That means that links within your site are described in *relative* terms. To use the phone number analogy: when you're inside an office, you need only to dial a person's extension—rather than her complete number—to reach her. Same goes for relative URLs: they need only to indicate the path in relation to the current page.

Relative Web addresses are pretty straightforward, but one thing that can help when you're trying to understand how they work is to think about how Web pages get stored when you're creating a Web site.

When you create a Web site, you store your files within folders (also called directories), as illustrated in Figure 3-1. You do this to help organize your pages. (Chapter 10 tells you more about why and how maintaining this organization is helpful.) In a relative hyperlink, you're letting the browser know how to navigate through this folder structure.

Imagine that your browser is visiting the *index.htm* page of the Web site illustrated in Figure 3-1. When you click the "gloves" link on the index page, you're telling the browser to open the *gloves.htm* page. How does your browser get there? By reading that link's relative URL: */accessories/gloves.htm*. This URL tells the browser to open up the *accessories* folder and display the *gloves.html* file.

Once you've checked out all the gloves, you click a link on the *gloves.htm* page to get back to the home page (*index.htm*). To go there, the browser needs to get out of the *accessories* folder and back into the *root* folder. In other words, the browser goes up one folder level. The link from *gloves.htm* to *index.htm* has this relative URL: *../index.htm*. The *../* in front of the file name tells the browser to go up one folder level. The URL *../../index.htm* would tell a browser to go up two folder levels and look for the *index.htm* file.

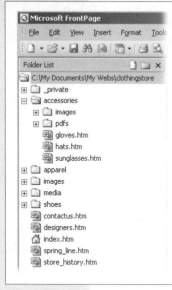

Figure 3-1:
Here's a simple example of a Web site's folder structure. The clothingstore folder contains the whole Web site. This folder is the first or main level of the site, often called the root directory. The index.htm file (the site's home page) lives in the root directory. The gloves.htm file lives one folder level down, within the accessories folder..

What all this means to you

Here's the bottom line: you use *absolute* URLs to link to pages on other Web sites. You use *relative* URLs to link to pages and files within your own site. Actually you won't really need to manage this yourself. When you create a link within your site, FrontPage automatically formats the URL as relative without any intervention on your part. However, when you have problems with hyperlinks, you can use your knowledge of URL types to troubleshoot.

FREQUENTLY ASKED QUESTION

Keep Your Site Together

I created a hyperlink to a PDF file. The link works when I'm testing the site on my own computer, but not when it's up on the Web server. What went wrong?

Most Web authors create and edit their sites on their own PCs and then publish them to a Web server so the public can see them. When a site contains a link pointing to a file on the PC but somewhere *outside* the Web site folder, the link won't work when the site gets moved onto a Web server.

For example, say the URL for that PDF file is something like *C:\My Documents\Reports\june\profits.pdf.* The link works

on your computer, because you have access to that particular file. But once you copy the Web site folder up onto the live server, that same URL causes a problem. In the server environment, there's no such place as *C:\My Documents\ Reports,* so a browser can't find the file.

The bottom line: you want to link to a file? Always *import it* into your Web site's folder structure first. (Select File → Import, then browse to and select the file.) Keep all your files stored together somewhere within your site's folder. That way, files in your site will live and travel together in one big package.

Creating Hyperlinks

Okay, so now that you know the theory behind URLs, you're ready to actually create a linking, breathing hyperlink. The first step is to select the element on your Web page that'll serve as the clickable link. You can create a hyperlink out of text or an image. (You've got a few other options for linking from images, which you'll learn about in the next chapter.)

Next, you'll set the destination for your hyperlink. Most often, links lead to other Web pages. But you can link to pretty much any type of file—Adobe Acrobat (PDF) files; Microsoft Word, Excel, or PowerPoint presentations; even zip files or actual programs (sometimes called *executables,* because they carry out a series of programmed instructions). Below, you'll learn to link to any page on the Web, to a page in your site, or to an email address.

Inserting a Hyperlink

To create a hyperlink:

1. **In the document window, select the text or a picture that you want to turn into a hyperlink.**

2. **Insert a hyperlink.**

   To do this, select Insert → Hyperlink, or press Ctrl+K, or right-click the selection and choose Hyperlink. You can also click the Hyperlink button on the Standard toolbar. All these commands open the Insert Hyperlink dialog box (see Figure 3-2).

3. **Set the Text to Display.**

   The Text to Display field, at the top of the dialog box, shows the text that appears on your Web page as the hyperlink. The field automatically displays any text you selected on the page. You can edit the text here, if you want.

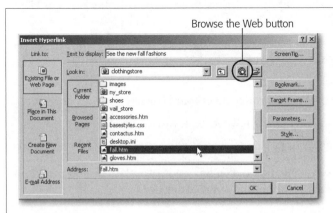

Browse the Web button

Figure 3-2:
The Insert Hyperlink dialog box includes many options for setting the destination of your hyperlink. Link to a file within your site, a URL out on the Web (by clicking the Browse the Web button, circled), or help a visitor email you by linking to your address.

Once you've opened the Insert Hyperlink dialog box, you can create any one of the types of hyperlink described in the following sections.

Linking to an Existing File Within your Site

After they get to your site, visitors will need to get from page to page. Follow these steps to link to any page or file *within* your site:

1. **On the left side of the Insert Hyperlink dialog box, click the Existing File or Web Page button.**

   The "Look In" browse box in the center of the dialog box shows your Web site's folder.

2. **Locate the page or file you want to link to.**

   Navigate to the page you want to link to just as you would to any other file in a dialog box: you can click the drop-down arrow on the right side of the "Look in" box or you can double-click any of the folders in the center of the dialog box.

3. **Double-click the file, or click it once and click OK.**

Linking to a Page on the World Wide Web

The World Wide Web is your oyster. You can link to *any* page, anywhere in the world.

There are two ways to link to a page out on the Web. The fastest is simply to type the address directly on the page you're editing. For example, type *www.google.com* followed by a space. FrontPage automatically creates the hyperlink and adds the *http://* prefix. You can use the Insert Hyperlink dialog box to edit the link later, if need be.

Or you can use the Insert Hyperlink dialog box to create the link:

1. **On the left side of the Insert Hyperlink dialog box, click the Existing File or Web Page button.**

   On the right side of the dialog box, just above the large browse box in the center, you see a Browse the Web button with a globe and magnifying glass (see Figure 3-2).

2. **Click the Browse the Web button to open your browser.**

3. **Navigate to the page on the World Wide Web you want to link to.**

4. **Copy the address from your browser's address bar.**

5. **Return to the Insert Hyperlink dialog box and paste the text you just copied into the Address field at the bottom of the dialog box.**

   Paste by pressing Ctrl+V. Then click OK and you're done.

Tip: If you've visited the Web page recently, FrontPage gives you an easier way to make the link. Click the Browsed Pages link on the left side of the dialog box to display a list of Web addresses stored in your browser's history menu. Select the address you want and then click OK.

Linking to a New Page

As you build a site, sometimes you'll need to link to pages that you haven't created yet. FrontPage includes a handy option for handling this. Instead of forcing you to create a new page, and then return to the page you were working on to create a hyperlink, the program lets you do both simultaneously.

1. **Within the Insert Hyperlink dialog box, click the Create New Document button on the left (Figure 3-3).**

   The dialog box changes to reflect your new options.

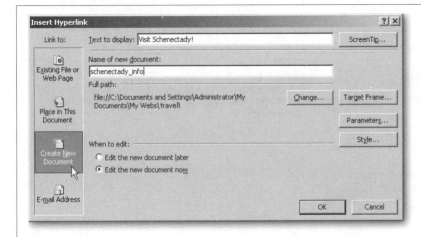

Figure 3-3:
When you're creating a hyperlink and a new page all at once, the Hyperlink dialog box lets you edit the text that'll serve as a link, and name the new file. Under File path, FrontPage displays the location in which it plans to save the file. If you want to change it, click Change and browse to another folder. Then type a file name in the bottom of the Create New Document dialog box and click OK.

2. **In the "Name of new document" field, type in a name for your new page.**

   Just type the name itself. FrontPage adds the .htm file extension for you. As always, don't include any spaces, capital letters, or special characters.

3. **Click the "Edit the new document later" radio button if you don't want the new page to open right away.**

4. **Click OK.**

   FrontPage simultaneously creates your page and your new hyperlink.

Tip: If you're working in Design view and want to edit a page you've linked to, just press Ctrl and click the hyperlink. FrontPage opens the destination page of the hyperlink in the document window.

Dragging Between Files to Create Hyperlinks

Sometimes you're too busy to bother with menus. If you're the point-and-click type, FrontPage gives you another option for creating hyperlinks. With the folder list active on the left side of your screen (page 378), just drag the file you want to link *to* onto the page that should contain the hyperlink. Poof! Your hyperlink appears, taking its text from the title of the file you dragged. The page title may not be exactly what you want, but you can edit this. Just right-click the link and select Hyperlink Properties. Then change the Text to Display field.

Tip: A Web page *title* is different from its *file name.* To view a page's title, open it in Design view and select File → Properties. The Title field shows you the page title and lets you edit it. (See page 184 for more details.)

Speaking of menus, FrontPage gives you a handy menu when you're dragging your new links around. Instead of dragging with your left mouse button depressed, drag while holding your right mouse button. A menu appears that gives you more choices, as illustrated in Figure 3-4.

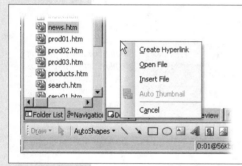

Figure 3-4:
This pop-up menu offers additional actions for dragged items and even lets you back out of your drag-and-drop operation with a Cancel option.

The right button drag offers the following choices:

- **Create Hyperlink.** Inserts a hyperlink just like dragging with the left mouse button does.

- **Open File.** Opens the file you're dragging so that you can edit it within the document window.

- **Insert File.** Inserts the contents of the file you dragged into the page that's currently open.

- **Auto Thumbnail.** If you've dragged a picture onto the page, this inserts the graphic as a *thumbnail,* or miniaturized image, that hyperlinks to the full-size version of the image

Linking to an Email Address

Say you want to provide site visitors with an easy way to contact you. Maybe you need to take orders, gather information, or you just haven't been getting enough email lately. Sure, you could just post your email address and invite people to write to you. But they might decide it's too much trouble to open their email program, copy and paste your address, type a subject line, and so on.

Thankfully, FrontPage provides a faster, more convenient option that makes this process almost effortless. When you create a link to an email address, what you're actually doing is giving the visitor an automated shortcut. When a visitor clicks an email hyperlink, the *mailto* code command in HTML launches the visitor's email program and creates a new message, already addressed to the email address you specify. All that's left for him to do is fill out the message and click Send.

WORKAROUND WORKSHOP

Spam Alert

Think twice before you add a bunch of mailto links to your pages. The Web is crawling with automated email address harvesters, called *spam bots* or *spiders,* that scour text across the Web for anything resembling an email address. Addresses they find end up in the databases of the nefarious spammers who dispatch these parasites. If you post your address within a mailto link, it won't be long before your inbox is inundated.

Fortunately, there are a few things you can do to protect yourself. One solution is to use numeric or named entities for all the characters in your email address (see page 25)

However, many newer bots can easily crack the code.

There are other workarounds that you can research on the Web by searching for "mailto + spam." Also, check out a FrontPage Add-in called Spam Spoiler at *www.jimcoaddins.com,* which masks and then recreates your email address in a way that seems to foil bots. Perhaps the best solution is to create a "Contact Us" form on your site instead. That way, visitors can enter the information on a Web page (which then gets automatically forwarded to you) and nobody emails you directly. (Read all about forms in Chapter 15.)

To create an email link within the Insert Hyperlink dialog box:

1. **Click the Email Address button on the lower-left corner of the dialog box.**

   A collection of email specific options appear in the dialog box.

2. **Within the Email address field, type in the destination email address.**

   Enter only the address. FrontPage writes the rest of the necessary code for you.

Note: If you're creating lots of email links, you'll be happy to discover that FrontPage saves addresses you've used within the "Recently used email addresses" box. Just click to select an address.

---

3. **In the Subject field, type the subject line that should appear in all messages generated by the link.**

   Use the subject line to help you sort your mail. For instance, you could give the link on your customer assistance page the subject line "Support Request," while you might give a link on another page the subject "Suggestion" or "New Order."

4. **Click OK.**

Fine-Tuning Hyperlink Properties

Say you've got a hyperlink on your page that links to an article somewhere on the Web that relates to what you're discussing. If a viewer clicks the link, she might get engrossed in the article and click further links within that page. Next thing you know, she's so far away exploring other Web sites that she forgets where she was in the first place. Point is, you may not want people to leave your site entirely. Maybe it would be better for you (and your fragile, neglected ego) if your viewer's browser opens up a *new* window when a visitor clicks on the article link, keeping your site open at the same time.

You not only have the power to send your visitors where you wish, you can control how destination pages display on their screen. For example, you can launch a linked page in a new, separate browser window. In this section, you'll also learn how to provide viewers with additional information about a hyperlink so they'll know whether or not they want to click it. You can even draw attention to your links using color and rollover effects.

Open a Target Page in a New Window

Unless you specify otherwise, hyperlinks open the destination page in the same browser window as the original page containing the link. The new page replaces the first page in the window. While a viewer can always press the back button on a browser, you may prefer to keep the original page open, while also displaying the destination page in a new window.

You can set this preference by adding a *Target* attribute to the hyperlink. This attribute specifies *where* the destination document opens—in this case, a new browser window. To do this, click Target Frame within the Insert Hyperlink dialog box. Then, from the list of choices, select New Window. Other selections under Target Frame let you control hyperlinks created on pages that exist within a frameset. You'll learn all about frames and what these target options mean in Chapter 6.

Adding Screen Tips

The more information you share with your visitors, the better their experience is bound to be. While text often serves as a hyperlink and indicates where the link might go, it's not always so clear cut. What if the hyperlink is a graphic? In some cases, you'll want to provide more info about a link. You can do this by creating a *screen tip*—a small yellow box of text that appears when a visitor passes his cursor over a hyperlink.

To add a screen tip to a hyperlink, open the Insert Hyperlink dialog box. Click Screen Tip, on the upper-right corner, and FrontPage presents you with the Set Hyperlink Screen Tip dialog box. Type in the text that you want to display and click OK.

Note: Screen tips may not work in older browsers—those that predate Internet Explorer and Netscape 4.0.

Changing Hyperlink Colors

Colors can really help your hyperlinks stand out on a page as well as provide some guidance to visitors. For instance, you can help people navigate your site, by displaying links they've already followed in a different color.

Use the Page Properties dialog box to set link colors. Start by selecting File → Properties and then click the Formatting tab pictured in Figure 3-5. Within the drop-down lists for each different hyperlink state (Hyperlink, Visited Hyperlink, and so on), select the color you want.

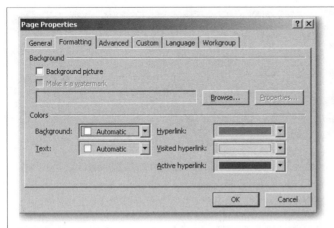

Figure 3-5:
On the right side of the Formatting tab, you can set up a color scheme for your hyperlinks. In the Hyperlink field, set the color that links should be when a visitor first opens the page. Links that a viewer has already visited display in the color you choose for Visited Hyperlink. Active Hyperlink controls the color that displays while a visitor is clicking on a link. Experiment with a few schemes and test them in your browser.

Cascading Style Sheets, which you'll learn about in Chapter 7, offer a better way to set hyperlink colors. Using CSS, you don't need to set colors on each and every page, but you can configure this setting just once in a style sheet and save yourself a ton of work.

Adding Rollover Font Effects

Later in this book, you'll read about lots of ways to add motion to your Web pages. But before you even start learning about some of these more sophisticated tools, you can easily add a simple touch of visual spice by animating your hyperlinks. FrontPage gives you the ability to change the font of a hyperlink when a visitor's cursor passes over it. The effect can be as simple as a change from normal text to bold formatting. Here's what you need to do:

1. Select File → Properties and click the Advanced tab.

2. Within the Styles section, turn on the "Enable hyperlink rollover effects" checkbox.

3. Click Rollover Style.

   A Font dialog box displays.

4. **Set the font style and color you want to display whenever a cursor passes over the hyperlink.**

   This style should be different from the regular hyperlink style already in place on the page.

5. **Click OK to save the font and then again to close the Page Property dialog box.**

Note: Font rollover effects work only in browsers that support DHTML (see Chapter 9) and aren't available on pages that use FrontPage themes.

FREQUENTLY ASKED QUESTION

Underlined Links

I hate the underlining applied to hyperlinks. Do I really need it?

When you turn text into a hyperlink, FrontPage automatically underlines the text. If this formatting doesn't fit in with your design scheme, you can get rid of it. Remove it as you would any other underline formatting. Select all the underlined text and click the underline button on the Formatting bar. The hyperlink remains, but the underlining is removed. Cascading Style Sheets can help you make this change across your entire site with one setting. To learn how, turn to page 122 in Chapter 7.

Adding Bookmarks

Suppose you'd like to link to another page, but the relevant material is so far down the page that your viewers won't see it when the file first opens in their browser. Your readers could get confused when the information they're looking for doesn't seem to be there.

You can solve this problem with a *bookmark*. A bookmark allows you to create a hyperlink that jumps to a specific location within a page. The location can be within the same page as the hyperlink or on another page altogether.

You have to set the bookmark first. Then you can create a hyperlink to it.

Note: You can create bookmarks only on pages that you yourself can edit. This means you can't bookmark to a passage within somebody *else's* page out on the Web.

Setting Bookmarks

When a visitor clicks a link that's keyed to a bookmark, the browser displays only a portion of the Web page. You get to designate what portion by placing a bookmark at the top of the part of the page you want viewers to see (see Figure 3-6).

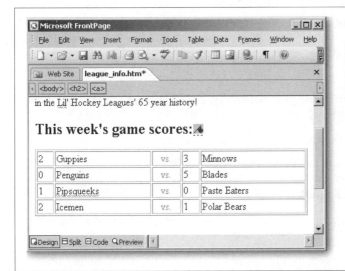

Figure 3-6:
To link directly to this page's game scores, you'd insert a bookmark anywhere on the heading line for that section of the page. A bookmark displays as a small flag icon that's visible in FrontPage's Design view, but not in a browser.

To insert a bookmark:

1. **Click to place your cursor at the point on the page where you want to place the bookmark.**

2. **Select Insert → Bookmark.**

3. **Within the Bookmark dialog box, type in a name for the bookmark and click OK.**

   Give each bookmark an original name that's easy to identify. Clear names and labels help you manage links throughout the life of your Web site. Keep bookmark names short (eight characters or less) and don't include spaces, capital letters, or special characters.

   A bookmark shows up in Page view as a small flag icon within the text.

Note: If your bookmark is too close to the bottom of the page, the browser may be unable to display the bookmark in the upper-left corner. Once a browser hits page bottom, it can't go any lower. This means text above your bookmark will display in the top of the browser window.

Linking to Bookmarks

Linking to a bookmark works the same way as creating a regular hyperlink—the only difference is you're specifying a specific location on the page you're linking to.

Link to a bookmark within the same page

Bookmarks can help you reign in text on a very long page. For example, you can create a list of hyperlinks at the top of a page that link to bookmarked headings farther down the page.

1. Select the text or image for the link and click the Insert Hyperlink button.

2. Within the Insert Hyperlink dialog box, click the "Place in this Document" button on the left.

   A list of bookmarks within the current page displays.

3. Select the bookmark you want to link to and click OK.

Link to a bookmark on another page

Even if you're linking from a separate page, you can send visitors to a specific location on the destination page.

1. Select the text or image for the link and click the Insert Hyperlink button.

2. On the left side of the Insert Hyperlink dialog box, click the Existing File or Web Page button.

   The Look In browse box in the center of the dialog shows your Web site's folder.

3. Locate the page or file you want to link to and click once to highlight it.

4. Click Bookmark.

   A list of bookmarks within that page displays.

5. Select the bookmark you want to link to and click OK.

   In the Insert Hyperlink dialog box, the target address for the hyperlink changes. A pound sign (#) and the name of your bookmark now follow the destination page information.

6. Click OK to save the link.

Working with Images

Graphics fill pages all across the Web. For better or for worse, if something can be photographed, illustrated, animated, or videotaped, you can probably find it online. Miss the news on CNN? Just go to their Web site and watch the streaming video.

Whether you plan to use images as an integral part of your site or just for visual accent, FrontPage makes it easy to include graphics. After you read about the basics of image file formats, you'll learn how to place a picture, video, or Flash animation anywhere on your page. Or why not let FrontPage create an instant photo gallery for you? You can then annotate each snapshot with your own clever commentary. Images can even display as a page background or act as hyperlinked navigation buttons. Read on to learn how.

Image Files on the Web

Know your medium. Before you start loading up your site with image files, it helps to know a little bit about the many graphical species roaming around out there and which ones make sense for you to use.

Image File Formats 101

Graphic files today come in all shapes, sizes, and types. Some high-quality graphic file formats, like *TIF* (Tapped Image Format) and *BMP* (Windows bitmap), provide terrific detail and color, which is a big reason why these formats are popular with people who want to print their images. But, as in real life, quality costs. The bandwidth and disk space these files require can slow the speed at which your Web pages load.

Tip: You can tell a file's format by its file suffix. For example, *house.jpg, house.gif, house.tif,* and *house. bmp* are all different formats of the same image file.

Most Web browsers are limited and can display only two image types: *GIF* (Graphic Interchange Format) and *JPEG* (Joint Photographic Experts Group). These two formats take image information and compress it, while retaining the most important details so that the image remains recognizable. FrontPage also supports a new technology called *PNG* (Portable Network Graphics). PNG is an improvement on the GIF format, but isn't recognized by all browsers, especially older ones. As you add images to your pages, you'll probably want to use the two more standard file types, GIF and JPEG. GIF files are best for displaying images that have flat areas of color and simple lines, like a cartoon or company logo. JPEGs are good for images that contain subtle color variations, like photographs.

Tip: GIF files can also include multiple images within a single file. These simple GIF animation loops are used—annoyingly, for some peoples' tastes—throughout the Web to add movement to pages. Viewers don't need any special software to view them.

The bottom line: go with a GIF or a JPEG and be careful not to use too many images on one page since they'll affect your page's download time.

Adding Pictures

FrontPage's talents as a visual Web page editor really start to shine as you begin to add graphics to your site. The program provides a few easy options for inserting images.

Inserting Pictures

To insert a picture on a page, place your cursor wherever you want the picture to appear and select Insert → Image → From File, or click the Insert Picture button on the Pictures toolbar. (To access the toolbar, select View → Toolbars → Pictures.) A Picture dialog box like the one in Figure 4-1 opens. Browse to your image file and click Insert. The picture then displays on your Web page.

Note: FrontPage lets you retrieve a graphic that's stored anywhere on your computer so that you can add it to a page on your site. The program prompts you to save the image file in your site when you save the Web page. However, you may want to import a graphic into your site's images folder *before* you insert it on a page–especially if the picture's a JPEG (see the "Editing JPEGs" sidebar on page 61 to learn why and how).

Figure 4-1:
If you're having trouble remembering what your images look like, use the Views button on the Picture dialog box toolbar to change the way files are displayed. Both the Preview and Thumbnails options show your actual pictures.

Dragging Pictures onto Your Page

You may find yourself using the same images over and over on many different pages throughout your Web site. To speed things up, FrontPage lets you drag images directly onto your page.

To insert a picture that's already saved within your site, find it within the Folder List and drag it onto your page within the document window. The image appears wherever you drop it.

You can also drag an image file from another location, outside your site's directory. If you've used Windows Explorer to find a file, just drag it onto the page you're editing. When you save your Web page, FrontPage prompts you to save the image file as part of your site. If you want to get a picture file into your site, but not necessarily onto a page right away, you can also drag a file directly into your images folder.

Or, you can drag your pictures around within an individual page. If you drag a picture from one page onto another page within the same Web site, FrontPage moves it to the new location. If the destination page is in a different Web site, the program copies the image, leaving the original in place.

Formatting Pictures

Okay, so you've got an image on your page, which is very exciting. But perhaps it came out larger than you wanted it to? Also, maybe it's shoved your text off to the side, and the page layout is now a disaster.

Inserting the image was a breeze, but you may need to work a bit harder to make it fit nicely and really look good. FrontPage is far from a sophisticated image editor, but it offers a handful of tools to help you edit, resize, and adjust the placement of your graphics.

Editing Appearance

Web designers who edit pictures extensively rely on software programs created for the job, like Adobe Photoshop. For best results, you should, too. But if all you need to make are simple edits or small tweaks, like cropping or rotating an image, FrontPage can save you the trouble of opening a separate program. To access FrontPage's rudimentary editing features, open the Pictures toolbar (see Figure 4-2). Select View → Toolbars → Pictures and run your cursor over each toolbar button to display a tool tip, which tells you what each button does.

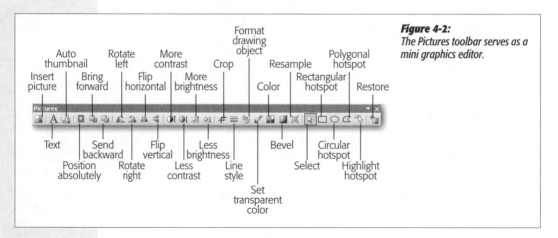

Figure 4-2:
The Pictures toolbar serves as a mini graphics editor.

To edit a graphic within FrontPage, select the image, and then choose from the following options on the Pictures toolbar:

- **Rotate** images with the four rotate and flip buttons. Rotate buttons turn the picture 90 degrees, while flipping creates a mirror image.

- To place text over a picture, click the **Text** button and type within the box that appears. Click and drag to move the text box around. FrontPage adds the text to the image itself, so you'll be prompted to resave the image when you save the page.

- Click the **Color** button and you can change an image from color to grayscale or black and white. Choosing Washout lightens an image, which may be handy for background pictures, or to show that a button on your page is temporarily inactive.

- Adjust **contrast** and **brightness** with the more and less buttons for each of these attributes. These two controls often work together to pep up an ailing image. For instance, if you have a dark, muddy image and increase the brightness, your picture can look washed out. You can fix this by upping the contrast, which increases the darkness of dark colors and lightens light colors. If, after trying these, your picture still needs help, turn to a real image editor.

- Click the **Set Transparent Color** button and click on a color within the image to make all similarly colored areas see-through. This button is great for eliminating a picture's monochrome background. This feature works well only if your picture has simple lines and areas of flat color. It doesn't work on photographs. In fact, if you try to use this tool on a JPEG, FrontPage converts it to a GIF. (Don't know the difference? See "Image File Formats 101" on page 57.) And converter beware: if you're converting an image in order to set a transparent color, don't bother—the results are lousy.

- To **crop** a picture, click the crop button, use the cursor to outline the area you want to keep, and click the crop button again. Anything outside the area you selected disappears.

- Click **Bevel** to bevel, or angle, a picture's edges. FrontPage lightens the top and left edges while darkening the bottom and right ones. This creates a 3-D effect, which is handy if you're using pictures as buttons.

UP TO SPEED

Editing JPEGs

One important thing to understand about JPEG files is that each time you edit one (in any program), you reduce the image's quality. That's because JPEGs stay lean and mean by automatically discarding data when saved. Not surprisingly, this data loss degrades image quality. Graphics professionals call the JPEG's format "lossy" because of this trait. (GIF files, in contrast, aren't lossy.)

Before tossing an image on a page, a lot of Web developers edit and compress their JPEGs as much as they can while still maintaining an acceptable level of quality. You measure compression in percent. For instance, you could tell a program that you want to compress a JPEG to 85 percent of its current size. The lower the percentage, the lower the quality. (Though even at 100 percent, some compression takes place.)

FrontPage has a bad habit of compressing JPEGs even further if you insert them on a page without first importing them into your site. When FrontPage saves a copy of the JPEG with your page, it automatically compresses the file up to 70 percent, which can really degrade your picture.

To avoid this:

- Import the image into your site *before* you place it on a page. To do so, select File → Import. Then click Add File, browse to the image file, and then click Open. Finally, click OK to save the picture in your site and move it into your images folder. FrontPage respects the sovereignty of an imported JPEG and won't try to compress it.

- Or, while saving your page, click the Picture File Type button, select JPEG, and change the Quality setting to 100 percent.

Due to the JPEG's talent for losing quality with each save, edit your JPEG files as few times as possible. You also might want to consider keeping unedited copies of these files in a safe place so that you can go back to the original file if the JPEG on your site grows worse for wear. Better yet, keep a backup copy of the picture in a format that doesn't lose information—like TIF, for instance.

Resizing

Even when you find the perfect picture for your page, it doesn't always fit perfectly. You'll often need to change a picture's dimensions to make it look good.

When it comes to resizing, you're almost always better off using a full-blown graphics editing program—especially if you're drastically changing the image size. FrontPage offers its own unique options for resizing pictures, which may suffice if your needs are very simple.

Resizing by pixel

You resize a digital image by changing the height and width of a picture, which are usually measured in pixels. FrontPage's pixel-editing controls look like those in any image-editing program. But they're deceiving.

To take a look, open the Picture Properties dialog box pictured in Figure 4-3. Right-click an image and select Picture Properties.

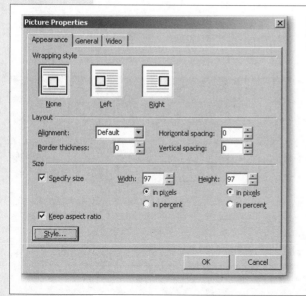

Figure 4-3:
Use the Picture Properties dialog box to set size, alignment, and other attributes.

On the Appearance tab, under the Size heading, you'll see two boxes, which display the height and width of the image. To activate these, turn on the "Specify size" checkbox. You can then readjust the size using pixels or percent.

Note: When you're resizing in pixels, make sure that the "Keep aspect ratio" checkbox is turned on. This keeps the height and width of your picture in proportion. Without it, you could distort the image, making it look squeezed in one direction or another.

When you resize in pixels, with "Keep aspect ratio" on, you need only edit one number. The other one changes automatically.

So far, these height and width fields look like resizing tools you'd find in any image editor. But in reality, FrontPage's pixel-editing controls are just a smokescreen. Say you go in and shrink a 400×400 pixel image down to half its size. You may believe you've changed the size of the image file, but you haven't. FrontPage has fooled you. The actual image remains 400×400 pixels. What you've changed is the space on the page that the picture occupies. The 400×400 image now displays on the screen within a 200×200 pixel space. FrontPage doesn't edit the file itself, but instead tells the browser to display the picture at whatever size you've specified. FrontPage adjusts what it calls the "appearance attributes" of a picture, not the actual size of the image.

If you're resizing by very little, this approach is fine. But if you're making a drastic change, your image will appear rough or distorted. If your picture looks bad after you resize, try resampling (explained below). Another important point: if your plan is to shrink your picture's size in order to speed page download, resizing by pixel in FrontPage won't do the trick. Again, resample instead—or use a real image editor like Adobe Photoshop or Photoshop Elements to change the actual picture size.

Note: While you can *shrink* a picture easily, you can't really make an image much *larger* than it already is—even in professional quality image-editing software. Doing so inevitably makes your picture jagged and distorted. The only thing to do is start over. Go back to your scanner or digital camera and create a larger picture.

Resize by percent

Resizing by percent may also not work as you expect. In other programs, like Photoshop and Microsoft Word, you can resize pictures by percent. The key question here is: percent of what? In Word, the percentage always refers to the image itself. The image begins at 100 percent. So, if you want it half as big, you enter 50 percent and Word shrinks it. In FrontPage, percent means something very different. The percentage is relative to the browser window (or—if the image is contained in a table—the table cell size). In other words, an image set at 100 percent takes up the entire browser. One set at 50 percent takes up half the browser window. This is your first taste of *fixed* (pixel-specific) vs. *relative* (percent) sizing on a Web page. Later in this book, you'll read more about these issues. For ease of use, you probably should stick with resizing in pixels for now, but keep your percentage option in mind. It may come in handy when you start using tables.

Resampling your picture

Unlike "resizing" by pixel, resampling *does* change the image's actual size. You can resample at any time by right-clicking on an image and selecting Resample. When you resample, FrontPage saves a new instance of the image file within your site, using the new dimensions. In other words, if you shrink a 400×400 pixel image down to half its size, FrontPage will resave it as a 200×200 pixel image.

When should you resample? If you've shrunk an image and want the page to download faster, resample. Resampling can also smooth out a resized image that looks rough or pixilated. But beware: after you resample, you won't be able to enlarge the image again. If you do, the picture will look terrible. In fact, resampling more than once can really blur a graphic and compromise image quality.

Tip: Keep backup copies of your graphic files in a folder outside your Web site. This way, if the FrontPage picture editor ruins an image, you can import a new copy and start over.

Resizing by dragging

If accessing Picture Properties seems like one step too many, you might want to resize by dragging directly on your image. In Design view, select the image. Resizing handles appear around the picture in the form of tiny squares around the edges. Grab a corner handle and drag it until the image is the size you want. (Why grab a corner? Because, if you grab a handle on a side, top, or bottom and drag, the picture expands only in one direction and becomes distorted.)

Resizing by dragging is the same as readjusting pixels in Picture Properties. This means that FrontPage doesn't change the size of the picture file—only the picture's display size on the page.

After you resize by dragging, FrontPage displays a Picture Actions box beneath the image. Click it to display a shortcut menu, pictured in Figure 4-4.

Figure 4-4:
The Picture Actions box offers a menu to assist with resizing. The first choice, Only Modify Size Attributes, is the equivalent of resizing by pixel (page 62). The second choice, Resample Picture to Match Size, is a shortcut to the resample command (page 63). The first option here is what FrontPage does with a picture resized by dragging anyway, so click the Picture Actions icon only if you want to resample instead.

Setting Picture Placement

When you plunk an image down on a page, your job has often just begun. You'll need to spend some time fine-tuning your picture's placement. The best way to control your pictures so they play nicely with the surrounding text is to place everything within a table, which you'll learn about in Chapter 5. Meanwhile, you can make do with a few simple tools that FrontPage provides to tweak your page layout.

Text wrapping

Whenever you insert a large picture on a line with text, it looks awkward and out of place. The cure? If you want your text to flow around your pictures gracefully, turn on text wrapping. If you do, words "wrap" around the side of your picture instead of treating the image like just another character on a line (one which happens to be huge). When you insert a picture, wrapping is automatically set to None. Unless a picture is going have a paragraph all to itself, the None setting tends to look clunky and unprofessional.

A simple click on either the Left or Right wrapping button in the Picture Properties dialog box (see Figure 4-3) can really help make a picture look like it belongs with the text around it. If you need to set a buffer between the picture and the surrounding text, use the Horizontal spacing and Vertical spacing fields.

Alignment

Alignment settings available in the Picture Properties dialog box (see Figure 4-3) control picture placement for *small* images plopped down in the middle of a chunk of text. If you place an image within a line of text, you can set the image to align with the bottom or top of the letters, or to be centered vertically within a line. You'll find that if a picture is larger than the text, inserting it within a line disturbs the line spacing of the paragraph. If you're inserting picture within a line of text, keep it small and use the alignment drop-down menu to reduce its impact on line spacing.

Absolute positioning

If you're a real control freak, simple alignment choices might not satisfy you. Absolute positioning is the final word in picture placement. You can set the position of your image at a precise location on your Web page and even position pictures in front of or behind each other. But this feature has its pitfalls.

Click to select an image and then click the Position Absolutely button on the Picture toolbar. A blue box surrounds the graphic. Drag the box to wherever you want it to appear on the page. If you're creating a collage of images, use the Bring to Front and Send to Back buttons on the toolbar to place images in front of or behind each other.

Note: FrontPage actually places your picture in a *layer* to allow you to position it. Chapter 8 covers layers and absolute positioning in depth.

Use absolute positioning with caution. While the positioning of these pictures may be absolute, other elements on your page may not be, resulting in hidden text or a confusing layout. Not to mention that some older browsers don't even support absolute positioning.

Alternative Representations

A picture illustrates something that you couldn't express with words. In spite of that, you may want to add some text that briefly describes your image. The truth is, on the Web, a picture is just not enough. You should always include a short description of whatever it is you're showing. Why? See the box "Accessibility on the Web."

So how do you include a text alternative? The way you'd add any other property: right-click the image and select Picture Properties. Then click the General tab. FrontPage offers options for adding additional property information, as pictured in Figure 4-5.

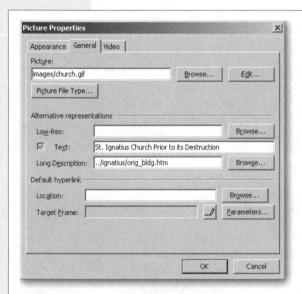

Figure 4-5:
Within the Picture Properties General tab, you can enter alternative representations for an image, like a text description. Sometimes the Text field isn't long enough. In that case, you can use the Long Description field to feature a link to another Web page that contains detailed information about the picture. Just enter the URL, or use the Long Description browse button to link to another page in your site.

FREQUENTLY ASKED QUESTION

Accessibility on the Web

Why do I need to write out a description for each of my pictures?

Common courtesy. There are people out there who might not be able to see your images. Visually disabled Web surfers use screen readers that read a page's text to them. A screen reader can't read a picture, but it can read a picture's alternative text and at least give a blind or partially sighted person a better idea of what's on your page.

Many people with perfect eyesight may also need this alternative text. For reasons of security, or to speed download

time, lots of folks set their browsers not to display images. Use a description to let them know whether or not they should take the extra step of actually displaying a graphic (see Figure 4-6).

You'll learn more about making your site fully accessible to people of all abilities in Chapter 12. Meanwhile, don't leave visitors wondering what's on your page. Create alternative text for all your pictures.

The Text field is where you'll enter a description of the image. This description displays as a screen tip when a visitor passes a cursor over the picture, or appears in place of the image when the browser doesn't or cannot display graphics (see Figure 4-6).

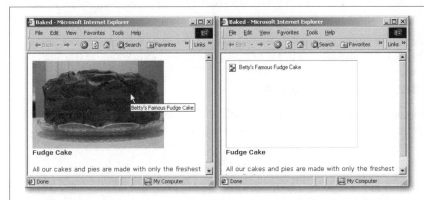

Figure 4-6:
Alternative text appears as a screen tip (left) or (if a viewer has configured the browser not to show images) inside the image's placeholder to explain what should be there (right).

Note: For pictures that serve as buttons, just enter the text that's on the button. If you've used transparent or one-color images to space out your page, don't bother to type any alternative text. You'll just confuse visitors.

Images can take a long time to load. If you want to give readers a preview of what they'll eventually see, you can designate a low-resolution image of the same picture as an alternative representation. A low-resolution image contains less color and detail, so it loads faster. For example, a simple black-and-white version of a picture might serve nicely. This simpler image displays temporarily in the time it takes for the actual image to fully load within the browser. If you want to use a low-resolution image, click the browse button to the right of the Low-Res field and select the alternative picture. Make sure that it has the same dimensions as the real image.

Adding Videos and Flash Movies

Static pictures don't seem to be enough in today's world. Flash animations and videos add life to Web sites around the globe. In fact, many sites' sole purpose is to present videos, movies, and other moving images.

FrontPage makes incorporating moving images just as easy as adding still pictures—all you need to do is click a button.

Inserting Video Files

It's easy to add videos to your site. But make sure you've considered all the angles first. Video files are large. As you'll see, it's easy to embed a video directly within your page, but your page could then take forever to download. To avoid frustrating your visitors, you might want to place a hyperlink to the video on your page, instead of inserting the file itself. This way, your page will load quickly but viewers still have access to the video.

Also, video files require their own players in order to function. Are your visitors likely to have this software installed on their systems? Even if you think so, make sure you provide information on what's required. You could even include a link to a site that offers downloads.

What kinds of moving images can you add? FrontPage can handle the following digital video file types: WMV, MPEG, AVI, RAM, and QuickTime (MOV files).

Displaying a video as a picture file

FrontPage lets you embed a video directly within your page. Inserting it is fast and easy. Place your cursor on the page and select Insert → Picture → Video. Once you browse and select the file, your video then appears on the page. You can also just drag a video file from the folder list onto the page.

If it seems almost too easy to be true, it may well be. The big drawback to using this method is that people who use Netscape Navigator won't see your video. When you use this shortcut method, FrontPage generates HTML that Navigator doesn't understand, so a broken picture icon will appear in place of your video. If that thought bothers you, then you probably want to display the video as a *plug-in*. When you insert the video as a plug-in, the file calls whatever separate software a viewer's installed with her browser to view video files—like Windows Media Player or QuickTime. One additional advantage is that your viewers now get controls so that they can stop, play, fast forward, and so on. To add a plug-in, see the section on "Inserting Plug-Ins" on page 69.

Setting video properties

If you've embedded your video on the page, you can control its placement as you would any other picture: right-click the video file and select Picture Properties. The dialog box you see now includes a Video tab, as illustrated in Figure 4-7.

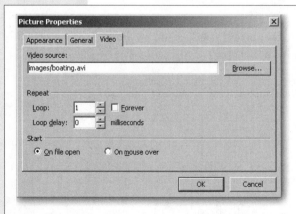

Figure 4-7:
The Video tab includes file information and other options. For instance, you don't need to limit the video to only one showing. Within the Loop field, select the number of times you want it to play, or turn on the Forever checkbox to have it loop continuously.

FrontPage automatically sets the video to play when the page opens. Your only other choice is to have it start when a cursor passes over the image. To change this setting, select "On mouse over" within the Start section.

Inserting Flash Movies

If you think videos are too large to include on your site, you have another animation alternative. Macromedia Flash movies (which bear the SWF file extension) are smaller than regular video files. Flash movies use vector graphics, which are composed of lines and geometric shapes (as opposed to videos, which are bitmapped, or made up of individual pixels).

To insert a Flash Movie, select Insert → Picture → Movie in Flash Format. Browse to your SWF file and select it. A blue box for the Flash graphic appears on your page. To view it, preview the page or right-click and select Play Movie in Flash Format.

Note: You must have the Macromedia Flash player installed to preview any Flash animations. Viewers must have this player, too, to see Flash content. Don't worry about directing them to download sites. Most browsers come with Flash, but for those that don't, your Flash movie includes an automatic link that will take a viewer where he needs to go.

Setting movie properties

Most likely, you'll want to keep all of FrontPage's automatic settings in place when you insert your Flash movie. However, if you want to change the movie's size or placement on the page, right-click and select Movie in Flash Format Properties. Selections under Layout are just like those for arranging any graphic and surrounding text (page 64).

Inserting Plug-Ins

A *plug-in* is a separate software program that works in conjunction with a browser. Plug-ins are helper applications that let Web surfers watch movies and listen to audio files that appear on Web pages. Macromedia Flash is actually a plug-in, but it's so common that FrontPage lets you insert it directly on a page. Likewise, videos often require the presence of RealPlayer or Windows Media Player on the system.

You can insert any file type you want as a plug-in. Plug-ins give visitors control over media files—video programs will open with controls to play and rewind, for example. But keep in mind that visitors might not have the necessary software installed on their system. If you think they won't mind, go ahead. But be sure to provide a link to the plug-in they may need to download.

To insert a plug-in:

1. Select Insert → Web Component and, within the Component type list, click **Advanced Controls.**

2. **Within the "Choose a control" list, select Plug-in and click Finish.**

   A Plug-in Properties dialog box appears.

3. **Browse to the file you want to insert and select it.**

4. **Enter a message for browsers without plug-in support.**

   You might want to say something like: "You need the QuickTime player in order to view this animation."

5. **Set preferred alignment and dimensions, then click OK.**

   FrontPage usually sets the dimensions automatically based on the file you selected, and so typically you don't have to make changes here. But if you do ever need to, you can return to this dialog box at any time to make adjustments. Right-click the plug-in file and select Plug-in Properties.

Saving Image Files

Though graphics are a part of your Web pages, FrontPage saves images as separate, individual files. Eventually—even if your site is small—you're going to have a whole lot of image files to contend with. You may need to use certain images on multiple pages or go back and edit a picture or two, so you'll want to find them easily and quickly.

Keep your picture management chores hassle-free by naming and organizing your image files intelligently. Give each file a name that's appropriate and describes the picture. Keep all your images in the same folder, called *images*. FrontPage even creates an images folder automatically when you create a new Web site. Put it to good use. If you have a lot of Flash or video files, gather them in a folder called *media*. You can manage this process as you go, saving image files in the correct folders as you insert them on pages.

Saving Files with a Page

When you've inserted a new image or video within a page and try to save the page, FrontPage displays the Save Embedded Files dialog box, illustrated in Figure 4-8. Since the graphic file hasn't yet been saved within the Web site, FrontPage needs to know where to put it.

Save your file by setting the following options:

- Click **Rename** to give the file a name that you can easily identify later on.

- Use **Change Folder** to browse to your site's *images* folder. Once you set this folder, it appears in the Folder column.

- Click **Picture File Type** if you want to change the file type to another Web-friendly format.

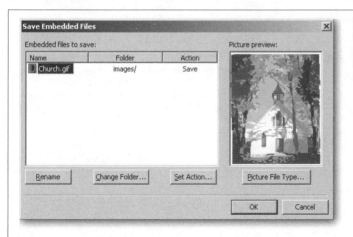

Figure 4-8:
Click any of the three buttons at the bottom of the Save Embedded Files dialog box to change the settings in the columns above.

Note: When you save a JPEG file with a page, FrontPage automatically compresses the file, which can diminish picture quality. To avoid this, click the Picture File Type button, select JPEG, and then change the Quality setting to 100 percent. Another way to avoid FrontPage's compression mania is to import the image into your Web site before inserting it on a page. The program doesn't attempt to compress imported images. (See the "Editing JPEGs" box on page 61 for details.)

- Steer clear of the **Set Action** button. The only option it offers is letting you link to the image file somewhere on your computer *outside* of your Web site. Why is that a bad idea? Because it means that when you upload your site to a Web server, the link to the image will be broken and the image won't display.

Note: The Save Embedded Files dialog box sometimes automatically changes the format of files so that they're appropriate for the Web. For instance, FrontPage converts clip art images from WMF files, which browsers can't display, into the GIF format.

Creating an Image Map

Using an image as a hyperlink can create a nice effect on a Web page. Even better, FrontPage lets you turn one picture into a collection of hyperlinks.

By divvying your image into what are called *hotspots* (invisible hyperlink areas), you can make separate clickable regions that link to different locations. These can be square, round, or any shape you wish. A collection of hotspots on an image creates what's known as an *image map*.

This is a great tool for creating a single reference point that leads a viewer to further details on separate pages. For example, if you sell bicycle parts, you could

---

place hotspots on a picture of a bike. Make the wheel a hotspot that leads to a page of wheel types for sale. If a visitor clicks on the pedals, your shop's selection of pedals displays. And so on. You may have seen this effect used on images like actual maps, as in Figure 4-9.

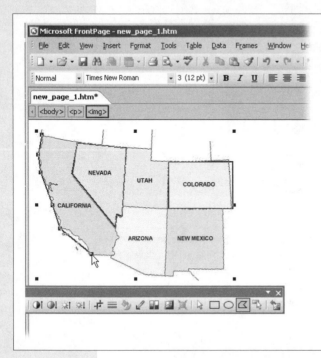

Figure 4-9:
Hotspots can be any shape. The polygonal hotspot tool outlines irregular shapes, like California. The square hotspot tool traces square or rectangular shapes like Colorado.

To create an image map, using buttons on the Pictures toolbar, follow these steps:

1. **Select the picture you want to use as an image map.**

2. **Select an image map tool.**

   Three buttons on the Pictures toolbar offer different shapes: rectangle, circle, and polygon. Click the button that's most appropriate for the shape of the hotspot you want to create.

3. **Draw the hotspot.**

   Draw rectangle and circle spots with one stroke, by dragging diagonally through the area you want the shape to cover. Polygons require more steps. Click to create a corner, then click to create another corner, and another, until you click back on the first spot again to complete a closed shape. After you've drawn a shape, the hyperlink dialog box displays. If you don't like the placement of a hotspot, just click cancel and try again.

4. **Choose a destination for the hotspot's hyperlink.**

   Set a hotspot hyperlink just as you would any other link (page 47).

Tip: If your image is intricate, you may have trouble distinguishing where you've applied hotspots. FrontPage can help. Select the image and then click the Highlight Hotspots button on the far right side of the Pictures toolbar. The image disappears temporarily, leaving only your hotspots visible.

Editing a Hotspot

You can change the shape of a hotspot by dragging one of its handles. To edit a hotspot hyperlink, right-click the hotspot and select Picture Hotspot Properties. An Edit Hyperlink dialog box appears. You can remove a hotspot entirely by selecting it and pressing delete.

Create screen tips for your hotspots

Don't leave visitors in the dark. Let them know where a link will take them. Sure, the pictures underneath your image map help, but you can also create a screen tip for each hotspot to make its destination even more obvious. To do so, right-click a hotspot, and then select Picture Hotspot Properties. Click ScreenTip on the upper right and enter the text that you want viewers to see when their cursor passes over the hotspot.

Creating Thumbnails

Sometimes you need to include a group of pictures on one page, but in trying to do this, you encounter some problems. Maybe the pictures are too big to fit on one page, or your page is taking ages to download.

FrontPage includes a handy feature for inserting pictures as *thumbnails,* which are just miniature versions of graphic files. This section shows you how to create thumbnails. For a similar effect, skip ahead to page 74 to learn about FrontPage's Photo Gallery option, which helps you add some nifty formatting and commentary options to a collection of photos.

AutoThumbail Feature

You can create a thumbnail out of any image file in your site. First, insert the full-sized picture on your Web page. Select it and choose Tools → Auto Thumbnail, or press Ctrl+T. You can also right-click and select Auto Thumbnail, or click the Auto Thumbnail button on the toolbar.

Tip: If you drag the picture onto the page with your right mouse button, a menu displays. Select Auto Thumbnail.

FrontPage converts the picture to a thumbnail. Thumbnails automatically link to their larger versions. During this process, FrontPage actually creates a new smaller image file, which the program prompts you to save next time you save the page.

FrontPage also adds a border to the thumbnail. If you want to get rid of it, right click the thumbnail and select Picture Properties. On the Appearance tab, change Border thickness to zero.

Sizing AutoThumbnails

FrontPage automatically formats thumbnails to be the same size: 100×100 pixels. You can resize these pictures (page 62) as you would any other. Chances are you'll want them to be consistent, so FrontPage lets you change the size for all thumbnails on a page with one setting. Select Tools → Page Options and click the Auto Thumbnail tab. Here, you can change size, set border width, and apply beveling. Unfortunately, these settings won't apply to any work you've already done. Only thumbnails created *after* you make changes in Page Options take on these settings.

Adding a Photo Gallery

Some people put up a Web site simply to display the pictures of their last trip to the mountains or their party at the Tiki lounge. Often the task of formatting a page to display and write about these photos involves more work than most people are willing to invest.

FrontPage now offers a quick, automated solution. A photo gallery is page of pictures and text with a professional-looking layout that FrontPage creates for you. The gallery page features thumbnail photos, which your visitors can click to see the full-size image, and includes space for you to name and discuss each picture.

Creating a Photo Gallery

You can place a photo gallery within an existing page, or on its own page. Here's what you need to do:

1. **Create a new gallery.**

    Select Insert → Picture → New Photo Gallery.

2. **Add pictures.**

    The Photo Gallery Properties dialog box displays (see Figure 4-10). Click Add to bring new images into your gallery. Browse and select the pictures that you wish to include. Enter a caption and description for each picture.

3. **Select a Layout.**

    Click the Layout tab to preview your layout options and select the one you prefer. If you find later on that you don't like it, you can come back and change it.

After you click OK, your gallery displays in FrontPage. You can continue to add pictures and edit the layout at any time. Right-click the Photo Gallery and select Photo Gallery properties to make changes.

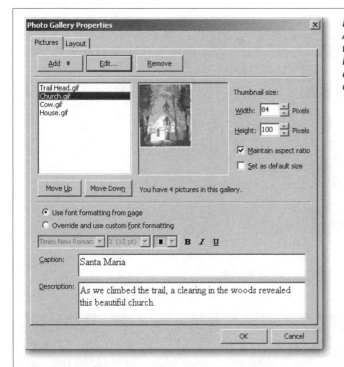

Figure 4-10:
Add and order your Photo Gallery images within the Photo Gallery Properties dialog box. Order pictures as you want them to appear using the Move Up and Move Down options.

Using the Photo Gallery template

FrontPage offers an already populated gallery for you. Select File → New and within the Task pane, click "More page templates" and select Photo Gallery.

The program creates a photo gallery that already contains a handful of pictures, as illustrated in Figure 4-11. This might be a nice way to preview what the gallery looks like, but otherwise, having to replace these photos with your own makes extra work for you. You might as well create a blank photo gallery following the instructions above.

Editing Pictures Within a Photo Gallery

You can't edit Photo Gallery pictures by using the Pictures toolbar. The gallery feature comes with its own, more limited editing feature. If you click Edit within the Photo Gallery dialog box, a special Edit Picture dialog box appears. Use it to rotate, crop, or change the size of a picture. Previous and Next options, at the bottom, allow you to access all your photos without leaving the dialog box, which you may find handy. If you need to edit a picture more extensively, use an image-editing program. Again, you may want to keep backup copies of your images in a folder outside your Web site for safekeeping. This way if FrontPage's editor mangles a picture, you can import a fresh copy.

Figure 4-11:
FrontPage's Slide Show format as it appears in a browser.

Getting Photos to Open in a New Window

The Photo Gallery (with the exception of the Slide Show layout) has one trait that's not really viewer friendly. When a visitor clicks a thumbnail, the large version of the photo opens in the same browser window. This forces the viewer to hit the back button to return to the page of thumbnails. If you want a full-size picture to open in a new instance of the browser, don't waste your time looking for that setting in the Photo Gallery Properties dialog box. Like other Web page features that FrontPage provides ready-made for you, the Photo Gallery isn't very flexible.

Fortunately, there's a workaround. To change the target of your thumbnail links, do the following: look in your site's folder list and locate the *photogallery* folder. Open the

folder and then open the folder that contains your Photo Gallery. (This folder's name begins with the word "photo" followed by a series of numbers. FrontPage creates one of these folders for each gallery in your site. If you have more than one, compare them by checking the folders' image file contents.)

Open the *real.htm* file, and you'll see your gallery appear in the document window. Right-click a picture and select Hyperlink Properties. Set a different target for the hyperlink (page 52). Repeat for each picture you want to open in a new window. While you have *real.htm* open, you can also turn any caption text into a hyperlink, if you want. When you're done, save the *real.htm* file.

Adding a Background Picture

Now that you know how to stick images all over your Web pages, you can get even crazier and place an image *behind* your page. In other words, you can use an image as your page's background. This can be a fancy landscape photograph or something subtle, like a washed-out image of you, pale from hours spent in front of your computer. A background picture displays behind all the other elements on a page, such as text and inserted images. If you do decide to use an image as a background, make sure that the image doesn't obscure your page's text (patterns often work well).

With your Web page open, select File → Properties or right-click the page and select Page Properties. Then click the Formatting tab. Turn on the Background Picture checkbox and browse to find and select the image. If you want the image to remain fixed in the background as a viewer scrolls down your page, turn on the "Make it a watermark" checkbox.

Note: If your background picture creates a *tile effect,* appearing multiple times within the page, then it's too small. Edit the image to make it large enough so that only one picture appears in a browser window. The problem is your visitors will all have different size windows. To keep the picture from tiling, you can give it a "no repeat" style. To do so, Select File → Properties and click the Advanced tab. Then click Body Style. Within the Modify Style dialog box that opens, click Format and select Border. Within the Borders and Shading dialog box, click the Shading tab. Under Background Picture, browse to and select the image. Then within the Repeat drop-down list, select No Repeat. Preview this effect in browsers with varying screen dimensions (page 234).

Part Two:
Improving Your
Web Page

2

Tables

So far, you've learned how to add attractive text and eye-catching images to your Web site, but they all appear in a more or less vertical line down your page. This probably isn't the gorgeous design you had in mind. How do you arrange these elements in an interesting and dynamic way that really gets the most out of a Web browser's screen space?

As you've seen, HTML isn't very helpful when it comes to page layout. To gain a modicum of control, Web developers have turned to tables to help them design and organize a page. Tables rise to a lofty purpose when it comes to designing a Web page. In lieu of holding boring data, they contain images, page headings, product offerings, and more. On many pages, designers use the simple trick of hiding the table, so their pages look masterfully laid out, but the viewer doesn't see all the scaffolding at work behind the scenes.

Learning how to insert and manipulate tables well is the most effective skill you can have in your design repertoire if you want your pages to look professional. FrontPage also offers a sophisticated improvement on the traditional HTML table—the *layout table,* which is surprisingly powerful. This chapter will explain when and how to use all these tools.

Tables 101

A *table* is a grid containing columns and rows. These columns and rows contain cells, which, in turn, can hold any kind of content you want to put inside them. Sure, you can use a table to list game scores, but a table can also provide you with a structure on which to organize your page. Tables help break up your page into separate regions. Any region can contain elements like text, pictures, and so on. A table used for page layout can be very simple. For example, it might consist of only two cells, a short narrow one on top containing a page banner, and a large one below for general page content.

Figure 5-1 illustrates the basic parts of a table.

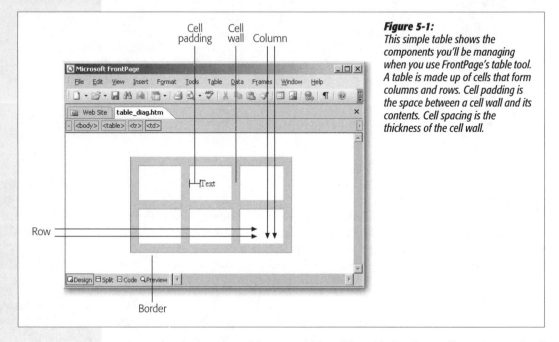

Figure 5-1:
This simple table shows the components you'll be managing when you use FrontPage's table tool. A table is made up of cells that form columns and rows. Cell padding is the space between a cell wall and its contents. Cell spacing is the thickness of the cell wall.

You need to know your table parts—things like table borders, cell spacing, and cell padding—because you'll manipulate each part to fine-tune the layout you want. FrontPage gives you two ways to control a table's appearance: you can format attributes of the *entire* table or you can manipulate the look and feel of *individual* cells. Many times, you'll want to do both.

HTML tables aren't like other tables you've encountered in Microsoft Word and similar programs. Once again, the browser is in charge of what your viewer sees and is quite capable of making your table look very different from what you envisioned. Even as you work with a table in Design view, you'll get a taste of this volatility. For instance, if you insert a large picture into a small cell, the cell expands to display the picture, enlarging the dimensions of the rows and columns that it sits in. And as you type in a table cell, the table may change its dimensions with each letter you add. These things happen because a table cell expands to display its contents. While this fluidity can be disconcerting at first, once you understand how HTML tables behave, you'll become a pro at managing them.

BEHIND THE SCENES

Tables in HTML

As you learn about tables, you'll appreciate how much time and hair-pulling agony FrontPage can save you from. Below is the HTML code for the table illustrated in Figure 5-1.

```
<table border="1" width="100%"
cellspacing="14" cellpadding="20">
    <tr>
        <td> </td>
        <td>Text</td>
        <td> </td>
    </tr>
    <tr>
        <td> </td>
        <td> </td>
        <td> </td>
    </tr>
</table>
```

What's happening here? Table tags contain row tags, which contain cell tags. The <tr> tags represent a table row. Notice how each set of <tr> tags contains multiple <td> tags ("td" is short for table data). Each set of <td> tags is a table cell. (Right now, all but one of these cells contain only a non-breaking space.)

This is actually a very simple table. Imagine the code for one that's more complex. Not only do manual coders have to type out all these mind-bendingly minute instructions, they have to keep track of what the table actually looks like and in which row they're working. Even professionals who love to work directly in HTML often turn to products like FrontPage to save them a lot of time and tedium.

Inserting a Table

Inserting a table is usually the very first step when it comes to laying out a page. FrontPage gives you a number of ways to add a basic HTML table, and each has its own pros and cons.

Inserting a Table with the Toolbar

The Standard toolbar sports a fast and convenient feature that lets you insert a table and set its basic layout all in one step. Place your cursor wherever you want the table to appear and click the Insert Table button. A small table menu appears, as illustrated in Figure 5-2.

Figure 5-2:
When you click the Insert Table button on the Standard toolbar, this grid appears. Use it to select the basic table layout you want.

Once you're looking at the table menu, you can do one of the following things:

- Pass your cursor over the grid to select the number of columns and rows you want.

- Keeping your mouse button depressed, drag across the grid to select the desired number of columns and rows. This option gives you the power to expand the grid, if you need to create a larger table than the one that you first see.

Inserting a Table Using the Table Menu

Often, when you insert a table, you'll want to specify more than just the number of columns and rows your table contains. For example, you might want to set cell padding or border thickness. In either case, you should use the Table menu.

Place your cursor in the document window and select Table → Insert → Table. The Insert Table dialog box appears, offering an abundance of settings that you can use to make the table of your dreams.

Tip: If you just accept the Table dialog box's standard settings and click OK, FrontPage creates a 2×2 table. You can modify it at any time with a right click, which gives you access to Table Properties. In fact, the Table Properties dialog box offers the same options as the Insert Table dialog box.

To set up your table, fill out the fields in the Insert Table dialog box as follows.

1. **Select a layout tools option.**

   Here, FrontPage is just asking: "What kind of table are you making?" If you're creating the table to structure a page, leave the standard setting called "Automatically enable layout tools based on table content" in place. If you'll enter data in the table, select "Disable layout tools." Selecting "Enable layout tools" creates a layout table (which is FrontPage's own variation on the table-as-layout-tool theme; you'll learn more about that later in this chapter).

2. **Type in the number of rows and columns you want in the respective fields.**

   You can estimate here. Columns and rows are easy to add and delete later on.

3. **Select alignment.**

   You can center, left align, or right align your table within your page. Choose Default, and FrontPage leaves it up to a viewer's browser, which usually picks left align.

4. **Set float.**

   This setting generally applies to smaller tables. If you want text outside your table to wrap around the table, use the Float box to select which side. For instance, select Right to have text wrap to the *left* of the table. If you're creating a table to help with page layout, leave this set at Default.

5. **Specify table width.**

If you don't know whether to set the width in pixels or percent, read the box "Fixed vs. Fluid Design" and see Figure 5-3. The standard setting for basic HTML tables is in percent. A table width of 100 percent stretches all the way across browser screen, 50 percent covers half the browser screen, and so on.

Fixed vs. Fluid Design

Depending upon what type of table you insert on your page, FrontPage uses either pixels or percentage to measure components like column width. Tables that the program sizes in pixels are a fixed size that won't change, even if a browser window is too small to display them. This could force a viewer to scroll across to see the whole page. Tables that FrontPage measures in percentage, however, tie their appearance to the size of the browser window. A table width of 100 percent always fills a browser window, whether that browser takes up the whole screen or just a fraction of it. You've probably seen this effect on many Web pages. If you reduce the size of your browser window, content doesn't disappear beyond the browser's edge. Instead it shrinks to the size of its new space.

Because it's often difficult to know what browser settings and screen resolution viewers are using, Web designers have traditionally used the percent setting's more fluid approach. Basic HMTL tables are always fluid. However, tables that you drag and drop into your document or FrontPage's layout tables (which you'll read about later in this chapter) are always fixed. Some designers like the control that a pixel-specific or fixed environment gives them. If you don't mind the fact that visitors might need to scroll across to see your page (as in Figure 5-3), you might want to use fixed tables. To decide which approach is best for you, think about your audience and test your pages across a wide variety of monitor resolutions.

Tip: If you disabled layout tools in the first step and don't make any changes to your table's dimensions, FrontPage creates a fluid table.

6. **Set cell padding.**

Cell padding is the space between content and a cell wall (see Figure 5-1). The higher the number you enter, the more white space that appears around the text or pictures in a cell.

7. **Set cell spacing.**

Cell spacing determines the thickness of table walls. This is the spacing *between* cells. The higher the number, the thicker the wall.

8. **Set border attributes.**

Borders are the lines that mark the edges of a cell wall and the outside of a table. If you want your table borders to be invisible, set Border Size to zero. (As you edit, FrontPage still shows you the table structure using dotted lines, but these lines won't show up in a browser.) Otherwise, set a pixel width here and select a color.

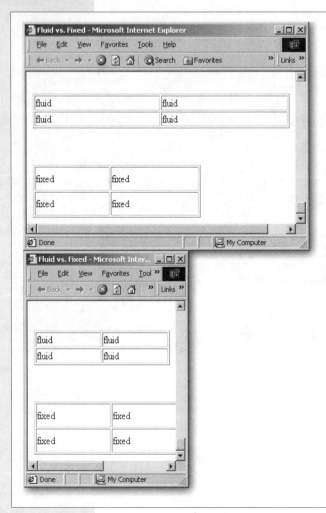

Figure 5-3:
Here's a look at a fluid and a fixed table, both displayed in the same browser window.

Top: When the window is wide, the fluid table expands to fill the window, while the fixed table retains its fixed dimensions.

Bottom: When the browser window shrinks, the fluid table shrinks to fit within it. The fixed table, on the other hand, retains its dimensions, which extend beyond, and therefore behind, the edge of the browser window. Notice how the browser adds a horizontal scroll bar when page elements are out of sight.

A fixed table used for page layout can fill an entire page. Large fixed tables like that force viewers with lower screen resolutions to scroll from side to side to see the entire page. Also, a printer processing a wide page might cut off the right side. You'll need to decide if the risk of display and printing problems is worth the more precise layout capabilities that fixed tables offer. (See "FrontPage Layout Tables" on page 96, to learn about the advantages that come with FrontPage's fixed layout tables.)

You can use the light and dark border options to create a subtle 3-D effect, making the table look slightly raised off the surface of the page. By "Light borders," FrontPage means the top and left sides of a table. Likewise the program considers "Dark borders" to be the bottom and right sides. These effects (light on top and left, dark on bottom and right) are used by designers to create a 3-D effect where a button or table looks raised up off the page. However, you can also set them in reverse (use a dark color in the top and left "light border" sides and a light color in the bottom and right "dark border" sides). If you do, your table will look as though it's cut into your page instead of raised up.)

Note: FrontPage's automatic settings create tables with a cell wall that is 2 pixels thick. What if you don't want any space between your cells? In this case, you may be tempted by the Collapse Table Border checkbox. Turning on this checkbox squeezes your borders together so that only a single line separates table cells. However, not all browsers display collapsed borders as you'd expect. Firefox won't even show any cell borders within the table, for example. There's a better solution. If you want cell borders to display as a single line, then set "Cell spacing" to zero.

9. **Set table background.**

Tables are transparent. In other words, the page background shows through. You can change this setting by making a selection in the Color drop-down list. If you want to use an image as your table's background, turn on the "Use background picture" checkbox and browse to select any image you have stored on your computer. Just like when you use a picture as a background for a page, any image smaller than the table repeats, creating a tile effect. To fix this, resize the graphic. Or, set a "no repeat" style rule on the image. To do so, click the Style button within the Insert Table dialog box. Within the Modify Style dialog box that opens, click Format and select Border. Within the Borders and Shading dialog box, click the Shading tab. Under Background Picture, browse to and select the image. Then within the Repeat drop-down list, select No Repeat.

Note: Various browsers handle background color or pictures in tables differently and some—most notably, Netscape Navigator 4 and earlier—cannot display these background images.

10. **Insert the table.**

Once you click OK, pat yourself on the shoulder and watch as FrontPage adds the table to your page. You can add text to any cell or insert an image (page 58) if you want. Table cells function like mini document windows. Text travels from left to right and left aligns unless you specify otherwise (you'll learn about how to control cell formatting on page 93). Press Tab to move from one cell to the next. As in Microsoft Word, pressing Tab in the very last cell of a table creates a new row.

Tip: As you work with tables, you'll probably want to have the Tables toolbar in view. If it's not displayed on your screen, select View → Toolbars → Tables.

Saving settings in the Insert Table dialog box

You may need to create exactly the same types of tables throughout your site. FrontPage is one step ahead of you and lets you save basic table settings, so you don't have to make the same adjustments over and over again.

At the bottom of the Insert Table dialog box, you'll see an option called Set As Default for New Tables. Turn this checkbox on to save all the settings you entered while creating your table. Next time you insert a table, the settings display automatically in the dialog box, and you just need to click OK.

Note: This feature has one irritating bug. Unfortunately, FrontPage won't save your entry for the number of columns and rows. No matter what figures you enter and set as default, this dialog box always shows table size of 2 rows × 2 columns–forcing you to edit these figures each time you want a new table.

It's difficult to know, as you create a table, whether or not it meets your needs as a table template. A good idea is to just wait and see how your table ends up looking. Since you can also find the Set as Default option within the Table Properties box, you can apply it at any time, using any table.

Drawing a Table with Your Mouse

FrontPage has a nifty virtual tool for all Web authors who miss their pencils. There's no need to create your table using the Insert Table dialog box. Instead, you can simply draw it in Design view.

Start off by selecting Table → Draw Table. Your cursor turns into a pencil. Drag it diagonally across the area where you want your table to appear. FrontPage responds by inserting a one-celled table.

You can add cells to the table, since at this point FrontPage is still in drawing mode. (Notice that your cursor still looks like a pencil.) Drag your cursor inside your new table, from one side to the other to create borders for columns and rows (see Figure 5-4).

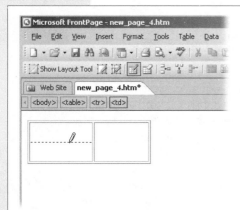

Figure 5-4:
FrontPage shows you where it will place the table line you're drawing by displaying a dotted line.

Note: This method inserts a fixed-size table. In other words, FrontPage measures the dimensions of this table in a fixed number of pixels that won't change. See the box "Fixed vs. Fluid Design" on page 85 for the full story. If you want to use a fluid table, create a table using the menu or toolbar instead. In the long run, you'll have an easier time managing tables inserted using the menu and dialog box, so drawing like this is usually not the best approach. Drawn tables also occasionally suffer from display problems like empty cells disappearing from view.

If you drag outside the table, FrontPage creates a new one-celled table. In fact, the pencil sticks around until you actively get rid of it. To get your cursor back to normal, select Table → Draw Table again or click the Draw Table (not Draw Layout Table) button on the Tables toolbar.

Converting Text to a Table

When you need to move a lot of existing text into a table, an afternoon of cut and paste might seem like the only tortuous option available. Microsoft Word veterans probably have their hands up and are thinking of the feature that makes quick work of turning text into tables. FrontPage, you'll be glad to know, is equally adept. As in Word, for this feature to work well, your text must contain some sort of uniform punctuation—like paragraph marks, commas, or tabs—that you can use to separate text into appropriate cells.

To convert text into a table, first select all the text that you want to put into the new table. Then select Table → Convert → Text to Table.

Tip: You can also convert text that you've pasted in from another program, like Word. Just make sure that when you paste, you keep whatever formatting you want to use to create the table (pop back to page 26 to review pasting options).

A Convert Text to Table dialog box displays. Here, FrontPage is asking you how you want to break down the text. Select whatever kind of character currently divides the elements you want in their own cells. For example, if there's a tab between each item, select tab and click OK. If you don't see the character you need, you can enter it yourself. If you want each word to have its own cell, for instance, select Other and type a space in the box.

Note: FrontPage doesn't recognize tabs from other programs. Only tabs you've created in FrontPage work as separators. If you're pasting in text from another application that contains tabs, try selecting Other and entering a space in the box instead.

You can also do the reverse: click in any table and select Table → Convert → Table to Text. FrontPage removes all table formatting and spills the text back out onto your page.

Formatting a Table

Invariably, tables require a lot of adjustments and edits, especially if you're using them to help lay out a page. This section shows you how to select and manipulate different parts of your table so you can change the table's shape and overall appearance.

Selecting Parts of a Table

A table is the sum its parts: the rows, columns, cells, and so on, each of which possesses its own unique properties (like height and width). Before you can modify a table's innards, you first have to select the part you want to work on.

Selecting a table

To select a table:

- Click anywhere inside the table and then select Table → Select → Table.
- Click anywhere inside the table and select the <table> tag within the Quick Tag toolbar (page 6).

Selecting a row

To select a row:

- Click anywhere inside a row and then select Table → Select → Row.
- Click anywhere inside a row and then select the <tr> tag within the Quick Tag toolbar.
- Place your cursor at the left margin of a row. When the pointer turns into a rightward arrow, click to select the column. Drag up or down to select multiple rows.

Selecting a column

To select a column:

- Click anywhere inside a column and then select Table → Select → Row.
- Place your cursor over the top margin of a column. When the pointer turns into a downward arrow, click to select the column. Drag across to select multiple columns.

Selecting cells

To select cells:

- Click inside a cell and then select Table → Select → Cell.
- Click inside a cell and then select the <td> tag within the Quick Tag toolbar.
- Press the Alt key and click the cell. To select additional cells, press Ctrl and click in the cells you want. Or press Ctrl+Alt and drag across cells to select all cells your cursor touches. (These cells don't have to make up a continuous span. You can stop dragging and click in additional cells, too—as long as you hold down the Ctrl and Alt keys.)
- Drag your cursor across a range of cells to select all the cells your cursor passes over.

Manipulating Table Structure

Even if you plan carefully, you're bound to end up adding, moving, or deleting table rows, columns, and cells.

Inserting rows or columns

To insert a row or a column, place your cursor within your table and select Tables → Insert → Rows or Columns. The Insert Columns or Rows dialog box that appears lets you insert however many rows or columns you specify on either side of your cursor.

The Tables toolbar offers a quick alternative: click in a cell to the right (for a column) or below (for a row) where you want the new row or column to appear. Click either the Insert Rows or Insert Columns button (or right-click the cell and choose either selection from the pop-up menu). If you select numerous rows or columns and then click one of these buttons, FrontPage inserts the number of columns or rows you selected.

Deleting rows, columns, or cells

The fastest way to delete rows, columns, or cells is to select them and press Delete. You can also click the Delete Cells button, or right-click the item once you've selected it and select Delete Columns, Delete Rows, or Delete Cells from the pop-up menu. As you select rows or columns, FrontPage also adds options to delete them to the Table menu.

Moving table components

You can copy or cut any table part—like a row, column, or cell—and paste it within another part of the table. If you want to create a new table from the excerpt, just paste it in an empty spot on a Web page.

Table Properties

FrontPage lets you change other table attributes, like size, alignment within the page, text wrapping, border, and color formatting, by using the Table Properties dialog box (page 84). The Table Properties dialog box offers the exact same choices you learned about in the Insert Table dialog box (page 84).

Adding a Table Caption

If you're using a table to display actual data, you'll probably want to label it. To tell people what you're showing them, FrontPage provides a caption feature. To use it, click anywhere within the table and select Table → Insert → Caption. A blinking cursor appears over the table. Type the caption text. If you'd rather have your caption beneath the table, right-click the caption, select Caption Properties, and change its position setting to "Bottom of table."

AutoFormat Feature

If you're not a design guru, or just don't have the time to play around with borders, colors, and shading settings, FrontPage has a nice feature that helps you decorate your table with only a couple of clicks.

Start off by clicking anywhere within a table to select it. Next, select Table → Table AutoFormat or click the Table AutoFormat button on the Tables toolbar. The AutoFormat dialog box that displays contains scores of format options for your table. Click on a format, and the Preview pane shows you what it'll look like. If you want to exclude a few of the settings, turn them off using the checkboxes in the lower portion of the dialog box. The Preview pane reflects any changes. Click OK, and your table sports the new look (see Figure 5-5).

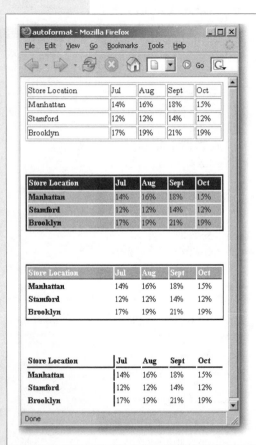

Figure 5-5:
AutoFormat can spruce up a plain table (like the one at top) in a jiffy. FrontPage offers a variety of AutoFormat styles, a few of which are pictured here. This quick formatting tool can really make the information you're presenting easier to read.

Nested Tables

Tables really help structure a page so you can place elements where you want them. However, you might find that you want to exercise that same control *inside* a table. For instance, you may find that a table cell in one spot is too big or the wrong size for the material you want to put in it.

You can enter anything in a table cell: text, pictures, and even other tables. If you have a large cell that you want to divide, you can insert a table within it to manage the space. That's known as *nesting*. You can even nest another table within that nested table. But before you let your M. C. Escher instincts run wild, it's best to stop here and refrain from nesting yet another within that last table. Excessive nesting can slow the loading speed of your page.

Before you resort to nesting, check out all the options for managing cells that the rest of this chapter covers. A simpler solution—like merging or splitting cells—might solve your problem.

Formatting Cells

FrontPage lets you control the appearance of each cell's contents, borders, and decoration (sounds festive, no?). Your control center for these maneuvers is the Cell Properties dialog box.

Alignment

Once your cells are holding text or pictures, they may not look quite as nice as you expected. Aside from bad writing or poorly shot pictures, sloppy or irregular cell alignment is often the biggest offender.

You can adjust alignment for one or more cells at a time. Select the cells, then right-click them and select Cell Properties from the pop-up menu. Within the Cell Properties dialog box, you can set vertical and horizontal alignment (see Figure 5-6).

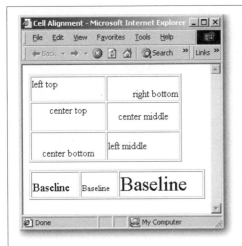

Figure 5-6:
Here's how some alignment combinations appear in a browser. Use the Cell Properties baseline setting to make text of different sizes line up horizontally.

Tip: If you've got multiple paragraphs within a cell and want to align one differently from the rest, FrontPage can handle it. Click anywhere in the paragraph and select Format → Paragraph and set the alignment to whatever you want. Paragraph formatting overrides cell formatting.

Cell Dimensions

Since a table is made up entirely of cells, you need to size cells to format your table. FrontPage makes changing cell dimensions easy. You can enter absolute pixel values or measure according to the percentage of a browser screen you want the cell to occupy. (What's the difference? Pop on back to "Fixed vs. Fluid Design" on page 85.)

FREQUENTLY ASKED QUESTION

Cellular Power

I don't see a setting to change column width. How do I widen a column?

FrontPage doesn't give you any settings for controlling column or row dimensions. The size of a column or row depends upon the cells within it. The widest cell in a column sets the width for the entire column. Likewise, the tallest cell in a row sets the height.

So, to widen a column, you must widen one or more of its cells. Do so by selecting a cell. (You can also select the entire column, but FrontPage is going to change each cell's dimensions.) Then right-click your selection and select Cell Properties from the pop-up menu to change the setting. You can also shrink a column using cell properties, but you must select all the cells, so none of them remain large and prevent the column from slimming down.

Control the display of your fluid HTML tables, by setting column width in percent. To do this, select a cell or column (again, if you're widening you can select one or more cells, but if you're shrinking you must select all the cells in the column), open the Cell Properties dialog box, and specify width by percent. This measure is the percent of horizontal space that the column takes up within the table. In a table with two columns, you can set one at 10 percent and the other at 90 percent. In a table with four columns, make each 25 percent. Whatever settings you choose, make sure all columns all add up to 100 percent.

Controlling column width in fixed tables works the same way, except instead of entering a percentage, you'll enter exact pixel measurements.

Always remember that table cells expand to show their contents. For this reason, table dimensions sometimes change as you type. If one cell expands—automatically or through your intervention—the row or column it sits in expands to that size as well. When you expand a row or column, its neighboring row or column expands, too.

In Design view, you can also resize a cell by clicking a cell wall and dragging it. FrontPage automatically changes the dimensions of the row or column in which the cell sits.

Cell Borders and Background

The Cell Properties dialog box lets you edit a cell's borders and background. If you've already set table borders, you may not need to set individual cell borders. But sometimes you might want to; the process works exactly the same way as it does for an entire table (page 85).

Note: Only Internet Explorer recognizes (and displays) certain special cell border settings like light and dark borders.

Setting a cell's background works the same way as setting a table's background (page 87). Thankfully, most browsers can display color or even picture backgrounds; the few that don't simply keep your cell's background the same color as the rest of the Web page.

Merging and Splitting Cells

Most self-respecting (and finicky) Web designers don't like the rigid, graph-paper like layout FrontPage gives them when it creates a new table. For example, say you've got a table heading that really applies to two columns that should sit beneath it. How can you create an extra wide cell above these two columns?

FrontPage is ready with a feature that solves this kind of problem quickly and easily. You can *merge* cells, turning them into one larger cell that encompasses the area formerly taken up by multiple cells. For example, you could merge two adjacent cells at the top of a column and create one heading. If need be, you can also split a cell in two, or four, and so on (that, as you might expect, is called *splitting*).

To merge cells, first select the cells you want to merge. You won't get away with any funny stuff here. These cells must form a square or rectangle. If you select cells that aren't connected or that form an L-shape, FrontPage won't let you perform the merge.

Once you've selected the cells, you can go ahead and merge them. To do this, select Table → Merge Cells or click the Merge Cells button on the Tables toolbar. (You can also right-click the selection and open Cell Properties from the pop-up menu, then specify a new number of columns or rows for the cell to span. But this is less intuitive—it's hard to see what you're doing.) Another method is to use the Eraser tool on the Tables toolbar. Click the Eraser button to activate it. Then drag your cursor across any cell wall to delete it. To deactivate the eraser, click the button again. Whatever your method, merging creates cells that span columns or rows (see Figure 5-7).

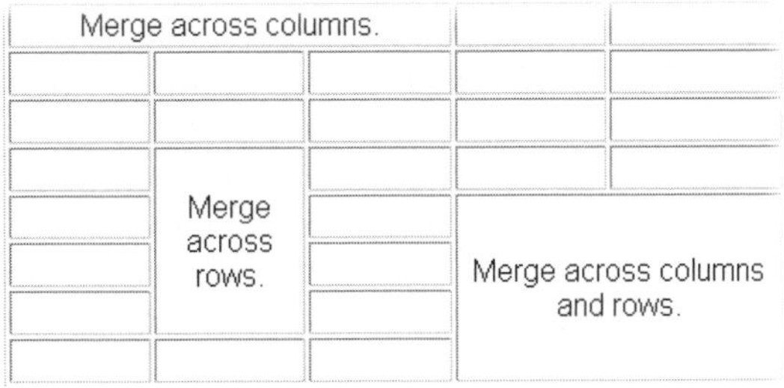

Figure 5-7:
Merge cells across columns, rows, or both to create larger cells like those in this table.

You may find that instead of merging, you actually need to divide a cell. FrontPage can split a single cell into two or more cells vertically or horizontally. To split a cell, click inside or select it. Select Table → Split Cells, click the Split Cells button, or right-click the cell and select Split Cells from the pop-up menu. The Split Cell dialog box appears. Choose whether you want to split the cell into rows or columns, enter a number, and you're on your way to splitsville.

FrontPage Layout Tables

For ages, Web designers have used regular HTML tables to help lay out their pages. Because these tables weren't originally designed to perform such duties, occasionally they buckle under the load—or, put another way, they're not always as nimble as most designers would like them to be. For example, positioning cells exactly where you want them can be an ordeal. To address these limitations, FrontPage has added a powerful set of tools, called *layout tables,* which are designed expressly for page layout. Layout tables don't function like the regular tables you've been reading about so far. FrontPage's layout tables are based on drafting programs that let designers place elements in precise locations on a design grid. All measurements are fixed and absolute, not fluid like traditional HTML tables.

Fixed width tables do carry some drawbacks, which you'll learn about in a moment. If you decide that you want to use layout tables, read on to learn how to insert and format them to suit your needs. You'll also learn about another layout tool, called a *tracing image,* which lets you trace an image from a picture file and use it to shape your page design.

Pros and Cons of Layout Tables

For all their advantages, regular HTML tables can still make page design a challenge. If you'd like to add text to a specific spot in the middle of a page, maneuvering a cell into that precise location can take a lot of work. FrontPage's layout table gives you much more control. You can create a cell of any size anywhere you want. Then you can just plunk it down without a care in the world, and FrontPage does all the grunt work of arranging cells to support it.

This is truly one of FrontPage 2003's most impressive features, but it does come at a price. Layout tables work because they use fixed pixel dimensions. Unlike HTML tables that shrink or expand within a browser window, layout tables are static and unchanging (see the "Fixed vs. Fluid Design" box on page 85 to understand the difference). If you use a layout table to create a page, not all browsers are going to be able to display it as you intend. For example, a page that looks great on your 1024×768 monitor won't fit on a Web surfer's 800×600 screen. She'll have to scroll to the right to see what's on the rest of the page. This may interfere with your graphics, hiding portions of pictures and text. FrontPage's layout tables can produce a great design, but not everyone can always enjoy it.

If you can deal with this, or if the allure of easy layout trumps any possible difficulties for your viewers, read on.

Inserting a Layout Table

FrontPage gives you a separate set of tools for layout tables, which are distinct from the HTML table controls covered earlier. You can manually create a new layout table or pick one from FrontPage's layout template selections. You can also turn an existing HTML table into a layout table, and vice versa.

Creating a layout table

You'll need the Layout Tables and Cells task pane to create and edit layout tables. To open it, select Table → Layout Tables and Cells, or click the task pane dropdown menu and make the same selection.

You can create a layout table using any of the following methods:

- **Use a template.** Scroll down within the task pane to view the many table layout templates that come with FrontPage. The display at the bottom of the pane previews how the table would structure things on your page. The tables you see here represent a variety of page configurations and will probably satisfy most of your design impulses. Click a selection, and FrontPage inserts the layout table on your page, instantly organizing your workspace. Using one of these preformatted tables could save you a lot of work.

- **Draw a layout table** by clicking the Draw Layout Table button (within the Tables toolbar or the task pane). Your cursor turns into a pencil. Use it to draw a table in the document window. A one-celled layout table appears to get you started.

- Click the **Insert Layout Table** link at the top of the task pane. A one-celled table appears in the document window.

Adding layout cells

Layout tables consist of rows, columns, and cells just like other tables. However, unlike HTML tables, not all cells are created equal. Layout tables differentiate between *layout cells* and *ordinary cells*. Layout cells contain text or graphic elements while ordinary cells are empty. FrontPage creates ordinary cells to space out layout cells. (Microsoft probably should've called them inert cells or worker bee cells.)

When you create a layout table, you start off with only one cell. (This one cell is an ordinary cell, but if you were to type in it, it would become a layout cell.) To see how layout and ordinary cells interact, add another cell to your new table. Click the Draw Layout Cell button and draw a small cell in the center of the layout table.

Though you drew one cell, FrontPage unleashes a flurry of cells—it actually creates nine cells within the table, as shown in Figure 5-8. The cell you drew is the only layout cell. The other, ordinary cells surround it to keep it in place. FrontPage manages ordinary cells as it sees fit and may delete or rearrange them to support your layout cells. If you type any text into an ordinary cell, it rises in stature and becomes a layout cell.

When you click in a cell and type something, FrontPage hides the layout formatting display. To view the measurements of a layout table, drag your cursor over the table border until a green outline appears and click anywhere along the green line. Or, in the Tables toolbar or the task pane, just click the Show Layout Tool button twice.

Note: Clicking the Show Layout Tool button converts your table to an HTML table only once (see the next section, "Converting tables").

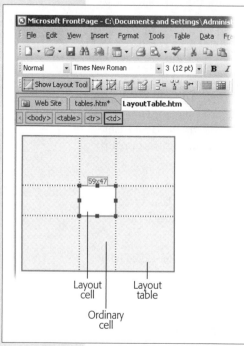

Figure 5-8:
When the Show Layout Tool is active, FrontPage displays layout tables with a green border (the dark line surrounding the table). Individual layout cells sport a blue border. Ordinary cells in a layout table are surrounded by dotted lines.

Layout
cell

Layout
table

Ordinary
cell

Converting tables

FrontPage makes it easy for you to transform your tables from HTML to layout tables. To convert an HTML table to a layout table, click anywhere in the table, then click the Show Layout Tool button within the Tables toolbar or the task pane. Or right-click anywhere in the table, select Table Properties, and then click the "Enable layout tools" radio button. Voilà. Your HTML table turns into a layout table. To verify this, select the table. Design view displays advanced handling options and measurements like those pictured in Figure 5-9. Though you may still see your table's dimensions measured in percent, you'll only be able to adjust the table's dimensions by using pixel measurements from now on.

Tip: If you're having difficulty selecting a table in Design view, try this shortcut: click once inside the table, and then click the Table tag icon in the Quick Tag Selector toolbar (page 6) just above the document window.

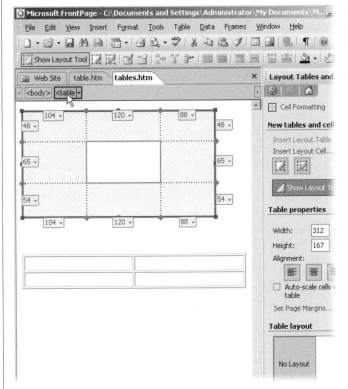

Figure 5-9:
Layout tables always feature the profusion of colored borders and cell dimension tags that you see in the top of this document window. To see them, select the table. Old-fashioned HTML tables (like the one at the bottom) never show their dimensions in Design view—even when you select them.

You can also do the reverse: turn a layout table into a normal HTML table. To do so, click anywhere in the table, and then click the Show Layout Tool button (within the Tables toolbar or the task pane) to deactivate it. (You can also right-click the table, select Table Properties from the pop-up menu, and click Disable layout tools.) The table is no longer a layout table, but FrontPage still measures it in pixels. If you want a fluid table, go into Table Properties and change table measurements to percentages.

Manipulating Layout Tables

Layout tables come with their own set of editing techniques, which are different from what you learned earlier about editing HTML tables. To edit a layout table, pass your cursor over the table border until a green outline appears and click anywhere along the green border. Or, within the Tables toolbar or on the task pane, click the Show Layout Tool button twice. Layout table and cell borders appear in green and blue with small square handles and dimension boxes.

You can drag the handles of layout cells and tables to whatever width and height you like or you can enter exact measurements. Click on any column or row measurement box and select either Change Row Height or Change Column Width. Within the dialog box that displays, enter the new number of pixels.

Setting more cell properties

To adjust cell properties like color and cell padding, select one or more cells and, in the task pane, click the Cell Properties and Borders link (or, if that's not visible, click Cell Formatting). A number of formatting options, including those for color and border, display in the task pane. FrontPage immediately applies the settings you make in the task pane to the cells you've highlighted.

To see additional decorative options, in the task pane, select the Cell Corners and Shadows link. Doing so displays controls that let you add L-shaped borders with a shadow effect that'll make your cell look 3-D. You can also add soft, curved corners to a cell. Click a curved corner button to turn it on and click it again to turn it off. When you turn on a corner button, you automatically activate the cell's header or footer setting, which you'll find if you click the Cell Header and Footer link in the task pane. The Header and Footer pane contains selections for formatting the top and bottom borders of a cell, with bands of color to frame cell contents. All these controls work together to create effects like those shown in Figure 5-10.

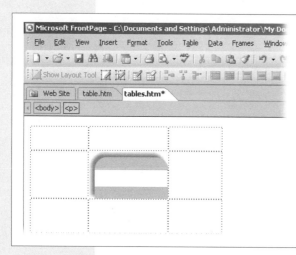

Figure 5-10:
Layout cell formatting can include 3-D shadow effects and curved corners. A header band blends in with curved corners at the top of this cell, while the bottom features only a plain thick footer strip. In a browser, the table's dotted lines won't show up, so the cell looks like it's floating alone over the page.

Setting Page Margins

Page margins set the distance between the edge of a browser window and wherever the content starts on your page. Most browsers automatically set margins of 8 or 15 pixels. There may be times when you want to control margin display. For instance, maybe you want your colorful company banner to stretch to the very edge. In that case, you'd want to set your margin width to zero.

To do so, pop over to the Layout Tables and Cells task pane where you'll find a link called Set Page Margins. You can also select File → Properties and click the Advanced tab to make the same settings on any page. Both commands open the Page Properties dialog box, pictured in Figure 5-11.

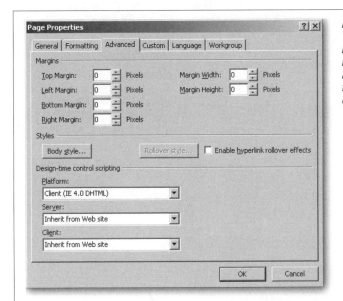

Figure 5-11:
The Page Properties dialog box seems to repeat itself: What's the difference, you might reasonably ask, between Margin Width and Left and Right Margin? The answer lies in the fact that different browsers respond to different margin settings. Details follow below.

Different browsers recognize different types of margin-setting instructions. For example, Netscape Navigator obeys your Margin Width and Height settings, but not your Top, Left, Bottom, and Right margin settings. The opposite is true of Internet Explorer. So, if you want your margin settings to work in a variety of environments, enter them in all the boxes that appear in this dialog box.

Adding Flexibility to a Layout Table

The fixed nature of layout tables can present you with some design challenges. Remember that layout tables are measured in exact pixels, which means that they're the same size, no matter how big or small your viewer's browser window is. If your page layout isn't large enough to fill a browser window, distracting areas of empty space may appear, as in Figure 5-12.

FrontPage helps you get around this problem with its *autostretch* feature. Use autostretch to allow one column in your table to be flexible instead of fixed. The column "stretches" to fill a browser window. Apply this to a column containing elements that expand gracefully, like long passages of text. In contrast, menu columns and fixed pixel graphics don't widen well. They can end up creating an unsightly blank space like the one you're trying to eliminate.

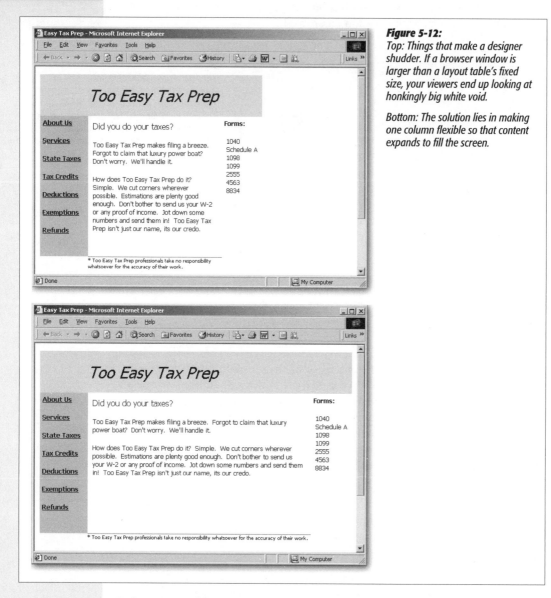

Figure 5-12:
Top: Things that make a designer shudder. If a browser window is larger than a layout table's fixed size, your viewers end up looking at honkingly big white void.

Bottom: The solution lies in making one column flexible so that content expands to fill the screen.

Before you try this maneuver, make sure that you click the Show Layout Tool button (within the Tables toolbar or the task pane) once or twice until you to see your layout table's measurements. To make a column autostretch, click its measurement box and select Make Column Autostretch (see Figure 5-13). Save the page and preview in a browser to see the difference.

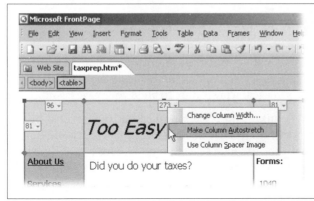

Figure 5-13:
When FrontPage's layout tools are active, you can click any measurement box to display this pop-up menu. FrontPage limits you to setting only one column to autostretch.

The spacer image

When you save your page, FrontPage prompts you to save an image file called *msspacer.gif*. What's that? This humble image file holds the key to your table's new flexibility. To make one column flexible, FrontPage sets it at 100 percent screen size. If left alone, that autostretch column would hog the whole screen and muscle out the other columns. To preserve the width of the fixed columns, FrontPage inserts a transparent graphic in each column. As you learned earlier, a column can't be smaller than any element it contains. FrontPage sets the width of the transparent GIF to the pixel width of the column and inserts it, preserving the column's fixed width against its flexible neighbor. Take a peek in your page's code, and you'll see *msspacer.gif* inserted in various pixel sizes.

If you want to insert a spacer image manually, click the measurement box at the top of a column and select Use Column Spacer Image (see Figure 5-14). You can use this menu to remove a GIF as well. Select Use Column Spacer Image to turn the checkbox off. Removing the autostretch setting from a neighboring column also removes the GIF files.

Figure 5-14:
A checkmark next to Use Column Spacer Image indicates that the column on the left contains a spacer GIF. The column next to it is the autostretch column, set to percent.

Web designers use transparent GIFs all the time to space out elements within table cells or text. Because these picture files are transparent, viewers never know they're there.

Using a Tracing Image to Create Page Layout

Some Web authors prefer to occasionally lay out a page by first drawing the design with pencil and paper. Or they may get Web page prototypes submitted to them by designers. If that happens to you—*honey, can you make the site look like* this?—you may want to use FrontPage's image tracing feature to build your page layout.

FrontPage lets you take any image and place a washed out version of it behind your workspace in Design view. It's just like the old tracing paper trick you learned in grade school. You then use the program's layout tools to trace over the image as you create your page's layout structure. FrontPage saves the image with the site, but the picture never appears in a browser window.

Start out by selecting View → Tracing Image → Configure to display the Tracing Image dialog box. Browse to your tracing image and then select it. Move the opacity slider left toward Transparent to avoid confusing the image with page content and click OK. The image displays in gray on your page. Then use the layout table tools to draw a table based on the image. If you find that you'd like to make the image more or less transparent, you can go back into the Tracing Image dialog box and adjust it. To do so, select View → Tracing Image → Configure at any time.

Hide the image when you're done by selecting View → Tracing Image → Show Image to remove the checkmark. You can also use this same menu command later on, if you want to see your tracing image again.

Frames

In your travels around the Web, you have probably seen pages that present a mix of never-changing parts (typically a menu on the side or top of the page) and a main section that changes depending on the link you've clicked. Welcome to the world of *frames*.

Frames don't just divvy up screen space like the tables you learned about in the previous chapter—frames actually present multiple Web pages simultaneously within one browser window. Using frames, you can divide a browser screen into sections and display a different Web page within each one. Each separate Web page appears within its own border, or frame. An additional page, called a *frameset,* serves as the host for all these pages. The frameset tells the browser how to apportion screen space and which pages to display in each section. A simple frames page is illustrated in Figure 6-1.

While frames can create interesting effects, they also come with serious disadvantages, all of which you'll learn about in the next section. If you decide to use frames, read on to learn how to create and manage them. Or check out the alternatives mentioned at the end of this chapter, on page 114.

Deciding Whether to Use Frames

While frames do offer an interesting way to divide a Web page, many Web designers hold their noses or shake their heads disapprovingly when looking at a site that uses frames. Some of their objections are aesthetic—akin to modern fashionistas who cringe at the big hair trends of previous decades. Other objections stem from frame-specific technical disadvantages, like the problems they create for search engines (more about that in a moment). And yet for some people, frames remain a helpful tool. What follows is a quick pros-and-cons tour so you can decide for yourself.

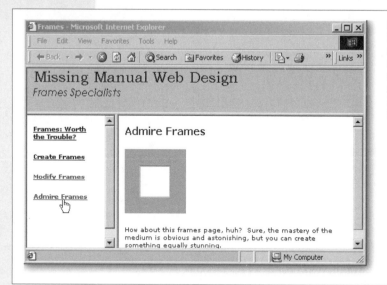

Figure 6-1:
This frames page displays three different HTML pages. As a viewer clicks links in the frame on the left, different pages display in the main window on the lower right. The banner at top and menu on the left never change.

Some advantages of frames:

- Frames save you from having to add a navigation menu to every page of your site. Using frames, you can save loads of time by creating the menu just once and placing its Web page in a frame.

- With frames, you can feature a page from another site, but display it surrounded by your own banner and menu offerings. This way, visitors may not even know they've left your site.

- With only one part of the browser window updating, readers don't need to reorient themselves, as they might on a site where every page changes. Using frames, menus and border elements remain constant.

Unfortunately, the drawbacks that come with using frames seem to outweigh the advantages. Many Web design veterans who have used frames end up redesigning out of frustration. Common causes of disenchantment include:

- Not all browsers can display sites that use frames. Visitors instead see an empty page or a message declaring that the browser they're using doesn't support frames. (These browsers are a tiny minority and include versions of Internet Explorer before 3.0 and pre-2.0 Netscape. Others are Mosaic 1.0 and Lynx, which displays framed pages as separate documents. And Opera lets you decide whether or not to view frames.)

- Many search engines have a hard time *indexing* (cataloging) content on sites that use frames. The reason? Each frame is actually a separate HTML file, and some search engines will mistakenly index only one frame—say, the one containing a banner—and ignore the content in the other frames. When people use the search site, their results would include only links to your banner frame and not to the important stuff elsewhere on your site.

- Web surfers won't be able to bookmark certain pages in your site. Say a reader has been merrily clicking away and is viewing deeply buried content in a frame when she *bookmarks* (or adds a favorite page to) her browser. The problem is, the browser won't necessarily save what she's looking at. As far as the browser is concerned, she hasn't left the frameset page (the page coordinating all the other, individually framed pages). So, when she clicks her bookmark later, she'll see the initial frameset page rather than the one she was looking at when she saved the bookmark.

- Printing frames is difficult, as most browsers can't tell which framed pages to print. If you've ever tried to print a page and ended up with only a picture of navigation buttons, frames were probably to blame.

If you're still game, or if you're just curious to learn more about how your Web forefathers and mothers designed many of their sites, read on.

Creating Frames and Framesets

When you build a site that uses frames, you're actually creating multiple Web pages for each browser window your viewers are looking at. Coordinating these pages can get confusing, but FrontPage helps by letting you create and edit framed pages directly from within the frameset. The program also lets you insert an alternative page for visitors whose browsers don't support frames.

Creating Frames

FrontPage simplifies the process of creating frames with its frames pages templates. These are canned frameset pages, each with a different layout, that include buttons and other aids to help you fill the frameset with pages.

To get started using one of these templates, select File → New to display the New task pane. Within the task pane, click "More page templates" and then click the Frames tab. Here, you'll find FrontPage's templates for frames. To preview and read a quick summary about each template, click each template. Then pick the frames template you want to use and click OK. FrontPage creates the empty frameset, as shown in Figure 6-2.

To help you fill the empty frames, FrontPage adds two buttons to each frame. You use the buttons to select or create the first page viewers will see when they come to your site.

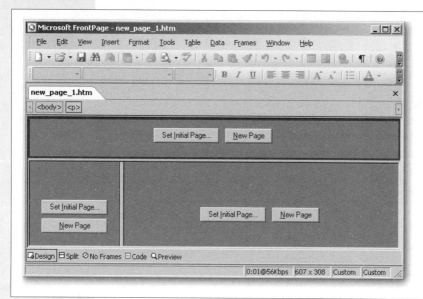

Figure 6-2:
FrontPage's Banner and Contents frames template creates this empty frameset. When you select pages to load into each of these three frames, you'll see them here in Design view. At that point, you'll be editing four separate HTML documents all at once within the same window.

- **Set Initial Page.** Click this button if you have an existing Web page you'd like to load into the frame.

Note: Don't let the terminology here confuse you. "Initial Page" means the page that initially loads in the frame. But if you haven't created it yet, you can click New Page (which will then become the initial page).

- **New Page.** Click this button to create a new Web page to load into the frame. FrontPage creates a new blank page and displays it within the frame, so you can edit it. Later, when you save the frameset, FrontPage prompts you to save any new pages.

That's all you need to do to get started creating a group of pages that use frames. Page 111 shows you how to add more pages to a frameset, but first you need to save your new frames.

Saving the New Frameset

Once you're done creating your new framed pages, you save them by first saving the frameset and then saving any new pages that you added. With the frameset open in Design view, save it as you would any other Web page (page 14).

When you save the frameset, FrontPage first prompts you to save each new page you've created, one by one, and provides a diagram on the right side of the Save As dialog box, as shown in Figure 6-3, to help you keep track of what you're saving.

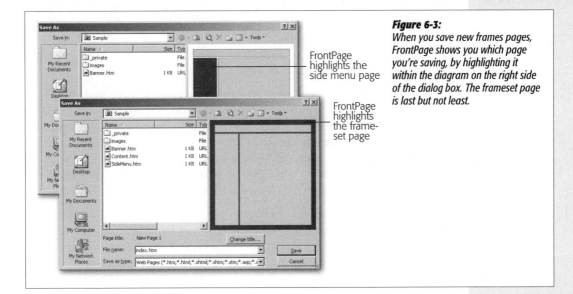

Figure 6-3:
When you save new frames pages, FrontPage shows you which page you're saving, by highlighting it within the diagram on the right side of the dialog box. The frameset page is last but not least.

FrontPage highlights the side menu page

FrontPage highlights the frame-set page

Pick a name for each new page and enter it into the File Name box. Since you may be looking at more than one dialog box (one for each new page, plus one for the frameset), make sure you know which file you're naming. Most people find that naming the frameset *index.htm* or *default.htm* works well, since it's usually the first page of their site. (See page 188 for details on naming a site's home page.)

Modifying Frames

Frames are just like any other design element on your site; if you don't like the way they look, FrontPage gives you lots of ways to change their appearance. For example, if the proportions of your frames look a little off, you can change the way they're laid out by using the Frame Properties dialog box (which is what you'll use to make most frame-related modifications). To get started making changes, first select a frame, then right-click it and select Frame Properties (or select Frames → Frame Properties).

Adjusting frame dimensions

The quickest way to modify the size of an individual frame is to drag and reposition its border. However, the Frame Properties dialog box gives you some better options. The Frame size boxes let you set precise dimensions by typing them in. Frames can use both percent and pixel values, like tables (page 85).

You can also use *relative sizing,* which lets you control the size of a group of elements, by assigning dimensions that are proportional to each individual element.

For example, a banner at the top of a page might have a relative height of 1, while a vertical menu below it has a relative height of 4. This means that the banner takes up one-fifth of the vertical window space while the menu takes up four-fifths.

The best bet? Stick with percentage or relative dimensions. This way you know your page will look more or less the way you intended—no matter what a viewer's browser size or screen resolution.

Frame scroll bars: To show or not to show

On some pages, like the one shown in Figure 6-1, scroll bars can mar and clutter up an otherwise lovely composition. To get rid of these unsightly controls, adjust the Show Scrollbars setting. You can choose to show them Always, If Needed, or Never. Before you make this change in Frame Properties, take a good look at the frame in question. If a viewer will definitely need to scroll, hiding the scroll bar is cruel and counterproductive, so weigh your priorities. You also might want to edit the dimensions of your frame (explained in the previous section) so that scroll bars aren't necessary.

He that taketh can also giveth. Bestow the power of frame resizing on your readers, enabling them to solve the problem themselves by moving frame borders around within their browser. To do so, in Frame Properties, turn on the "Resizable in Browser" checkbox.

Hiding frame borders

Even without scroll bars, frame borders look clunky and obvious. If you want to elevate your game and do like the professionals do, hide your frame borders (see Figure 6-4).

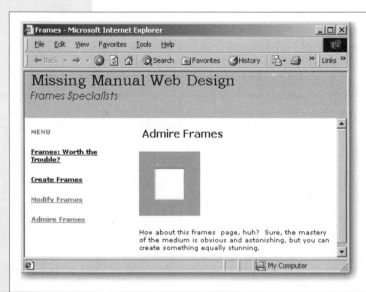

Figure 6-4:
Compare this page to its border-showing twin in Figure 6-1. Hiding borders makes a page look sleek, unified, and more professional.

Tip: To change the amount of space between a frame border and its content, use the margin settings in the Frame Properties dialog box.

With the frameset open, select Frames → Frame Properties and click Frames Page on the lower right. Turn off the Show Borders checkbox in the Frames tab.

You can set the width of your borders on the Frames tab, too. The Frame Spacing field controls border thickness in pixels. This setting applies to visible and invisible borders. If you've hidden your borders, frames are still separated by the number of pixels you enter here.

Splitting frames

If you need to add a frame to a frameset, you have to split an existing frame in two to make room for it. To do so, first click in the frame. Then select Frames → Split Frame. Specify whether you want to split the frame into rows or columns, and click OK. A new blank frame appears.

Creating a No Frames Page

Not all browsers are on good speaking terms with sites that use frames. The typical response from browsers that can't handle frames is to show a big blank page. Fortunately, FrontPage is capable of helping you reach across this browser divide. Take a look at the Views buttons on the lower-left corner of the document window. Just when you were getting bored with your choices, a new option appears there called No Frames. You can see it in Figure 6-2. Click the No Frames button, and a terse message appears: "This page uses frames, but your browser doesn't support them." This message, which is just an alternate view of your frameset, will appear in browsers that don't display frames. If you'd like to let these browser owners down a bit easier, reword the message. If you don't want to lose them, create an alternate site that doesn't use frames, enter a message about that alternate site here, and include a link to it.

Editing Frameset Content

Okay, so you know how to create a frameset and change its appearance. What about the pages your frameset displays? You'll probably want to edit these initial pages you created earlier in this chapter and you might also want to add a few *new* pages. This section shows you how.

Editing Pages

To edit any page that's already part of a frameset, just open up the frameset page and click the page you want to edit. You can also open individual framed pages on their own, as you would any other Web page, and edit them within the full document window.

Creating Additional Pages

Say you created a frameset that contains three frames. Eventually, you'll want to display more pages than just those initial three pages. For example, the frameset in Figure 6-1 features a large window on the lower right. As a viewer clicks menu items in the frame on the left side of the screen, the large frame on the lower right displays different pages. So if you were building this site, you'd want to create new pages for each menu link on the left-side frame.

Fortunately, adding new pages to a site that uses frames is easy. Just create additional pages the same way you'd create any other page (page 9). The next section shows you how to create the links between existing pages and any new pages you've created.

Using Save As to Add Pages

If you really want to see how this page appears in the frameset as you create it, and you like to live on the edge, you can use a slightly riskier method: FrontPage's Save As feature. This approach lets you edit directly through the frameset while you're creating your page. All you'll do is replace the content of an existing page (the one currently open in the frameset) and save it as a new page.

To do this, select all the content within the desired frame (Press Ctrl+A or select Edit → Select All) and delete it. (Be careful *not* to click Save or Save Page at any point during this procedure.)

Enter content for the new page and, when you're done, select Frames → Save Page As. Enter a name for the new page and save the file in the appropriate folder.

Hyperlinking from Frames

A hyperlink within a frame is more complicated than the usual plain vanilla hyperlinks you first learned about in Chapter 1. A link that appears within a frameset must tell the browser not only *what* page to open, but *where* to open it. Or, as FrontPage would put it, you don't just select the hyperlink *destination*, you also identify the *target*.

Setting Targets for Frames

The target attribute of a hyperlink specifies what frame the new page will open in. Open up the Hyperlink Properties dialog box (by clicking the Hyperlink button on the Standard toolbar) to edit the target.

Within the Hyperlink Properties dialog box, click Target Frame. The Target Frame dialog box appears, sporting a new feature called "Current frames page" (see Figure 6-5).

Depending on what template you've chosen, FrontPage makes an intelligent guess at what your target frame should be (based on the template's automatic settings). But you can override this choice and select any one of your frames to serve as the hyperlink's target. Just click the diagram to make a selection or enter the frame name in the Target Setting field. If you select Whole Page from the list on the upper right, then the new page will take up the entire browser window, replacing your frameset completely. The regular hyperlink target selections also still appear here, and you're free to choose any of them instead. For example, if you wanted the hyperlink to launch a new browser window, the Target Frame dialog box gives you that option (see Chapter 3 for a refresher on hyperlinks).

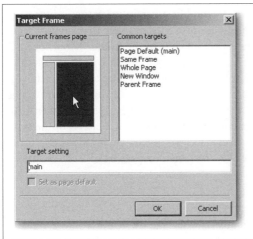

Figure 6-5:
The Target Frame dialog box displays an interactive diagram of your frameset. Click the frame in which you want the linked page to load.

Creating Inline Frames

Perhaps you've grown fond of the idea of guiding your visitors with the constant, reassuring presence of frames. Maybe you're already confidently envisioning one page, majestically sitting atop every page on your site, while the other pages below it scurry about, making brief appearances as they're summoned by link clicks. And then you snap out of it, alarmed at the thought of having to deal with so many different frames. If that sounds familiar, you may want to consider using a kind of pseudo-frame solution: *inline frames.*

An inline frame allows you to insert a frame within a regular Web page. Doing so is kind of like placing a window in your Web page that lets viewers see and scroll through the content of another page—the one you place in the frame.

The biggest problem with inline frames is that, like regular frames, not all browsers support them. So be sure to create a No Frames page (page 111) for inline frames as well.

Adding an Inline Frame

You can add an inline frame to any Web page. To do so, place your cursor where you want the frame to appear and select Insert → Inline Frame. Select (or create) pages to appear in the frame, just as you would for any frame: click the Set Initial Page button to select an existing page, or click the New Page button to create a new one.

Modifying an Inline Frame

You can enlarge or reduce the size of your inline frame by selecting it, then dragging one of its small square handles until it appears just as you want it.

Use the Inline Frames Properties box to modify other inline frame settings (like your scroll bar preference or the alternate text for browsers that don't support frames). To open it, move your cursor over an edge of the frame. When your cursor turns into a regular white pointer, double-click. Or click once to select the frame, then right-click and select Inline Frame Properties. The choices in this dialog box work just like the ones you learned about earlier in this chapter on page 109. One option you have here that you don't get in other Frame Properties dialog boxes is Alignment. Use this to set alignment—left, right, or center—of the frame within your page. Other alignment choices let you line up the frame with a line of text just like you can do with a picture (as explained on page 64).

Alternatives to Frames

Maintaining navigation bars and menus on your site often turns into a full-time job. That's why so many people were originally attracted to frames in the first place. But as their charm (the frames, not the people) wore off, Web designers started looking for other options. Fortunately, FrontPage has got you covered and is ready to help you out with two tools that you'll learn about later in this book:

- **FrontPage Link Bars.** Let FrontPage do your work. Link bars are site menus and navigation links that FrontPage creates and updates for you. As you'll see when you read more about site navigation in Chapter 10 (page 182), you have to set up a navigation structure for link bars to function properly, but after that, FrontPage does all the work.

- **Included Content.** This special feature lets you take content from one page and include it within another or many other pages. Because you edit this content only on its original page, included content is a great way to create one navigation menu that you can insert on many pages. Make a change once on the original page, and FrontPage automatically updates all other pages that "include" this menu content. Page 206 shows you all the details.

Cascading Style Sheets

When HTML receives its lifetime achievement award from the World Wide Web Academy, it surely won't be for the gorgeous documents it helped produce. As you learned in Chapter 2, HTML's layout capabilities are pretty limited. So now that you understand basic HTML formatting, you're probably wondering how some Web sites manage to look so sleek.

Cascading Style Sheets, or CSS, have advanced the cause of Web design enormously. With CSS, an author gains greater control over what each page looks like. Style sheets contain specific typographic and color controls to improve your site's appearance, and most of these CSS tools surpass regular HTML formatting capabilities. But styles go beyond controlling text and color. You can also use styles to do things like precisely position images and add margin and alignment settings to page elements. Best of all, you can apply style sheets to many pages at once. By implementing site-wide changes on the style sheet only, you won't need to edit each and every page. If you frequently need to update the look of your site, CSS can save you loads of time.

As you learn to implement styles in this sophisticated manner, you'll be amazed at the power Cascading Style Sheets bring to your bag of tricks. This chapter will introduce you to styles and teach you to create, modify, and apply them across a page or an entire Web site.

Styles: An Introduction

A style is a group of formatting specifications identified by a name. You can create a style and then apply it to characters, paragraphs, images, tables, or HTML tags.

For example, you can create a style for a paragraph that specifies maroon 10-pt Verdana font on a yellow background. And you can keep on going—by setting spacing before and after the paragraph, making it right aligned, and even giving it a border. Once you're done creating your style, you pick a name for it—Maroon-VerdanaGrafs, for example—and then you can apply it to any paragraph with a click.

If you've worked with programs like Microsoft Word or Adobe FrameMaker, you may be familiar with this method of applying a style to specific elements. Similarly, in FrontPage, styles help you centralize the formatting of your Web pages. For instance, if you want all your Heading 1 paragraphs to be blue, you could apply blue color style to the <H1> tag using an external style sheet (more on the particular types of style sheets in a moment). After doing this only once in the style sheet, you'd then be able to change all the Heading 1 paragraphs throughout your site. Any paragraph with an <H1> tag anywhere in your site would then be blue.

Styles are that powerful, but the technology behind them isn't very complicated. A style is just a *rule* (or group of rules) for formatting some HTML. Rules are written in simple text, as in this example, which specifies that all Heading 1 paragraphs should be blue:

```
H1 {color: blue}
```

Note: Some older browsers don't support CSS. Both Netscape Navigator and Internet Explorer supported CSS as of their 4.0 releases. In earlier versions of these browsers, your pages display fine, just without the styles.

The Scope of Your Styles

Once you create a style, you might wonder whether its rules extend to every page throughout your site. That depends on *where* you create a style rule. These snippets of text can live within the HTML on an individual page, or within a separate style sheet. As you'll see, location is everything.

Inline, embedded, and external styles

Styles can be applied at three basic levels:

- **Inline styles** apply directly to one specific HTML tag on a page and affect whatever text the tag contains. Inline styles control only one element at a time. The style rule lives within the element's HTML tag.

- **Embedded styles** (sometimes called *internal styles*) apply to an entire page. You'll use an embedded style to control elements across a whole page. These kinds of style rules live between the page's <head> tags (page xvii).

- **External styles** apply to multiple pages. These types of style rules live within a separate file called a *style sheet*. A style sheet is a simple text file (whose file extension is .css) composed of nothing but rules. Any Web pages that you link to a style sheet adopt the formatting rules contained within the style sheet. You can use external styles to control elements across multiple pages or even your entire site.

UP TO SPEED

Creating an Inline Style

You've actually already created an inline style. You often do so when you apply formatting to an HTML tag. To see this for yourself, create a hyperlink page 47). Right-click the link, select Hyperlink Properties, and then click Style. Click Format → Font. Change the color to Red, then close all the dialog boxes. Select the hyperlink and switch to Split view (page 5). Your <a> hyperlink tag now contains a style tag:

```
<a style="color: #FF0000" href="info.htm">
Click here</a>
```

But FrontPage doesn't always create an inline style when you apply formatting. For instance, when you select some text and pick a font or color, FrontPage applies a <font> tag containing your formatting. The <font> tag adds extraneous decorative information that's considered outside the bounds of HTML, so it's losing favor on the Web (mostly because authors are always looking for ways to trim code out of their pages so they'll download as quickly as possible). Inline styles aren't much better than the <font> tag, as they still clutter your document with presentation details. But once you implement page- and site-level styles, you'll use inline styles only to override these other settings.

Style Selectors

Inline style rules are stored inside an element's tag, so a browser knows immediately what element they affect. When you work with embedded and external styles, on the other hand, you need to specify which elements the styles will control. To do so, you'll use a *selector*. Selectors are just different methods for telling FrontPage where to apply a style. There are a few different types of selectors.

Tag selectors

You can apply a style to any HTML tag, such as <H1>, <H2>, <p>, <table>, <a>, <li>, and even the <body> tag.

Look again at this sample style rule, which you might put in either an embedded or an external style sheet:

```
H1 {color: blue}
```

The style actually begins with the selector information, which is the <H1> tag. This is an example of a tag selector. In other words, this style rule is saying: *Hey, browser. Wherever you find an <H1> tag (on this page, if you're using embedded styles; or throughout a collection of pages, if you're using an external style sheet), make it blue.*

Class selectors (user-defined styles)

The ability to apply styles to tags gives you a lot of formatting power, but it doesn't cover all bases. You may also have your own unique text elements that don't have

---

tags associated with them but which require their own distinctive style. For example, say you created a page to display a collection of t-shirts and you want to give all the shirt descriptions a uniform, special style all their own.

In this case, you'll have to create your own custom style, name it, and then go into your pages and manually apply the style name to each shirt description. Web professionals call these tags *class selectors*. FrontPage sometimes calls class selectors *user-defined styles*.

ID selectors

You may need to define a style for an individual element on a page, like a particular image or (as you'll learn in Chapter 8) a layer. This type of selector uses an element's ID (located within its HTML tag) to apply a style to it. Unlike the other style selectors, FrontPage doesn't make it easy to create an ID selector even though the program supports applying styles to IDs. You might never need to use this selector. But if you do, and the ID is missing, you'll have to create it manually (which you'll learn how to do later in this chapter in the "Applying a Class Style" section on page 126).

Creating an External Style Sheet

If you want to apply styles to multiple pages, you'll need to create a style sheet to contain them. (If you don't plan to use style sheets and just want to create embedded or page-level styles, skip ahead to the next section, "Creating Styles.") External style sheets sit within a site alongside all your other image and HTML files and provide formatting for the HTML files that you've linked to them. A site can have multiple style sheets, if you want.

FrontPage makes it easy to create external style sheets and even provides some templates for you to use. Below are the basic steps for creating an empty style sheet. In the next section, you'll learn how to add styles to your sheet.

Creating a New Style Sheet

A style sheet is just a plain old text file that contains a bunch of style rules. You could open a file in Notepad, start typing in style rules, and save it as a CSS file, but FrontPage makes it easier than that.

To get started, first select File → New to display the New task pane. Within the task pane, click "More page templates" and then click the Style Sheets tab. FrontPage offers some canned CSS files here that are already filled with styles. To read their descriptions, click once on each template. To create a blank style sheet, click Normal Style Sheet. A blank page appears within the document window. The next section explains how to add styles to your sheet, which will eventually look like the one shown in Figure 7-1.

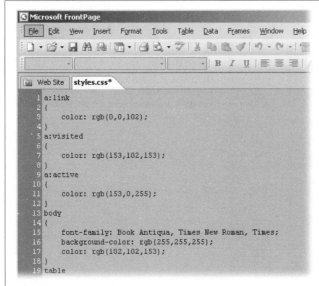

Figure 7-1:
A style sheet looks like—and in fact is—a regular text file. If you're comfortable writing your own style rules, you can type in a new style setting directly onto the style sheet. Otherwise, use the Styles dialog box (page 120).

Saving your style sheet

When you're done creating your style sheet, save the file in your Web site. To do so, select File → Save or press Ctrl+S. If it's going to be the only style sheet in your site, name it something like *styles.css*. If you'll have multiple style sheets, pick a more descriptive name, so you can identify it easily when you link it to various HTML pages. It's also a good idea to create a folder named *css* to store all your styles sheets in.

Creating Styles

When you create a style, you're really just creating style rules. If you want, you can type rules directly into a style sheet or into an HTML file. But, once again, there's no need tax your keyboard—FrontPage walks you through the rules-creation process with its Style dialog box. You'll use the Style dialog box to create a style, set formatting, and even preview the effects.

Creating a Style

Whether you're creating an embedded (page-level) or external (site-level) style, the process is the same. Begin by opening the HTML page or style sheet and selecting

Format → Style. The Style dialog box displays (Figure 7-2), which you'll use to set the characteristics of a style and to name it.

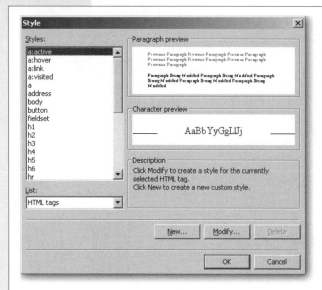

Figure 7-2:
The Styles dialog box features a pane on the left called Styles, though at first, it doesn't show any styles. Instead, it shows HTML tags to which you can apply a style. Use the List drop-down menu, beneath it, to switch between HTML tags and user-defined styles. If you select a style or tag, you get a preview of what it looks like on the right side of the Styles dialog box.

To create a new style:

1. **Choose a style selector so that FrontPage knows what element this style will modify.**

   - If you're applying a style to an HTML tag, select the tag from the list and click Modify.

   - If you're creating a class (user-defined) style (page 117), click New.

2. **Confirm or name the selector.**

   - If you selected Modify in step 1, confirm that the tag you want to modify appears in the Selector Name field.

   - If you selected New in step 1, type in a name for your class selector (don't use any spaces in the name). Class selector names always need to be preceded by a period, but FrontPage inserts this for you automatically. Use the drop-down listbox on the right to specify whether the style will apply to paragraphs or characters.

3. **Define the style.**

Click Format to display a list of style properties (see Figure 7-3). Each of these selections opens a dialog box, which lets you set specific formatting. For details on all your formatting options, see "Setting Style Properties" on page 122.

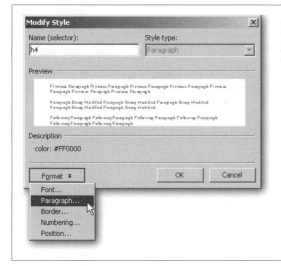

Figure 7-3:
Click Format to display the Style Properties menu, which lets you control a style's settings for things like position, border and shading, and font style.

4. **Save the style.**

To confirm that you've created a new style, you can click the List drop-down menu below the Styles pane and select User-Defined Styles. Your new style should appear in the Styles pane. (Switch between the tags and styles lists at any time, using the List drop-down menu.) Click OK to save and close the dialog box.

BEHIND THE SCENES

Embedded Styles in HTML

Embedded style rules are stored inside the <head> tags of a Web page (page xvii). To see what an embedded style looks like, switch to Split or Code view and locate the <head> tags. Nested within the <head> tags are <style> tags. For instance, if you created an embedded style to make hyperlinks red, you'd see this:

```
<style>
<!--
a { color: #FF0000 }
-->
</style>
```

As you can see here, FrontPage does you the favor of placing embedded style rules within comment tags (<!-- and

-->) as a safety measure. Why? Browsers never display text within comment tags, so coders use this trick to hide style rules from browsers that can't display CSS. Otherwise, the rules might appear as text within older browsers.

Embedded styles work only for the pages in which they're stored. If you want to copy an embedded style to another page, just copy the HTML code. To do so, select the <style> tags and their contents, copy, and then paste the selection into the <head> section of another Web page. If you find yourself frequently copying styles between pages in that way, you're probably better off using an external style sheet.

Setting Style Properties

Cascading Style Sheets provide many more formatting options than plain old HTML. Click Format within the Style dialog box (page 120) to launch the style properties dialog boxes that are described next.

Fonts

The Font dialog box (see Figure 7-4) is pretty similar to the one you get by selecting Format → Font. Some options—like Strong, Emphasis, and others—are missing here, because those are HTML-specific tags, whereas the ones in this dialog box show all the options CSS gives you.

Tip: To remove underline formatting from all your hyperlinks, modify an <a> tag style font by turning on the No Text Decoration checkbox.

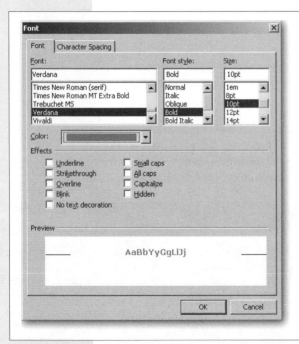

Figure 7-4:
When you're setting a style's font attributes, FrontPage offers the dialog box pictured here. If you want to condense characters (bring them closer to together so they take up less horizontal space) or spread characters out, click the Character Spacing tab and select your preference.

While CSS gives you a few new font formatting options, the basic rules that govern how text displays within a browser still apply. If you select a font that's not loaded on a viewer's system, the browser replaces it with a similar font (or what it

thinks is a similar font). Again, stick to the common fonts you learned about back
on page 27.

WORKAROUND WORKSHOP

Adding Font Families

A font won't display in a browser, unless a viewer has that font on his system. A lot of Web designers get around this problem by specifying a family, or group of similar fonts, from which a browser can choose. That way, if a viewer doesn't have the first font in the list, the browser loads the second, or third font, and so on.

While this is a common practice, FrontPage doesn't give you an easy way to include these font families. Your only option is to type alternative fonts in your style sheet yourself.

The program does give you a small head start, though. When you add a font to a style sheet, it appears like this:

```
h1  { font-family: Verdana }
```

What you need to do is type additional fonts after your first font and separate them with commas. (If the family name includes a space, be sure to enclose it in quotation marks.) You'll end up with something like this:

```
h1  { font-family: Verdana, Arial,
Helvetica, sans-serif; }
h2  { font-family: "Book Antiqua", "Times
New Roman", serif; }
```

How do you know which font family to use? An old-school, ink-stained finger designer would probably tell you the following: Serif fonts, like Times New Roman, feature small flourishes at the ends of each letter to help lead a reader's eye to the next letter. This makes these Serif fonts easier, especially when it comes to long paragraphs. Sans-serif fonts don't have these flourishes, or serifs, and are more often used as headings due to their bold, blocky appearance.

Those guidelines were gospel back in the days of print-only typesetting. But Web authoring has changed the rules of font selection. Reading on a *pixilated screen*—that is, one made up of thousands (or millions) of tiny dots—differs from reading print on paper. Because a screen *pixilates* (renders in little squares) serifs, they're actually harder to read on a computer screen. Most Web designers therefore now use a sans-serif font, like Verdana, for large passages of text.

Paragraph

FrontPage's CSS paragraph settings are identical to those you saw on FrontPage's regular paragraph format dialog box (page 34). In fact, when you're editing a Web page and select Format → Paragraph, you actually create an inline style. Setting paragraph spacing and alignment works the same on a style sheet, except that you get to apply it across your entire site, of course.

Border

You can set borders for any page element, including the entire body of a page, text, pictures, tables, rows, and cells. Speaking of cells—you can also use the Border dialog box to set cell padding by creating a style for the <td> tag (page 83) and editing the Padding fields. (As you learned in Chapter 5, padding is the space between a border and its content.) Setting cell padding on a style sheet instead of on every table in your site can save you tons of time.

Want to set the background of a particular element? Just click the Shading tab. The Background Color field sets the color behind any elements you've specified. This might be the background of a cell, list, paragraph, or an entire page—depending on the tag or selector you've chosen. Foreground Color sets the color of the element itself, like text.

The Shading tab also gives you more control than HTML property settings if you want to use background images. For example, if you don't want your picture to tile (appear multiple times when it's not big enough to fill the space), select No Repeat from the Repeat drop-down menu. You can also have the background picture scroll along with content by selecting Scroll within the Attachment drop-down menu. Neither of these settings is possible if you're just using HTML.

Note: Netscape Navigator 4.0 doesn't support most border background settings.

Numbering

Because you can control more than just numbering, a better title for this style properties dialog box might be Lists. You already know that numbered and bulleted lists work in pretty much the same way (page 38). Use this styles dialog box to format both. As with the standard List Properties box, you can control the appearance of numbered or bulleted lists, and include picture bullets if you want.

Position

While you'll want to use HTML tables (Chapter 5) for complex layout, CSS is better for controlling the positioning of individual elements.

CSS gives you two types of position control options:

- **Relative positioning** places objects according to the position of elements that precede and follow them on the page (see Figure 7-5). HTML automatically arranges items relatively, so—unless you've "absolutely positioned" an element (see below)—everything on your pages should already be positioned relatively. But you can make adjustments here. For example, you can set wrapping (page 65) and width options for relatively positioned objects.

- **Absolute positioning** lets you set an exact location on your page's x-y axis for the placement of an object. For example, to position an image, click the Absolute button in the Position dialog box and set Top = 20 and Left = 40. This sets the location of the top-left corner of the image at 20 pixels from the top of the page and 40 pixels from the left side of the page. Be careful with absolute positioning. Text won't flow around an absolutely positioned item, but will appear behind or, if you specify, in front of it (see Figure 7-5).

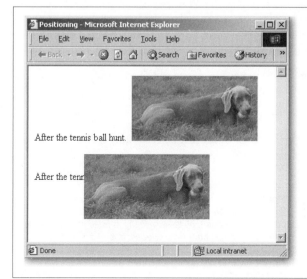

Figure 7-5:
The picture on the first line is positioned relatively. The text pushes it across the page and determines its position. The second picture is positioned absolutely. It sits in an assigned spot that you've selected, uninfluenced by the position of other elements—even to the point that it obscures a line of text.

You can position elements like paragraphs, images, and tables. Web developers use absolute positioning most often when they're working with layers. For detailed information on positioning layers and using other controls in the Position dialog box, see Chapter 8.

Tip: Many developers are using CSS positioning to lay out pages instead of using tables. This is the next big wave in page design. Advantages include quicker page load times and easier access for handheld browsers like cellphones, which often can't read tables. While you can attempt this kind of layout in FrontPage 2003 using layers and CSS, many hope that the next FrontPage release will include features to make this method a lot easier.

Applying Styles

The whole point of styles is to enhance your pages. Now that you've created a few styles, the last step is actually applying them to page elements. How you do so depends upon what kinds of styles you created.

Inline and embedded styles with tag selectors show up immediately without any further action on your part. FrontPage automatically applies the proper formatting to the specified tags. Steps for getting your external and user-defined styles onto your pages follow.

Linking to an External Style Sheet

If you want your pages to adopt external styles (page 116), you've got to link your HTML pages to the style sheet that you've created. The fastest way to do this is to open a Web page in Design view, locate the .css file in your folder list, and drag it into the document window.

However, you probably want to link *multiple* Web pages to a particular sheet. To do so, first pop over to Folder view (page 17). Select the page(s) that you want to follow the external style rules, and then select Format → Style Sheet Links. A Link Style Sheet dialog box opens (Figure 7-6).

- If you want to link all the pages in your Web site to the style sheet, click the "All pages" radio button.

- To link just those you've selected, click "Selected page(s)."

Then click Add and browse to the style sheet file. Select it and click OK. You can add as many style sheets to your site as you want.

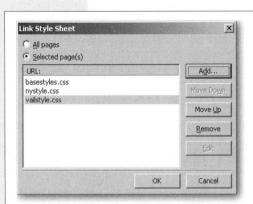

Figure 7-6:
You can link more than one style sheet to the same Web page(s). For instance, all three style sheets listed here will apply to whatever pages have been selected. If you have more than one style sheet, use the Move Up and Move Down buttons to pick the order in which you want browsers to follow the rules (that's important in cases where multiple style sheets contain conflicting rules). Styles in sheets higher on the list take precedence over those below. For more about how multiple sheets interact, see "Understanding Style Behavior" on page 128 at the end of this chapter.

If a Web page you've linked to the style sheet is currently open in Design view, you'll immediately see it take on the new styles.

Note: If you're linking multiple pages, some may already have links to style sheets. If they're all linked to the same style sheet(s), no problem. But if separate pages have different style sheet links, FrontPage can't handle the confusion. The program displays a confirmation prompt, asking if you want to overwrite existing links. The prompt gives you an option to cancel, continue, or examine a links report to see what links are in place. If you choose to continue, FrontPage overwrites links for all pages with the new style sheets you choose.

If you don't like the effect, or chose the wrong style sheet, unlink it. Return to the Link Style Sheet dialog box, select the style sheet, and then click Remove.

Applying a Class Style

FrontPage automatically applies any styles you associate with a tag, but when you create a user-defined style (page 117), you must manually apply it to elements on your Web page. To do this, it helps to have the Style toolbar active (View → Toolbars → Style).

You can apply styles in various ways. It all depends upon the target element.

To apply style to text—for example, say you want to apply a rule to every snippet of text that describes one of your products—select the characters or paragraph that compose a description, and then do one of the following:

- Select the style from the Style drop-down list on the Formatting toolbar.

- Select the style from the Style toolbar's Class drop-down list.

Note: You can apply the style to only one selection at a time. In other words, if other types of text separate each product description, you won't be able to select all your product descriptions at once and apply the style. You'd have to select one chunk of text, apply the style, and repeat.

If the element is a picture, table, or layer, applying a style can be trickier. Try the method above, but if it doesn't work, you've got a couple other options:

- Right-click and select the Properties option for the item, such as Picture Properties. Click the Style button in the Properties dialog box and make your selection from the Class drop-down list.

- With the Style toolbar displayed, select the item. If an ID for the item appears in the toolbar's ID field (as in Figure 7-7), select it. Then select the style from the class drop-down list on the left.

Note: An ID is a unique label for an item that lives inside its HTML tag. FrontPage often creates IDs automatically. If the item has no ID, you can assign one. For details on creating an ID, see the box "ID Your Elements" on page 165 in Chapter 9.

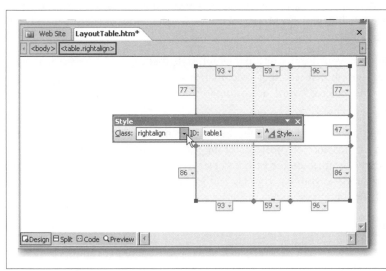

Figure 7-7:
The Style toolbar helps you apply styles quickly. It also features an ID field to help you select individual elements. If you need more options than the toolbar offers, click the Style button on the right to open the Style dialog box.

Removing a Class Style

Perhaps you've grown bored with the pink boldface you've applied to the text throughout your site? The steps you need to take for removing a class style depend upon the element affected by the rule.

To remove a class style from text, select the text and select Format → Remove Formatting.

Note: You must select all the text in order for this to work, even for a paragraph style. You can't just click inside a paragraph to remove a style (though that's all you need to do to apply one). You must select all the text the paragraph comprises.

To remove a class style from an image or table, right-click the object and then select the Properties option for the item, such as Picture Properties. Click the Style button in the Properties dialog box and delete the style from the Class drop-down list. Click OK to close and save settings in both dialog boxes. If that doesn't work, select the item, and then select Normal from the Style drop-down list.

Understanding Style Behavior

So you've created an external style sheet and linked your HTML files to it, but you also have some embedded and inline styles on your Web pages. How do they all interact? Who's the chief stylist? To answer that question, first you have to get your head around the two basic tenets of style: *inheritance* and *cascading*.

Inheritance

Style inheritance, like human inheritance, passes from parent to child. In other words, style attributes of HTML elements pass styles onto smaller elements that they contain.

For example, say you've got a <p> paragraph style that calls for blue Verdana font. Within a paragraph that uses that style, there's a word you've italicized (using <i> italic tags). The italicized word, according to rules of inheritance, also gets the blue Verdana font.

As you design your site styles, keep this behavior in mind. Inheritance can save you a lot of work. For instance, if you want all the text on your site to appear as Tahoma font, don't set this attribute for each and every tag like <H1>, <H2>, <p>, and so on. Apply the style to your <body> tag and let the law of inheritance take over and do the work for you.

Cascading

Inheritance is easy enough to understand when you're thinking about parent-child style relationships (at least HTML ones). But what if you have conflicting style settings for the same element? Imagine that you've created an external style sheet and formatted <H2> as green, 12-point Verdana font. On one of your site's pages, you've embedded an <H2> style as red Times New Roman font. When a browser displays this page, it sees two different style settings for the very same tag. What's a browser to do? Simple. The browser displays the embedded, or page-level, style. The heading on that page shows up as red Times New Roman.

Style power structure dictates that the style closest to the element takes priority. Therefore, an inline style overrides an embedded or page-level setting, and a page-level setting overrides a site-wide or external style.

However, it gets a little more complicated than that. In the example above, not all properties conflicted with one another. Font size is specified on the external style sheet as 12 pt, but the embedded style specifies nothing. So, though the heading on that particular page follows the page-level rule, appearing in red Times New Roman, it takes the directive from the external style sheet to size the text at 12 point.

When you link multiple style sheets to the same Web page, cascading behaviors also apply. Within the Link Style Sheet dialog box, you can specify the order in which style sheets will be applied (see Figure 7-6). The style sheet on the top overrides those below it, just as an embedded style sheet overrides an external one. Style rules on the additional sheets can fill in the blanks as in the scenario above. Often, site developers create additional style sheets to hold style rules designated for a few specific pages in a site. These supplemental CSS files can work in harmony with a master style sheet.

Take advantage of the cascading behaviors: create general rules to control your site's overall appearance, and at the same time, use embedded or inline styles to customize individual pages.

Layers

Chapter 5 showed you how tables can help lay out a Web page. All in all, they do a pretty good job, but they do have some limitations. Complex tables with lots of cells slow a page's download time. And a lot of new Web browsers—like those in cellphones and palmtops—can't handle tables. And then there's all that tweaking. You could spend a whole afternoon fine-tuning columns and rows to position a cell just so. After spending a little time working with tables, perhaps you'll find yourself wishing for some kind of magic table cell that you could just draw and place anywhere on your page. Well, in a way, you can. Instead of using table cells, use a *layer*.

A layer is an invisible container that you can place anywhere on your page. It can hold anything you want—like text, pictures, tables, or even a video. Why bother to put these things in a layer? Because layers give you control—like the ability to position them absolutely anywhere on a page—that you just can't get with regular page elements on their own.

Unlike table cells, you can easily move and rearrange layers as you edit your page. Layers can even sit on top of one another. Try *that* with a table. To see how this is all possible, take a look at Figure 8-1. In FrontPage's document window, layers appear as blue boxes. After you fill the box—say with text or a picture—you can drag it around and place it anywhere.

Meanwhile, your viewers have no idea that you used layers to create your page. Figure 8-2 shows the same page as it appears in a browser. No layer boxes are visible. You can create a layout like this with just a few clicks. It's so fast, and so direct, that many Web designers are turning to layers to handle page design and abandoning tables altogether.

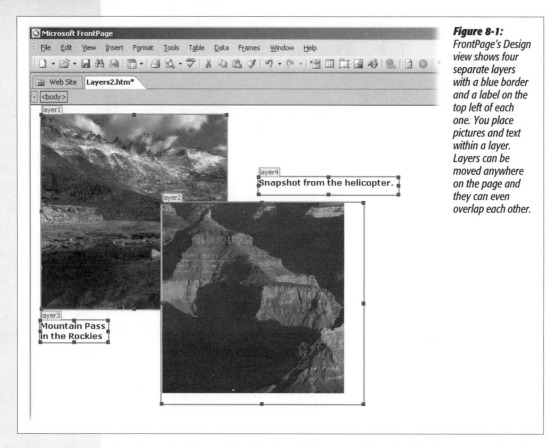

Figure 8-1:
FrontPage's Design view shows four separate layers with a blue border and a label on the top left of each one. You place pictures and text within a layer. Layers can be moved anywhere on the page and they can even overlap each other.

But layers don't stop there. When FrontPage adds a pinch of *JavaScript* (a coding language that works alongside HTML to spice up your pages), layers can bring motion and interactivity to your Web pages. Want a click on a menu heading to unfurl submenus? Or have a car zoom across the screen when a page loads? Layers can deliver these slick effects.

In this chapter, you'll learn to create and position layers. Once you know how to use layers to control *placement,* move on to Chapter 9 to see how designers manipulate layers to create *action.*

Note: Older browsers don't support layers. Instead, viewers using browsers that predate IE 4.0 or Netscape 4.0 will likely see a hapless jumble of text and images. If you know you'll have a lot of such visitors, you shouldn't use layers and may want to turn off absolute positioning (page 124) options altogether. To do this, select Tools → Page Options and click the Authoring tab. Turn off the CSS 2.0 (positioning) checkbox.

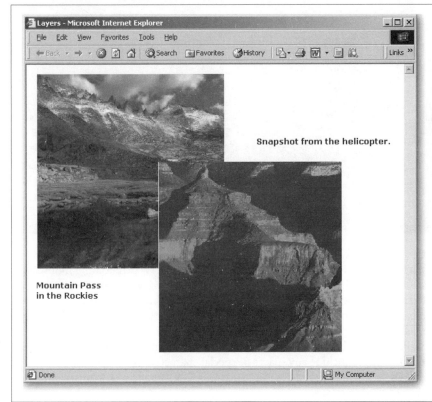

Figure 8-2:
The same layers that you saw in Figure 8-1 appear here, but their borders are now invisible when the page displays in a browser. Page elements overlap and sit exactly where you place them.

Creating Layers

One reason layers are so popular is that creating them is a snap. It's just as easy to add content to them as well. The easiest way to create layers is in Design view, using the invaluable assistance of the Layers task pane. To open it, select Format → Layers or open the Task pane menu and select Layers.

Inserting Layers

You can create a layer in one of three ways:

• In the Layers task pane, click the Insert Layer button.

- In the Layers task pane, click the Draw Layer button, and then drag your cursor diagonally across the space on the page you want your layer to occupy.

- Select Insert → Layer.

FREQUENTLY ASKED QUESTION

What's in a Name?

A Web maven I met says that "layer" is not a proper Web term. What's he talking about?

Technically, your friend is right. Here's the story.

In 1997, Netscape invented the layer and created a <layer> tag in the version of HTML that their browser recognized. This creation did pretty much everything you read about in the introduction to this chapter. Meanwhile, the folks over at the Web standard-settings group, W3C, were busy tackling the same positioning issues and came up with their *own* solution. They decided that a <div> division tag (a tag that divides out, or partitions, a portion of a Web page), when used in combination with CSS (covered in Chapter 7),

could do the same job more elegantly than an HTML layer. Since W3C's standards carried (and, in fact, still carry) more juice than Netscape's initiatives, the <layer> tag died a quick death.

To create a layer, FrontPage takes a <div> tag and gives it special positioning properties, which make it display as a pretty, blue, malleable box in your document window. While the term *layer* isn't technically correct, programs like FrontPage and Dreamweaver still use it. As do many Web professionals, because—face it—as a term, "layer" is more apt than "division." Just don't look for any <layer> tags behind the scenes.

Once you create a layer, it appears on the page as a blue box, and it also shows up in the task pane list. FrontPage automatically gives layers such exciting monikers as *layer1, layer2,* and so on. To avoid confusion, give the layer a proper and descriptive name—something like *Fido,* if it'll contain a picture of your dog, or *Product-Menu,* if it'll be part of a series of menus. To rename a layer, double-click it within the task pane, or right-click the layer in the task pane and then select Modify ID. FrontPage highlights the layer name to show it's editable. Type a new name (and remember not to include any spaces or special characters).

Adding content to a layer

Layers can contain a variety of content, such as pictures, video, or text. You add these items to a layer just as you would to a table cell. Within the document window, click inside the layer and start typing, or insert a picture (select Insert → Picture → From File or just drag a graphic into the layer). Poof! Your content appears in the layer. If you enter a lot of text or insert a picture that's larger than the layer, the layer expands to contain it. That's all there is to it. FrontPage saves changes you make to a layer whenever you save the page.

Selecting Layers

Before you can resize, move, or modify a layer, you first need to select it. Use one of the following methods:

- In the Layers task pane, click the layer's name.

- Run your mouse over the layer's border. When your cursor turns into a four-headed arrow, click.

- Click the layer's label, or handle, in the document window. You'll find the label on the upper-left corner of the layer.

When eight little blue boxes appear around a layer's edge, you know you've selected it.

Resizing and Positioning Layers

Each time you insert a layer, FrontPage plops a 100 × 100 pixel layer in the upper-left corner of the document window (unless you've manually "drawn" the layer's shape, as described above). So in most cases, you'll need to make some adjustments. Everything you need to know about resizing and positioning layers follows.

Resizing

When you select a layer, eight small, square, resizing handles appear along the edges. Drag any handle to change the dimensions of the layer. Dragging like this is the quickest, most direct resizing method.

If you're a precisionist and prefer typing in exact dimensions, then in the task pane, click the Positioning link (or select View → Toolbars → Positioning) to display the Position dialog box. The Position dialog box and the Positioning toolbar (both pictured in Figure 8-3) offer Width and Height fields that you can use to resize a layer.

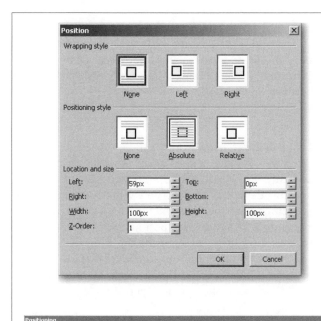

Figure 8-3:
Control layer placement and size with the two tools pictured here. The Position dialog box (at top) includes controls you don't really need for layers, like wrapping and relative positioning. Use only the absolute positioning controls, which appear in the lower portion. The Positioning toolbar (at bottom) features handy buttons, like the Bring Forward and Move Backward options on the far right.

Note: Within the Position dialog box, don't select Relative Positioning. If you do, your layer will disappear, leaving only its content. To FrontPage, a layer is nothing without absolute positioning—literally. (See the "Layer Positioning and CSS" sidebar on page 137.)

Placing Layers

To move a layer, first select it. Then you can drag the layer anywhere you want. When you set a layer down in the document window, FrontPage sets the location *absolutely*, meaning that it measures, in pixels, how far the layer is from the top and left side of the page.

Tip: If you need to fine-tune layer placement, use the arrow keys on your keyboard to nudge a selected layer into the right spot.

If you want to adjust these coordinates, you can enter pixel measurements in the Left and Top fields of the Position dialog box or in the Positioning toolbar. FrontPage always places layers by measuring from the left and top of a page. Why? Because you read a page from left to right and from top to bottom (in Western countries, anyway). So, your browser window expands out to the right and bottom, making those two axes unpredictable. If you're tempted to position a layer in relation to the bottom and right side of a page, don't. Results are erratic—not just due to varying browser window size, but also because various browsers handle settings in these fields differently. If you enter values in all four of these fields, FrontPage takes control and uses the Left and Top field measurements to place the layer.

Also, be careful about combining layers with regular page content. As you now know, FrontPage positions layers *absolutely*. At the same time, the program positions regular page content *relatively*. As a result, your layer might float over your page and block out text beneath it. If you're using layers, you're usually better off absolutely positioning everything on the page.

X, Y, and Z

Because layers can overlap, a designer must work in three dimensions. So far, you've set elements along a page's x and y axis. (Algebra nostalgia alert: dust off your high school math skills.) In other words, you've positioned elements horizontally, along the x axis, by aligning them left or right. You've also situated them vertically, along the y axis, by setting items between the top and bottom of a page. Now, you're going deeper. An object's *stack level*, or position from front to back, is known as the *z-index*. Adjust a layer's z-index by using the Bring Forward and Move Backward buttons on the Positioning toolbar (see Figure 8-3), or by entering a numerical order within the z-index field, at the far-right end of the toolbar. (In a lapse of continuity, the Position dialog box in Figure 8-3 calls this field *z-order*. It controls the same thing.)

Numbers in the z-index rise in order—lowest to highest—up from the page. In other words: the smaller the number, the closer the layer is to the page. The larger the number, the closer the layer is to the viewer. For example, if you have two layers and you want one to display on top of the other, give the bottom layer a z-index of one and the top layer a z-index of two. (Actually z-index numbers don't need to be sequential. Just make the second number larger than the first. Entering 11 and 32 has the same effect.) The Bring Forward or Move Back buttons actually increase or decrease the z-index number by one. You may need to click the button more than once to bring a layer forward many levels.

You can even go negative, if you wish. Enter –1 in the z-index field, and that layer will appear *behind* any other content on the page, such as regular text that's not positioned in a layer. The z-index of regular page content is zero. Work up or down from there.

Tip: If two layers have the same z-index value, the layer that appears first within a page's HTML code appears behind the one that follows.

BEHIND THE SCENES

Layer Positioning and CSS

Select a layer and then take a quick peek at your layer page's HTML code. How does FrontPage set exact coordinates for layers?

The <div> tag is your layer. The tag is short for *division,* representing a portion of a Web page that you can position or move in a block (layer). The <div> tag has style attributes that look something like this:

    Style="position: absolute; top: 50px;
    left: 30px;"

When you position a layer, you create an inline style (page 117). FrontPage positions your layers using CSS.

In fact, when absolute positioning is changed to relative (be it through a code edit or the Positioning dialog box), the layer evaporates in Design view. While the <div> tag still

exists behind the scenes, the FrontPage Layers pane won't recognize it as a layer without the absolute positioning attribute.

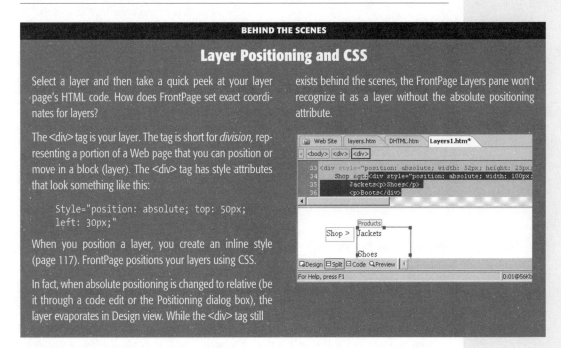

Modifying Layers

Layer appearance can range from completely invisible (yes, you can even hide a layer's content—more soon on why you'd want to do that) to a "look at me" bright pink background with a chartreuse border. To learn how to achieve effects like that, or anywhere in between these two extremes, read on.

Setting Layer Appearance

Layers created in FrontPage are automatically transparent. In other words, no one can see the outline or background of this invisible container—only whatever objects you put in it. Most designers prefer layers this way, because a layer's content is the real star of the show. But, if you want, you can give your layers a little personality by adding a border or a background (see Figure 8-4).

Figure 8-4:
Layers don't have to be invisible. You can add a background color to set off one area of a page (upper left). Or you can use borders to do the same thing and make it look like a picture frame (upper right). By adding background color, foreground color, and a border you can even make a layer look like a button (lower left). Though a much better way to include buttons in your layer is to insert FrontPage's interactive buttons into the layer (lower right), which you'll learn about in the next chapter.

To do so, first select the layer. Then, within the Layers task pane, click Borders and Shading. The Borders and Shading dialog box that appears offers the following options:

- **Set border style.** If you want to outline the edge of your layer, give it a border. When you make a selection, FrontPage previews its effect within the Border tab.

- **Set layer padding.** Layer padding is like cell padding. (Recall from Chapter 5 that padding is the distance between a border and its content.) But you can be more persnickety here than you can be within a table cell. FrontPage lets you specify a *different* setting for each side of the layer. This might be useful if you want to set text away from the left edge of a layer, for example.

- **Set layer background and foreground.** Click the Shading tab to access options for setting the background of your layer. Then choose a color or use a picture. If a picture is smaller than the layer, it will tile (appear multiple times) just like it does in a cell. Use the Foreground color field to control text color in a layer.

Tip: The Layers task pane doesn't give you any way to align content within your layer. Instead, you need to use the alignment tools you learned about earlier (page 33). First, select the text or picture that you wish to align. On the Formatting toolbar, click the alignment button (left, center, justify, or right) you want, or select Format → Paragraph and set alignment within the Paragraph Properties dialog box.

Visibility

When FrontPage creates a layer, it makes layer content visible automatically. But there are times when you want a layer to be entirely *invisible* to viewers. This is usually so you can pull off some masterful sleight of hand. Imagine this: on your Web site, a visitor's cursor passes over text that says "Grand Canyon" and a picture of the canyon appears in the middle of the screen. The cursor then passes over text that says "Yellowstone," and a picture of Old Faithful replaces the photo of the Grand Canyon. You can easily create this impressive effect by using FrontPage *Behaviors* (which you'll read about in the next chapter) to make a layer—like the one containing the picture of Old Faithful—invisible and then visible.

To see your visibility options, right-click a layer within the Layers task pane. Three visibility choices appear on the pop-up menu:

- **Visibility: Default** is the automatic setting FrontPage gives to any new layer. In other dialog boxes, FrontPage calls this option *Inherit*. Under this setting, the layer is visible, but if you give it a parent layer (a way to make one layer share another layer's attributes, which you'll read about in the next section) the layer automatically takes on the visibility setting of its parent.

- **Visibility: Visible** means that the layer is visible no matter what (even if its parent is invisible).

- **Set Visibility: Hidden** makes the layer invisible no matter what (even if its parent is visible).

Right-clicking gave you access to all those choices, but there's actually a much easier way to set visibility—with a simple click in the Layers task pane (see Figure 8-5).

Nesting Layers

Nesting layers is not like nesting tables. One layer doesn't sit inside another. Instead, nesting is a way to group layers within parent-child relationships. In this arrangement, child layer settings—like display and positioning—are linked to those of their parent layer. Why would you want to group layers like this? The advantage is that parent layers manage the attributes of their children (just like in real life—yeah, right).

Figure 8-5:
The far left side of the Layers task pane features a visibility column topped by an eye icon. This column provides a handy way to set visibility and is also great for viewing the visibility properties of all your layers at a glance. Click in the visibility column to the left of a layer. An open eye appears. This is the pictorial equivalent of the Visibility: Visible command, explained above. The open eye indicates that the layer is visible. Click again, and the eye closes, setting the layer to hidden. Click one more time, and the eye disappears, returning to default (inherited) visibility.

For instance, if you move a parent layer (say, a long menu bar), all its children (submenus for the menu bar) move with it. So, if you've spent the morning setting up a beautiful multi-layered composition and find you need to move it in its entirety over to the right, you can do so in one move. Child layers also inherit some display attributes from a parent layer. For instance, if you set a parent to be invisible, all its children are invisible as well (unless you specify otherwise). Or, if you set a parent's foreground color to green, then the text in any child layers becomes green, too.

Note: Nested layers stick together. This remains true even when you're positioning nested layers along the z-index. If you lower the z-index setting of a parent layer so it appears behind all other layers, all its children will also display behind other layers. In other words, FrontPage won't let you insert an outside layer between nested layers.

Inserting Child Layers

You can give any layer one or many child layers. Even a child layer can have its own children.

To create a child layer, select the layer that you want to make the parent and then click the Insert Layer button or select Insert → Layer. FrontPage creates a new layer. In the document window, it looks like any other layer, but you can tell that the new layer is a child of your existing layer because within the Layers task pane, the child layer is indented below its parent, as illustrated in Figure 8-6.

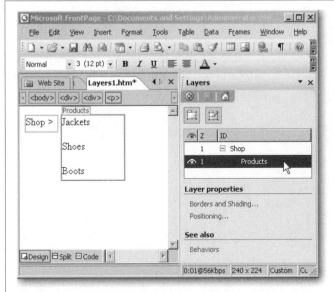

Figure 8-6:
The Products layer is indented below the Shop layer, indicating that Shop is the parent layer. Control layer properties using either the "Borders and Shading" link or the Positioning link within the Layers task pane.

Changing Parent-Child Relationships

Even if you've already created layers, it's not too late to organize them into parent-child relationships. For example, you can easily give a layer a new parent. First, create the parent layer. Then, in the Layers task pane, click the layer that you want to turn into a child layer and drag it onto the layer you want to make its parent. FrontPage moves the layer beneath its new parent and indents it. The child layer will take on the attributes of the parent layer.

If the relationship isn't working out, go ahead and free a layer from its parent. Select the child layer in the Layers task pane and drag it up onto the column heading bar just above the pane, or down into the empty space beneath the list of layers. Now you've got two completely independent layers.

DHTML: Adding Interactivity

The average Web surfer has clicked through thousands of Web pages. Your visitors have seen it all, and getting them to notice your site and its content can be a challenge. One trick still seems to grab the attention of even the most jaded reader: *action*. FrontPage lets you animate page elements in response to visitors' clicks and the pages they visit. For instance, if a mouse passes over a button, you can make the button pop up and become 3-dimensional. Or if a visitor clicks on the name of a neighborhood—poof!—a map of the area can suddenly appear out of nowhere.

FrontPage makes it easy to bring your pages to life. Animating Web elements used to require complex scripting, but once again, FrontPage saves you from all that by providing you with easy-to-use dialog boxes.

In this chapter, you'll learn how to create rollover buttons, cascading menus, play sounds, and display pop-up windows and messages. You can even automatically reroute your visitors to a different Web page. You'll learn to do all these things with FrontPage *DHTML* (short for Dynamic HTML) effects and behaviors. At the end of the chapter, you'll put all these skills to work with a tutorial that helps you create one of those slick, cascading drop-down menus that you see on really professional-looking Web sites.

Tip: Use the animation and interactive behaviors presented in this chapter with care. Overloading your viewers is a big danger here. Too much movement on a site distracts people from the point you're trying to make and can even annoy them.

DHTML Effects

DHTML, the engine behind all the activity you're going to learn how to create in this chapter, is a combination of two main ingredients: HTML (the building block of almost every Web page), and JavaScript (a nimble coding language that can manipulate the elements on a Web page).

You can use DHTML to do things like have text and pictures drop into place, slide on and off a page, or change the font in some text. You can animate a variety of other items, like buttons, page banners, hit counters, and even forms.

All DHTML effects consist of the following:

- An **event** occurs, like the click of a mouse or a page loading in a browser. FrontPage lets you pick events from a list of keywords, all of which begin with the word "on." For example, *onpageload* means "when a page loads," and *onmouseover* means "when a mouse passes over" an element.

- This event triggers an **action,** like a word flying onto the screen or a picture changing.

- The event and action both work together to manipulate a particular **HTML tag.**

An example DHTML effect would be something like a mouse clicks (onclick *event*) on a picture (contained within the <img> *tag*) and the picture moves off screen (*action*).

DHTML Tools

Where do you start? FrontPage has two main control centers for all this activity: the DHTML Effects toolbar (for basic effects) and the Behaviors task pane (for more complex functions).

Why aren't all these controls in one location? The DHTML Effects toolbar is a relic from earlier versions of FrontPage. It used to be the only way to create interactive behaviors until Microsoft introduced the Behaviors task pane in FrontPage 2003—an addition that's brought a lot more power and professionalism to FrontPage. The Behaviors task pane lets you create effects that are light years beyond the capabilities of the DHTML toolbar. But the toolbar remains—maybe to show you how good you've got it nowadays (and for those who want to edit effects they created using previous versions of FrontPage).

Creating Basic DHTML Effects

You apply the most fundamental effects using FrontPage's DHTML Effects toolbar. These are mostly one-move animations that can make an element on a page slide, hop, or fly in or out of view. The toolbar also easily creates slick effects like *rollover images* (pictures that change when a mouse passes over them). If you want to create rollover images for any navigation buttons you're using, FrontPage gives you a specially designed shortcut: interactive buttons. This section will show you how easy it is to create all these bells and whistles.

Note: FrontPage DHTML effects on the DHTML Effects toolbar have one major flaw: they often work only in Internet Explorer. This is because the jury (the Worldwide Web Consortium, which sets standards for the Web) is still out on a lot of DHTML standards, so Microsoft has gone ahead and created what it *thinks* DHTML should be. Some effects may work in Netscape 4.0 or later, but things may not work the way you expect them to. As with any other browser compatibility issue, consider your audience and test your pages. (See Chapter 12 for a whole chapter's worth of advice on page-testing strategies.)

Using the DHTML Effects Toolbar

You can unleash a handful of simple animations quickly using the DHTML Effects toolbar (Figure 9-1).

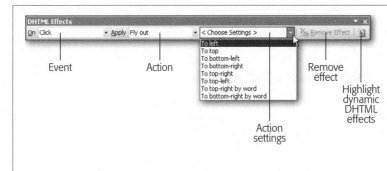

Figure 9-1:
The DHTML toolbar forces you to select items from left to right. Your selection determines options in the next drop-down list. Unsure of what dynamic effects you've placed on a page? On the toolbar's far right, click the Highlight Dynamic HTML effects button, and they appear highlighted in blue right on your page in Design view.

To open the DHTML Effects toolbar, select View → Toolbars → DHTML Effects. Then:

1. **Select the object on the page.**

   First, you need to choose a page element (by selecting its tag) that will trigger the action. Choices on the DHTML toolbar remain grayed out until you select an item on the page, like a paragraph, a hyperlink, or a picture. FrontPage forces you to choose a tag here. For instance, if you just select some words within a paragraph, the program applies the effect to the entire paragraph.

2. **Set an event.**

   The "On" field of the toolbar is the only active field (at least initially). Click the drop-down menu next to it to select the event that will trigger the action. For instance, if you select "Mouse Over," then a cursor passing over the element you chose in step 1 will trigger the action you'll select next, in step 3.

3. **Select an action to apply.**

   Once you've made a selection in the "On" field (where you set the event), FrontPage activates the "Apply" drop-down menu to its right. This menu is where you set the action. Your choices depend upon two things: the tag you initially chose to modify, and the event you just chose in the "On" field.

For example, if you selected a picture and choose "Mouse over," then "swap image" is your only choice under actions to apply (details on swapping images follow). If you select some text and then choose "Mouse over," the only action available is formatting. Most of the one-move animations that let you do things like gradually reveal an element (Wipe) or have it "fly in" or "spiral" onto the page can be set only on the "Page load" event (which is when a page initially appears in the browser).

4. **Select action settings.**

   Once you choose an event and an action, you use the final drop-down menu to finish setting your effect. As with the other menus, options here depend on your previous selections. Choose the direction in which an element will fly or the special formatting a text will adopt in response to a cursor pass or click.

Note: To test these effects, you must preview your page in a browser, not in FrontPage's Preview view.

Creating a Rollover Image (Image Swap)

How do you attract attention to your hyperlinks? Adding color works, but having a picture serve as a hyperlink is even better. And if that picture changes when a mouse passes over it, your readers are sure to take notice.

Web designers call this a *rollover* or an *image swap*. When you set up an image swap, FrontPage generates a script that replaces one image with another. The change can produce a subtle effect, like adding a shadow to a button to make it look 3-dimensional, or the new image can be completely different.

Tip: To make this effect look smooth, be sure to use pictures that are the same size.

To insert an image swap, first insert a picture on a page (page 58) and select it. In the DHTML toolbar, click the On drop-down menu and select "Mouse over." To the right, click the Apply drop-down menu, and then select Swap Picture. Then click Choose picture and browse to another image and select it. Save your page and preview the effect in a browser.

Tip: The Behaviors task pane includes a more advanced image swap action. See "Swap Image" on page 161.

Interactive Buttons

Web authors swap images all the time to attract attention to hyperlinks. But you don't need to go to all the trouble of creating images and swapping them out. Right out of the box, FrontPage offers you an assortment of working *rollover buttons,* whose appearances change automatically when a cursor passes over them. To

---

preview and choose buttons, select Insert → Interactive Button. The Interactive Buttons dialog box, pictured in Figure 9-2, appears.

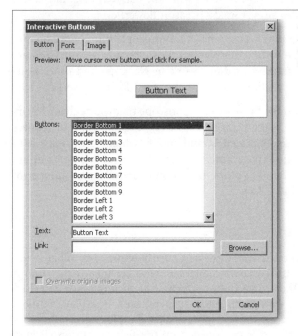

Figure 9-2:
Select a button style and it appears in the Preview pane at top. Pass your cursor over it to preview its "mouse over" effect.

Use the Text field to name your button. This text will show up as the button label on your Web page. Click Browse to the right of the Link field to set a button's hyperlink.

Note: An interactive button's visual rollover effects won't display in Netscape Navigator, but hyperlinks will work correctly.

The Interactive Button dialog box gives you loads of ways to customize and configure your buttons. If you don't like the color and font settings of a particular button, change them within the Font tab. Click the Image tab to change button dimensions. To edit a button, click it, and then select Format → Properties. Or right-click it and select Button Properties. You can even double-click a button.

If you want to add even more interactivity, check out the tutorial at the end of this chapter. It shows you how to mix these buttons with layers and behaviors to create cascading menus.

Page Transitions

When a Web page changes or refreshes, the new page pops up all at once. FrontPage has a special feature that lets you customize this transition with some special effects. For example, you could have parts of your new page first appear in a pattern, like vertical blinds or a checkerboard, until the whole image eventually changes. Or you can have the new page begin as a small circle in the middle of the page and expand out to the edge of the browser window. You may be familiar with these kinds of transitions if you've ever used Microsoft PowerPoint.

Not everyone's a fan of these page transitions. A lot of people find them unpleasantly distracting—kind of like surfing the Web via the billboards in Times Square. Even more seriously, these transitions don't work in Netscape and other non-Microsoft browsers. Finally, transitions also slow your page download speed.

But maybe you have a page on the history of the periscope that you're dying to circle in on. If you want to set a special transition for a page, open it, and then select Format → Page Transition. Select the effect and specify whether you want it to appear when the page is opened (Page Enter) or closed (Page Exit). You can use the Duration field to set the duration of the transition by entering the number of seconds you want the transition to last.

Creating Behaviors

The toolbar's simple effects are cute, but not particularly impressive. What if you want to offer visitors some truly dynamic interactions—like menus that unfurl when a cursor passes over them or a button people can click to rewind a Flash movie? Back in the bad old days (before the 2003 release), FrontPage authors would have to write custom scripts to incorporate such complex effects. But with the addition of *Behaviors,* FrontPage has opened up the field to button-clicking greenhorns. Behaviors are advanced scripting options that FrontPage has gift-wrapped for you in dialog boxes and task pane controls.

The Behaviors task pane goes beyond the capabilities of the DHTML Effects toolbar, by letting you control specific variables. For instance, the Behaviors task pane features a swap image option, like the DHTML toolbar, but offers a far greater selection of trigger events to choose from. Behaviors also enable you to have an event on one element affect the display or action of another (great for your "the knee-bone is connected to the thigh-bone" type pages).

This section walks you through the basic steps of creating a behavior. Then you'll learn all about the actions you can create, the events you can base them on, and how to bring it all together to animate your pages.

Note: Some browsers won't show FrontPage behaviors. Whether or not a viewer will see your handiwork depends not only on what browser she has, but what version. Because results vary, always test your FrontPage behaviors in multiple browsers. Fortunately, most behaviors work in recent versions of most browsers (after Internet Explorer 5 and Netscape 6).

Creating a Behavior

You create and manage behaviors within the Behaviors task pane. To open it, select View → Task Pane, and then select Behaviors from the task pane drop-down menu.

1. **Select the object on the page.**

   You have to apply a behavior to a particular HTML tag. To select a tag, click an object on the page, or use the Quick Tag Selector toolbar (which you'll find just above the document window—if not, select View → Quick Tag Selector). The Quick Tag Selector helps you be precise and makes it easy to select elements like the <body> tag. FrontPage shows you what tag you've selected in the Behaviors task pane (see Figure 9-3). If you want an event on one element to influence another element, select the trigger element here. For example, if you want a cursor passing over a picture to reveal some nearby text, select the picture.

Figure 9-3:
When you pass your cursor over an event in the Events list, a drop-down arrow appears on the right. Click the arrow to access this menu and select other events.

Whenever you want to see an event/action combo in the Behaviors task pane list, you first need to select the tag you want to set as its trigger. Once you select a tag, all behaviors connected with it appear in the list below. To see what tag is active, glance above the list, to the right of "Scripts on tag."

2. **Select an action.**

   Within the Behaviors task pane, click Insert, and then choose the action you want. See "Creating Actions" on page 151 for details on all your choices here.

3. **Configure the action.**

   Depending on what action you select, FrontPage needs different information. Each action has its own dialog box, where you set specifics. This chapter includes details on how to configure each action (see "Creating Actions" on page 151). Once you've entered all the details, click OK to set the action.

4. **Change the event.**

   In the Behaviors task pane, the action you just created appears, with an event to the left of it. Depending on what choices you've made so far, FrontPage makes an educated guess in the event column and automatically sets it to something like the onclick event. If you want to change it, right-click the action and select

Choose Event. Or, pass your cursor over the event field and then click the drop-down arrow that appears. At that point, you can make another selection from the event drop-down list (see Figure 9-3).

Events

The list of triggers in the event drop-down list are different depending upon what behavior you're implementing. Here's a rundown of the most basic events.

Mouse and keyboard events:

- **onclick.** A visitor clicks the element.
- **ondblclick.** A visitor double-clicks the element.
- **onmousedown.** A visitor clicks the element, but doesn't release the button.
- **onmouseup.** A visitor clicks and releases the button while on the element.

Tip: Use onclick instead of onmouseup. Both events create the same effect, but onclick works in more browsers.

- **onmouseover.** A cursor passes over an element.
- **onmouseout.** A cursor moves off the tag or element.
- **onkeydown.** A visitor presses a key on the keyboard but doesn't release it. (You'll use keyboard events when you have visitors filling out forms, which you'll read about in Chapter 15.)
- **onkeypress** and **onkeyup.** A visitor presses and releases a key on the keyboard.

Page events:

- **onabort.** A page download stops prematurely.
- **onload.** A page finishes loading. You'll use this most often for triggering actions after a page loads (just select the <body> tag and configure the behavior on it). But the onload event can also apply to images or video. For instance, if you select an image and then choose this event, whatever action you specify is linked to the completion of the image download.
- **onunload.** A page is about to disappear because a viewer clicked a link to another page or entered another URL.
- **onresize.** A viewer changes the size of the browser window.
- **onerror.** An error occurs during a page or image load, or in the running of a script.
- **onscroll.** A visitor moves the element's scroll bar. This could apply to a <body> tag or frame.

Form events (though you may not know much about forms yet, you can probably imagine that a visitor filling out a form is an action rife with potential events; you'll learn all about forms in Chapter 15):

- **onchange.** A visitor changes text in a form field.

- **onfocus.** A visitor focuses on an element like a form text field by clicking or tabbing into it.

- **onblur.** A visitor takes focus off of an element. For example, he clicks or tabs out of a text field.

- **onsubmit** and **onreset.** A viewer clicks a form's Submit or Reset button. You can apply these two events only to a <form> tag (see Chapter 15).

Most of the other events you'll find in this list have to do with live data connections. For instance, the ondataavailable event occurs when a database has updated information to send to a Web page. For now, don't worry about these advanced functions. (In fact, you probably won't need them. Even if you'll be using FrontPage's data display features, the program handles this kind of programming for you.) Read on to learn about the real heart of behaviors—actions.

Tip: For a comprehensive list of events and more information on DHTML, crack open *Dynamic HTML: The Definitive Reference* by Danny Goodman.

Creating Actions

When you look at a group of complicated menus and dialog boxes, like the Behaviors task pane, you might have a hard time connecting the hodgepodge of choices to real world problems and solutions.

Behaviors can add a lot of valuable and impressive features to your Web site, and *actions* are the fuel behind this magic. As you'll see, actions can help you route viewers to the pages you want them to see and shoot visitors specific messages based on choices they've made. You can also check to see if they have the software they'll need for a plug-in (a special program, like a video player) you've included in your Web page, or wow them with magically appearing images and menu selections.

Again, when creating a behavior, you first select a *tag* on the page and then you pick the *action.* In the following pages, you'll learn what each action can do for you and how to configure it. After you set any one of these actions, it will appear in the Behaviors task pane, where you then set the *event* you want to trigger the action.

Actions to Control Navigation

You already know how to get visitors moving around your site using the trusty old hyperlink. As you'll see, a lot of actions in the Behaviors task pane let you take this kind of in-site navigation to a whole new level.

Creating a drop-down menu

Numerous hyperlinks on the same screen can create clutter and confusion. But sometimes you don't have a choice—say you've got 26 cousins, and you've got to include links to all of them on your Favorite Relatives page. Text for all these hyperlinks can take up a lot of screen real estate.

Why not consolidate? Instead of including a long list of hyperlinks on a page, you can create a drop-down list of links. This way the list, like the one shown in Figure 9-4, displays only if a viewer clicks on it.

Figure 9-4:
This drop-down list contains links to four other pages in this site: Tables, Chairs, Bookcases, and Cabinets. The list's drop-down arrow and the text above it help you guide your visitors' actions.

FrontPage calls this feature a *jump menu* and provides a dialog box to help you make one. To create a jump menu:

1. **Insert a Jump Menu.**

   Place your cursor at the spot on the page where you want the menu, and within the Behaviors task pane, select Insert → Jump Menu. A Jump Menu dialog box, like the one in Figure 9-5, appears.

2. **Add Choices to your menu list.**

   Click Add to open the Add Choice dialog box. Within the Choice field, enter the text that you want to display as an item in the list. In the Value field, browse to or type the URL for the link and click OK. Repeat for every entry you want to include in your menu.

3. **Set target properties for your list items.**

   Within the Jump Menu dialog box, you can set the link's target—specify whether or not a browser should open the link in the same window, open a new one, or display the page in a frame (see Chapter 6 for more about frames). Select the destination page and make your choice within the "Open URLs in" drop-down menu.

4. **Set list order.**

   Select an item and click Move Up or Move Down to rejigger the order of your list items.

5. **Save the list.**

   Click OK, and your list appears on your Web page.

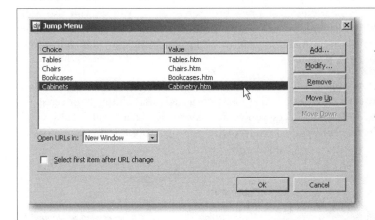

Figure 9-5:
Create your drop-down list using the Jump Menu dialog box, which is also where you configure list items, and set their order and target window. To have the list display the first item again when a visitor returns to the page later on, turn on the "Select first item after URL change" checkbox.

Note: Links in a jump menu don't behave like regular hyperlinks. They won't show up in Hyperlinks view and they won't update automatically if you move a file into a different folder. So, if you want your menu to work, don't move any files (including the page that contains the menu) after you create this feature.

Jump Menu Go

If a visitor selects an item in a jump menu, she's immediately taken to the destination page. But what if you want to give her more time to think about it? You can pause things by adding a Go button next to your drop-down list. This way, when your visitor makes a selection from the list, she first has to press Go to open the page. If a visitor is a keyboard-only type person (as many visually disabled people are), she'll need a Go button to make a selection from the list.

To add a Go button next to your jump menu, select Insert → Interactive Button (page 146). Once you've got the button on your page, select it. Then, within the Behaviors task pane, select Insert → Jump Menu Go. A Jump Menu Go dialog box displays. Select the jump menu you want the button to affect from the drop-down menu and then click OK.

Now, the button will act as the hyperlink, connecting to whatever link a user chooses from the jump menu. But you've still got one more step: for the viewer to have a chance to click the Go button, you have to modify the jump menu itself to stop it from linking when a viewer clicks one of its choices. To do so, in the document window, select the jump menu. Its "onchange" behavior setting displays in the task pane. In the actions column, click on the jump menu to select it. Then, at the top of the task pane, click Delete.

Open Browser Window

Say you want a hyperlink's destination page to open in a new browser window, rather than replacing the current page. You already know how to do that after reading Chapter 3. But maybe you don't want your viewers to contend with the usual menu and toolbar clutter of a new browser window. And say you also want to specify how big the window will be. No problem. The Open Browser Window action gives you all the control you want by letting you create and launch windows like the one shown in Figure 9-6.

This action usually opens off a link, but you can base it on another event, like a page load, if you want. After all, all those pop-up ads that clutter your screen as you surf the Web aren't choices you've actively made. That's right. Now you'll know how to pester beleaguered readers with pop-ups, too. For the sake of Web-kind, please use your power for good only.

Figure 9-6:
Here's one effect you can achieve with the Open Browser Window action. This is a plain browser window, stripped of all menus and toolbars. The window size corresponds exactly to the picture dimensions to create a tidy, controlled look.

Note: Keep in mind that many people configure their systems to block pop-ups (those based on a page-load event) and some browsers, like Mozilla's Firefox, block them automatically.

After you've chosen your trigger element (a hyperlink or <body> tag), and selected Open Browser Window from the Behaviors task pane's Insert menu, the relevant dialog box opens. Then you can set the following options:

- **Go to Url.** Browse to the page that you want to open in your new browser window.

- **Window Name.** Text you enter here won't appear anywhere in your window, but may come in handy if you want another page to open in your new browser window. FrontPage uses this name to add a Target attribute to a link. So, you could have a second page open in this same window, replacing the initial page (as long as this window remains open). You can also use this field to target frames (see Chapter 6), by typing in the name of the frame. Because this text is a link target, you can't include any funny characters here—just letters and numbers.

- **Window width, Window height.** Type in exact pixel dimensions for your new window. FrontPage automatically sets these measurements to 200 pixels and won't let you enter a blank. Keep your sizes reasonable. A window that exceeds a visitor's monitor room will be impossible to read.

- **Attributes.** Decide which browser elements and menus you want to give viewers. If you turn on a checkbox, they'll have access to that browser feature. Don't know what all these attributes are? Take a look at Figure 9-7.

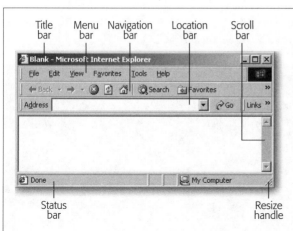

Figure 9-7:
These are the basic browser window attributes that you can choose to display (or not) when you use the Open Browser Window action. One exception: you can't get rid of the title bar, which displays your page title. (Title is different from the HTML file name. See page 184 for more on the difference.)

Tip: Taking away browser attributes isn't always cruel. Sometimes visitors lose track of what browser screens they have open. Say you've posted a special note or report that, for some reason, shouldn't appear on a regular page—one with links to the rest of your site. Taking away the navigation and menu bars is an easy way to communicate that a reader is at the end of the road. When he closes the new window, he's back where he belongs.

Go to URL (Redirect)

Imagine that your company has been bought out, and your old name has been scrapped. What about people still trying to go to your company's old Web site, *www.DowJones36000.com*? It's a simple matter of redirecting them to your company's *new* site.

Much like a hyperlink, the Go to URL behavior sends a browser to the URL you specify, but it provides more options. For instance, you can have the change happen when a viewer's cursor passes over something, or, more helpfully, when a page loads for the first time in a browser window. With DowJones36000.com, for example, you could create a barebones home page at this address and then redirect people to your new site (*ShortSelling.com*).

To set up a redirect, select the <body> tag of the initial page you expect people to arrive at, and within the Behaviors task pane, select Insert → Go to URL. Specify the destination URL and click OK. Then under Events, select onload from the drop-down menu.

Note: The onload event is triggered only *after* the entire page loads. So, if your page has a lot of images or content, viewers may get a glimpse of it before the action takes them to the new URL. This can look sloppy and disconcert your visitors, who may worry that the browser's been hijacked. If you want a lightning-fast, imperceptible transition, then put very little on the dormant page. However, you should include some text and link to your new site, just to be thorough.

If setting the action on the onload event creates a switch that's too fast for you, or you want to be sure your visitors know your site has moved, you could base the Go to URL behavior on another event, like a click on a link or picture. You can also set your own schedule. See the box "Redirect on a Time Delay."

BEHIND THE SCENES

Redirect on a Time Delay

Imagine that you don't want to use a link or page load event to trigger your Web page redirect. Maybe you'd rather just set the redirect after a certain amount of time has elapsed.

While the Go to URL action uses JavaScript to hustle your visitors on to their next destination, there's an old-fashioned HTML tag that you can add to the <head> section of your page that will redirect according to the number of seconds you specify.

```
<meta http-equiv="refresh"
content="10;URL=http://www.newcompanyname.
com">
```

The meta "refresh" tag can load a new page this way, or you can use it to refresh the same page. For example, many developers use this tag to update pages with links to live information, like stock quotes.

Always let your visitors know what's going on. For example, you may want to display a message that tells them something like "You will be redirected in 10 seconds" so they're not alarmed when their browser goes to a completely different page. Also include a hyperlink to your new site in case your visitor's browser doesn't support the meta "refresh" tag.

Check Browser

Throughout this book, you've been hearing over and over about browser support—or lack thereof—for certain features. If you've already tested pages in a variety of browsers, you've probably seen how differently they can display the same page. Web designers sometimes get around this problem by creating more than one version of all or parts of their site. These alternate pages are identical but designed specifically for different browsers. In other words, one company may have two separate, but identical Web sites: one for Internet Explorer and one for Netscape. Designers then implement the Check Browser Behavior to direct a visitor to the appropriate site. (After which they go drink buckets of soothing herbal tea, in order to calm nerves jangled by the existence of so many different browsers.)

Did you ever wonder why some sites on the Web have a home page that contains only one link that says something like "Click to Enter"? A hyperlink like this can serve as the trigger event for the check browser action. Say you've loaded a page with the IE-only DHTML effects covered earlier in this chapter. You can do other browser owners a favor and use such a trick to steer them to an alternate page.

Tip: While you might be tempted to have a page load event trigger this action, don't forget that the onload event starts only *after* the entire page has loaded. If you're trying to steer viewers away from the page in question, it'll be too late.

To implement this behavior, select the tag (usually a link) that will trigger your event. Then, within the Behaviors task pane, select Insert → Check Browser. Use the dialog box in Figure 9-8 to set your preferences.

Unfortunately, you can set only one browser apart from the pack here. Also, your choices are limited to those that Microsoft has provided—you can't add a browser here as you can when you're previewing pages.

In the "If current browser type is" drop-down menu, select a browser and version you'd like to set as the target. Then turn on the Go to URL checkbox beneath that field and browse to the correct page. To set another page for all other browser types, turn on the Go to URL checkbox on the bottom and, in the corresponding field, browse to the alternative page. Then click OK and set your event as you would for any behavior.

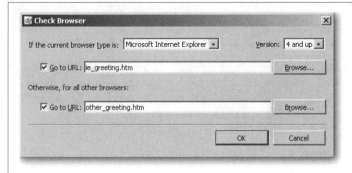

Figure 9-8:
This dialog box lets you detect a viewer's browser and route her to a page made just for her. Choices are limited here, but you can separate out one major browser, at least. Use the version drop-down menu, on the upper-right corner, to steer older browsers away from pages that contain new technology.

Actions to Control Multimedia

If your site includes Flash or video files, you may want do to more than just throw them up on a page and hope your viewers can see them. FrontPage offers a few

---

actions to help make sure your bells and whistles are actually jingling, blowing, and moving properly.

Check Plug-in

If you can't tell what browser a viewer might have, how would you know what other software he has loaded on his machine?

Just as you might want to create different pages to accommodate different Web browsers (page 156), you might also want to separate versions of pages for visitors who've got different kinds of *plug-ins*. (Plug-ins are miniature programs that play audio, video, and other specialized files directly within a browser's window.) For example, you might create two copies of the same page, one featuring a video in QuickTime, while the other shows it using RealPlayer. Use the Check Plug-in action to direct your viewers to the appropriate page.

This action works a lot like the Check Browser action. First, select a trigger tag—for instance, a link to a video. Then, in the Behaviors task pane, select Insert → Check Plug-in. As with Check Browser, you can only separate out one plug-in. Select it from the drop-down menu at the top of the dialog box and enter the corresponding URL. Then enter an alternative URL for all other programs and click OK.

Play an Audio File

Maybe you want an event to play a sound? You're in luck. The play sound action supports WAV, MIDI, Real Audio, AIFF, and AU sound files. Unfortunately, this behavior works only in Internet Explorer. Select the page element that'll trigger the sound and, within the Behaviors task pane, click Insert → Play Sound. Browse to select your sound file and set your event, as you would for any behavior.

Tip: You may want to add a sound that plays in the background while visitors have your page open in their browser. You don't need an action to do this. There's a setting in Page Properties (page 369) that lets you have the sound loop continuously while the page is open. Think twice, however, before creating this racket. Your visitors may find such noise intrusive and annoying, since they have no control over it (other than hitting their computer's mute button or, worse, leaving your site).

Also, depending on the size of the audio file, adding sound could really slow down your page, and it won't work in Netscape Navigator. But sound might be appropriate in certain situations. To add it, first select File → Properties. Locate the Background Sound setting on the bottom of the General tab. Click browse to find the audio file you want and use the Loop field to set the number of times you want it to play.

Control Properties in Flash

When you learned to insert Flash movies in Chapter 4 (page 69), you saw that FrontPage gives you basic control over Flash properties like height and width. The Control Properties in Flash action lets you control more obscure Flash properties. For instance, you could have the display window zoom in on the movie or pan across it.

To implement this action, select the trigger tag. This could be a button that says Rewind or Stop, depending upon what controls you want to give your viewers. Then within the Behaviors Task pane, select Insert → Control Properties in Flash, and then complete the dialog box:

- **Movie.** This drop-down list shows every Flash movie you've inserted on the page. Select the one you want to control.

- **Method.** This field features a list of all the properties you can adjust. Chances are you'll use one of the most common methods, which are:

    — **Rewind.** Movie goes back to the first frame.

    — **Tplay.** The movie plays.

Tip: Any method that begins with T lets you target a nested clip within your Flash movie. (For instance, if your movie shows a moving car belching smoke, the car and smoke are probably separate clips. You could target only the car clip to stop, while the smoke would continue.) Just enter the target name in the field provided. If you want to play or stop the entire movie, don't enter anything in the target field.

- **TStopPlay.** The movie stops.

- **LoadMovie.** Have a movie replace the one that's already there or play another Flash movie on top of it. Just browse to select the additional SWF file and enter a layer number (page 136)—zero for replace, and one or greater to superimpose it over the original.

- **Zoom.** The display zooms in on the movie by the percent you specify.

- **Pan.** The display pans (moves across) an already zoomed-in movie. Specify the coordinates for the pan in pixels or percent.

To learn more about the selections above and the others in this dialog box, visit *www.macromedia.com* and type "Flash methods" in the site's search box.

Note: The Control Properties in Flash action works only in Internet Explorer 6.0. Some methods, like zoom, may work in earlier versions of IE, so you can give them a try, but your audience for this action is pretty much limited to those who've got Microsoft's latest browser.

Actions to Send Messages

You may find yourself occasionally wishing you had additional ways of reaching out, across the Web, and sending small notes to your site's visitors or quickly changing the information they're looking at. The following methods may be just what you're looking for.

Pop-up Message

If you need to alert your visitors to an important issue, use this action to make a pop-up message box appear in front of a viewer, based on a click or other trigger.

These pop-ups aren't pretty windows like the ones you can make with the Go to URL action (see Figure 9-6). Instead, these look like regular Windows error message boxes that contain whatever text you specify. (Consider this your chance to write something slightly more friendly than the typical Microsoft missive.)

Select the element that'll act as a trigger, then within the Behaviors task pane, click Insert → Popup Message. Enter the message in the dialog box that appears and click OK. Then set the event.

Set Text of Frame

You can use this action to replace the content of a frame (pop back to Chapter 6 for a refresher on all things frame related). The term "set text" doesn't really convey the power of this action. The fact is you can include images, tables, or whatever you want. You're essentially replacing the HTML in the frame with new HTML. It's like loading a new page in the frame, but because the HTML is already part of the page, it's lightning fast.

To apply this action, you'll need to have a frameset in place. Select the trigger tag or object and then, within the Behaviors task pane, select Insert → Set Text → Set Text of Frame. Then complete the fields in the dialog box:

- **Frame.** This drop-down menu features all the frames available to you. Select the target frame.

- **New HTML.** Paste or type the HTML that you want to appear. If you're not comfortable working directly with code, just create your content on a blank page in the document window and copy the source code from Split view or Code view. Copy only content that's within the <body> tags. This action won't replace any code that you'd put in the head of page, like styles or behaviors, for instance.

- **Preserve background color.** If your frame features a background color that you want to keep when the new content displays, turn on this checkbox.

Set Text of Layer

The Set Text of Layer action works like the Set Text of Frame action, but—as you might guess—replaces the content of a *layer* with whatever HTML you want.

To implement this action, first select a tag. Then, within the Behaviors task pane, select Insert → Set Text → Set Text of Layer. The Set Text of Layer dialog box appears:

- **Layer.** This drop-down list shows every layer on the page. Pick the one whose content you want to change.

- **New HTML.** Type in your message and format the text using HTML commands. Or paste in some source code from a page you create.

Set Text of Status Bar

Use this action to have a message appear in the status bar. Where's the status bar? It's the strip at the bottom of your browser (see Figure 9-7). For instance, you can use this action to have a description or credit for an image appear when a visitor passes her cursor over it.

To create this action, first select the trigger tag (like <img> for an image). Then, within the Behaviors task pane, select Insert → Set Text → Set Text of Status Bar. In the dialog box that appears, type in the message and click OK.

Set Text of Text Field

You'll read all about forms when you get to Chapter 15, but you've probably filled out hundreds of them yourself. You visit a page, fill in a few blanks, and then click Submit. Next thing you know, the fishing lures you ordered are en route to your cabin in the woods—all based on the information you entered in the form. When it comes time to create your own forms, you can use the Set Text of Text Field action to help visitors out by adding text to certain fields in response to viewer actions. For instance, say you ask a visitor "Do you have an alternate address?" and provide radio buttons for Yes and No. If a viewer clicks on the No radio button, you can trigger the Set Text of Text Field action to fill the alternate address field with a note that says "Please proceed to the next question."

To do so, first select the radio button that'll act as the trigger. Then, within the Behaviors task pane, select Insert → Set Text → Set Text of Text Field and fill out the dialog box that appears:

- **Text Field.** This drop-down list shows every text field on the page. Pick the one whose content you want to change.

- **New Text.** Type in the message that you want to appear.

Click OK and set the event you want.

Image Actions

If you think graphics can spice up a Web page, just wait until you add a few actions to your pictures.

Swap Image

You've already read about a couple of ways to swap images. For example, FrontPage's interactive buttons automatically add image-swapping behavior to a page to generate a rollover effect. Then there's the DHTML Effects toolbar, which also provides a handy shortcut.

But neither of these methods quite measure up to the Swap Image action in the Behaviors task pane, which gives you loads more fine-tuning options. For example, say you have a page all about your trip to Alaska that opens with an impressive landscape photo you took. You can place a list of towns you visited down the left side of your page. When a viewer clicks on Skagway, a picture of that town replaces the landscape photo. Using the Swap Image behavior, you've made your own Alaska slideshow.

Tip: To achieve a similar effect, you could insert your pictures in layers (see Chapter 8) and use the Change Property behavior to control layer visibility settings (see "Advanced Action: Change Property" on page 163).

To create an image swap action follow these steps:

1. **Select a trigger tag.**

   This could be a <p> paragraph tag that—to follow the example above—contains a word like Skagway. Or (depending on the effect you're after) it could be the image you want to swap out, a different image, or any tag.

2. **Set the action.**

   In the Behaviors task pane, select Insert → Swap Image, and then fill out the dialog box:

   • **Image Name.** The top portion of the dialog box lists all the images on the page. Click to select the original image that you want to swap *out.*

   • **Swap Image URL.** Browse to the image that you want to swap *in* to replace the original.

   • **Preload Images.** FrontPage turns on this checkbox automatically and you should leave it on. See the description of the "Preload Images" action, next, to understand why.

   • **Restore on mouseout event.** If your trigger event will be a mouseover, you can turn on this checkbox to have the original image return once a cursor passes off the trigger element.

3. **Set the event.**

   In the Behaviors task pane, select the event that'll trigger the image swap.

Note: If you do set the event to be a click on a paragraph, be aware that—as with collapsible menus—your viewer may have trouble knowing that he needs to click in that spot, because his cursor won't change into a "click here" pointing hand like it does when he hovers over hyperlinks (see Figure 2-12, back on page 40). For this reason, you may want to use the onmouseover event instead.

Preload Images

As anyone with a slower Internet connection knows, images can take a long time to download. The Preload Images action downloads image(s) onto a viewer's machine *before* they display on a page. Why would you want to do this? Say you've added a rollover button or other image swap to your page. When a viewer's cursor passes over it, the second image is supposed to replace the first. If your visitor had to wait for that second image to download, this effect would be ruined (it'd be kind of like a magician saying "ta-dah!" and then making her audience wait for the payoff spectacle). By the time the image appears, the cursor might be off on another part of the page, creating confusion. In fact, when you insert FrontPage's interactive buttons (page 146), the program automatically adds this action to ensure that the buttons work properly.

You want to attach this action to the body tag's onload event. Once you've selected the tag, open the Behaviors task pane and select Insert → Preload Images. Then complete the dialog box:

- **Image Source File.** Click Browse to locate the image and then click Add to insert it in the Preload Images list. Click Browse again to find another picture. You can add as many images as you want.

- **Preload Images.** Images you've added appear in this box. If you want to get rid of one, select it and click Remove.

When the list is complete, click OK, and then set the event to onload (if FrontPage hasn't already done so).

Advanced Action: Change Property

Now that you're familiar with all these different actions, you're ready for one that's slightly more intricate and bursting with possibilities.

The Change Property action lets you modify the appearance and/or placement of an object. This behavior changes font style, visibility, borders, or position. You can do something simple, like have a layer background change color on a cursor pass, or you can use this action to create complicated screen choreography—a click on one button makes multiple pictures move around the screen.

The basic steps for changing properties of an element are the same as setting any other behavior, but you'll have to go through a bit more work when adjusting the settings in the dialog box. The following steps take you through the basic guidelines for completing the dialog box. To see this "action" in action, follow the tutorial at the end of this chapter, which shows you how to use Change Property to animate a cascading menu system consisting of layers.

After you've selected the element that you want to trigger the Change Property action and accessed the Behavior pane's Insert → Change Property command, the dialog box in Figure 9-9 appears.

Now follow these steps:

1. **Select the element you wish to modify.**

   If you want to modify the item you selected on the page, leave this radio button set at Current Element. If you want an event on the item you selected to modify *another* object on the page, click Select Element. Next, identify the element. Click the Element Type drop-down menu and select the HTML tag for the element (img for an image, div for a layer, td for a table cell, and so on). Finally, from the Element ID list, select the element itself.

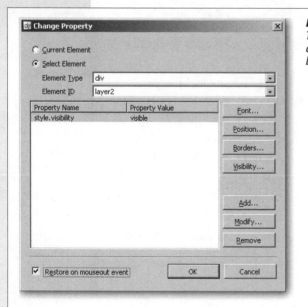

2. **Set properties for the modified element.**

   How will the element change following the trigger event? Specify modifications now by clicking one of the following options:

   • **Font** lets you change the typeface, color, and appearance of text elements.

   • **Position** lets you set alignment or absolute positioning. You could have an element move to the right side of the page, for example—or click absolute positioning and set the exact coordinates to get a picture or layer to move to a specific spot.

   • **Borders** lets you add or remove a border and set shading options, including background color and picture.

   • **Visibility** lets you hide or reveal an element.

   You can add multiple properties for an element. For example, you might want to have a picture move and gain a border at the same time.

   Note: You can't edit more than one element at a time.

   ---

3. **Specify mouse out behavior, if applicable.**

   The dialog box includes a checkbox ("Restore on mouseout event") in the lower-left corner that can save you the trouble of setting an additional event.

For example, if the pass of a cursor over a picture will reveal a layer, but you want the layer to appear only while the cursor sits over the picture, turn on the "Restore on mouseout event" checkbox. This means that a browser will restore the element to its original property setting when a cursor passes off it.

FREQUENTLY ASKED QUESTION

ID Your Elements

I can't find the element I want to modify in the Element ID list. Where did it go?

The Change Property dialog box displays all the elements it can see. In order to be seen by the dialog box, an element needs to have an *identity attribute* within its HTML tag. An identity attribute is a unique name for the element. The problem is, while FrontPage often assigns IDs automatically, just as often, it doesn't.

If an element is lacking an ID attribute, or if you don't know what its ID is, you can find it or add it yourself. Unfortunately, FrontPage supplies no helpful dialog box for this job. You must add an ID by editing the HTML code directly.

But you don't have to slog through all the code on your page. Instead, just use the Quick Tag Editor. To get to it, use the Quick Tag Selector, which is located directly above the document window. If it's not visible, select View → Quick Tag Selector.

If you select the element in the document window, the element's tag (img for an image, div for a layer, and so on)

should display in the Quick Tag Selector toolbar. Click the tag's drop-down menu and select Edit Tag. The Quick Tag Editor, like the two illustrated here, appears.

Find the ID information for the tag. As illustrated, ID information will be something like:

```
ID="layer1"
ID="img2"
```

If there's no ID attribute, you can type it in. Click to place your cursor between any attributes, or at the end of the tag. Follow the format above, using any text you want between the quotation marks (as long as no other page element has that same ID). To save the ID, click the checkmark on the right side of the Quick Tag Editor. The ID now appears in the Change Property dialog box's ID drop-down menu.

Note: The "Restore on mouseout event" checkbox actually creates a Change Property Restore behavior, which you'll see appear in the task pane. In fact, you can choose Change Property Restore from the action menu, but it does the exact same thing as the "Restore on mouseout" checkbox.

If you want an event other than mouseout to restore an element to its original state, don't turn on the checkbox; use the menu selection instead. To do so, wait until after you've set the initial Change Property action, then select the trigger tag again. In the Behaviors task pane, select Insert → Change Property Restore and then click OK. Once the Change Property Restore behavior appears in the task pane, you can change its event.

---

4. **Save the change property setting.**

   Click OK to close the dialog box.

5. **Set your trigger event as you would for any other behavior.**

Within the Behaviors task pane, the event is often automatically set to onclick. Click it and select another, if you wish.

POWER USERS' CLINIC

Call for Scriptwriters

So far, you've read about a lot of tricks FrontPage creates for you by inserting scripts based on your settings in the Behaviors task pane. But what if you've got some JavaScript of your own you'd like to run? No problem. In Code view, insert the script into the <head> section of your page. Choose your trigger tag, and in the Behaviors task pane, click Insert → Call Script. Then type the name of your script (like *myscript()* or *greateffect()* or whatever you name it) and click OK. Then set the event. Note that JavaScript is case sensitive. Get the name right, or a browser won't be able to find your script.

If it's just a single line of JavaScript that you want to call, type it directly in the box. For instance, you could create a "Print this Page" button on your page, and have it trigger a Call Script action that lets a viewer print your page with a click. Type *window.print()* in the Call Script action dialog box, click OK, and then set the onclick event.

Deleting and Editing Behaviors

If a behavior you've added isn't working out, you can easily get rid of it or modify its settings. You do both in the Behaviors task pane.

To display a behavior, you need to select the tag or page element you first attached it to. Then you'll see all related behaviors set on that tag appear in the Behaviors task pane. To delete a behavior, right-click it, and then select Delete. Or click the action and then, at the top of the task pane, click Delete. Be careful here—don't press the Delete key. If you do, FrontPage deletes the entire element, not just the action you attached to it.

If all you need to do is make a change, it's easy to modify a behavior. To change a behavior's *event*, just click the event in the Behaviors task pane, and then make another selection from the drop-down menu that displays, or right-click the action and select Choose Event. To edit an *action*, just double-click it in the task pane and make changes in the dialog box that opens.

Tutorial: Creating a Cascading Menu

Now, it's time to play around with the skills you've learned in this and the previous chapter. To get things moving on your page, you just need to create a few layers and toss in a handful of Change Property behaviors. Follow the steps below to create an interactive menu using layers, behaviors, and FrontPage's interactive buttons.

Creating the Main Menu

First, you'll create a horizontal menu bar containing a few basic choices. Later, submenus will unfurl from this main menu.

1. **Create a new blank page.**

---

2. **If the task pane isn't open, select View → Task Pane.**

3. **Click the task pane drop-down menu and select Layers.**

4. **Draw a layer at the top of your page. Make it stretch horizontally across the top.**

   Need a refresher on inserting layers? Pop back to Chapter 8.

5. **In the task pane, right-click the layer you created, and then select Modify ID.**

   The layer name in the task pane becomes editable.

6. **Type in a new name for the layer, like Menu.**

7. **Within the document window, click inside the layer, and then select Insert → Interactive button.**

   The Interactive buttons dialog box appears.

8. **Select a button type.**

   FrontPage starts you out with the BorderBottom style, which is fine. These buttons are designed to form a horizontal menu bar, like the one you're creating in this layer. If you want, take a look through all your choices here. If you select a button type, it previews in the dialog box. Some are designed for horizontal menus and others for vertical menus. Many are even labeled "row" or "column" to help you out.

9. **In the Text field, type a name for the button, like Home, and click OK.**

   The button appears in your layer. Your cursor sits to the right of the button, where you'll add a second button.

10. **Select Insert → Interactive button again.**

11. **Select a button type and name it something else, like Clothing, and click OK.**

    Your second button appears. Add one more button by repeating steps 10 and 11. All your buttons should now form a single horizontal line near the top of the page (see Figure 9-10).

Creating a Submenu

With the main menu in place, you're ready to create a submenu. In the steps that follow, you'll make a submenu for your second menu button (Clothing, in Figure 9-10). As you might suspect, the process involves a new layer.

1. **Draw a layer below the middle button, in the shape of a vertical rectangle.**

   If it's not quite where you want it, don't worry—you can set exact placement later.

2. **Right-click the layer in the task pane, and then select Modify ID.**

The layer name in the task pane becomes editable.

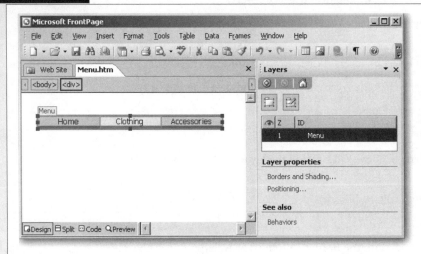

Figure 9-10:
The first level of your menu should look like this. If the shape of your layer has caused a button to wrap beneath the others, just expand your layer out to the right by dragging the handle on the right border. (For help with resizing, see page 135.) You'll also want to shrink your layer box so its edges line up with the edges of your buttons.

3. Type in a new name for the layer, which corresponds to the button, like ClothingMenu (avoid using spaces or special characters in layer names).

4. Within the document window, click inside the new layer, and then select Insert → Interactive button.

   The Interactive buttons dialog box appears.

5. Select a button type.

   Here you're creating a vertical menu, so select one of the buttons that's designed for drop-down menus, like the Border Left style.

6. In the Text field, type a name for the button, like Shirts, and then click OK.

   The button appears in your layer. Your cursor sits to the right of the button.

7. Press Shift+Enter, so your cursor sits just below the button.

8. Select Insert → Interactive button again.

9. Select a button type and name it something else, like Pants, and click OK, and then repeat this step, adding a new button, called something like Jackets.

10. Make the main menu a parent to the submenu.

    In the task pane, drag the submenu onto the main menu. You'll recall from Chapter 8 that the advantage to grouping layers this way is that later, if you need to move the main menu, the submenu will move with it.

11. Resize and move the submenu layer.

You want layer edges to line up with button edges. Place the submenu just beneath the middle button on the main menu—so it looks connected.

12. **Set the visibility of the ClothingMenu layer to Hidden.**

Because you want the ClothingMenu layer to appear later—as if by magic—you need to set its initial visibility to Hidden. Remember how? In the Layers task pane, click in the visibility column on the left until a closed eye appears (see Figure 9-11). See page 139 back in Chapter 8 for more details on layer visibility settings.

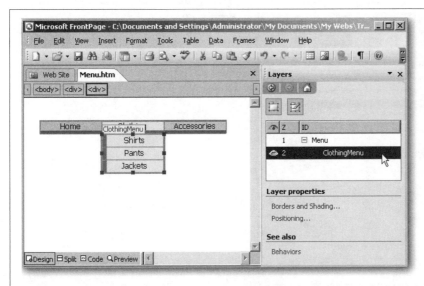

Figure 9-11:
The main menu now has a submenu that will be connected to the Clothing button. In the Layers task pane, on the right, the ClothingMenu is indented beneath the Menu layer because you've made it a child layer. The closed eye to the left of ClothingMenu shows that it's hidden.

Adding Behaviors to Animate the Menu

Layers! Visibility! *Action!* Now, you'll really make things happen. Again, the effect you're after is this: when a cursor passes over the Clothing button, the submenu appears.

Since an event on the Clothing button is the agent for this change, you'll begin setting this behavior with that button. To do so:

1. **Select the Clothing button, then click the Behaviors link at the bottom of the task pane.**

   The Behaviors task pane displays. Since FrontPage interactive buttons automatically create swap image behaviors for themselves, you'll see some behaviors already listed here for the Clothing button.

2. **Within the task pane, click Insert, and then select Change Property.**

   The Change Property dialog box appears. It's set to Current Element, which is the Clothing button you selected. In the next step, you'll change this. You want the event on the Clothing button to "change the property" of the Clothing-Menu layer, switching it from hidden to visible.

3. **Click Select Element.**

   Make sure the Element Type field is set to div (the layer tag). If it's not, click the drop-down menu, and then select div.

4. **Within the Element ID drop-down menu, select the layer that contains your submenu, as illustrated in Figure 9-12.**

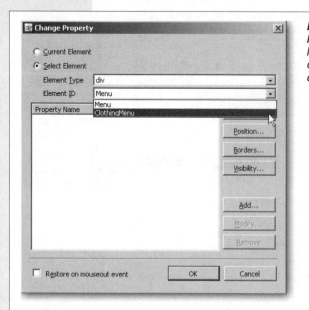

Figure 9-12:
In this example, ClothingMenu is the name of the layer that contains the submenu. You select it here in order to change its visibility property in reaction to an event on the Clothing button.

5. **Click Visibility, and within the dialog box that appears, select Visible. Then click OK.**

   Your setting appears within the dialog box.

6. **Turn on the "Restore on mouseout event" checkbox.**

   This will ensure that once a viewer's cursor moves off the Clothing button, the submenu will disappear.

7. **Click OK to save the change property setting.**

   Within the task pane, your change property setting appears in the Actions column. To its left is the event that triggers the property change. It's set to onclick, meaning when a mouse clicks on the Clothing button, the Clothing submenu layer will appear. But you want the submenu to appear when a cursor merely passes over the button. So, change the event.

8. Within the events column, pass your cursor over onclick and click the drop-down arrow that appears on the right.

9. Select onmouseover.

10. Save the page and preview it in multiple browsers to test your effect (Figure 9-13).

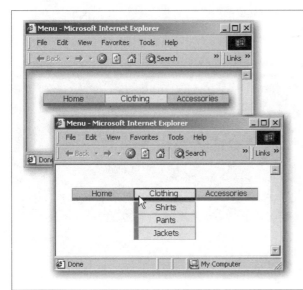

Figure 9-13:
Before and after: the submenu is hidden (above left), until a cursor passes over the Clothing button (below right).

If you followed all the steps above, your submenu appears every time a cursor passes over it. Everything's great, right? Well, almost. You may have noticed a problem. When you try to run your cursor down the submenu, the submenu disappears. FrontPage needs some more direction from you. You need to specify that the Clothing submenu should *remain visible* while a cursor passes over it. Otherwise, how would a visitor select an item on the submenu? To make this change, add the following action to the submenu layer:

1. **Select the ClothingMenu layer.**

   Since the submenu is a hidden layer, FrontPage doesn't display it in the document window. You'll need to switch back to the Layers task pane and select it from the list. At the bottom of the task pane is a Layers link. Click it and then select the ClothingMenu layer from the list in the Layers task pane. Then, at the bottom of the task pane, click Behaviors to return to the Behaviors task pane. (Because you often need to switch back and forth like this, FrontPage provides these handy links at the bottom of related task panes to speed your work.)

2. **Within the Behaviors task pane, click Insert, and then select Change Property.**

3. **Click Current Element.**

4. Click Visibility, and within the dialog box that appears, select Visible, and then click OK.

5. Turn on the "Restore on mouseout event" checkbox.

   You do this so the submenu won't hang around when a cursor passes off it.

6. Click OK to save the change property setting.

7. Change the onclick event to onmouseover in the Behaviors task pane.

8. Save the page and test in a browser.

WORKAROUND WORKSHOP

Problem with Renamed Layers

You may encounter one bug when animating layers. If you change the name of a layer within the Layers task pane, any behaviors or dynamic effects that involve that layer no longer work. This is because FrontPage changes the name of your layer, but it doesn't change code that refers to that layer.

Fortunately, this name confusion is easy to fix. Switch to Code view and select Edit → Replace. Within the "Find what" field, type the layer's old name. Within the "Replace with" field, type the layer's new name. Click Replace All. Close the Find and Replace dialog box, save the page, and then test out your layer behaviors in a browser.

Part Three: Building and Managing a Web Site

3

Creating and Structuring Your Web Site

It's time to take a step back from working on individual Web pages and look at the big picture. All the files that you've learned how to create—HTML pages, graphics, and style sheets—are designed to work together. So FrontPage automatically groups these files within a folder, classifies it as a Web site, and even helps you tame this many-headed file beast wherever it can—through a lot of features that you've already read about (like site views and the folder list) and ones you'll learn about in this chapter (like site templates).

But FrontPage can't do everything. As you work on your site, the program constantly prods you for information and answers to questions, ranging from where to save your entire Web site, all the way down to the name of your tiniest GIF image.

This chapter will help you tackle important decisions that rear up when you start building a Web site: what FrontPage tools should you use to create your site? Where should you save your site? What should you name it? Once you get going, you'll also need to know how to store and organize all the files that you're creating.

Where to Create Your Web Site

FrontPage stumps many new Web authors right from the start. The program prompts you to save a Web site before you really even know what you're doing. So where should you put it?

The best place to create and edit your site is out of the public eye, of course. There's no reason to subject visitors to your typos, or that chartreuse color scheme that seemed like such a good idea at first. So, to start, save your site in a private location. Later, when you're ready for others to view your work, you'll transfer your site to a live Web server where the masses can see it. The initial, or working, location for your Web site is called the *development environment.* Your development environment can be your computer's C:\ drive (a *disk-based* location), or you can use a Web server that's not public (a *server-based* site). The process of transferring your site from the development location to a live server is called *publishing.*

You'll read all about publishing in Chapter 13. Meanwhile, where should you set up your development environment? Your options, and what you should know about them, follow.

Creating a Disk-Based Web Site

You may have no choice but to create and edit Web pages on your regular desktop or laptop computer. After all, very few people have a full-fledged Web server at home, and renting space on somebody else's Web server can cost you. When you save your Web site on your local computer, you create what's known as a disk-based site, and FrontPage is happy to help. You can save your site in any folder you want (with the exception of the root of your C:\ drive).

Warning: *Do not* save a FrontPage Web site directly on the root of your C:\ drive (meaning the location should never be something like *C:\mysite*). When you delete a Web site, FrontPage removes *everything* that's in the folder where the site is stored. Plenty of unseasoned FrontPage owners have experienced the stomach-sinking feeling of turning their PCs into expensive paperweights by, in effect, performing a lobotomy on their machine. Save your Web site anywhere *but* the root of C:\.

If you work in a disk-based environment, you'll encounter one drawback. Some Web site features—like a form to collect data from visitors, for instance—require software that exists only on a Web server. FrontPage lets you add Web features like this within a disk-based site, but you won't be able to see them in action or test them until you transfer your site to a Web server.

Creating a Server-Based Web Site

You can do fine working with a disk-based Web site, but if you develop your site on a Web server (a server-based site), you gain some advantages. First of all, most Web servers come with special software that some components of a Web site need in order to function. For instance, if you want visitors to be able to search your site, you can add a search box to one or more of your Web pages. It doesn't matter if you're creating your site on your own computer or on a Web server—you can add this feature either way. However, in a server-based development environment, you could *test* your search function right away—there's no need to wait until you upload your site to see if it works.

Also, if you want to do something like have your Web pages pull information from a database (useful, for example, if you're site publishes a catalog of constantly changing products), you'll want a server-based development site. Data retrieval functions like these work only on a Web server. This Web server might be part of your corporate or home network, or you might access the server from home, over the Internet (see Figure 10-1).

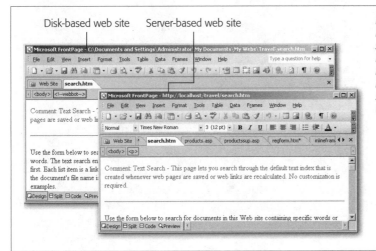

Disk-based web site   Server-based web site

Figure 10-1:
Depending on where you create your site, you'll see a different path in FrontPage's title bar. At top, the disk-based site shows a path on your local computer. At bottom, the server-based site shows your site's URL.

FrontPage Server Requirements

So, certain Web features require a Web server to run. That makes sense. But, beyond that, FrontPage has its own special requirements. To help FrontPage execute advanced Web functions like site searches, Microsoft developed its own custom software for Web servers. The company offers two varieties of this *server-side* technology: FrontPage Server Extensions (FPSE) and SharePoint Services. Even if you're working in a disk-based development folder, your live Web server needs to have one of these programs for some advanced features to run. Chapter 13 tells you all about which features these two server-side programs control. You'll also want to make sure that if you're renting Web server space, you do so from a Web-hosting company that's friendly to FrontPage authors. (Check out Microsoft's list at *www.microsoft.com/office/frontpage/prodinfo/partner/wpp.asp*).

Using Site Templates and Wizards

FrontPage already does a lot for you, with its friendly workspace and easy shortcut buttons that translate your design choices into HTML code. In fact, the program can do almost *everything* for you, if you want. FrontPage includes templates that create entire Web sites complete with multiple pages, a navigation structure, and design scheme. All that's left for you to do is fill in your name.

The program offers many different flavors of templates. These options range from complete ready-to-view sites to an empty site template that lets you do all the work from scratch, if you prefer. This section explains all your options and how to get started using templates.

Can Your PC Be a Web Server?

Maybe you don't have your own personal IT department. It's just you and your laptop. But suddenly you find yourself wishing for a local Web server so you can see all the wondrous things your site can do as you create it. Well, don't despair—you may have hidden powers.

If your computer's operating system is Windows 2000 Server or Professional, Windows Server 2003, or Windows XP Professional (not XP Home Edition), you can install or may already have Web server capabilities. (Owners of other Windows operating systems are out of luck.) To check, open your PC's Control Panel and double-click Add/Remove Programs. Click Add/Remove Windows Components and scroll down the list that appears until you see Internet Information Services (IIS). (In Server 2003, this is located within Application Server → Details.) If the IIS checkbox is turned on, your PC is ready to get to work as a Web server. If not, read on if you want to install IIS.

To install IIS on Windows 2000 or XP Professional, you'll need your Windows CD. After inserting the CD, highlight IIS within the Add/Remove Windows Components dialog box, and then click Details. Turn on the checkboxes for all components you want to include—at a minimum, you should choose Common Files, Documentation, IIS Snap-in, and World Wide Web Sever. (When you perform this installation, make sure that the FrontPage 2000 Server Extensions checkbox is turned off. That version is out of date.) Click Next and follow all the installation prompts. Then, if you want to install the latest FrontPage Server Extensions (FPSE

2002) too, go to *www.Microsoft.com/downloads/* and type "FPSE 2002" in the "Search for a download" box.

You can install IIS on Windows Server 2003 in the same manner. Select IIS within the Add/Remove Windows Components dialog box and click details. Server 2003 comes with the latest version of the server extensions, so turn on the FrontPage 2002 Server Extensions checkbox, if you want to install them. If you want to install Windows SharePoint Services instead, don't turn on the 2002 Server Extensions checkbox. Instead, you need to get a copy of Windows SharePoint Services later and install it. (To get the software, go to *www.microsoft.com/downloads/* and type "SharePoint" in the "Search for a download" box. SharePoint Services works only on Server 2003.)

If you do decide that you want to make your PC a Web server, you should click on over to Microsoft's Web site and read more about the ins and outs of installing IIS. (Visit *www.microsoft.com/windowsserver2003/iis/* and also check out *www.iisfaq.com*.) For example, once you've got IIS installed, you've got to make a host of choices about things like server configuration and site security—topics that others have written thick volumes about. (Two particularly good volumes are *IIS 6.0: The Complete Reference,* by Hethe Henrickson and Scott Hoffman [McGraw-Hill Osborne Media], and *CYA Securing IIS 6.0,* by Chris Peiris, Bernard Cheah, and Ken Schaefer [Syngress]). You should also read Chapter 13 (of this book) first, to figure out whether or not you actually want to add FrontPage Server Extensions or SharePoint Services.

Understanding Templates and Wizards

FrontPage's Web site templates are groups of predesigned pages, many of which come out of the box as working Web sites. Pages in these sites already link to one another and come completely formatted with a fully coordinated graphics scheme. It's kind of like having your mom lay out your Web site for you.

A *wizard* is also a template, but you and the program work together to create the site. FrontPage prompts you for information—like site display preferences, company name, address, and so on. Then the program creates a Web site based on the answers you've given. Figure 10-2 shows a sample screen from one FrontPage wizard.

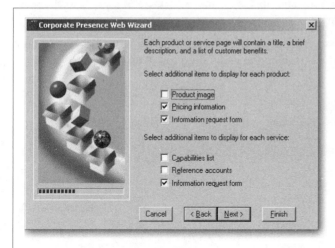

Figure 10-2:
This is a typical Wizard dialog box. To determine how to configure your Web site, FrontPage poses questions to you on a series of screens like this one. Turn on checkboxes, enter information, and click Next to proceed through these dialog boxes, and you've got yourself one genuine Microsoft-composed Web site.

To see all your automated Web site creation options, select File → New. Within the New task pane, select "More web site templates." FrontPage presents you with the following choices:

- **Empty Web Site** creates a Web site with no pages in it. This option gives you the most flexibility. If you want to do all your own design and formatting, pick this template.

- **One Page Web Site** creates the equivalent of an empty Web site, but gives you a start with one blank, unformatted home page.

- **Corporate Presence Wizard** takes your responses and uses them to create a simple corporate Web site with pages set up for contact, service, and product information.

- **Customer Support Web Site** creates a basic site designed to help companies provide support services to clients.

- **Database Interface Wizard** walks you through the creation of a Web site that taps into a database and uses the information to build the site's pages. See Chapter 17 for details.

- **Discussion Web Site Wizard** creates a site that hosts online discussion boards. Visitors can view entries posted by others and add their own thoughts.

- **Import Web Site Wizard** lets you suck in the contents of an existing Web site from the Internet or from your own computer or network. You can also import a regular folder that you'd like to turn into a Web site. Be aware that this method won't deliver all site components. For example, it leaves out FrontPage configuration files that control special functions like navigation. If you've lost the local copy of your Web site and want to get a copy off the live Web server, try reverse publishing it (remote to local) instead (see Chapter 13 for details). In other words, use the import function as a last resort only.

- **Personal Web Site** generates an "about me" site, including pages to showcase your hobbies and photos.

- **Project Web Site** is designed for use by a group of people collaborating on a project (see Figure 10-3). One page lists the project team, others feature the project schedule, status, and discussion area.

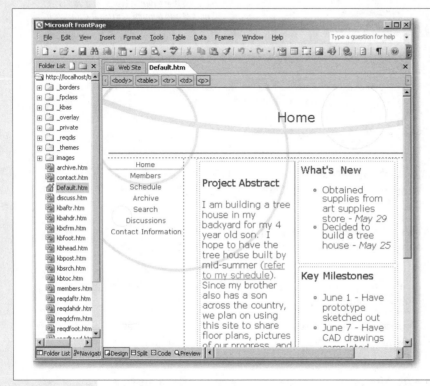

Figure 10-3:
This is how Microsoft's canned Project Web site looks right after you use the template to create it. It comes with fully structured and designed pages that are linked together and decorated with a FrontPage theme. You'll replace boilerplate text with your own.

- **SharePoint Team Site** is similar to the Project Web site, but is much more extensive. This isn't just a Web site template, but an active application that a large staff can use to post documents, discussions, and project information. This option requires Windows SharePoint Services (page 251).

- The **Packages** tab features Web packages that also require the use of Windows SharePoint Services on your Web server. Like the SharePoint Team Site, these packages are actually interactive Web applications that come bundled with FrontPage. The Packages tab features two kinds of sites: the News and Reviews site includes interactive features like discussions and reviews, and, the Web log package helps to create a blog site that includes search and discussion.

Note: Windows SharePoint Service programs offer a world of options for groups of people who want to coordinate their online activities and projects. In fact, you don't even need FrontPage to use them. For full-fledged coverage of SharePoint, a good starting point is Jeff Webb's book, *Essential SharePoint.*

How to Use a Template

Of course, FrontPage makes using a template easy—that's the whole point. To get started with one of these templates or wizards, launch it—select File → New, click More Page (or Site) Templates, then double-click the template in the Templates dialog box—and fill out any prompts that follow. After that, you can add content to your site. In many cases, that means replacing FrontPage's generic text with your own information.

Tip: If you realize, after creating a site, that you've answered one or more questions incorrectly, FrontPage doesn't give you an easy way to instantly change all the template-generated info on your site. Your best option is to just delete the Web site and start the wizard again.

Other Options

Microsoft's a great software company, but it's not likely to win any design awards in this millennium. If you really like the idea of using a template but find these Microsoft designs unattractive, unsuitable, or just too limited for what you want your site to say, the Internet is teeming with additional templates. Many independent vendors design FrontPage templates and sell them online. The files usually come in a package that installs the template right in your FrontPage templates directory, so you can select them as you would any other template. Shop around and check out all your options. (Start at *www.pixelmill.com*, *www.classythemes.com*, or *www.myartsdesire.com*.)

Creating a Site Manually

Since the dawn of the Web, authors have built Web sites one page at a time. They start with a home page, then create other pages, and add links to connect those pages. This page-by-page process is still the way most Web professionals work, since it offers the greatest flexibility and control.

If you want to start from scratch, creating and designing pages on your own, you don't need to use FrontPage's templates. However, (in a Microsoftian twist of logic) you still need to begin in the Templates dialog box. Select File → New, and within the New task pane, click More Web Site Templates. Instead of using a template that contains content, select Empty Web Site or One Page Web Site.

FrontPage presents you with a sparkling brand-new site that includes no intrusive elements. Use the tools you've already read about to create, design, and link pages as you wish.

Creating a Site in Navigation View

Imagine your boss has asked you to create a Web site. You're going to plan it, design it, and stamp it with your personal flair, but most of the actual content—the words and pictures—you're going to get from your co-workers. You *could* create the site manually, page by page, but FrontPage provides another, more helpful approach—*Navigation view.*

When you start a site in Navigation view, you can create and structure your site simultaneously. Essentially, you're creating the shell of a site—making empty pages and telling FrontPage how they relate to one another. You do all this in a diagram format like the one shown in Figure 10-4.

Read on to determine whether or not Navigation view is right for you. Then see how to create a site or just manage your site's hierarchy using this feature.

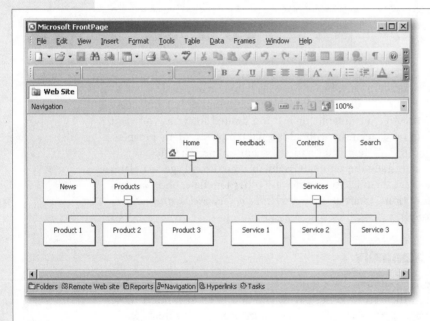

Figure 10-4:
This page presents the Navigation view of FrontPage's Corporate template. The Home page includes links to the second tier of the site's information—the company's three major departments: News, Products, and Services. To use FrontPage's Navigation-view lingo, Home serves as a parent to News, Products, and Services. These pages have subtopics of their own; for instance, the Products page features links to a third tier of information—details on each product offered. Consequently, the pages on each product page (Product 1, Product 2, and so on) are children of the Products page.

Why Use Navigation View?

If you need to create an empty site structure quickly, Navigation view provides a handy alternative to building your site page by page. Another reason you'd create a navigation diagram is if you want to use FrontPage's automated navigation aids, like link bars and page banners. These features supply your site with automated hyperlinks to other pages and sections within your site. (Chapter 11 tells you all about how to use them.) The important thing to know about Navigation view is that the links FrontPage creates in a link bar pull their information from the navigation diagram you create.

You probably don't want to bother creating a navigation scheme if your site consists of only a few pages, or if you plan to create all the navigation links yourself. If you've incorporated frames into your site, you can also skip this option, since Navigation view can't handle framed pages.

Note: Navigation view isn't just for new sites. If you have existing Web pages, you can still create a navigation diagram for them. But there is one drawback. Even though your pages may already be linked to each other and organized in folders, you have to build the diagram manually. FrontPage can't infer from hyperlinks or your site's folder structure what the hierarchy of a site should be. It seems like double the work, but setting up a navigation diagram does let you use the automatic site navigation links that you'll learn about in Chapter 11. And if you're creating a diagram just so you can add link bars, the good thing is you need only to include those pages that you want link bars to appear on.

Creating a Home Page in an Empty Site

Sites designed in Navigation view always need to start with your home page. If your site has no pages, Navigation view prompts you: "To create a Home Page, click New Page on the toolbar." This message refers to the Navigation toolbar, which appears automatically in Navigation view, just above the document window (see Figure 10-5). Click the New page button on the Navigation toolbar. A page appears in Navigation view called Home Page. If you have the folder list open (View → Folder List), the same page appears there, called *index.htm* or *default.htm*.

Figure 10-5:
Use the New Page button on the Navigation toolbar to add pages to your diagram. Other buttons on this toolbar let you change the Navigation display. For example, if you choose a smaller percentage from the zoom drop-down list (on the right end of the toolbar), FrontPage shrinks pages in your diagram so you can fit more on the screen.

Adding Child Pages in an Empty Site

Once you've established your home page, you can create the next tier in your site's hierarchy. Since these pages will link to the home page, but live one level down in the hierarchy, FrontPage calls them "children" to the home page (their "parent"). Whenever you want to create a child page, do the following: in Navigation view, select the parent, and then click the New Page button on the Navigation toolbar. Or right-click the parent and then select New → Page.

File names

Navigation view slaps generic names like "new page 1" on each page. Assuming you have a personality (or a need to keep organized), you'll probably want to rename these. In Navigation view, right-click the page, select Rename (or click once on it), then click again to edit the name. Next, type the title you want for the page. To speed up the process, lay out your navigation pages first, and then use the Tab key to hop from page to page, renaming as you go.

UP TO SPEED

Page Titles vs. File Names

Navigation view displays page *titles*, not HTML *file names*. File names (like *prometheus.htm, mountsthelens.htm, rossperot.htm,* and so on), which appear in your folder list, are for your benefit. You (and the browser) use them to find and organize Web pages. The title, on the other hand, is there for the benefit of your site visitors. A page title displays in the—you guessed it–title bar of a browser, above the menu. Preview a page and take a look. Even more importantly, the page title serves as the name of your Web page within search engine result lists, so you really want titles to express page content accurately.

Often, FrontPage automatically titles pages with lackluster and irrelevant names like New Page 0, New Page 1, and so on. Avoid a bad first impression. Enter appropriate and descriptive names for your pages in Navigation view or within the Title field of the Page Properties dialog box. (To open Page Properties, select File → Properties.)

Now that you understand that, you've got to deal with a minor FrontPage annoyance. Navigation view creates and uses page titles, yes. However, once a page is saved in Navigation view, page title and navigation name actually exist separately. Making changes to one has no effect on the other.

Creating HTML files for child pages

Unlike the Home page that FrontPage automatically creates in your folder list when you use Navigation view to start a site from scratch, FrontPage doesn't create the actual files for child pages as you add them in Navigation view. This gives you an opportunity to arrange and name files before FrontPage actually creates them. Naming pages properly in Navigation view before you create their actual HTML files will save you a ton of renaming work later on.

When you are ready to create these pages, right-click the Navigation background and select Apply Changes. Or double-click on a page to create and simultaneously open it within the document window.

Adding Top Pages

Not all pages fit neatly into a navigation structure. There'll be pages that you want to include in your diagram, but that don't require a parent—usually a contact or search page. Why would you include a page like this in your navigation map even though it's outside the hierarchy? Because you want it to have a link bar, so visitors can get back to the main pages of your site. Navigation view calls these floaters *top pages* (see, for example, the Feedback, Contents, and Search pages in Figure 10-4).

To add a top page, click on the Navigation background so that no specific page is selected. Then click the New Page button, or right-click and select New → Top Page. Then name the page and save it.

Creating a Navigation Diagram for Existing Pages

If you've already created all or most of the pages in your site, you can still create a navigation diagram. You really need to include only those pages to which you'll add link bars or page banners.

To get started, open your site in FrontPage and switch to Navigation view. The program should recognize your home page. If it doesn't, this might be because it can't recognize the file name as a home page. To correct this problem, locate your home page in the folder list, right-click, and select Set As Home Page. FrontPage changes the name of the file to *index.htm* or *default.htm* (see the "Home Page Names" sidebar on page 188 to understand why).

You build a site from the top down. Once you've got your home page, create child pages by dragging files from the folder list into Navigation view. If you have a page you'd like to add, drag it onto the Navigation diagram, over the page you want to make its parent. FrontPage shows which page it'll set as the parent by displaying a temporary dotted line connecting parent to child (see Figure 10-6). If you're a fan of browse boxes, you have a couple of other options: you can select a parent page and click the Add Existing Page button on the Navigation toolbar, or, right-click the parent and select Add Existing Page. Then browse to and select the desired child page.

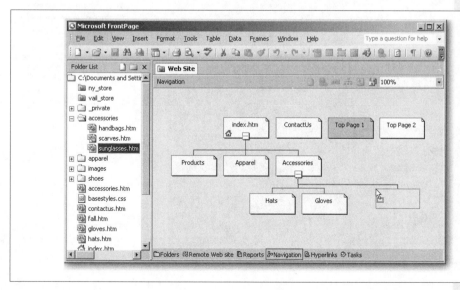

Figure 10-6:
When you drag a page from the folder list onto a page in Navigation view, FrontPage displays this dotted line, indicating where it'll place the page within your site's hierarchy.

Note: As you add existing pages to Navigation view, their names may surprise you. Page names in Navigation view are *page titles,* not *file names.* Refer back to the "Page Titles vs. File Names" sidebar on page 184 for details.

Planning Your Web Site's Structure

Experts judge embroidery not just by the pretty picture a needle worker creates, but by the jumble of threads—neat or not so neat?—that can be seen on the back side of the stitching. Similarly, building and maintaining a Web site can either generate a tangled mess of files and folders or an easy-to-follow collection. What you end up with can make your life as a Web maven a whole lot easier.

No doubt you'll use smart page design and well-placed hyperlinks (as in Figure 10-7) to make your site easy to understand and navigate for viewers. Behind the scenes as well, you should have just as easy a time getting around—meaning that you'll want to organize files into a clear folder structure so they're easy to find. You'll also want to name everything clearly so your files are easy to identify.

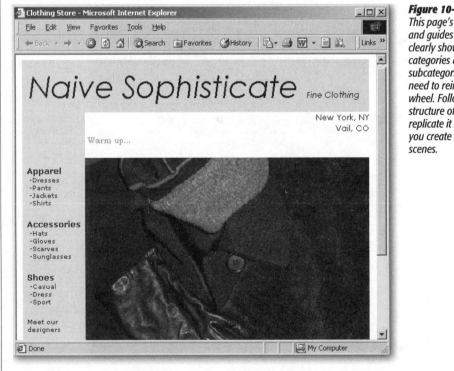

Figure 10-7:
This page's layout informs and guides viewers. Links clearly show product categories and subcategories. You don't need to reinvent the wheel. Follow the innate structure of your site and replicate it in the folders you create behind the scenes.

As you'll see, FrontPage takes an active hand in managing your site. But creating an orderly site structure is still up to you. Guidelines for sorting and handling files follow.

Note: As you learn FrontPage, you may occasionally encounter the term "Web" when it seems like FrontPage (or grizzled FrontPage veterans) should be referring to a "Web site." Microsoft used this confusing term in previous releases of FrontPage. Finally, the company abandoned it and now speaks the same language as the rest of the Web (the World Wide Web, that is). Within FrontPage, instead of *web* and *subweb,* you'll now see *Web site* and *subsite*.

Naming Your Site

FrontPage does its best to squelch your originality at times. Save a new site, and the program tries to name it "myweb4" or "myweb5" (there's that old Microsoft-speak rearing up—see the previous note). Take control and name your site in a more meaningful way. Come up with a short, descriptive name. Use only lowercase letters, and don't include any spaces or unusual characters, like symbols or punctuation marks. Following these guidelines insures that your site will live in harmony with wide variety of Web servers (some of which don't look kindly on things like capital letters, spaces, and so on).

Naming Files

While Microsoft Windows lets you create long file names that include spaces and strange characters, Web servers won't stand for such shenanigans. When you're naming files, consider the following:

- **Don't use special characters.** Many characters, like &, @, and %, actually mean something to Web servers. Using them can create errors. Stay away from special characters and don't use any punctuation marks like quotation marks, apostrophes, parentheses, or slashes.

- **Never include a space in a name.** If you need a space, use an underscore or a dash.

- **Use lowercase letters.** Many Web servers are case-sensitive, meaning they regard *About.htm, about.htm,* and *ABOUT.htm* as three different files. To reach a page, your visitors must get the name exactly right. Avoid confusion and stick to lowercase.

- **Keep file names relatively short.** Twenty-five characters is the outside limit.

- **File names should make sense and be specific.** Use them to describe file content. You may know that *34er.gif* is your company's logo, but does anybody else? If you name it *logo.gif,* you and your coworkers will be able to find it later. If you have a navigation button that leads to the *hats.htm* page, don't call it *hats.jpg*. That sounds like a photo of the new product line. A name like *nav_button_hats.jpg* is more precise.

Creating Folders

A folder containing a FrontPage Web site stands out from the other folders on your computer. A blue globe on a folder indicates that it contains a FrontPage Web site or subsite (page 190). The blue globe appears even if you're browsing your computer's directory outside of FrontPage, using Windows Explorer, or opening files within other applications.

UP TO SPEED

Home Page Names

When you enter a simple URL like *www.microsoft.com*, your Web browser opens a Web page, even though you didn't specify a particular page. So how does your Web browser know where to go?

Actually, the Web server leads the way. When given a general address like *www.microsoft.com*, a Web server automatically delivers a site's home page (also called a default page). The server can identify a home page by its name, which is usually *index.htm* or *default.htm,* depending upon the Web server.

So FrontPage automatically names your home page based on your Web site's environment. If your Web site is on an IIS Web server (page 178), FrontPage names the home page *default.htm*. On another Web server, or in the absence of a Web server (as in a disk-based site), FrontPage names the home page *index.htm.*

Problems arise when your development environment (page 176) and the live Web server use different home page names. For example, if you edit a disk-based site and upload to an IIS server, what happens to all those *index.htm* pages?

Thankfully, FrontPage executes an automatic name change for you—as long as you use the program's publishing feature, which you'll read about in Chapter 13. In the process, the program also updates all hyperlinks relating to the page. But what if you're publishing *outside* of FrontPage and you encounter this problem? You can implement a quick solution: create a page with the name that the Web server wants to use and insert a redirect (Go to URL) behavior (page 155) on the page, to route visitors to your real home page.

One core folder (with just such a blue globe on it) contains your entire site. All your Web pages and their associated files sit in this root folder. As you add more and more files to this folder, it can get cluttered and chaotic, unless you create an organizational system to manage it.

What's the best tool for the job? The same one you use to organize the rest of your computer files: the folder. Use folders to group Web files in a way that speeds your work and makes sense to collaborators. A simple Web site folder structure appears in Figure 10-8.

A couple of tips:

- **Let your site content guide you as you create a folder structure.** Organize by category. In the Clothing Store example (shown in Figure 10-8), each product line, like accessories and apparel, has its own folder. These categories derive directly from links on the home page of this site. Each category folder has its own set of pages and subfolders.

- **Group like files.** FrontPage tries to be a good influence in this area. The program creates an *images* folder automatically, even when it creates an empty Web site. Place all your images in one folder so you can locate them quickly and easily. Or, if you have a huge number of images, you can create image folders for each section of your site. For instance, the *accessories* folder in Figure 10-8 has its own *images* folder. Multimedia files, like video, audio, and Flash files, can all go in a *media* folder. If your site features multiple CSS files or PDF files, group them together as well.

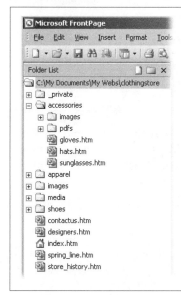

Figure 10-8:
The clothingstore folder at top is this site's root directory. Other folders contain pages grouped by category and file type.

To create a new folder, go to the folder list and select the existing folder in which you'd like to create it. Right-click the folder and select New → Folder. Name your folder in lowercase, and don't include spaces or special characters. The guidelines for naming files (page 187) also apply to folders.

FrontPage's Territory

You may not be collaborating with anyone on your Web site. But you're never really working alone. FrontPage toils beside you whenever you're editing your pages. You can see evidence of this right in your Web site's folder list. The program has its own set of folders (such as _derived, _fpclass, _overlay, and _private) that it uses to manage your site. You shouldn't move or interfere with these folders.

Because FrontPage tracks and manages aspects of your site behind the scenes, you must always keep the program in mind whenever you're thinking about making any changes (like deleting folders whose names you don't recognize). In other words, never edit folders or file names from outside FrontPage in an application like Windows Explorer. If you use your operating system to copy a graphic file into your site's *images* folder, FrontPage won't recognize it. Instead, you should use FrontPage to import the file, or insert it onto a page while you're editing.

Subsites

Some areas of a site require special security considerations. If you want to set separate permissions (access restrictions) to certain portions of your site, you'll need to create a *subsite*. A subsite is a Web site within a Web site. You can turn any folder within your site into a subsite.

Designers also use subsites to shield contents of a folder from settings that affect an entire site. For example, if a site features a theme (see Chapter 11), but you don't want to use this theme within one area, make a subsite to contain that group of pages.

Note: Before you run off to create subsites, consider this: when you publish a site, subsites aren't automatically included. You'll have to publish them separately, or turn on the "Include subsites" checkbox when you're configuring publishing options (see page 257). This can create confusion (not to mention, some extra work), so create a subsite only if you really need to.

You create a subsite as you would any other Web site. In fact, a subsite is really just a Web site. Its presence within the parent site's folder is the only thing that makes it a subsite. Select File → New and choose from FrontPage's Web site templates. Save the subsite within its parent site.

You can also turn any existing folder within a site into a subsite. Right-click the folder and select Convert to Web. FrontPage warns you of the consequences involved. (Specifically, the program tells you that it won't treat everything in your root folder as a whole. So automated elements like themes and link bars—which you'll read about in the next chapter—won't carry over to the subsite.) Click OK. Your subsite now features the blue globe, pictured in Figure 10-9, which denotes a Web site folder. If you change your mind later, you can switch the subsite back into a regular folder. Just right-click the subsite and select Convert to Folder.

Figure 10-9:
The blue globe on the clothingstore folder in the "Look in" box indicates that it contains a Web site. Blue globes on two folders within the clothingstore folder, ny_store and vail_store, reveal that they're subsites.

Themes, Link Bars, and Templates

Imagine that a visitor is exploring your Web site. He clicks link after link, traveling from page to page. As he moves along, how does he know he's still in the same Web site?

Usually a site has its own design scheme, a unifying look and feel that remains constant from page to page—that's one clue. Another tip off might be a fixed navigation bar at the top, side, or bottom of the page. This tells him how to get back to where he started, and where he is in the grand scheme of your site.

When you're creating pages—if you care at all about keeping your visitors oriented and surrounded by consistent visual cues—you need to consider your site as a whole. You've already read about lots of ways you can implement site-wide design and navigation plans. For example, you could set up a single decorative format for your site using a CSS style sheet. You could also create a site navigation menu with interactive buttons or simple hyperlinks and put it on every page, or display it in a frame.

So far, so good. But FrontPage can give you even more help. The program offers a bunch of automated solutions to handle site-wide display and navigation issues, including tools like FrontPage themes, link bars, shared borders, Dynamic Web Templates, and more. This chapter shows you how to use all these options, and examines the tradeoffs when you accept FrontPage's helping hand.

Note: If you're collaborating with authors who use non-Microsoft products like Dreamweaver, you shouldn't use themes, link bars, page banners, or shared borders. These features depend upon FrontPage technology, and if you hand off your FrontPage-designed pages to someone who plugs them into, say, a Dreamweaver-designed site, you're guaranteed to see a spectacular mess. On the other hand, included content (page 206) and Dynamic Web Templates (page 216) should work regardless of what Web design program you or your colleagues are using.

FrontPage Themes

If you're not a talented designer or just don't have the time to choose colors and special formatting flourishes, you can have FrontPage decorate your Web site for you. FrontPage *themes* contain preselected colors, graphics, and text style settings that the program applies to every page on your Web site. Coordinated colors set off hyperlinks, text, and page borders. Graphic files provide elements like page background, banners, bullets, and buttons.

FREQUENTLY ASKED QUESTION

Themes Like Old Times

I created themes using a previous version of FrontPage. Now that I'm using FrontPage 2003, will the old theme work?

Older versions of FrontPage added some HTML to Web sites in order to implement themes. The program now applies themes using CSS. This is a real improvement because CSS uses less code, which means that your pages download a bit faster. Also, the CSS method more closely

follows Web standards set by the World Wide Web Consortium (for more on these standards, see page 231). FrontPage 2003 recognizes your old theme, but for best results, update your site by removing the theme (page 197 shows you how), and then reapplying it using FrontPage 2003. If your old theme doesn't appear in the FrontPage theme list, try customizing another one (page 197) to suit your needs.

Should You Use a Theme?

Themes make site design a breeze, but not everyone's a fan. Themes mostly appeal to beginners or those who simply don't have time for graphic design decisions. Most advanced Web developers tend to worry about what files and code FrontPage will add to their site to achieve a theme's effects. Others wouldn't dream of using a FrontPage theme—maybe because they don't like FrontPage controlling parts of a site, or they're very particular and want to set every design detail themselves.

The pros

Themes automate page design and your site's overall appearance instantly and easily. You can apply a theme to your entire site or just a portion of it. Even if you don't like the packaged themes FrontPage offers, you can still take advantage of the feature's formatting automation. Just customize an existing theme to suit your needs, or create your own theme from scratch (you'll learn how to do both those things in a moment).

The cons

FrontPage themes tend to have a "made by Microsoft" canned look that a lot of designers and even average Web surfers find uninspired (others have used the terms "soul-killing," "drone-like," and, well, you get the idea). Also, because there are so few themes to choose from, it might be painfully obvious to many of your visitors that you've used a FrontPage theme (see Figure 11-1). The result? Your site could look less professional than you want.

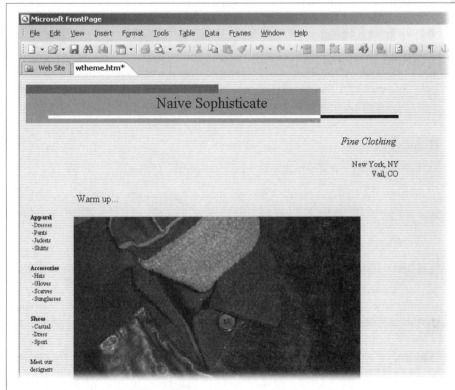

Figure 11-1: This is a typical FrontPage theme. A banner at top incorporates the page title in a graphic. A background image provides texture and color—here it's horizontal stripes.

Themes also restrict your freedom. You make a real commitment when you apply a theme. FrontPage takes control of a lot of page elements, keeping you from making design tweaks where you may want them.

If you're wary of themes, check out these alternatives:

- **Dynamic Web Templates** let you create pages with the shared look and features that you get when using a template (page 214). After that, any page created from the template continues to take its design directives from the template file. This means you can make one change (to the template file) and control the look of your entire site. Details follow later this chapter.

- **Cascading Style Sheets** offer great design flexibility, as you learned in Chapter 7. You can create your own style sheets to give your site a uniform design. But don't forget that FrontPage features a few canned style sheets, too. Applying one of these is just as quick and easy as applying a theme.

- **Included content** is a nifty FrontPage feature that lets you take the content of one page and drop it into many other pages. This tool, which is covered below, provides an alternative way to create the same elements that themes do—like banners and other headings. If you use included content in combination with CSS, there's no theme you can't recreate or surpass.

Applying a Theme

FrontPage can apply a theme to a Web site, subsite (page 190), or individual pages. Once you apply a theme to a page, it takes over the entire page. In other words, you can't pick and choose what elements the theme will control. Banners, bulleted lists, background, headings, and other elements automatically fall under a theme's control.

To apply a theme:

1. **Select the page(s) to which you want to apply the theme.**

   Within the folder list, select a page, multiple pages, or a site (by selecting the folder that holds the site). If you want to apply a theme to one page only, open the page in Design view. As long as no files are selected in the folder list, FrontPage applies the theme only to the page you're working on.

2. **Display themes.**

   Select Format → Theme to open the Themes task pane. It features a scrolling list of theme thumbnails (see Figure 11-2), which give you some idea how each theme will look when applied to your pages.

Tip: You may want to see how a theme looks when it's applied to *your* Web pages, not just some sample page. To see how the theme looks with your content, open a page in Design view. As you select themes within the task pane, the page adopts their style elements. If you don't see something you like, just cancel at any time without saving.

Checkboxes at the bottom of the Themes task pane offer the following options:

- **Vivid colors.** If you turn on this checkbox, FrontPage amps up the brightness and variation of theme colors. Depending on the theme, activating this checkbox can turn a black heading to blue or make yellow hyperlinks orange.

- **Active graphics.** Turn on this checkbox to activate a theme's animated pictures—like rollover buttons. Doing so can change the appearance of some navigation buttons and banners.

- **Background picture.** Many themes feature a background picture, which is usually a pattern. If you like the theme, but not the background, turn this checkbox off. FrontPage substitutes a solid color.

3. **Apply a theme.**

To apply a theme, you can just click a theme thumbnail, but you also have additional options. When you pass your cursor over a theme thumbnail, a down arrow appears on the right side of the thumbnail. Click the arrow, or right-click the theme itself to display a menu (Figure 11-2).

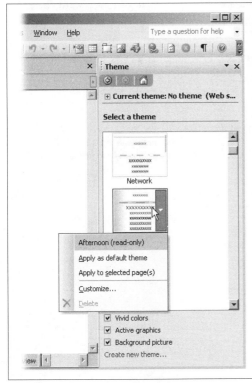

Figure 11-2:
Apply themes using the Theme task pane. Right-click any theme thumbnail to display a pop-up menu, which lets you tweak some of the theme's settings. The first line of the pop-up menu, shaded in gray, shows the theme name. If you can't quite make out the theme's details in the thumbnail, select Customize to see a full-sized preview. (You can always just look and click Cancel.)

The menu shows the name of the theme you selected, and offers the following two ways to apply the theme:

- **Apply as default theme.** This selection applies the theme to the entire Web site, even if you've selected just one page.

- **Apply to selected page(s).** Use this command if you've selected pages or folders within Folder view, or have a single page active in the document window. Themes applied to single pages override a site-wide theme.

Other available options include:

- **Customize.** This option lets you modify a theme. See the next section for details.

• **Delete.** Don't try to use this option to remove a theme from a Web site or page. This command just removes a theme from the list of options in the Theme task pane. (FrontPage won't delete any themes that came bundled with the program, only those you create or import yourself.)

Once you've applied a theme, FrontPage takes over. Not only do your pages take on the appearance of the theme, but FrontPage grays out (disables) formatting options that the theme now controls, like bullet style. If you ever want to retake control of these options, your only option is to remove the theme.

Themes are pretty dictatorial, but they don't control everything on a page. For those elements outside a theme's control, FrontPage still tries to help you to stay within the color scheme, as shown in Figure 11-3.

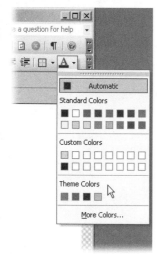

Figure 11-3:
For elements a theme doesn't lock down—like text color, for instance—FrontPage offers an additional feature to help you work in harmony with any theme you're using. The program adds a Theme Colors section to your palette to help you color coordinate your pages.

Things to keep in mind when applying a theme

Themes can be pretty helpful, but they don't always behave exactly as you might expect. Consider the following:

• If you apply a theme to a Web site, it won't affect subsites.

• Themes applied to specific pages override a site theme.

• When you apply a theme to a Web site, FrontPage obliterates formatting already in place. Even if you remove the theme later, you won't get a lot of your prior settings back.

• If your Web site contains pages controlled by Dynamic Web Templates, Themes won't affect them. If you want to apply a theme to these pages, apply it to the Dynamic Web Template itself. (You can even do this after you've created the template and pages based on the template. When FrontPage saves the template, it updates the pages. See the end of this chapter for details on Dynamic Web Templates.)

Customizing a Theme

Say you've found a theme that you like, but the colors don't quite match your corporate colors. The packaged themes FrontPage offers may not seem like a perfect fit at first—but you can tweak them to suit your needs. FrontPage lets you change the color, graphic files, and font settings associated with any theme.

Your customization work begins in the Themes task pane. Click the "Create new theme" link at the bottom of the task pane, or right-click a theme you like and then select Customize. The Customize Theme dialog box displays (see Figure 11-4).

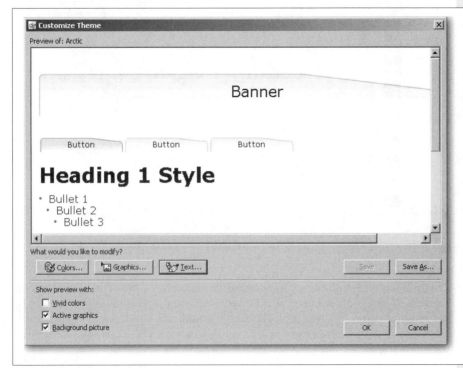

Figure 11-4:
The Customize Theme dialog box lets you modify theme color, graphics, and text. You control each of these settings using the corresponding buttons, in the lower-left corner. FrontPage previews all your changes in the large pane at top.

Changing colors

To change colors within the theme, click the Colors button. The dialog box displays the theme's color settings (see Figure 11-5).

The three tabs that appear offer varying degrees of color customization. The Color Schemes tab offers preset schemes (sets of colors) from which you can choose. Click a scheme for a preview (in the right-side pane) of what it looks like.

If you want to really customize what colors you're using, click the Color Wheel tab. Here you can drag a small white dot to any point you like on the *color wheel,* a circle that presents all the colors available on your computer. The color you select will be the Normal text color for the theme. Based on your selection, FrontPage sets the rest of the theme colors automatically. The resulting scheme appears back at the top of the Color Schemes tab under the label (Custom). Use the Brightness slider control to adjust the intensity of the colors.

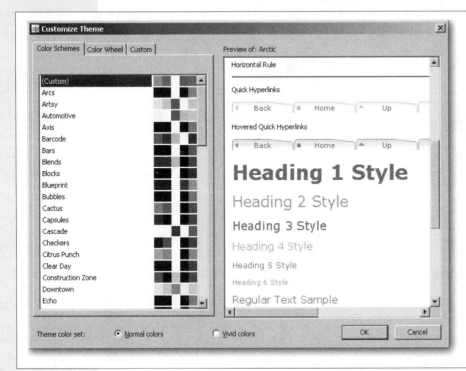

Figure 11-5:
Select a color scheme on the left and FrontPage previews it on the right. Click the Vivid colors radio button to see how that setting punches up the color in each scheme.

Say you like every color in a theme, except the hyperlink color. You can change the setting for that one element only. Or, you can even pick your colors element by element, if you want. To do so, click the Custom tab. The Custom tab features a drop-down list of Items and a corresponding drop-down list of colors. Select an item, then select a color.

Note: Not all theme colors—especially customized colors—are Web safe. For more information on Web Safe colors, see page 31 back in Chapter 2.

If you're changing colors, keep in mind that any packaged graphics that come with the theme will remain the same and may not match your new color scheme. To fix this inconsistency, you may want to change some of the theme's graphics, which is what the next section shows you how to do.

Changing graphics

Theme elements like bullets, buttons, and sometimes even the background are actually graphic files. If you don't care for one of these images, change it within the Customize Theme dialog box by clicking the Graphics button.

To customize a graphic, select an element from the Item list at the top left of the dialog box (see Figure 11-6). FrontPage then lets you browse for alternate graphic files.

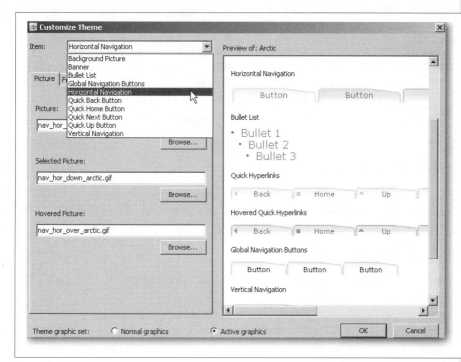

Figure 11-6:
The Items list within the Customize Theme Graphics dialog box includes all theme elements that use graphics, like bullets and navigation buttons. When Active Graphics is turned on (at the bottom of the dialog box), buttons have two images: one at rest and a "Hovered Picture" that appears when a cursor passes over it.

Many of these graphics, like banners and navigation buttons, include text. To change the typeface, size, or alignment (within the graphic), select the element. Then click the Font tab (see Figure 11-7).

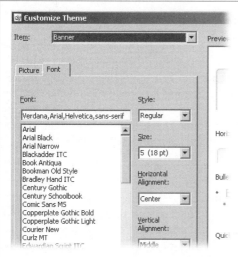

Figure 11-7:
The Font tab on the Customize Theme dialog box lets you select a new font for text that appears on a theme's graphics. Use the drop-down menus on the right to set font size and alignment within buttons and banners. What if a viewer doesn't have your chosen font loaded on her system? To ensure that she'll see the alternative that you want, type it in this dialog box, following the first font. Enter as many fonts as you want, separating them with commas.

Changing text

If you don't like the fonts a theme uses to display text on the page, you can change those as well. Back in the main window of the Customize Theme dialog box (see Figure 11-4), click the Text button.

A simple font dialog box, like the one illustrated in Figure 11-7, displays. Select a page element from the Item drop-down list at top, then select a font from the font list. FrontPage previews the effect in the pane on the right. You can enter multiple fonts here, just as you can when you adjust the font for graphic elements.

To create or access CSS styles (page 115), click the More Text Styles button on the bottom left.

Saving a custom theme

Once you've set all your preferences within the Customize Theme dialog box, click Save As. Enter a unique name for the theme in the Save Theme dialog box that appears, and click OK.

Removing a Theme

If you've grown disenchanted with a theme, you can remove it.

Note: Removing a theme doesn't restore pages to their original design. Any previous graphics, color, or font settings you had in place won't automatically return. All your content will remain, just looking a lot plainer than before. For example, a picture bullet wouldn't survive this process. You'd see a regular bullet in its place.

To remove a theme, select the site folder or pages that should no longer feature the theme. Select Format → Theme. The Themes task pane displays. Choose No Theme and click Yes to confirm your choice.

How Themes Interact with Style Sheets

How will your pages react when you apply a theme? Theme formatting follows the basic laws of cascading styles (page 128): formatting that lives closer to the element takes precedence. You've already read that a theme applied to a page trumps a site-wide theme. The rule applies to formatting for smaller elements, too. For instance, say you have an embedded style (page 116) for Heading 1 on a given page, making the headings bold and bright pink. If you apply a theme that features a Heading 1 formatted as black, your bright pink headings will remain.

If you have Web pages you've already filled with content, be careful with themes. When you apply a theme, some of your page elements stay as you've set them, while others change. This can create some unexpected problems. For example, say you've formatted some text to be yellow and set it against a blue page background. Then you apply a theme, which doesn't change your text color but replaces your blue background with a yellow and white graphic. The light background would render your text indecipherable.

Link Bars and Page Banners

How will your visitors navigate your site? By following hyperlinks, of course. To help readers out, Web authors usually include a menu along the side or top of a page that features links to a site's important pages. As you update your site, editing, deleting, and renaming pages, keeping up with all those hyperlinks can become a real chore.

If you want, FrontPage can automate the hassle of maintaining your site's navigational menus. *Link bars* are navigation menus that FrontPage controls and manages for you. Link bars get their information from the navigation diagram you read about in Chapter 10 (see page 182). To go along with link bars, the program offers the *page banner* (see Figure 11-8). A page banner is an automated page heading that shows the title of a Web page in a graphic across the top of the page. Because page banners also take their page titles from Navigation view, banner displays will always perfectly match the text in your link bars.

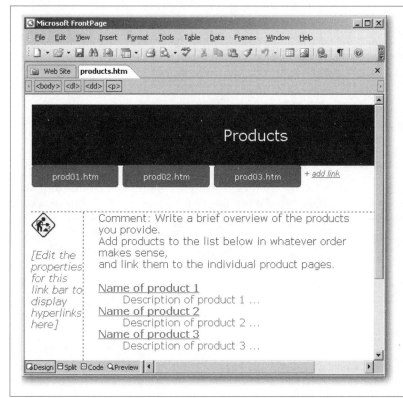

Figure 11-8:
This page is from FrontPage's Corporate template. It has a banner at top that proclaims the page title: Products. A link bar appears just beneath the banner, featuring navigation buttons that lead to other pages. In Design view, link bars feature an "Add link" shortcut at the end that you can use to create additional navigation buttons. (This text won't show up in a browser.) Another link bar appears on the left edge of the page, but doesn't yet contain any links. (Text telling you to configure a link bar would show up in a browser if you don't edit it.) To edit this link bar, just double-click it.

Steps for creating link bars and page banners follow. Before you create these elements, you must open your site in Navigation view and set up a hierarchy and flow for your pages (see Chapter 10, page 182 for details). FrontPage uses the page relationships and titles in your navigation diagram to build links that make up a link bar. If you hate the idea of having to create a navigation diagram first, skip ahead to the "Link Bars with Custom Links" section on page 204 to see how you can make a link bar without it.

Tip: You can't create link bars or page banners until you've established your site's navigation in Navigation view. However, the navigation diagram you create doesn't need to include every page in your site. Feel free to create a navigation scheme only for those pages that will feature link bars.

Creating a Link Bar Based on Navigation Structure

With some guidance from you, FrontPage can manage your site's navigation links. You need to get the process started by first creating a navigation diagram (page 182). Once you've done that, you're ready to place your link bars.

1. **Specify a location for your link bar.**

   Place your cursor on a page where you want to insert the link bar, and then select Insert → Navigation.

Note: If Navigation is grayed out, that means that navigation features are disabled within FrontPage. To fix this, select Tools → Page Options and click the Authoring tab. Turn on the Navigation checkbox. (You may need to turn on the Author-time Web Components checkbox first.)

   The Web Component dialog box displays. The pane on the left, Component Type, is set automatically to Link Bar. In the pane on the right, select "Bar based on navigation structure" and click Next.

2. **Select a style for your link bar.**

   The dialog box that follows features formatting options. You can use the page's theme or select another. Scroll down the list for a preview of all your choices. If you prefer a look that's more "Spartan" than "Microsoft," check out the text-only choices end of the list. Select the look you want and click Next.

3. **Choose an orientation.**

   You can make your link bar spread horizontally across the top of the page or fall vertically down the left edge of the page. If you choose vertical orientation, FrontPage puts a return between each item. Click on the preferred orientation preview and then click Finish.

Tip: Each dialog box you encounter while creating a link bar features a Finish button. If you don't need to set style or orientation, click Finish instead of Next to skip ahead to the Link Bar Properties dialog box.

4. Specify navigation.

Now that you've set a look for your link bar, FrontPage needs to know what links to include. The Link Bar Properties dialog box displays (see Figure 11-9).

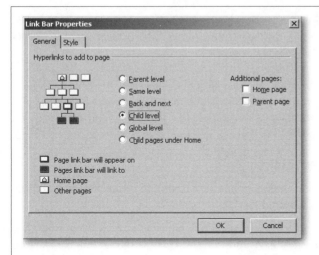

Figure 11-9:
Use the Link Bar Properties dialog box to preview your link bar navigation options. Click on a radio button, and the diagram on the left shows the effect within a sample site. Pages that will get links appear in blue.

FrontPage creates links in relation to the current page. Select from the following options:

• **Parent level.** Creates links to all pages one level above the current page.

• **Same level.** Creates links to all pages on the same level as the current page.

• **Back and next.** Creates links to pages on the same level as the current page that appear to the right and left of it. Use this scheme if you want to lead readers through your site in a specific page order. If this option appeals to you, check out a more flexible variation: see "Creating a Link Bar with Custom Next and Back Links" on page 205.

• **Child level.** Creates links to all pages to which the current page is a parent.

• **Global level.** Creates links to the home page and any top pages. *Top pages* exist outside the directory structure and often include search or contact forms.

• **Child pages under home.** Creates links to all the home page's first-level children. Depending on your site structure, this selection might be useful for providing general category links.

You have additional options here, too:

• If you want to feature a link to the home page even though it may not be part of the navigation structure you've chosen, turn on the "Home page" checkbox on the upper-right corner.

- If you want to include a link to the page one level above the current page, turn on the "Parent page" checkbox. The text for the link to the Parent is "Up" instead of the page title. If you want to change this, select Tools → Site Settings and click the Navigation tab.

Tip: If you find that you need to include multiple link bars on a page, go ahead and do so. For example, you may want all pages to include home and parent links, but only a designated few to offer links to their child pages. Create a separate link bar for each circumstance.

Once you set your navigation scheme, click OK. The link bar appears on your page. To edit a link bar, double-click it. The Link Bar Properties dialog box pictured in Figure 11-9 displays again. Repeat the steps above on each page on which you'd like to feature a link bar.

Link Bars with Custom Links

Many people like the idea of link bars but hate having to create and maintain the navigation diagram that's required.

Link bars with custom links let you create a link bar of your own design that lives independently from your site's navigation diagram. These special link bars let you include whatever links you want, with no interference from FrontPage. Even better, you can use a custom link bar over and over again. Here's how:

1. **Specify a location for your link bar with custom links.**

   Place your cursor on a page where you want to insert the link bar and select Insert → Navigation.

   The Web Component dialog box displays. The pane on the left, Component Type, is set automatically to Link Bar. In the pane on the right, select "Bar with custom links" and click next.

2. **Select a style and orientation for your link bar.**

   In the dialog boxes that follow, select a look and layout for your link bar. (See steps two and three in the previous section, "Creating a Link Bar Based on Navigation Structure" for details.)

3. **Name the link bar.**

   A Create New Link Bar dialog box presents you with a Name field. Type in a short, descriptive name. You'll use this name later to add this link bar to other pages.

4. **Add links.**

   The Link Bar Properties dialog box displays (see Figure 11-10).

Tip: If you've already created a link bar, you can select it from the "Choose existing" drop-down menu at the top of the dialog box. Any custom link bars you create are always available here for you to insert on any page.

Click Add Link and the hyperlink dialog box displays. Select the URL (within your site or on the Web) and enter the text to display. In a link bar with custom links, you—not your navigation diagram—set the text of a link.

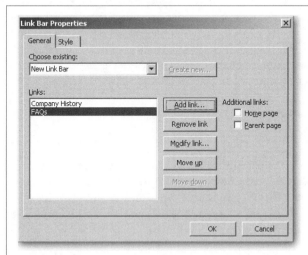

Figure 11-10:
When you create a link bar with custom links, the Link Bar dialog box gives you direct control over links and link order. Add, modify, or remove a link using the buttons on the right. Set link order using the Move Up and Move Down buttons.

Creating a Link Bar with Custom Next and Back Links

If you want to lead your visitors page by page through your site (which is great for Web-based picture slideshows), use back and next links. When you create a link bar based on navigation, you can use back and next links, but they work only on one navigation level at a time. If you use this custom option, you can set any order you wish. The flexibility can't be beat.

To get started, first select Insert → Navigation. The Web Component dialog box displays, with the left pane set to Link Bars. In the pane on the right, select "Bar with back and next links" and then click Next. In the dialog boxes that follow, choose style and orientation, and then click Finish. The Link Bar Properties dialog box pictured in Figure 11-10 displays. Use it to add links as you would for a link bar with custom links. Once you've added all your links, use the Move Up and Move Down buttons to set browse order for your pages. The order in which pages appear in the links list is the order in which viewers will see them when they click Next.

Page Banners

As you're discovering in this chapter, FrontPage is chock full of features that help you help visitors navigate your site. One key to a good navigation system is letting readers know where they are. A page banner goes a long way toward this goal. If a huge graphic at the top of the page says "Products," then your visitors know they've made it to the list of products.

Of course you can create a page heading like this yourself with special font effects, or by making your own graphic, but FrontPage has an automated solution that works hand in hand with link bars and Navigation view.

FrontPage banners are page headings that the program creates and controls. You'll get the most bang for your banner buck if you use banners in conjunction with link bars. Both these features take their page names from page titles in Navigation view. So link names in a link bar will always match the text in page banners. Often banners proclaim a page's identity with text set in a fancy graphic. However, if you aren't using a theme, the "banner" effect is somewhat anticlimactic. Without a theme, a page name shows up as just plain text.

Note: Don't forget—in order to include a page in a link bar or banner, you first must place the page in a navigation diagram (page 182).

To add a page banner, open the page in Design view and place your cursor at the top of the page. Select Insert → Web Component to open the Insert Web Component dialog box. Within the list of Component types on the left, click Included Content. Within the list on the right, select Page Banner, and then click Finish. The Page Banner Properties dialog box opens.

- If you have a FrontPage theme applied to your site, select Picture, and then confirm or change the banner text. (Changing text here will also change the page name in Navigation view.) If you select text, the banner won't be very flashy—it'll appear as plain text.

- If you have no FrontPage theme in place, a plain text banner will result, even if you select Picture.

- If your page doesn't exist in the navigation structure, the text box is grayed out. When you click OK, a message appears on your page telling you to add it to the navigation structure.

To edit a banner name, double-click it in Design view. This opens the Page Banner Properties dialog box again.

Included Content

Say you have a company logo that you want to put at the bottom of all your pages, right beside your corporate motto. Or maybe you have a copyright blurb or a simple navigation menu that needs to appear on lots of different pages. Recreating these same elements over and over again on hundreds of pages can be a downright pain in the mouse.

Banner Ad Manager Is Gone

If you've used previous versions of FrontPage, you may have used the program's Banner Ad Manager. This feature let Web authors include rotating ads on a page. Microsoft phased this feature out in FrontPage 2003. Why? Because in order for visitors to see the ads this feature creates, their computers need to have Java Virtual Machine, which used to ship with Windows but no longer does. This means that any visitor using Windows XP and/or Internet Explorer 6 will see a gray box instead of ads.

If you want ads like this on a Web page, your best alternative is to create the same effect using JavaScript or Flash. A lot of JavaScript Web sites feature-free scripts, including those to create a rotating banner ad. Try looking around online at sites like *www.javascript.internet.com*. If you want to use Flash, you must purchase the program at Macromedia (*www.macromedia.com*), or find some kind soul to provide you with a Flash movie.

If you're desperately addicted to FrontPage's Banner Ad Manager and want to use it just a bit longer, don't despair. Microsoft hasn't gotten rid of this feature, they've just stashed it out of site to discourage you from using it. To get Banner Ad Manager back, you can create a program short-cut to it. Right-click any toolbar and select Customize. The Customize dialog box opens with the Command tab on top. In the Categories pane on the left, click Insert. Scroll down the list of Commands that appears on the right. Once you find the Banner Ad Manager, drag it onto any toolbar or menu. If you want to remove it later, just open the Customize dialog box again, right-click the shortcut, and then select Delete.

There's a much easier way. Whenever you want the same information to appear in many places, you'll probably want to use FrontPage's *Included Content* feature. This tool lets you create one chunk of HTML (including text, pictures, tables, or whatever you want) that FrontPage can then take and slip into any page(s) you want.

But that's not all. The real beauty comes when you need to make a change. Say your company motto changes and you need to edit the text on every page across your entire site. Even though the phrase appears on hundreds of pages, you can make all those changes in a snap. All you need to do is edit the included content in one spot. The logo and motto that appears on all those other pages is really just a copy of the original HTML. When you change the source, FrontPage automatically updates the copies wherever they appear.

Note: FrontPage creates included content using only HTML, not special FrontPage-dependent code. So, if you're collaborating with colleagues using Dreamweaver or other Web editors, this option is your best bet for creating elements that will be shared by lots of pages.

Inserting Included Content

Included content is just a Web page that you can drop into other Web pages. This page can have just two words on it, or your life story, complete with photos and a Flash movie of your birth. But generally, you'll want to use this feature for shorter passages that'll appear in lots of places, like a copyright notice. To include one page within another Web page:

1. **Create the content.**

   Create the source content (the page that you want to include within other pages) just as you would any Web page. Usually your source page will be a small amount of text, which serves as a header, footer, menu, or text snippet.

   Note: Don't include any DHTML effects or behaviors within your included content. FrontPage includes only content between the <body> tags. So anything that resides between <head> tags, like JavaScript and some styles, won't copy over.

   Save the page anywhere you wish. You may want to create a specific folder to hold your "includes" so you always know where to find them. Since these snippets aren't meant to exist on their own, you may want to tuck them out of site in the _private folder, so they won't show up during a search of your site.

2. **Set the destination for included content.**

   Open the page in which you want to include the content. Place your cursor where you want to insert the source page.

3. **Insert included content.**

   Select Insert → Web Component. Within the component list on the left, click Included Content. Then, in the pane on the right, select Page. Click Finish and browse to (or type the path) of the page you want to include. Click OK.

   The included content appears on the page. Included elements take on the formatting properties of the page in which they're included.

Tip: You can put an automated link bar (page 202) within an included page and have the bar appear on as many pages as you want. And of course the link bar hyperlinks will all connect to the right pages.

Inserting a Scheduled Include

Say you have a special sales offer that ends at midnight. Will you be up editing and publishing your pages at that hour? Probably not. But FrontPage can help you out (or at least, try to help you out).

The *scheduled include* is similar to the regular include page feature, but comes with additional options. You can set a start and end time for the content you want to display and replace the included page with another page at a time you specify (Figure 11-11).

Note: Scheduled include options require FrontPage Server Extensions (page 177).

The big problem with scheduled includes is that they don't always follow the schedule you've cooked up. Since the Web page can't track time on its own, it needs to be manually updated to show the new content. This means that the change will take place only if you publish your site *after* the time specified for the content swap. You can also run Recalculate Hyperlinks on your live Web site (Tools → Recalculate Hyperlinks), or ask your server administrator to create a batch file (a script that can tell functions to run at a certain time) to do this automatically.

Figure 11-11:
Here's a before and after picture of a scheduled include. The President's Day sale announcement doesn't appear on this page until it's scheduled. It will disappear again when the sale is over.

To set a scheduled include, create the content as you would for a regular include page (explained in the previous section) and place your cursor on the page where you'd like to insert it. Then:

1. **Insert the scheduled content.**

   Select Insert → Web Component to open the Insert Web Component dialog box. Within the component list on the left, click Included Content. Then, in the pane on the right, select Page Based On Schedule. Click Finish and the Scheduled Include Page Properties dialog box displays.

2. **Set included pages.**

   Here you'll specify the two pages that will exchange places. In the "During the scheduled time" field of the dialog box, browse to and select the page you want to include for a limited time—say, for your one-day sale. Below that, in the "Before and after the scheduled time" field, browse to and select the page you want to precede and replace the first page. You can leave this field blank, and nothing will appear.

3. **Set the schedule.**

   Next, you set the time period during which the first page should appear. Enter starting and ending dates in the fields at the bottom of the dialog box. The time fields display two-digit increments: by hour, by minute, and by second. FrontPage won't let you enter numbers directly here. Select a figure and use the up and down arrow buttons in the dialog box or the corresponding keys on your keyboard.

Inserting a Scheduled Include Picture

You can include a picture at a particular time just as you'd include a page, though you might as well just stick your picture on a page and include that entire page instead. One reason is that pictures you include this way can't have their own paragraph breaks, which means that pictures included by schedule always appear smack dab in the middle of surrounding text.

But, if for some reason you decide you want to add a scheduled include picture, select Insert → Web Component to open the Insert Web Component dialog box. Within the component list on the left, select Included Content. Then, in the pane on the right, select Picture Based On Schedule.

The Scheduled Picture Properties dialog box that displays is similar to the one for regular scheduled included content (page), and you should fill it out accordingly (see the previous section for how to do that). This dialog box offers two additional options under the Alternative Text heading. These set the picture's alternative text (text that appears in a tool tip and in place of the image) both before and after the picture swap.

Scheduled picture includes come with the same glitch that regular scheduled pages do: they require you to publish or run Recalculate Hyperlinks before the update kicks in.

Shared Borders

Say you want all your pages to have a banner at top and a vertical menu down the left side. Pages within a site often share common elements like this. FrontPage has a feature called *shared borders,* designed to help you feature this kind of arrangement on many pages, in just one step.

Shared borders are just what they sound like—page border areas (top, bottom, left, or right) that a group of designated pages share (see Figure 11-12). Shared borders also can work in conjunction with link bars and page banners. If you insert a link bar within a shared border, the navigation buttons on the bar will be different for each page it's on. In other words, the link bar knows what page it's on, so (depending on the navigation scheme you selected) it links to the correct pages and not back to itself, for example.

Figure 11-12:
The top banner and side menu on this page can be repeated on the site's other pages by activating shared borders.

Note: If you do feature a link bar in a shared border, that link bar appears on every page that's using those borders. Be sure that's what you want. For example, if a page isn't in the Navigation diagram, the border displays text instructing you to add the page to the diagram. This text will appear in a viewer's browser if you don't heed the instructions, so make sure you do so.

Why Not to Use Shared Borders

Since their introduction, shared borders have tormented many FrontPage Web authors (more on the reasons why in a moment). Save yourself time and trouble by skipping this feature. You can create the same effect using included content instead.

Some of the reasons shared borders have a bad rep:

- **They often behave unpredictably.** For instance, you thought you removed shared borders from all pages, but they still appear on some. Or your borders show up in FrontPage, but not in a browser. With a little effort, you can usually fix these issues (often by delving into the page's code). But since you can achieve the same effect with included content or another option, save yourself the hassle.

- **Shared borders can be edited from any page they appear on.** This means that anyone opening one of your Web pages (from within FrontPage) could potentially mess up shared borders across your entire site. Yikes!

- **FrontPage manages shared borders.** This means that shared border settings and controls live in the murky netherworld that the program controls—namely the secret folders like _private that FrontPage creates and uses to help you manage your site. As a result, you'll have a tough time troubleshooting the mercurial behavior of this feature. Included content, on the other hand, is simple HTML that lives within your domain—the regular folder structure of your site.

Activating Shared Borders

FrontPage doesn't automatically enable shared borders. You've got to flick a "shared borders on" switch, if you want to use them. To activate shared borders, select Tools → Page Options and click the Authoring tab. Turn on the Shared Borders checkbox.

Applying Shared Borders

As mentioned, you're better off avoiding shared borders, but if you must use them, follow these steps:

1. **Select the pages that you want to use shared borders.**

   If you want to feature borders on a limited number of pages, select them within the folder list. If you want borders on all your site's pages, don't select anything. Next, select Format → Shared Borders. The Shared Borders dialog box displays. It features a radio button, which lets you apply borders to all pages or selected page(s). Select your preference.

2. **Configure shared borders.**

The Shared Borders dialog box also features four checkboxes for each side of the page. Turn on the checkboxes for each side where you want a shared border (see Figure 11-13).

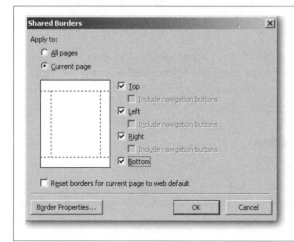

If you want to give a border a color or picture background, click Border Properties on the lower-left corner. In the dialog box that appears, select the border and the color you want or the graphic file you want to use as background.

3. **Set navigation.**

If you want a link bar to appear within any border, turn on the Include Navigation Buttons checkbox just below it. Turning this on inserts a link bar, so you'll need a navigation diagram (page 182) in place for this to work. Without it, unsightly text appears telling you to add the page to the navigation structure. Visitors to your Web site will also see this text, so definitely go ahead and create the navigation diagram to make it disappear.

4. **Apply shared borders.**

Once you've made all your settings, click OK. Shared borders show up in Design view, set off by dotted lines. If you're adding text or pictures to the border, now's the time to do so. Make changes on any page, and they'll show up on all pages that share the borders.

5. **Check border pages.**

Preview all the pages that now feature borders. If you've included a navigation bar, make sure that no pages contain errant text instead of links.

Editing and Removing Shared Borders

If you want to change the content of shared borders, just edit one of the borders anywhere it appears. All pages that feature the border reflect your changes.

If you want to change settings that you made in the Shared Borders dialog box, or if you want to get rid of shared borders entirely, do the following: if you've applied shared borders to a specific group of pages, select them within the folder list. If you've applied shared borders to your entire site and want to edit them all, don't bother selecting any pages. Next, select Format → Shared Borders. In the dialog box that displays, let FrontPage know the scope of your changes by clicking either the "All Pages" or "Selected page(s)" radio button. Make whatever other changes you want. To remove shared borders, just turn off all the border checkboxes.

To change shared border settings within one page, open it, and then select Format → Shared Borders. Click Current Page in the dialog box and select the settings you want. Use this method to remove shared borders from individual pages. Just turn off all border checkboxes, and the page loses them.

Creating a Page Template

Back in Chapter 10 (page 178), you learned all about how FrontPage site templates can furnish you with a ready-made collection of pages, waiting for you at the click of a button. Just add content to each page, and you're good to go. FrontPage lets you perform a similar trick with individual *page templates,* which are especially helpful if you're creating lots of pages that you want to look alike.

Page templates are like blueprints: you design the page's structure, add in any design elements you want, and then every time you want a replica, you just click the template. Violà, a pristine copy awaits you, to which you can then add any additional content you like. If your site has, say, separate pages for the 28 kinds of emu vests you're selling, templates can be a great timesaver: just create one emu-vest template, and then you can quickly fill in the details on each new page you create from the template.

Templates come in two varieties: static and dynamic. Static templates, which you'll learn about in this section, work like a photo copier: you can create as many copies as you like, but once a copy has been made, you can only change it by modifying the copy. For instance, if you've generated your 28 emu pages, and then you decide you want to include a different color for the heading that's on each page, you have to change each and every page separately. Dynamic templates, which you'll learn about in the next section, let you apply changes to all the pages that use your template, even after they've been generated.

Creating a Template

To create your own static page template:

1. **Create the page.**

   Create the page as you would any Web page. Add any elements like tables, pictures, and text that you want every page created from the template to have.

2. **Name the template.**

Select File → Properties. On the General tab, enter a name within the Title field. You'll use this name to select the template in the future.

3. **Save the page as a template.**

Select File → Save As. Within the "Save as type" drop-down menu at the bottom of the dialog box, select FrontPage Template (*.tem). FrontPage automatically saves this with other application files in a folder called Pages. Don't change this setting, or your template won't be available in the templates list. Click Save and a Save As Template dialog box appears. Verify the name of your template, and enter a description, if you want (see Figure 11-14).

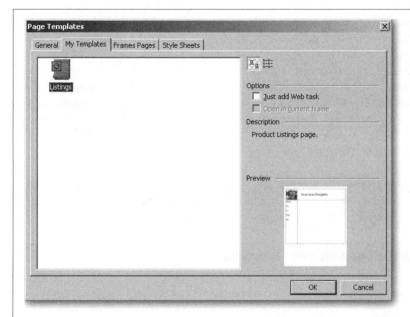

Figure 11-14:
Once you create a template, a new My Templates tab appears within the Page Templates dialog box. Your template description appears on the right side along with a page preview.

Note: FrontPage saves your template on your computer's C:\ drive in a FrontPage program directory outside your Web site. Of course, this means that you're the only one who can use it. If you want to grant access to others working on your site, then (once you get to the Save As Template dialog box) turn on the "Save Template in Current Web site" checkbox. This way, FrontPage saves the template within the site's directory, where your colleagues can find it.

Editing a Template

Modifying a template is pretty easy: create a new page using the template and make the changes you want to show up in the template. Then, save the file, using Save As (File → Save As), just as you did when you first created the template. In the Name field, enter the exact name of the old template. If you turned on the "Save Template in Current Web site" checkbox the first time you created the template, turn it on again. When you click OK in the Save As Template dialog box, FrontPage asks you if you're sure you want to replace the existing template file. Click Yes.

Note: Remember, modifications to a static template don't affect any pages already created with the template.

Creating Pages with a Template

Any FrontPage template you create appears with the other FrontPage templates. Select File → New and then, in the New task pane, click "More page templates." Open the My Templates tab, and then double-click the template to create a page.

Dynamic Web Templates

Dynamic Web Templates work similarly to static templates. They let you generate multiple fresh copies based on your original design. But they also do a lot more than their static brethren: not only do Dynamic Web Pages let you make changes to individual pages *after* you've created them (making it easy to propagate changes across groups of template-spawned pages), but the Dynamic templates also let you designate certain regions of these pages as un-editable—thereby protecting parts of your site from careless colleagues. Also, unlike shared borders, you can have as many Dynamic Web Templates as you want within one site, which lets you give separate sections their own look and page features.

Note: If your development environment (page 176) is a Web server loaded with FrontPage Sever Extensions 2002, the Dynamic Web Template update process won't work correctly. The "Dynamic Web Templates Won't Work" box on page 219 tells you how to get around this compatibility problem.

Creating a Dynamic Web Template

You start a Dynamic Web Template by adding elements like you would to any other page.

1. **Create the page.**

   The first step is to set the page structure, then create and fill the regions that you want to remain fixed when pages are generated from the template. Create this page just as you would any other page. The best way to manage areas in a Dynamic Web Template is to lay out the page using tables (page 81). This setup helps a lot later on, when it comes time to set editable regions.

2. **Save the page as a template.**

   When you've finished designing your template, select File → Save As. Save the file anywhere in your site. (If you're going to have multiple template files, you may want to create a folder named "templates" for easy access.) In the "Save as type" drop-down list at the bottom of the dialog box, select Dynamic Web Template (*.dwt). Name the file and click OK.

3. Set editable regions.

At the outset, no part of a Dynamic Web Template is editable. You've got to tell FrontPage which areas you want people to be able to edit. For instance, select a table cell or paragraph(s). (For precision, try using the Quick Tag toolbar to select a cell <td> or paragraph <p> tag.) Next, within the document window, right-click the element you selected and select Manage Editable Regions. Type in a name for the region and click Add. (If Add is grayed out, you haven't selected a valid element. For instance, FrontPage won't make multiple cells editable at once. You'll need to select each cell separately.)

Note: The doctitle editable region—which lets you edit your page's title—appears automatically within the Manage Editable Regions dialog box. FrontPage includes doctitle here so an author creating pages from the template isn't blocked from changing the page title.

If you really want to keep the people who use this template on a tight leash, just click inside an existing paragraph and create an editable region. FrontPage then lets an author add some text to that particular spot, but he can't insert a return. FrontPage surrounds editable regions with an orange border (see Figure 11-15).

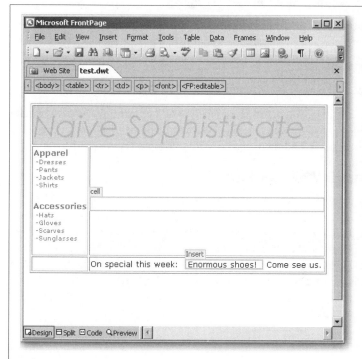

Figure 11-15:
FrontPage indicates editable regions by surrounding them with an orange box and adding a label just above and to the left of the box. This Dynamic Web Template has two editable regions. The first, called Cell, looks small but applies to the entire table cell in which the word "cell" resides. If you created a page from this template, you could type anywhere within the box containing the word "cell" and put anything you want (text, pictures, and even a table) into the cell.

The second editable region, called Insert, limits your page user's editing options. On a page created from this template, FrontPage only allows text to be typed in the box that currently includes the text "Enormous shoes!" FrontPage won't even let the user of this page insert a paragraph return in this spot.

Tip: If you're chomping at the bit to edit your template and don't want to go through all the steps of saving the document as a Dynamic Web Template first, you can use a shortcut. If you create a new page, add some content, and then add an editable region, FrontPage catches on and gives the page a temporary status as a Dynamic Web Template and a name like *new_page_1.dwt.* When you do finally save the template, you should give it a more descriptive name, of course.

Creating Pages from a Dynamic Web Template

The easiest place to create a new page using a Dynamic Web Template is in the folder list. To do so, right-click the template in the folder list and select "New from Dynamic Web Template."

Attaching pages to a template

Another way to generate a new page based on a Dynamic Web Template is to create a new blank page and attach it to the template. You can even attach existing pages that already contain content. (Doing so with complex pages can be dicey, because FrontPage takes content on the page and crams it into the template's editable regions.)

1. **Select or create the page that will use the template.**

   Open an existing page or blank Web page. If you want to attach the template to many pages at once, select them in the folder list.

2. **Attach the template.**

   Select Format → Dynamic Web Template → Attach Dynamic Web Template.

   If you have existing content on the page, FrontPage prompts you to specify which editable region should contain the content. If the program displays the wrong region, select it, and then click Modify to choose the correct region.

Editing a Dynamic Web Template

You can edit a Dynamic Web template at any time. Just open the template (as you'd open any other file in FrontPage) and make whatever changes you want. When you save the template, FrontPage prompts you to update all attached pages. Click Yes. If you click No, but find that you do need to update each page later, you can go back and select Format → Dynamic Web Template → Update Attached Pages at any time. If it's a single page you want to update, select it in the folder list (or open each one) and select Format → Dynamic Web Template → Update Selected Page.

TROUBLESHOOTING MOMENT

Dynamic Web Templates Won't Work

Dynamic Web Templates work fine in a disk-based site or if you're working on a server with Windows SharePoint Services. However, if your development site is on a server running FrontPage Server Extensions 2002, you may run into trouble, since Dynamic Web Templates came along *after* FPSE 2002. (Flip back to page 176 if you need a refresher on these development environments.)

If you find that your pages aren't showing changes you've made to the template, you can try a workaround. First, publish your site to a disk-based location. (To do so, select File → Publish Site, choose File System and enter the local computer path, such as *C:\My Documents\My Webs\copy\mysite*. See Chapter 13 for detailed instructions on how to publish a site.) Once you've done that, close your server-based site and then open your new disk-based site in FrontPage. Open your template and click Format → Dynamic Web Template → Update Attached Pages. All pages attached to the template should update. After that, publish the site back up to the server. (Do so with your disk-based site open in FrontPage. Select File → Publish Site, but this time, select the first option, "FrontPage-based site," as your remote Web site. Again, check out Chapter 13 for full publishing details.).

Detaching a Dynamic Web Template

Oops! You made a mistake and attached the wrong page to your Dynamic Web Template. No problem—you can call off the marriage. With the page open in the document window, select Format → Detach Dynamic Web Template. FrontPage severs the page's relationship with the template, rendering the entire page editable. However, the formatting of the page stays. If your goal was to change the look, you'll now have to edit the page.

Testing Your Site

Lots of companies dedicate entire departments to quality control. For instance, when you buy a new pair of boxer shorts, you have to peel off that sticker that says "Inspected by Number 5." That way, if there's a problem with the product, everyone knows who to blame. OK, you won't have a sticker like that on your Web site. But you still want to do everything in your power to ensure that your pages look great, and that all your links work correctly and lead to the right destinations. You also want to double-check that any interactive features, like animations or forms (which you'll read about in Chapter 15), are all working without a hitch—and doing so in the wide variety of browsers that your visitors are sure to be using.

Ensuring you've got a no-kinks site boils down to this: test your pages frequently as you create them, so you can catch problems before you bury them deep within your HTML. You should also test your pages after you publish your site (Chapter 13) to make sure your site works in its new environment, too.

This chapter covers the fundamentals of testing and proofing. The good news is that you're not alone in this endeavor. FrontPage can help you out. The program offers a variety of special tools to help you check for and correct errors on your pages. You can also get help preparing for all the different types of browsers that you expect to visit your site. In addition, you'll learn about FrontPage reports, which are great for tracking problems and getting the big picture of what's going on with your site.

Making a Good Impression

Nothing shouts "amateur" like a page filled with misspelled words or missing pictures. How can you avoid such mortifying embarrassments? For starters, do yourself a big favor and examine your pages carefully. But even then, you still might miss a few problems. That's where FrontPage's spell checker comes in handy. But that's not your only shield against typos and blunders. When it comes time to correct a site-wide error (you've been spelling the boss's name how?), nothing beats the program's Find and Replace tool, which helps you catch and fix errors all in one step.

Basic Proofreading

As you'll see, FrontPage offers lots of tools to help you present a polished, professional site. But, your best tools are your own two eyes (or, even better, enlisting someone else as a dedicated proofreader). Read each page carefully as you create it. Test all your pages in a browser to make sure everything works correctly (you'll learn how to do that on page 234). Does everything look the way it should? Confirm that the page has the right color scheme and that pictures appear where they're supposed to.

Checking Spelling

If your eyes tend to fail you now and then, you can lean on FrontPage. Even a crack proofreader might miss an error or two. In any case, FrontPage can help you check your spelling.

Checking spelling automatically as you type

You may already have noticed that as you type, FrontPage underlines misspelled words with a red squiggly line. This is your first line of defense. As soon as you see the line, ask yourself "Is it me? Or is it FrontPage?" FrontPage doesn't recognize a lot of words—like your unusual last name, or other items that don't show up in its dictionary. On the other hand, if you see the word "galoses" where you meant to type "galoshes," go back and fix it by right-clicking the word to make a speedy correction (see Figure 12-1).

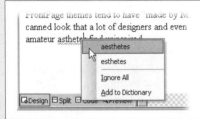

Figure 12-1:
Right-click a misspelled word to display this menu. Select a correction from the list, or add it to the dictionary so FrontPage never objects to the word again. FrontPage saves dictionary entries on your own PC only. A colleague editing the site from a different machine won't have your dictionary entries.

If those squiggly lines annoy and distract you, you can turn this feature off. Select Tools → Page Options and click the General tab. Then turn off the "Check Spelling As You Type" checkbox. But actually, there's a sneakier way. If you leave that checkbox on, and then also turn *on* the checkbox underneath it, "Hide Spelling Errors in All Documents," FrontPage stops pestering you with squiggly lines, but the program continues to tally up your errors. This can help later on, if you decide to run FrontPage's spell checker yourself. FrontPage will already have all the information, and you won't need to wait for the program to run a full check.

Manually running FrontPage's spell checker

Maybe you don't mind a few spelling errors while you're composing your pages; you prefer to leave proofreading until you're ready to publish. If so, it's easy to run the spell checker yourself. FrontPage tosses up a dialog box for each misspelled word, forcing you to correct or actively ignore it.

Just follow these steps:

1. **Open the page you want to check.**

Tip: If you want to check only one word or a paragraph, you can start by selecting the suspect text.

---

2. **Unleash the spell-checking hounds.**

   To trigger the spelling command, select Tools → Spelling, or click the Spelling button on the toolbar, or press F7. FrontPage displays a prompt asking if you want to check selected pages or the entire Web site. Make your pick and click Start.

   The Spelling dialog box displays, showing the first word it's found that's not in the program's dictionary (see Figure 12-2).

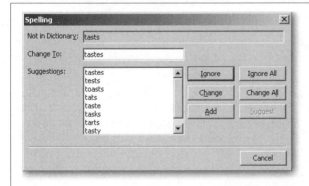

Figure 12-2:
The Spelling dialog box lists likely alternatives for your misspelled word. If you know you misspelled the word more than once on your page, click Change All, and FrontPage corrects all instances at once.

3. **If the "Change to" field is correct, click Change.**

   FrontPage shows a list of suggestions, with the most likely candidate already in the "Change to" field. If you want to replace the mistake with a word from the Suggestions box, double-click it, or select it and click Change. If FrontPage gets all its suggestions wrong, but you still want to change the word, you can type your own correction by just typing right in the "Change to" field.

4. **If the word is correct, tell FrontPage to ignore it.**

You can tell FrontPage to ignore a word in one of three ways:

- Click **Ignore** and FrontPage doesn't change the word, but will flag it again the next time it sees it spelled that way.

- Click **Ignore All** and the program ignores all instances of the word throughout the rest of the page.

- Click **Add** to add the word to FrontPage's dictionary. If you do so, the program will never flag the word again. You may want to add items like company or staff names to the dictionary, so they don't keep popping up.

5. **End the spell check.**

When the spell check finishes, FrontPage alerts you with a small prompt letting you know you've completed the check. Click OK.

Checking spelling on multiple pages

You can also check spelling on many pages at once—even across your entire site. To do so:

1. **Select the pages you want to check.**

Within the folder list, select multiple pages or highlight the folder that holds your entire site.

2. **Check spelling.**

To trigger the spelling command, select Tools → Spelling, or click the Spelling button on the toolbar, or press F7. FrontPage displays a prompt asking if you want to check selected pages or the entire Web site. Select your preference and click Start.

The dialog box then displays a list of pages that contain misspellings (see Figure 12-3).

Note: Attention procrastinators! If you turn on the "Add a task for each page with misspellings" checkbox and click Start, FrontPage ends the spell check and creates a task for each page's spell check (see Chapter 14, page 274, for more on tasks). Later, you can double-click one of these tasks to re-initiate the spell check and pick up where you left off.

---

3. **Make corrections.**

If you double-click the first page in the list, FrontPage opens it in Design view, so you can correct spelling errors (pop back to steps 2 and 3 in the preceding section for instructions).

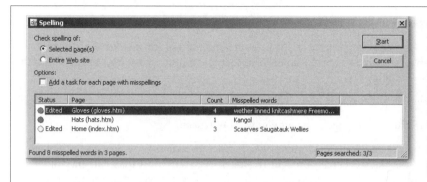

Figure 12-3:
FrontPage shows you the number of errors it found on each page in the Count column and lists misspellings in one continuous line to the right. Once you make some corrections, the Status column on the far left tells you which pages you've already edited.

Note: Most of the time, you'll want to begin with the first page in the list. This way, FrontPage leads you in order through each page's corrections. If you start in the middle, the program won't include the pages that precede your starting point in the list. However, the Spelling dialog box always shows you which pages you've edited and which you haven't (see Figure 12-3), so you can initiate another correction session to tackle the rest of the list.

Once you've corrected all misspellings on one page, FrontPage displays a "Continue with Next Page?" dialog box. To move on and make corrections on the next page, click Next Page. You can continue like this through all the pages that feature errors. If you want to return to the Spelling dialog box (in Figure 12-3) instead, click Back to List. Once you've made all your corrections, click Back to List (your only option).

4. **Click Cancel to close the Spelling dialog box.**

Note: FrontPage's spell check scours your pages for errors, but the tool doesn't examine elements like page titles and comments. While only other developers will see an error in a comment, page titles display in a browser's title bar for all the world to see, so make sure you check for errors on your own.

Find and Replace

Imagine that you've spent many weeks creating a series of Web pages about your new product, which is called the *Amazing Doohickey*. At the last minute, the bigwigs at corporate HQ order you to change the name to the *Marvelous Thingamabob*. Meanwhile, the old name already appears throughout your site. It's in included content snippets, in regular page text, and…well, you don't even remember all the places it pops up—there are so many. How are you going to find all the instances and correct them?

Easy—you're not. FrontPage is going to find and replace them all for you.

Find and replace does just what it sounds like. It takes one word or chunk of text (like *doohickey*) and replaces it with another (*thingamabob*). This feature is great for correcting mistakes, making site-wide edits to specific terms, and even sometimes just locating a snippet of text that you may be looking for.

Finding text

The first step in the process, is of course, searching for instances of the text you want to replace. You can also use this feature to hunt down a word or phrase that you're looking for.

To locate text:

1. **Decide which page or pages you want to search.**

    If you just want to search one page, place your cursor at the top of the page. If you'd like to search your entire site, select your site's folder in the folder list. You can also search through a collection of pages by selecting them in the folder list (press the Ctrl key as you select each page to highlight a group of pages).

2. **Initiate the search.**

    Select Edit → Find, click the Find button on the Standard toolbar, or press Ctrl+F. The Find and Replace dialog box opens (see Figure 12-4).

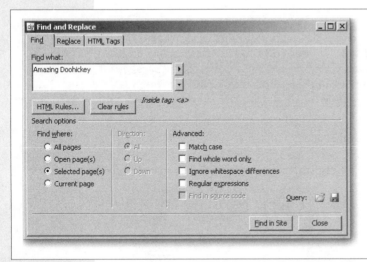

Figure 12-4:
The Find and Replace dialog box features three tabs. Use the Find tab if you just want to track down a particular word or phrase. Use the Replace tab to find and replace text. If you want to find or replace HTML tags, click the HTML tags tab.

3. **Tell FrontPage what you're searching for.**

    In the "Find what" field, enter the text you want FrontPage to locate.

4. **Set your search parameters (optional).**

    If you need to, you can create a very specific search that includes information about *where* an item appears within your HTML code. Say you want to find a word or phrase, but only where it occurs within a hyperlink. To set this parameter, click HTML Rules. (HTML Rules tells FrontPage exactly where or where not to look.) In the dialog box that opens, click "New rule" in the main box. In the drop-down list on the bottom left, select "Inside tag" (because you want to find the word only where it appears *inside* a hyperlink tag). In the drop-down list that appears just to the right, select the <a> hyperlink tag, and then click OK.

You could also do the opposite. Say you want to find some text, but in any place *except* where it appears in a hyperlink. Just follow the steps above and select "Not inside tag" instead of "Inside tag." FrontPage then ignores all instances of the text wherever it's part of a hyperlink.

You can narrow your search even further, if you want. Once you've selected a tag within the HTML Rules dialog box, FrontPage displays some additional choices in the New rules drop-down list on the lower-left corner of the dialog box. You can specify whether or not the tag you're searching within (or excluding, depending on your first choice in this dialog box) has special attributes (for example, the destination of a hyperlink or a style you attached to a tag). You can even tell FrontPage which attribute it should have (see Figure 12-5). You can also specify whether or not a tag contains some other text or an element like an <img> image.

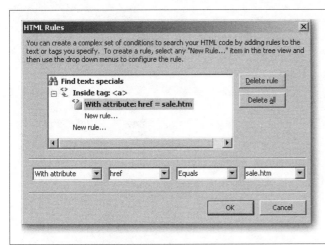

Figure 12-5:
You can customize rules to search for instances of text inside a tag and even specify tag attributes. For example, the rules attached to the search shown here require that FrontPage find the word "specials" only where it occurs inside a hyperlink <a> tag and only when that link leads to the sales.htm page (attribute href). To add another attribute rule here, you'd click the "New rule" entry indented beneath the tag. If you want to add another tag, click the "New Rule" entry at the bottom.

5. **Choose additional settings (optional).**

Once you return to the Find and Replace dialog box (see Figure 12-4), you can use some checkboxes to help you modify your search:

- **Match case** creates a case-sensitive search. In other words, if you turn this on, a search for "Caboose" wouldn't find "caboose," because the latter doesn't start with a capital letter.

- **Find whole word only** returns the text where it's surrounded by spaces. For example, a search for "are" would return the word "are" but not "aren't" or "tartare."

- **Ignore whitespace differences** treats all spaces as one. So, the search would find instances of a string of words with any number of spaces—1, 3, or 10—between them. For example, a search for "enormous herring" would return both "enormous   herring" and "enormous   herring."

POWER USERS' CLINIC

Finding a Pattern

Say your boss doesn't like the way you've entered telephone numbers. You've included them in this format: 800-555-1212. But your boss prefers phone numbers to be written like this: (800) 555-1212. You'd like to do a search to find all the phone numbers, but they're made up of all different numbers. How can you find them all?

FrontPage 2003 has a new search feature that saves the day. You can search for a *pattern* of text. In the situation above, you'd search for chunks of text that fall in the pattern: xxx-xxx-xxxx. The actual content of the text *string* (the collection of characters) doesn't matter. Instead FrontPage searches that particular 10-digits-broken-up-by-two-dashes format.

But if you want, you can also specify some specific characters. Say you want to find a certain kind of word. For instance, a co-worker has been including contractions in her prose, which isn't the formal tone your boss prefers. You can search for any word that includes an apostrophe. When you search for a pattern like this, you're using what mathematicians call a *regular expression.*

To conduct such a search, select Edit → Find and turn on the "Regular expressions" checkbox. Next, enter your search parameters in the "Find what" field. You'll do this using a special combination of characters. Here are some of your building blocks:

- A period stands for "any character." So, to find a phone number pattern, you could enter: ...-...-.... to find instances of telephone numbers.

- An asterisk means that the character that precedes it ("i" in the example that follows) can appear any number of times—even zero. Search for "tri*p" and you'd find "trip," "triiip," or even "trp."

- A + stands for one or more of the character that directly precedes it. So a search for "ha+t" would bring "hat," or "haaaaa,t" but not "ht" or "hart."

- A backslash tells FrontPage that the character following the backslash should be exactly that character. For example, entering "poo\c\h" would return only "pooch." Of course, you can achieve the same effect by just searching for the word "pooch," so why bother? Well, what if you wanted to search your site for a +? In the Find dialog box, FrontPage treats a + as part of a regular expression. You can use the backslash to say to FrontPage "Hey, I'm really looking for an actual plus sign." Do so by entering "\+" in the "Find what" box.

- Square brackets can find any one of the characters you put between them. If you enter "p[oiu]t, FrontPage would return "pot," "pit," or "put," but not "pat" or "pet."

If you want to learn even more expressions, check out FrontPage's Help file (select Help → Microsoft Office FrontPage Help or press F1) and type "Regular expressions" in the search box.

Once you've entered your expression, set the scope of your search in the "Find where" section and click Find Next (or Find in Site). FrontPage returns all results.

- To learn about the **Regular expressions** option, see the box "Finding a Pattern."

- **Find in source code** looks through regular page text and HTML code, too.

6. **Find.**

Click Find Next or Find in Site to spur FrontPage into action.

Find and Replace HTML

Say you get a new boss, who's an absolute HTML purist. She wants you to get rid of all <font> tags in your Web site. The staff will be using straight CSS from now on. No problem. You can do a find and replace operation within your site's HTML code just like you can in your site's regular content.

Open the Find and Replace dialog box (by pressing Ctrl+H, or using any of the methods you learned in the previous section). Click the HTML tags tab. In the Find tag drop-down list, select the tag you want to find. In the Replace Action drop-down list, choose from the following options:

- **Replace tag and contents** replaces the tag and anything the tag contains (even other tags and their contents).

- **Replace content only** replaces all text that the tag encloses.

The next four options do just what each one says:

- **Add before (after) start (end) tag** lets you slip in some content just in front of or behind a start or ending tag.

- **Remove tag and contents** deletes a tag and everything it contains.

- **Remove tag** deletes only the tag. Contents remain.

- **Change tag** lets you change one tag into a different tag. For instance, change all your <i> italics into <b> bold format.

- **Set attribute value** adds or replaces a tag's attribute. For instance, <table> could become <table width="50%">

- **Remove attribute** strips the tag's attribute out. You could use this setting to remove the background color of table cells (<td> tag), or change the alignment of <h1> (Heading 1) paragraphs, for instance.

You might not always want to find a tag. Maybe you're looking for some other passage of HTML code—like a phrase that appears in an HTML comment, for instance. If so, open the page in Code view and do a find and replace just as you would in Design view.

So, armed with all this information, you can easily get rid of those font tags mentioned earlier. To do so, open the Find and Replace dialog box and click the HTML tag tab. Click the "Find tag" drop-down list and select Font. Then within the "Replace action" drop-down list, select "Remove tag" and click Replace All. FrontPage strips all the font tags out of your pages, leaving a lot of text unformatted. Now you can go ahead and apply CSS styles to jazz up your site efficiently. (Flip back to Chapter 7 to learn about using CSS.)

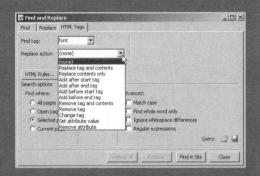

If you're searching within one page, the program highlights the first instance it finds. Click Find Next to move to the next match. Then repeat that sequence for the entire page. FrontPage tells you when it can't find anymore occurrences.

If you're searching many pages or an entire site, FrontPage lists (within the Find dialog box) search results grouped according to each page. Double-click a page to open it and see each instance that's been found.

Replacing text

If you want to replace text that you've found with some other text, you can start by selecting Edit → Replace or pressing Ctrl+H. Or, if you've already set up your search, you can also just click the Replace tab within the Find and Replace dialog box. The only new field that appears in the Replace tab is the "Replace with" field. Here you'll enter the text that should take the place of the text you asked FrontPage to find. To proceed from there, the dialog box offers the following options:

- If you want to make all the changes in a snap, click Replace All. FrontPage finds every instance of the term you searched for and replaces it with the text you entered in the "Replace with" field.

- If you'd rather make changes on a case-by-case basis, click Find Next. FrontPage takes you to the first instance. If you click Replace, the program makes the change. If you don't want to edit a particular instance of the search term, just click Find Next again to move on to the next instance.

Validation

Think about the World Wide Web and everything that goes into the mix: You've got browsers—made by software developers. You've got Web pages—made by you (and millions of others). You've even got programs like FrontPage that turn button clicks into HTML pages. All these groups need to speak the same language— HTML.

You may think HTML, like French or Farsi, is an established language—and for the most part, it is, but just like any language, HTML isn't set in stone. Here's a simple example of what can happen—and why subtle changes can lead to problems. Suppose a company making browsers wants to introduce a new feature that lets text scroll across the screen. The company's developers tweak their browser to recognize a new HTML tag they created called <marquee> that generates this effect. Millions of Web page designers, grateful for the chance to scroll text across their pages, include the <marquee> tag on the pages they create. Super!

Or maybe not. The problem is, if none of the other browser-making companies know about or—more to the point—support the <marquee> tag, then anyone using one of these non–marquee-supporting browsers won't see the scrolling text.

What's needed is a higher authority to say either: "Yes. Everyone wants scrolling text! All browsers should recognize the <marquee> tag." or "No. That tag clutters up HTML unnecessarily. Use JavaScript instead."

Enter the World Wide Web Consortium (W3C). As the Internet has grown, the W3C has set standards for HTML syntax and best practices. (See *www.w3c.org* for lots of information about their mission and about Web design in general.) The W3C sets these standards to ensure that browsers and Web pages can interact. The W3C not only determines what constitutes proper HTML, but also what other standards, like CSS or scripting languages, will be encouraged to flourish. Through agreed upon standards, developers create browsers that can read all the approved tags and scripts, and you can be assured that any browser can handle your Web pages.

Still, not everyone agrees on every issue. Remember the <marquee> tag story? Well, it's a true story of one initiative that Microsoft took with Internet Explorer. It was never approved by the W3C. As a result, <marquee> works only in Microsoft's Web programs: Internet Explorer and FrontPage. Netscape has also created tags that were never approved and work only with their browser. These kinds of dialect skirmishes happen all the time, for reasons ranging from innovative developers to monopolistic urges, but the good news is that most major browser developers recognize the need for agreed upon standards and generally defer to the W3C.

Validating Pages

To help folks meet the standards they set, the good people at the W3C provide a way for you to check the quality of your HTML code. Making sure that code meets the standard is called *validation*.

It's easy to validate a page. Just hop online and visit *http://validator.w3c.org/*. You can enter a URL or upload a page for validation. The W3C site then spits a report back at you telling you whether or not your code is "well-formed." If the validator finds errors, the report lists every instance, so you can make corrections.

Should You Validate?

The world won't fall apart if you don't validate your pages. As long as you test your pages in a variety of browsers, you can be sure they're working correctly. Also, if you've used FrontPage-specific Web features (like themes, shared borders, link bars, and so on), your page won't validate, so don't bother. (However, you can ignore those errors and use the validator to check the rest of your page.) The only FrontPage authors who sometimes truly need to validate their Web pages are those trying to meet accessibility guidelines (see "Accessibility" below). If this is you, your boss might tell you that you're required by law to validate all your pages, to ensure accessibility.

Accessibility

When developers talk about making sites accessible, they're referring to the laudable goal of designing pages so that disabled visitors can explore a site. For example, many blind people use a screen reader (which translates the text into a synthesized computer voice) or a Braille display program. These devices depend on site designers who take the time to label their graphics with alternative text tags (page 66).

FrontPage and DOCTYPE

I tried to validate my Web page and got the error "no document type." What does this mean?

The truth is that no Web page produced by FrontPage passes the well-formed HTML test. For starters, FrontPage never begins a page with a DOCTYPE declaration, so the validator immediately shoots out a "NO DOCTYPE FOUND!" message (complete with the alarmist capital letters). DOCTYPE is short for document type. This snippet of code tells the browser what version of HTML the page is written in. (The most recent HTML version sanctioned by the W3C is HTML 4.01. Past versions are HTML 3.2 and HTML 2.0, which can't handle more recent Web technology like CSS.) This way, in interpreting a Web page's HTML, the browser sticks to the established standards for that version of HTML. The advantage is that all browsers know what those standards are and there won't be so many differences between the way they interpret and display your page. When a browser renders (displays) a page that has a DOCTYPE declaration (in what's called "standards mode"), it ignores invalid tags or attributes.

So how could Microsoft decide to neglect such an important item? Well, you actually don't *need* a DOCTYPE declaration. If it's missing, a browser displays the page in *quirks mode.* Anything goes in quirks mode. If a tag or attribute isn't official HTML, the browser takes a crack at it anyway and tries to display all the elements it sees in a particular page. As you can imagine, in quirks mode, the page can look pretty different in each browser.

So what should you do? First, keep in mind that you don't really need a DOCTYPE, and adding one out of the blue can cause more problems than it solves. Pages that FrontPage creates may not follow the strict guidelines of "standards mode." If you insert a DOCTYPE declaration, then the browser expects your code to be in line with the version of HTML that you've specified. In other words, the browser won't display elements that aren't sanctioned. However, if

you decide that you want to bring your HTML in line with strict W3C standards, you can add one. But which version of HTML should you tell the world you're using? To choose the correct DOCTYPE, visit W3C.org and read up on all your options. In most cases, you can probably use the following common declaration:

```
<!DOCTYPE HTML PUBLIC "-//W3C//DTD HTML 4.
01 Transitional//EN"
    "http://www.w3.org/TR/html4/loose.dtd">
```

That last line refers the browser to the DTD (document type definition) file that contains the standards. A DTD lists the legal elements that define document structure and syntax. There are different DTDs for framed pages. You can also choose from DTDs that enforce stricter adherence to the HTML version's standard. Read about the different types of DTDs on the W3C Web site (*www.w3schools.com/tags/tag_doctype.asp*).

Use Find and Replace (see page 225) to add the declaration to existing pages. You add a DOCTYPE declaration at the very beginning of the page—before the first <HTML> tag. Make sure you include that last line with the URL. A DOCTYPE declaration must reference a DTD file. Without it, a browser reverts to quirks mode.

To automatically add the declaration to any of your future pages, create a FrontPage template (page 214) or Dynamic Web Template (page 216), add the declaration to it, and then use the template to create new Web pages.

Even if you decide you don't want to add a DOCTYPE, you can still validate your pages to look for other errors. FrontPage also helps you check pages with its accessibility checker (see the next section). But if you're legally required to make your pages accessible, you probably need to add DOCTYPE declarations to all your pages.

FrontPage may not help you much when it comes to validation, but it does try to help you comply with accessibility standards. This is important, since many companies and organizations are legally bound to make their sites accessible. To help you—and your visitors—out, FrontPage comes with an accessibility checker. To use it, select Tools → Accessibility.

The accessibility checker analyzes your site and displays a report containing errors it finds. To run a report:

1. **Decide which pages you want to perform an accessibility check on.**

   If you want to check just a few pages, start by selecting them in the folder list, then select Tools → Accessibility. Within the "Check where" section, tell FrontPage which pages you want to check. Most often, you'll want to check your entire site, of course.

Tip: If your site has pages with included content (see page 206), you may want to check included pages first and then check the rest of your site. The reason? When the accessibility checker examines a page with included content, it doesn't check the include page.

---

2. **Select an accessibility standard for FrontPage to measure against.**

   Within the "Check for" section, FrontPage gives you three options. You can select them all, if you want:

   - **WCAG Priority 1** includes the basic Web Content Accessibility Guidelines (WCAG) set forth by the W3C. Priority 1 guidelines are the most basic. If your page doesn't meet them, a disabled visitor will be unable to use the page at all, and your site will be inaccessible to him.

   - **WCAG Priority 2** is a less stringent level of guidelines. If a page doesn't rise to this level, a disabled visitor would have a difficult time using the Web page. You should try to meet these guidelines, too. The more accessible your site is, the larger the number of people who can enjoy it.

   - **Access Board Section 508** is for sites published under the aegis of the U.S. Federal Government. Section 508 of the Rehabilitation Act requires that any technology used by the Federal government comply with the standards set by the Access Board. You'll need to check this box if you're designing a site for the Feds.

3. **Tell FrontPage what feedback you want.**

   In the Show section, select one or all of the following:

   - **Errors** reports situations in your Web site that definitely fall short of the standards you selected in step 2.

   - **Warnings** reports situations in your Web site that might possibly fall short of the standards you selected in step 2.

• **Manual Checklist** lists items that you need to review (FrontPage can't check all issues automatically). These can range from general accessibility guidelines for making your pages accessible (like "Provide sufficient contrast for low vision users") to specific items you should check on each page.

4. **Check accessibility.**

Once you've made all your settings, click Check. Results appear within the Accessibility dialog box (see Figure 12-6).

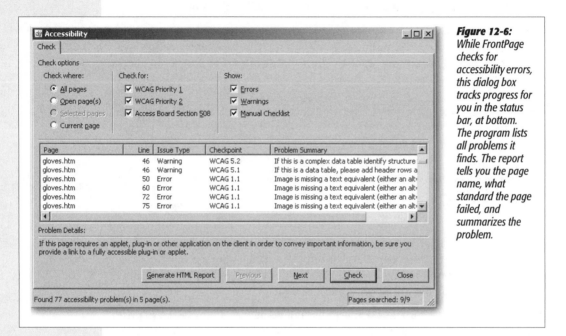

Figure 12-6:
While FrontPage checks for accessibility errors, this dialog box tracks progress for you in the status bar, at bottom. The program lists all problems it finds. The report tells you the page name, what standard the page failed, and summarizes the problem.

5. **Make changes.**

Double-click an entry to go to the page where the problem's been flagged. FrontPage opens the page in Split view and highlights the code in question. Edit or remove elements as you wish (you can add alternative text to a graphic, for instance). You can also proceed in order through the list. Double-click the first entry. Then click Next to address each item down the list. Click the Previous button to go back an entry.

Tip: If you want to generate a paper checklist from this report, click Generate HTML Report. You can print the resulting HTML page or open it in a browser and check off issues as you resolve them.

Testing with Different Browsers

After reading the tale of the <marquee> tag (page 230), you probably understand why different browsers display your pages in slightly (and sometimes not-so-slightly) different ways. As you've read, a lot of effects that FrontPage creates show up only in Microsoft's Internet Explorer. And it's not only browser variations that can throw cold water on your best design intentions. How your visitors have set the resolution on their monitors can also change your page's look. *Resolution* is the number of pixels (dots of color) that make up a computer screen. For example, an 800×600 pixel screen displays 800 dots across each of its 600 horizontal lines. Different settings can make a Web page expand beyond the sides of a browser window (forcing viewers to scroll) or the page can end up scrunched on the left side, leaving a big empty space on the right.

The best way to prepare your pages for the wide variety of browsers in which they're inevitably going to appear is to preview your pages in each one, as you're creating your site. By using a "check as you go" approach, you'll be able to make fixes as you develop your site.

Since not everyone has fleets of computers at their disposal (to help realistically mimic all the conditions your pages are going to encounter), FrontPage helps you out with a variety of testing tools, which are covered in the following pages.

Preview in Browser

From within FrontPage, you can launch any browser that's loaded on your PC so that you can see what your Web pages will look like in each of these browsers. To use this tool, select File → Preview in Browser and pick the browser you want. Or you can click the arrow to the right of the Preview in Browser button on the Standard toolbar (Figure 12-7). (When you install FrontPage, the program automatically adds any browsers it finds on your system to this list. If you install a browser later, you'll need to add it yourself, which you'll learn how to do in a moment.)

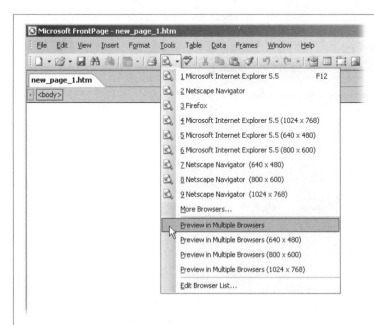

Figure 12-7:
The Preview in Browser menu features all the browsers loaded on your system. FrontPage gives you screen resolution choices for each browser it added during installation. If you don't see a resolution you want for a particular browser, select "More browsers" and choose the browser from the list that appears. If you select Preview in Multiple Browsers, FrontPage opens the page in all the browsers on your PC.

Preview in Browser also lets you pick from three different screen resolutions to use when previewing your page: 640×480, 800×600, and 1024×768. A page that works on your 1024×768 screen may not work on a monitor set to 640×480 (see Figure 12-8). This enhanced preview capability means you don't need to change the settings on your computer or get access to a different monitor each time you want to replicate real-world browsing conditions.

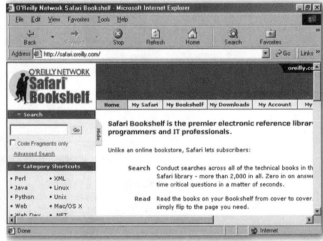

Figure 12-8:
This Web page clearly works best in a 1024×768 pixel monitor (top). If you came along with a 640×480 pixel resolution and opened the page (bottom), you'd see only a portion of it. Most Web authors create pages for an 800×600 pixel screen. However, as hardware technology advances and Web surfers splurge on increasingly larger monitors, pages targeting1024×768 pixel displays are more and more common.

Adding a browser

To add a new browser to the list, first install it on your computer. Then select Edit Browser List from the Preview in Browser menu. Click Add and then browse to the file that launches the program (like *firefox.exe*, for example).

Setting Authoring Options

Imagine that you're creating a site that provides emotional support to those who can't bring themselves to update their software. So you know from the start that your site's likely visitors are people who have very old browsers. How can you keep yourself from inadvertently including recent Web advancements like rollover buttons?

FrontPage can help you save yourself from yourself. The program lets you limit your own actions, by making certain features off-limits to you. The only real reason to limit your options here is if you know your visitors' browsers are all very old or only Netscape, for instance. You can set these restrictions in FrontPage's Authoring tab. To check it out, select Tools → Page Options and click the Authoring tab (see Figure 12-9).

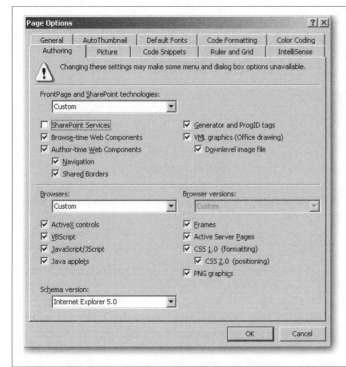

Figure 12-9:
If you turn off a checkbox here in FrontPage's Authoring tab, the program grays out the menu choices you've selected, limiting which features you can add to your pages.

Microsoft software-related authoring settings

The top half of the Authoring tab includes options for excluding or allowing features that rely upon Microsoft server software that you may or may not have available to you. If you want to avoid using Microsoft proprietary features, you'll want to take a close look at these options (details on most of them are covered in Chapter 13).

Browser settings

The bottom half of the Authoring tab lets you set target browser options, which is how you tell FrontPage what browsers you expect your visitors to be using. You probably wouldn't want to, but conceivably, you could do something like limit yourself to designing pages that work in the elderly Internet Explorer 3.0. Once you tell FrontPage that this is your model browser, the program helps you design a site for that environment. For instance, if you insert an interactive button, the program adds the button to the page, but leaves off the special rollover effects.

Note: If you impose restrictions here, FrontPage won't let you add certain features in Design view. However, if you were to go to Code view and enter some HTML code for a restricted element, the program wouldn't stop you. Nor do the rules you set here cover pages you import into the site.

Your options in the Browser section include:

- **Browsers.** This list of browsers is short and, unfortunately, you can't add any. You won't find Safari, Opera, or Mozilla here. All you get are variations on Internet Explorer and Netscape. You can select one or both. But, actually, your best bet here is to choose Custom. Then you're free to activate or exclude the feature checkboxes listed below the Browser pull-down menu. More on these options in a moment.

- **Browser versions.** Select the latest version of the browser(s) for which you want to design. Again, unless you have a very specific audience, select Custom. Custom gives you added flexibility in the choices that follow.

Note: If FrontPage has grayed out any feature checkboxes here, it's because the option that's active in the FrontPage technologies drop-down list, at the top of the Authoring tab, requires them (like Active X controls and JavaScript). Also, you can turn on the CSS 2.0 checkbox only if the CSS 1.0 checkbox is on.

- **Active X controls** are small program components (parts), which a browser can automatically download and run. Only Internet Explorer recognizes these controls. A lot of sites and computers block or limit these controls for security reasons. Unless you've designed your Web site to use an Active X control, you can turn off this checkbox. (If FrontPage has grayed out this box, it's because the SharePoint Services checkbox is turned on at the top of this dialog box. Many SharePoint site features require ActiveX controls, so FrontPage turns on this checkbox and then blocks your access to it.)

- **VBScript** (short for Visual Basic Scripting Edition) is a Microsoft programming language that can give commands to browsers. If you want to use a feature like the Database Interface Wizard (explained in Chapter 17), you'll need to turn on this checkbox. Only Internet Explorer supports VBScript.

- **JavaScript/Jscript.** Jscript is just Microsoft's version of JavaScript. If you turn off this checkbox, you won't be able to incorporate any JavaScript features (see Chapter 9). Leave this on unless you know for sure you don't want to include

JavaScript. (If FrontPage has grayed out this box, it's because the SharePoint Services checkbox is turned on at the top of this dialog box. Some SharePoint site features need JavaScript to work, so FrontPage turns on this checkbox and then blocks your access to it.)

- **Java applets.** The only reason to leave this on is if your site includes Java applets or you're still using FrontPage's Banner Ad Manager. Microsoft is phasing out Banner Ad Manager because Windows no longer includes the Java Virtual Machine, which is required to view Java Applets. (See the "Banner Ad Manager Is Gone" box in Chapter 11 on page 207.)

- **Frames.** If you turn off this checkbox, FrontPage grays out all menu options that help you create framed pages (see Chapter 6).

- **Active Server Pages** are Web pages that can interact with data. If you're working with data, you'd better turn this box on. Even if you never plan to work with data, you may as well leave this checkbox on to keep your options open. You never know how your site may grow.

- **CSS 1.0 (formatting).** Turning on this checkbox lets you add the Cascading Style Sheets and embedded styles that you read about in Chapter 7.

- **CSS 2.0 (positioning).** Only recent browsers can display CSS 2.0. This is the technology that enables you to create layers (Chapter 8). Unless you're sure that you have lots of older browsers out there, turn on this checkbox. If it's off, FrontPage grays out layer commands.

- **PNG graphics.** As you read in Chapter 4, PNG graphic files are the new gifs. Problem is—a lot of browsers out there didn't get the word yet. Turn off this checkbox, so you don't inadvertently include one in your site.

- **Schema version** controls which version of HTML FrontPage will churn out for you. Each version has its own syntax and rules. Choosing Internet Explorer 5.0 usually makes the most sense here.

Settings you make on the Authoring tab won't affect any pages you've *already* created. FrontPage imposes the new restrictions on new pages only. To find old pages that break the new rules, run a browser compatibility check (see the next section).

Browser settings: the bottom line

So what should you do? If you select Custom in the Browser drop-down menu and enable all the checkboxes underneath it (except Active X, Java Applets, and PNG graphics), you'll be able to use all the ingredients to satisfy both your creativity and most viewers who are using recent browsers. Unless you know most of your audience is using an old or very particular browser, you'll probably want to give yourself the freedom to include all these features. In other words, when in doubt, err on the side of inclusion. As always, preview your pages (often) and judge the effect for yourself.

Checking Browser Compatibility

Say you're creating a family reunion site and you know that all your cousins are avid Netscape Navigator fans. Of course, you'll want to preview all your pages in Netscape to see for yourself how things look. You have the latest version, so why not? But will things look the same to Aunt Minnie, who hasn't updated her computer (or browser) in a few years?

FrontPage's Browser Compatibility report runs through the code on your pages and spits out a list of features that won't work in certain browsers. It's especially useful when you're wondering how your pages will display in older browsers that you probably can't get a hold of anymore. The idea is, you can figure out who'll be able to see what.

Sounds like a real help, but in reality, the value of this report is limited. One problem is that FrontPage doesn't give you many browser choices. Also, the report doesn't actually test your pages in these browsers, it just compares your site's code with code that these browsers officially recognize. As a result, the report may show problems that aren't that serious and at the same time ignore issues that you might find important. For instance, running this check won't tell you that a table you've designed to be invisible actually shows up in all its boxy, ugly glory in Netscape. No, this report goes totally by the book. All it does is spit out tags and attributes that aren't part of a browser's repertoire. Again, there's no substitute for tracking down browsers and installing them on your system to test pages properly. A great resource for finding even older browsers is *http://browsers.evolt.org/*.

To run a compatibility report:

1. **Pick the page(s) you want to inspect.**

   If you just want to check a few pages, start by selecting them in the folder list (select multiple pages by holding down the Ctrl key). Then select Tools →
   Browser Compatibility. Within the "Check where" section, tell FrontPage which pages you want to check.

2. **Set the target browser.**

   Click Change and FrontPage opens the program's Authoring tab. Set your preferences for FrontPage browser types in the lower portion of the tab. (See the previous section for details on these settings.)

3. **Check compatibility.**

   Click Check. FrontPage displays a list of problems (see Figure 12-10). Don't get bogged down thinking that you need to address and correct every problem here. Most will be minor issues. Consider your site as a whole and use your best judgment. Whenever possible, open your pages in these browsers to look for yourself.

4. Make changes.

If you do want to make changes, you can double-click an entry to get to it. FrontPage opens the page in Split view and highlights the code in question. Edit or remove elements as you wish (delete a rollover effect from a button, for instance). You can also proceed in order through the list. Double-click the first entry. Then click Next to address each item down the list. Click the Previous button to go back an entry.

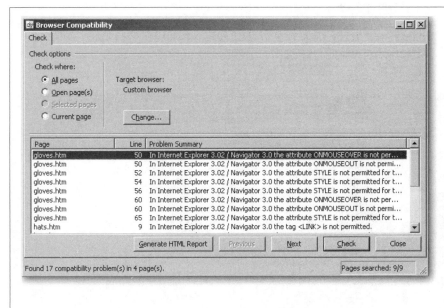

Figure 12-10:
This browser compatibility report lists problems that a collection of pages would encounter when viewed in an old version of Internet Explorer. The list shows the page and line the problem appears on. If you want, convert this list into a Web page by clicking Generate HTML report. FrontPage creates a Web page listing the problems organized by page. Checkboxes next to each issue let you track your corrections manually.

Optimizing HTML

In a bid to satisfy Web site developers who think FrontPage adds too much unnecessary code to Web pages, FrontPage 2003 features an HTML cleanup feature that lets you strip out extraneous HTML so your pages download faster. (Extraneous code is anything your page doesn't need to function in a browser. This can be something simple like a comment tag that developers use to communicate with each other, or the code FrontPage adds to administrate your pages using FrontPage Server Extensions.) To see the cleanup feature, select Tools → Optimize HTML.

FrontPage lets you optimize HTML when you're designing your site (meaning in your development environment) or when you publish your site to a live Web server. If you take the latter path, FrontPage cleans up only the HTML that resides on the server. Your development site stays as is.

There's no reason to optimize HTML at design time. If you do so, you could permanently disable even very basic features you've added and wreak havoc throughout your site. The only time you should even contemplate using the Optimize HTML feature is when you're ready to publish your site. Chapter 13 covers the ins and outs of optimizing.

FrontPage Reports: Monitoring a Site

Even if you test every page diligently, you still can't know everything about your site. Often, you'll want to get a bird's eye view of your Web project. For instance you may want to check the flow of your hyperlinks or see what kinds of files you've amassed over time. (You'd be amazed at how much dead wood—files that you no longer need—can collect in an aged site.)

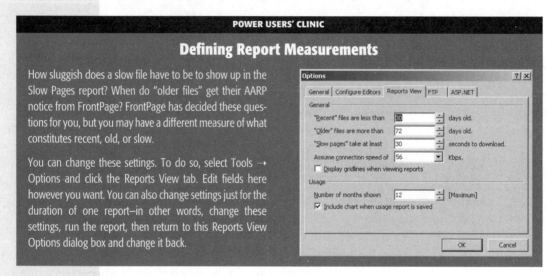

POWER USERS' CLINIC

Defining Report Measurements

How sluggish does a slow file have to be to show up in the Slow Pages report? When do "older files" get their AARP notice from FrontPage? FrontPage has decided these questions for you, but you may have a different measure of what constitutes recent, old, or slow.

You can change these settings. To do so, select Tools → Options and click the Reports View tab. Edit fields here however you want. You can also change settings just for the duration of one report—in other words, change these settings, run the report, then return to this Reports View Options dialog box and change it back.

FrontPage reports help you track work progress and potential problems across your site so you can keep on top of maintenance tasks. As you'll see, you can find and correct problems in a variety of ways.

Site Summary Report

See it all at a glance! Whenever you open a site in Reports view (click the Web Site tab and then at the bottom of the window, click Reports), you'll see the Site Summary report. This view shows you a wide range of information that'll help you keep your site ship shape, without forcing you to run a bunch of reports one by one (see Figure 12-11).

The Reports

You can get to most reports through the Site Summary report. To run other reports, you'll need to work from the Reports menu. To get to this menu, select

View → Reports, or click the shortcut drop-down menu on left side of the Reports toolbar. Both reveal the same menu choices.

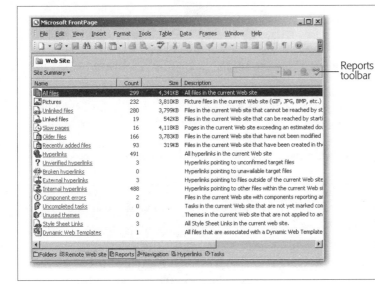

Reports toolbar

Figure 12-11:
The Site Summary report gives you a quick overview of your site. Any item that's underlined is linked to a more detailed report. With other items, what you see is what you get. Reports view has its own toolbar that appears just above the list, within the Web Site tab. The left side has a shortcut drop-down menu to other reports (like Unlinked Files and Hyperlinks)—just click Site Summary to reveal the menu. The right side of the toolbar contains shortcuts to report commands like Edit Hyperlink and Verify Hyperlinks. Use the Report Setting drop-down menu to change report parameters. The Usage Chart button changes a usage report into a graphic.

Below is a list of FrontPage site reports. (Unless otherwise noted, you can run the report from within the Site Summary screen.)

- **All files.** Shows all the files in your site. This report helps you get an overview and see what file types you've got. For instance, you can sort the list by file type to see how many PDF files your site contains.

- **Recently added files.** Lists all files in the site created after a fixed date. (You can change this date within the Reports toolbar. See the note below.)

- **Recently changed files.** Lists any files you edited after a certain date. Select View → Reports → Files → Recently Changed Files.

Note: Change the time frame for the above two reports using the Report Setting drop-down menu on the right side of the Reports toolbar.

- **Older files.** Shows you all files that haven't been edited in a long time. This helps alert you to files that might be out of date. (What's old? See the box, "Defining Report Measurements.")

- **Slow pages.** Lists pages whose download speed exceeds a certain amount of time.

- **Unlinked files.** Shows you "orphaned" files that no page in your site links to. This is a good way to find out-of-date files, or those that have lost their links. This report has one major drawback. If you've linked to an image or page within some JavaScript, FrontPage won't be aware of this link, so the file(s) will show up in this list. So, examine the Unlinked Files list carefully and make sure that a file isn't called by some JavaScript before you delete it.

- **Internal hyperlinks.** Shows all links that lead to pages inside your site.

- **External hyperlinks.** Lists all links that lead to pages outside your site.

- **Hyperlinks.** List all hyperlinks in your site (both internal and external).

- **Unverified hyperlinks.** These are links (mostly outside your site) that FrontPage doesn't automatically verify as valid and working. Clear out this list by having FrontPage run Verify Hyperlinks. (See "Verifying Hyperlinks" on page 248.)

Note: For more on using FrontPage's hyperlink reports, see the next section, "Testing Hyperlinks," on page 247.

- **Component errors.** Finds problems involving FrontPage components (like search boxes or forms).

- **Dynamic Web Templates.** Lists all HTML files in your site and shows you which ones you've linked to a Dynamic Web Template (page 216).

- **Shared Borders.** Shows you all pages that contain shared borders (page 211). Thought you removed them all? Better run this report to make sure. Select View → Reports → Shared Content → Shared Borders.

- **Style Sheet Links.** Lists all HTML files in your site and shows you which ones you've linked to a style sheet (CSS file; see Chapter 7).

- **Themes.** Shows you pages to which you've applied a theme (page 192), and tells you which one. Select View → Reports → Shared Content → Themes.

Tip: If you run a report and want to return to the Site Summary, just select View → Reports → Site Summary. Or, on the left side of the Reports toolbar, click the name of the report and select Site Summary from the drop-down menu.

Workflow reports

Workflow reports help you manage and track how work on your site is progressing and who's responsible for outstanding tasks. You can run the following reports only from the Reports menu. Select View → Reports → Workflow to get to these options. See Chapter 14 for details on taking advantage of the workflow features that make these reports valuable.

- **Review Status.** Lists all pages tagged for and awaiting review.

- **Assigned To.** Shows who's working on what files.

- **Categories.** Shows your pages and what (if any) categories you've assigned them to.

- **Publish Status.** Shows you if FrontPage is going to hold back any pages from being published.

- **Checkout Status.** Lists which, if any, files are checked out by colleagues.

Usage reports

Usage reports give you information on who's visiting your site and what pages they're looking at. As you might suspect, these reports get their information from your live Web server where that activity takes place. For these reports to work, your server needs to be running FrontPage Server Extensions 2002 or SharePoint Services. If your server meets these requirements and the usage reports still aren't working, get in touch with your server administrator and ask her to activate "usage analysis" settings within the Microsoft server-side software (whether it's FPSE or SharePoint).

You can run the following reports only from the Reports menu. First, open your remote site—that is, the copy of your site that lives on the live Web server (see Chapter 13, page 260). Then select View → Reports → Usage to access these options. The available reports are:

- **Usage Summary.** Shows an overview of site traffic.

- **Monthly, Weekly, or Daily Summary.** Lists the total number of site visits and page hits.

- **Monthly, Weekly, or Daily Page Hits.** Shows page-by-page visits. You can see exactly where your visitors are going.

- **Visiting Users.** Tells you who's visiting your site. For this report to work, you'll need to implement a sign-in procedure where viewers enter a name and a password. Keep in mind that this practice can turn away casual visitors.

- **Operating Systems.** Gives you statistics on the operating systems that your visitors are using.

- **Browsers.** Tells you what browsers your viewers are using. These statistics can really help you design your pages for your true audience. For instance, if you find that most of your visitors are using Firefox, you might cut out any IE-specific features you've included.

- **Referring Domains.** See where your visitors are coming from. This tells you the name of the site that contained the link they clicked to get to your site.

- **Referring URLs.** Like referring domains, but gives you the exact page that contained the link, not just the site.

- **Search Strings.** Find out what your visitors are looking for. Use this report to see what text strings (words or phrases) they've entered into your site's search function.

Viewing and Filtering Reports

You can arrange, sort, and filter the report display to see exactly what you want.

- Move columns by dragging the heading to another location in the heading bar.

- To sort a row, just click the heading. If you want to reverse the sort order, click the heading again.

- To filter, click the down arrow to the right of the heading and select your filter preference. You can choose individual items or all of them (which clears the filter), or Custom. Selecting Custom opens the Custom AutoFilter dialog box (see Figure 12-12).

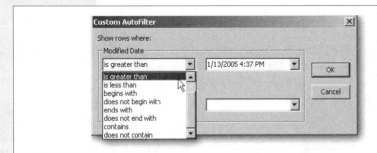

Figure 12-12:
Choices in the Custom AutoFilter dialog box depend on what column you're filtering. You can set up to two parameters. Require FrontPage to meet both (by clicking the "and" radio button between them) or either one (by clicking the "or" radio button). (Both the "and" and "or" buttons are hidden in this figure.)

Most reports show a list of files that are in your site (which files you see depends on what report you chose). If you want to open a file or preview it in a browser, right-click to access these and other options.

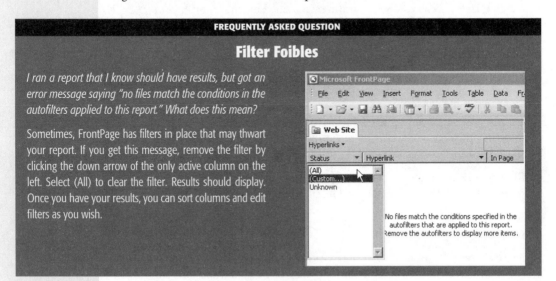

FREQUENTLY ASKED QUESTION

Filter Foibles

I ran a report that I know should have results, but got an error message saying "no files match the conditions in the autofilters applied to this report." What does this mean?

Sometimes, FrontPage has filters in place that may thwart your report. If you get this message, remove the filter by clicking the down arrow of the only active column on the left. Select (All) to clear the filter. Results should display. Once you have your results, you can sort columns and edit filters as you wish.

Testing Hyperlinks

A hyperlink that goes nowhere or (horrors!) to the wrong page can really frustrate even your most devoted fans and turn them off.

Again, your best defense is testing all links yourself in a browser, but for the benefit of your mouse-clicking hand, FrontPage can help out. You can check out the flow of your links in Hyperlinks view (page 17). This is a handy way to get a quick overview of your link pathways. FrontPage also gives you a bunch of reporting options to help you avoid broken links.

Finding Broken Links

When you're moving and editing pages, FrontPage updates links automatically. But broken links can still occur. If you sometimes type URLs in yourself, for instance, you might make a typo and not know it.

It's a good idea to run a quick site-wide check from time to time to make sure all your links lead somewhere. Since it's so easy, you don't have any reason not to.

When you open your site in Reports view, you can see the number of broken links at a glance. Within the Site Summary that automatically appears, find the "Broken hyperlinks" entry and look at the count. If the number is zero, you don't need to worry. If it shows that you've got broken links, click "Broken hyperlinks" to see what they are and correct them.

Checking for Orphaned Files

Sometimes Web pages fall out of the loop. Inevitably, you'll wind up with pages in your site that are *orphaned*. In other words, no other page in your site links to them. That means it's impossible for a viewer to navigate to the page using hyperlinks. Often, these are pages that have grown out of date. Maybe you removed all links to a page, but never got around to deleting it. Running a check like this could also alert you to links that should be made or fixed.

Checking for and deleting orphaned files can really reduce the size of your site. If you want to keep these pages, but put them back into rotation, you can do that, too. Or you may have a reason for keeping them unlinked. Whatever the case, if you want to see a list of these files, open the site summary report and click "Unlinked files." FrontPage shows all files that have no links leading to them.

Tip: You can also select View → Reports → Problems → Unlinked files.

To delete a file, right-click it in the list, and then select Delete. If you want to edit a page in the list, double-click it.

Verifying Hyperlinks

So you included a link to your favorite online surf shop, but your friend just told you that they went out of business months ago. You could have avoided frustrating all those visitors who clicked that link to nowhere.

FrontPage works hard to track and maintain all links within your site (internal hyperlinks). But it has less control over links that lead to other sites (external hyperlinks). Since it can't track them as you edit, FrontPage calls these "unverified hyperlinks." However, if you specifically ask it to, FrontPage can verify that these links do lead to working sites. This way, you'd have known about the surf shop ages ago, and you can also be sure that you haven't misspelled a URL somewhere along the way.

To check these links, you'll need to make sure you're connected to the Internet. Then open your site in Reports view (in the document window, click the Web Site tab and click the Reports button at the bottom of the program window) and select Unverified Hyperlinks from the list of reports. FrontPage prompts you to let it verify hyperlinks. Click Yes. If FrontPage can't find the destination, FrontPage changes the links status to broken. After verify runs, FrontPage clears out the unverified hyperlinks list.

Note: If your site contains unverified hyperlinks, FrontPage asks if you want to verify them whenever you select "Internal hyperlinks" or "External hyperlinks" from the Site Summary report.

Recalculate Hyperlinks

As you work on your pages, FrontPage constantly updates the information it uses to maintain your site. But sometimes things fall through the cracks. For instance, say a colleague edits an included content snippet in Notepad. Since FrontPage doesn't know the file changed, it won't update all the pages that include that snippet.

The program's Recalculate Hyperlinks command reindexes the site. This means, for example, that included content (page 206) refreshes on all pages, showing the latest changes. You can also use this feature to trigger a scheduled include (page 208). Run Recalculate Hyperlinks any time you suspect that someone has edited site content outside of FrontPage, or when your site's not behaving as it should.

To do so, select Tools → Recalculate Hyperlinks and click Yes at the prompt. Your cursor changes into an hourglass while the program runs. When the hourglass disappears, the process is complete.

Publishing Your Site

Once your site is everything you want it to be, how do you get it out in front of the world?

As you read in the beginning of Chapter 10, you should create your Web site in a *development environment* that's private and inaccessible to the public. This can be your laptop or desktop PC, or a Web server with no connection to the Internet. Eventually, though, you'll want to unveil your handiwork. To go public, you've got to post a copy of your site up on a live Web server—one that's connected to the Internet, where Google and your grandma can find it. This is your live *production environment,* where the real action takes place. Here, visitors from around the world can see and interact with your pages through their Web browsers. The process of getting your site from development to production is called *publishing* (see Figure 13-1).

Note: Learning how to publish your site will help you do more than just get your site online. For example, if you want to make a backup of your site, you'd publish it to a disk drive—like another folder on your computer, or onto a CD or other storage device (see "Publishing to a disk-based site" on page 257). And once your site is up and running, you'll also republish regularly to update your live public site with changes you've made in your development environment (assuming you've made some changes).

Things to Know Before You Publish

You can't publish a site until you have a live server to publish it on. Where will your live production site reside? Unless you're planning on running a Web server of your own (page 178), you'll need to find a *Web host.* Web-hosting companies offer space on a Web server that's connected to the Internet. These companies administer your Web server and often help you with related tasks, like purchasing a domain name. (A domain name is a unique Web address that you purchase. For instance, if you type *www.microsoft.com* in your browser's address bar, you'll see only information published by the folks who brought you FrontPage.) There are a lot of hosts out there—even some who provide free hosting (usually in return for permission to place an ad on your site). Shop around online to find a Web host that suits your needs. (Check out Microsoft's list at *www.microsoft.com/office/ frontpage/prodinfo/partner/wpp.asp.*)

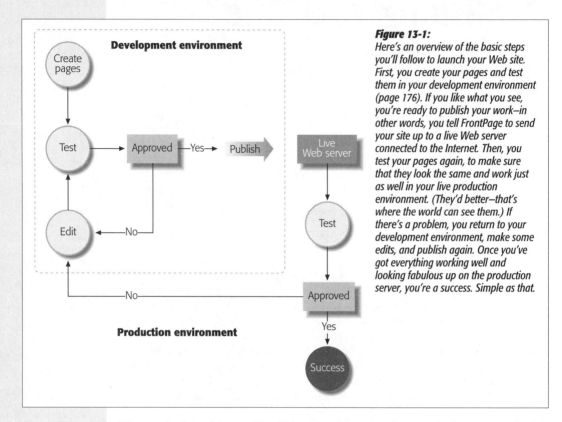

Development environment

Production environment

Figure 13-1:
Here's an overview of the basic steps you'll follow to launch your Web site. First, you create your pages and test them in your development environment (page 176). If you like what you see, you're ready to publish your work—in other words, you tell FrontPage to send your site up to a live Web server connected to the Internet. Then, you test your pages again, to make sure that they look the same and work just as well in your live production environment. (They'd better—that's where the world can see them.) If there's a problem, you return to your development environment, make some edits, and publish again. Once you've got everything working well and looking fabulous up on the production server, you're a success. Simple as that.

If your site is a plain-vanilla affair—simple pages of text and pictures, employing basic HTML—you don't have to be too discriminating about who you pick as your Web host. That's because your Web pages are pretty self-sufficient: all they need is some Web-based food and shelter, and they'll work just fine. But if you've included more advanced features (like letting visitors search your site, collecting information through forms, or displaying data from a database), you'll need to make sure the server you use is loaded with at least one of the Microsoft Web server technologies described on the following pages. It's easy to find out. Generally, Web-hosting companies advertise the availability of the FrontPage-related software you're about to read about. If not, just ask before you choose a provider.

The Microsoft Web Server Technologies

Microsoft's Web server technologies (special software that lives on your live Web server) enable some special FrontPage Web site features to work. The Microsoft

Web technologies fall into two basic camps: FrontPage Server Extensions and SharePoint Services.

FrontPage Server Extensions

FrontPage Server Extensions (FPSE) are a set of program files that enable a Web server to provide some FrontPage-specific services, like adding forms (Chapter 15) or a site search (Chapter 16) to your site.

Previously, Microsoft released a new version of the server extensions to support each new version of FrontPage. However, with the release of FrontPage 2003, Microsoft made no improvements to the server extensions. The company still supports FPSE 2002, but its focus is now centered on SharePoint Services, a new and improved server technology, which you'll read about next.

However, your FrontPage 2003 Web site is still compatible with FrontPage Server extensions, and in fact, many features still rely only on FPSE. But, some new advanced data-manipulation tools work only with SharePoint Services. Confused yet? Table 13-1 on page 252 provides a list of Web features and the server-side technology that supports them.

Windows SharePoint Services

Windows SharePoint Services (WSS) has taken over where FPSE left off. SharePoint is a souped-up, all-around more capable server extension that lets you perform fancy maneuvers like integrating live data sources into your site.

If you'll be working with a lot of data, or want to use XML (Extensible Markup Language, another type of publishing language that structures and organizes data in a file), SharePoint brings a lot more to the table than FPSE. But again, some Web functions still work only with FPSE and not with SharePoint. Think about what you want your site to do, and use Table 13-1 to help figure out whether you need FPSE or SharePoint on your Web server.

A lot of large organizations use Windows SharePoint Services to create large Web sites that let their staffs share information quickly and easily. In this sense, Windows SharePoint Services has taken over where SharePoint Team Services (which you'll read about next) left off. In fact, with SharePoint, you don't even need FrontPage to create a site like this.

Note: To use Windows SharePoint Services, the Web server you're using needs to be running Windows Server 2003.

SharePoint Team Services

Both FPSE and WSS work for the benefit of your Web site: they carry out their duties behind the scenes so that visitors to your site never actually interact with either of these programs. By contrast, SharePoint Team Services (STS) is purely a

---

self-contained Web program that, say, members of a large staff would use to communicate with one another. STS is essentially an intranet in a box that lets you create sites in which visitors can add and edit page content directly through their browser windows. (See the box "Net Differences" for more on intranets.)

A SharePoint Team site includes things like discussion lists and document libraries, which let many different people see and edit content. You don't need FrontPage to create or edit SharePoint Team Web pages. Because SharePoint Team Services is its own separate program, independent of FrontPage, this book covers it only briefly. You can't actually purchase SharePoint Team Services anymore. Microsoft now encourages you to use Windows SharePoint Services to create team sites. However, the presence of SharePoint Team Services supports some special Web site features that SharePoint Services doesn't. Also, some FrontPage owners may still be working on a SharePoint Team site, so it's included in Table 13-1.

Table 13-1. Feature Support from Microsoft Web Server Technologies. These features are available only when you or your Web-hosting company have installed FPSE or SharePoint on your Web server.

Feature	FPSE	WSS	STS
Top 10 Lists	Yes	Yes	Yes
Hit Counter	Yes	No	Yes
Save Form Results to E-mail or a File	Yes	Yes	Yes
Site Usage Reports	Yes	Yes	Yes
User Registration template	Yes	Yes	Yes
Database Results/Interface wizards	Recommended	No	Yes
Save Results to Database	Yes	No	Yes
Search Current Web	Yes	No	Yes
Full Text Search	No	Yes	Yes
Table of Contents	Yes	No	Yes
Search Form and Table of Contents options for various wizards	Yes	Yes	Yes
Include Page or Picture Based on Schedule	Yes	No	Yes
Table of Contents template	Yes	No	Yes
Bulletin Boards/Discussion Groups	No	Yes	Yes
Survey	No	Yes	Yes
Document libraries	No	Yes	Yes
Modify rules for document libraries	No	No	Yes
Data Source Catalog	No	Yes	No
Data View Features	No	Yes	No
XML Support	No	Yes	No
Web Packages	No	Yes	No
Web Parts	No	Yes	No

Note: Although FPSE don't support the advanced Discussion Group feature available under SharePoint, FrontPage does offer a Discussion Web site that works fine with FPSE. See page 310.

UP TO SPEED

Net Differences

What's an intranet? What's an extranet? For starters, you've of course heard of the *Internet*—the world-wide network that lets millions of computers all over the world speak to one another.

An *intranet* is a private Web network that exists behind a *firewall* (a protective tool that keeps out unknown network traffic and visitors). Many corporations and universities have created vast intranets that help their members share and send information quickly and easily. These networks are not available to the public.

An *extranet* is a special portion of an intranet that's accessible to outside visitors. These outsiders can only gain access with a user name and password. Companies often use extranets to share select information with clients. For instance, imagine you're a lawyer. You might share information with other attorneys on your firm's intranet. But if you wanted to show a client a document, you'd post it on an extranet and tell them how to access it.

Setting Publishing Preferences

Before you actually send your files out onto the Web, you need to supply FrontPage with some important information: what technology exists on the server you're publishing to and where exactly you're sending your files. You also have a few different options for specifying which pages FrontPage will publish.

Selecting a Remote Web Site

To access FrontPage's publishing options, open your site and select File → Publish Site. (You can also click the Web Site tab and, at the bottom of the document window, select Remote Web site view.) The Remote Web Site Properties dialog box appears (see Figure 13-2). If you don't see it, click the Remote Web Site Properties button on the upper right of the document window.

Before you can set all your Remote Web site details, you'll need to get the following information from your Web-hosting company or whoever is running your Web server:

• **The server address.** If you're publishing to a site administered by a Web-hosting company, this is probably just your domain name (*http://www.mysite. com/,* for example).

- **The folder or directory in which your site should go.** (If you're publishing to a server with FrontPage Server Extensions, you usually don't need to enter this info.)

- **Any user name and password you'll need to publish there.**

Figure 13-2:
This dialog box lets you tell FrontPage what software is on your destination server and how you want to send files there. Enter the exact destination location in the box at bottom. For example, if you've registered the domain name www.fleapower.com, you'd enter http://www.fleapower.com.

Publishing to a server with FPSE or SharePoint

If your server has FrontPage Server Extensions or SharePoint services on it, publishing is a breeze. On the Remote Web Site tab, just select the "FrontPage or SharePoint Services" radio button and enter the Web address for your site in the location box below.

Whenever possible, you should publish this way. Of course, if your site has any features that rely on Server Extensions or SharePoint, you have to publish using this option, or they won't work. But even if your site doesn't contain any of these special features, you should still use this method, if you can (that is, if the technology exists on your server). This method helps FrontPage keep track of all the info it uses to manage your site. Other publishing options will work, but they're a lot less helpful.

Note: Your Web server can't have both FPSE and SharePoint services loaded on it—only one or the other. FrontPage lumps both methods together in the same radio button, because FrontPage communicates with both types of servers in the same way.

WebDAV

If you don't have FrontPage Server Extensions or SharePoint services installed, you may want to publish via *WebDAV* (Web Distributed Authoring and Versioning). WebDAV provides more control than FTP or disk-based publishing (both of which you'll read about in a moment), because it features additional controls (like document locking and version control) that let authors collaborate and edit files on a remote Web server without erasing each others' work.

Note: FrontPage won't let you publish using WebDAV if your remote server features FPSE or SharePoint Services.

If you're publishing a personal or small business site through a Web host, you probably won't be using WebDAV. But if your site is part of a large corporate intranet, your administrator might choose this method. Publishing via WebDAV is pretty straightforward. In the Remote Web Site Properties dialog box, select Web-DAV and then enter your site's URL in the "Remote Web site location" box.

FTP

FTP (File Transfer Protocol) is a relatively ancient, but still fairly dependable system for exchanging files between computers. Before Web-authoring programs like FrontPage helped with publishing, authors hand-coding HTML in text files had to publish their files using a separate program, entirely dedicated to FTP. Many Web design graybeards, as well as folks who use other Web site–creation tools like Dreamweaver, still use FTP since it's all they really need. (See the box "FTP vs. HTTP" for more on the difference between FTP and FrontPage-specific publishing methods.)

When you select the FTP option, FrontPage asks you for a server address and provides a second field in which you need to enter a folder directory (see Figure 13-3). Before you fill out the dialog box, get this information from your Web-hosting company or whoever is running your Web server.

Also ask your host or server person whether or not you should turn on the Passive FTP checkbox. Passive FTP lets a computer communicate with a server, without requiring the server to initiate any commands. Microsoft added this feature because a lot of firewalls require it.

Note: Once you publish via FTP or WebDAV, your site is no longer, technically speaking, a FrontPage Web site. This means you won't be able to use the "Open Remote site in FrontPage" option discussed later this chapter (see page 260). You will, of course, still be able to edit your site using FrontPage (if your development environment is on your own computer). But the point is that the version of your site that's now up and running on an FTP or WebDAV server is no longer anything you can get at with your FrontPage tools. Also, these two publishing methods won't let you use any Web elements that rely on FPSE or SharePoint.

Figure 13-3:
Note that the Web site location begins with FTP instead of HTTP. To learn more about the difference between these two systems, see the box "FTP vs. HTTP."

FREQUENTLY ASKED QUESTION

FTP vs. HTTP

What's the real difference between publishing via FTP and entering an HTTP address under the FPSE/SharePoint option?

Imagine that the publishing process is like sending a delivery guy to bring your site up to the server. FTP is the courier who doesn't know anything about what's in his bag. He delivers the goods, but that's it—he doesn't share any details, and he doesn't hang out to chat about the quirky little preferences of what he's delivering. FTP is the Sergeant Schultz of Web delivery systems: it knows *nothing* about what it's delivering or why.

FrontPage's HTTP process, on the other hand, is a devoted, smart delivery man who anticipates your Web site's every need. He tells your remote Web server what he's delivering,

where it should go, and passes on special requests from FrontPage to make sure your pages function correctly.

Since this process is built into FrontPage and works with Microsoft software on the server, it's no surprise that it's very smart about your FrontPage Web site. As you publish, this method doesn't just copy your site folder to the remote destination. It processes your site, adjusting indexes and links so they'll work in the remote location. In fact, if you compare code from the same page between your development site and your live Web server, it'll often be different. (A good reason *not* to use your published site as a backup.)

If a server has FPSE or SharePoint on it, always use that option to publish your site—even if your site contains no special bells and whistles that require either of these tools.

Publishing to a disk-based site

Need to make a backup of your site? Using the publish command is the best way. If you select "File System" as your remote site, you can copy your site to another folder on your hard drive or a storage server. If you're on the move, you can even copy your site onto a CD, DVD, or any other kind of storage device.

Once you select File System in the Remote Web Site Properties dialog box, browse to or type the path. If you type in folder names that don't yet exist, FrontPage creates them. Then click OK. If the destination folder isn't already a FrontPage Web site, FrontPage asks you if you want to create a "web" (meaning "Web site") at that location. Click Yes.

Configuring Publishing Options

The basic sequence of steps involved in publishing (often called *workflow*) follows a consistent pattern: you publish your site, you make some more changes in your development environment, and then you need to publish again. But once most of your site's already up on the live server and you've edited only a handful of pages, you might ask yourself: why bother to replace the pages and files that *haven't* changed?

Fortunately, FrontPage lets you publish only those pages that have changed. To do this, FrontPage compares the copies of your site and uploads only new and updated files. This process can save you loads of time.

To set your file update preferences, open the Remote Web Site Properties dialog box and click the Publishing tab. Then tell FrontPage what it should publish.

Changed Pages only

If you select this radio button, FrontPage will push only new material up to the destination site. How does FrontPage tell what's new? In one of two ways, which you choose, in the Publishing tab's Changes section:

- **Determine changes by comparing source and destination sites.** FrontPage compares actual site content. This method is the more accurate of the two, though it takes a little longer.

- **Use source file timestamps to determine changes since last publish.** This process compares time and date information on each file and uploads only those whose edited time is later than the existing file. This method is more prone to error because timestamps on various machines are not always consistent or accurate.

Note: Selecting "Changed Pages only" is the only publishing method in which FrontPage prompts you to delete any files that exist on your remote site, but not in your local site.

All pages, overwriting pages already on destination

If you select the "All pages" radio button, FrontPage copies over all the files in your site, both old and new. You won't need to wait around for FrontPage to compare the sites, but you may wait quite a while for the site to publish. Obviously, the first time you publish, you'll need to publish all pages. After that, you can opt to publish changed pages only, if you want.

Tip: If you've created subsites (page 190) within your site, you'll need to publish them separately—unless you turn on the Include Subsites checkbox on the Publishing tab.

Publishing Your Site

You've laid the groundwork. You set up a remote destination and configured your preferences. Now it's time to pull the trigger.

To publish:

1. **Open the Web site you want to publish in FrontPage.**

2. **Initiate the publish operation.**

   Select File → Publish Site, or click the Web site tab and select Remote Web site view at the bottom of the screen. If you've configured your remote site and are connected to the Internet, you should see two panes: your local site (the one you opened in FrontPage and intend to move to the Web server) appears on the left, and your remote (or destination) site appears on the right (see Figure 13-4).

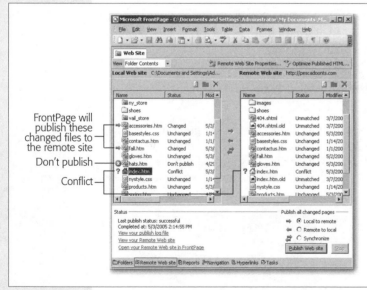

Figure 13-4:
Remote Web Site view shows your local site on the left and the remote site on the right. Updated files that FrontPage intends to publish have an arrow next to them, indicating the direction the program will send them. Conflicts (files that have changed in both locations) have a question mark next to them—like the index.htm file pictured here. A red circle with an X in it indicates a file that you've held back from publishing—like hats.htm in the left pane.

FrontPage will publish these changed files to the remote site

Don't publish

Conflict

Note: If you haven't configured your publish settings yet, the Remote Web Site Properties dialog box opens instead. The previous section explains how to configure these options.

3. **Set the direction in which you want to send your files.**

On the lower right of the screen, FrontPage gives you three choices. Most likely, you'll be publishing "Local to remote" (*from* the development site you have open in FrontPage up *to* your live production Web site). But FrontPage does let you publish in the other direction, "Remote to local." Generally, you want to stay away from the latter. (A live Web site should not be used as a backup; publish to another disk location instead.) However, you may need to occasionally go the "Remote to local" route. For instance, if someone edited a file or two up on the live server, you may need to copy the new files down to your development site.

If you've told FrontPage to publish only changed files, you'll have a third choice: Synchronize. This feature publishes in both directions at once, insuring that both the local and remote site contain the same copies of each file. The most recent copy of each file always wins out.

4. **Click Publish Web Site.**

As FrontPage publishes your site, the program keeps you apprised of its progress in the lower left of the screen. If it encounters a problem—say, a page that won't work on the destination server because the server lacks FPSE—FrontPage lets you know. You'll need to address these problems yourself later on.

Note: You may see other prompts asking you whether you want to overwrite files that conflict with each other. These are files that have changed in both locations since you last published. (Perhaps a colleague edited a file up on the live server and you didn't know about it.) In Remote Web site view, these files appear with question marks next to them. If you're unsure what the conflict is, click Ignore and Continue. Later, you can compare conflicting files manually, make the proper edits in your local site, and then publish those select files. If you're sure the copy you're publishing is the one you need, click Overwrite Destination Files.

5. **Test your site.**

The publishing process and new environment can affect your pages. Test your site thoroughly on the live Web server to make sure pages look and act the way you expect.

Tip: Before you publish, always make sure your settings are correct—that is, you're publishing in the direction you want, replacing the files you want, and have selected the criteria that you want.

Excluding Files from Publishing

There may be some files that you don't want to publish along with the rest of your site. For instance, you probably don't want to publish pages that are still under construction.

FrontPage makes it easy to hold back specific files. Just select them in the Local Web site page, right-click, and select Don't Publish. A red circle with an x in it appears to the left of the file, letting you know that FrontPage will hold it back the next time you publish. When you're ready to publish it, right-click it and select Don't Publish again. Doing so removes the checkmark and signals to FrontPage that you're ready to release this page in the wild. If you want to see a list of excluded files, click the View drop-down menu in the upper-left corner and select "Files not to Publish" (see Figure 13-5).

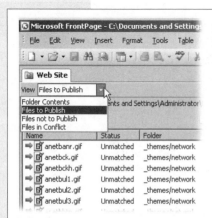

Figure 13-5:
If you want to see what files are in conflict, or held back from publishing, you can change your view. To do so, click the View drop-down menu on the upper-left corner of Web Site tab.

Publishing Selected Files

Say you made changes to just one page that you want to send up to the live server. There's no need to wait while FrontPage compares your site or uploads unchanged files. Just publish the file in question.

To do so, open your site in Remote Web site view (page 17). Within the Local Web site pane, select the file(s) you want to publish. Right-click and select Publish Selected Files or click the Publish arrow button in the center of your screen, between the local and remote panes.

Open Your Remote Web Site in FrontPage

It's bad practice to edit your site on the live Web server, since doing so earns you a free ticket to Version Control Hell. But there may be times when you want to open your remote site in FrontPage (to run a usage report, for example). FrontPage gives you this option in the form of a link on the lower left of Remote Web site view. Click the "Open your Remote Web site in FrontPage" link and the remote site opens in a new instance of FrontPage. Unfortunately, this option isn't available for sites published via FTP or WebDAV.

Tip: The "View Your Remote Web site" option just above the "Open your Remote Web site in FrontPage" link opens the site in Windows Explorer.

Authoring Modes

Suppose you don't want to mess around with FrontPage Server Extensions. You just want to create a plain-vanilla, text- and pictures-only HTML site. How can you be sure you're not adding a feature that requires special software on the server, that'll end up making your Web site look broken?

FrontPage lets you set your *authoring mode,* which lets you develop your site for specific server technologies and also browsers. Once you make authoring selections, FrontPage grays out all the choices to conform with the mode you've selected. For instance, if you don't want anyone working on your site to add shared borders, you can disable this option.

Note: Settings you make on the Authoring tab won't affect any pages you've already created. FrontPage imposes the new restrictions on new pages only.

Select → Tools → Page Options and click the Authoring tab (see Figure 13-6). Within the top section, take a look at the FrontPage and SharePoint Technologies drop-down list. You'll use this list to tell FrontPage what software you expect to have on the Web server. The choices here affect your choices in the checkboxes below. For instance, if you select Complete, FrontPage turns on all the checkboxes below. You're telling the program that you expect to have either SharePoint or FrontPage Server Extensions on the server. You might think then, if you click None, you're telling FrontPage that you don't want to be able to create *any* features that rely on FPSE or Sharepoint. Not so. Selecting None turns off all checkboxes below. Unfortunately, this cuts out some run-of-the-mill options as well. For instance, you won't be able to add included content (which doesn't rely on FPSE); you lose this feature when author-time Web components are turned off.

What's an author to do when it comes to making choices on the Authoring tab? Your best bet is to select Custom, and then turn on the boxes you want:

- **SharePoint Services.** Turn on this checkbox if you'll have SharePoint services on your Web server. If not, turn it off.

- **Browse-time Web Components.** These are Web elements that require help from software on the server to run. These actions take place on the live Web server when a browser accesses them (hence, "browse-time"). For instance, if you have a form that sends info to your email box, it needs the server to run a script for that to happen. If you won't have FPSE or SharePoint on your Web server, you can turn off this checkbox.

• **Author-time Web Components.** These components help you create a variety of page elements, ranging from forms to themes and included content. These components run while you're editing in FrontPage (hence, "author-time"). Almost everyone will want to turn on this checkbox. Disabling this option affects all Web components—even those that don't require special software on the server, like included content (which is just simple HTML that FrontPage helps you write).

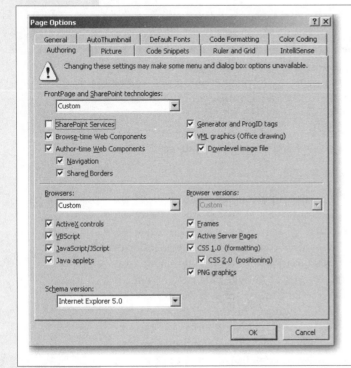

Figure 13-6:
You can use the Authoring tab to configure what features FrontPage lets you add to your pages. For most authors, the settings that FrontPage has on automatically after you install the program will be fine. However, if you're editing pages and find that FrontPage has grayed out certain menu options, the Authoring tab is usually the culprit. Check to see if the feature you're trying to use is turned off here.

• **Navigation.** If you turn off this checkbox, Navigation view and all that goes with it—link bars, banners, and so on—will be unavailable.

• **Shared Borders.** As you learned in Chapter 11 on page 212, you'll only create trouble if you use shared borders. FrontPage's automatic setting is to disable this option. If you're a glutton for punishment and decide you want it available, just turn on this checkbox.

• **Generator and ProgID tags.** In the course of creating pages, FrontPage adds some <meta> tags inside the head section of HTML pages. Meta tags contain basic descriptive information about the Web page. For instance: <meta name="GENERATOR" content="Microsoft FrontPage 6.0"> indicates what software created the page. These tags aren't exactly W3C standard, and many HTML purists disdain them. Turn off this checkbox and FrontPage will keep your pages meta-tag free.

- **VML graphics.** If you turn off this checkbox, you won't be able to use the Drawing toolbar or FrontPage WordArt. This is for the best (see the box "A Word on WordArt"). If you love working with this toolbar, turn on this checkbox, but use it in conjunction with the Downlevel image file option (see next entry). Or better yet, try the workaround below.

WORKAROUND WORKSHOP

A Word on WordArt

VML (Vector Markup Language) creates graphics like line art and charts that are saved as XML, not image files. The advantage is that these images load much faster than regular GIF files. Whenever you use features on the Drawing or WordArt toolbars, you're making this kind of image. The problem is that only other Microsoft Office programs and Internet Explorer understand this kind of image notation. Any other browser won't see it. You'll be a happy person if you steer clear of these features altogether.

But maybe you just love WordArt and you can't break the habit. If you're going to indulge, save yourself some cross-browser difficulties. Create your VML masterpiece with your favorite tools and then take a screenshot (press Ctrl+PrtSc). Paste the result into a graphics program, crop, and save as a GIF file. Voilà! Now everyone can see your handiwork.

- **Downlevel image file.** This option works together with the VML Graphics box just above it. If you turn on both of these checkboxes, you can avoid the problem discussed in the box "A Word on WordArt." When this option is turned on and a browser that can't display VML graphics comes along, FrontPage sends your VML graphics as regular GIF files. This is a really nice way to accommodate all visitors to your site. But to avoid glitches, you're better off using GIF images instead.

Code Cleanup: Optimizing HTML

A lot of Web purists will give you an earful on how FrontPage produces sloppy, overloaded HTML code. While older versions of the program were definitely guilty of this crime, the accusation has lost some of its bite with FrontPage 2003. The code the program now produces is relatively clean and efficient.

However, FrontPage still gives you an opportunity to clear out HTML elements that you don't want around. A lot of these elements happen to be FrontPage-specific HTML that rankles the aforementioned purists.

This section helps you decide whether or not you'll want to optimize, and what all your options are.

Should You Optimize?

The main reason you'd optimize is to trim the size of your pages so they download faster. Also, if you are using FrontPage to create simple HTML pages and don't want to include *any* of the program's FrontPage-specific coding, you should optimize.

As you read in Chapter 12, FrontPage lets you optimize HTML in your development environment. Since many optimization options disable important editing abilities, you should *never* do this. The only time to even think about using this code cleanup tool is at publish time.

But, unless you have a specific code-cleaning goal in mind, you're better off bypassing most of these cleanup options. Optimizing has two important ramifications you should consider:

- Most optimizations will render parts of your site uneditable. For instance, removing Dynamic Web Template comments cuts connections between Dynamic Web Templates and dependant files.

Note: Many a misguided author counts on using a published site as a backup for the development site. This is a very bad idea, because the act of publishing changes some files. In other words, your published site differs slightly from your development site. Turning optimization options on exacerbates the difference. If you optimize, your published site will differ drastically from your development site—turning what was just a bad idea (using the live Web copy of your site as backup) into a catastrophically bad idea.

- If you let FrontPage strip elements out of your HTML, your pages may end up looking and functioning quite differently than they did on the development site. Check your site's pages thoroughly after you've published.

Simple alternatives to optimization

Before you resort to code cleanup options, there are some simple things you can do to reduce download time. The following basic practices are more effective in reducing download time than most of the optimization settings.

- **Small image sizes.** Make sure that all your images are small—in byte size, that is. JPEG and GIF formats already give you a head start. None of these images are going to be very big. However, if you're asking FrontPage to display a file with large dimensions (say, 500×500 pixels) in a much smaller space (100×100 pixels), you're wasting precious download time. Make sure all your files are sized appropriately. (See Chapter 4, page 62, for details on resizing images.)

- **Use external style sheets to format your pages instead of inline formatting.** Chapter 7 tells you all about how to do this.

Optimizing HTML During Publish

If you want to include code cleanup as part of your publishing process, do the following:

1. Select View → Remote Web site (or click the Web Site tab and, beneath the document window, click Remote Web Site view).

2. Just above the document window, click the Optimize Published HTML button (if it's not grayed out), on the upper right; or click the Remote Web Site Properties button, and in the dialog box that opens, click the Optimize HTML tab (see Figure 13-7).

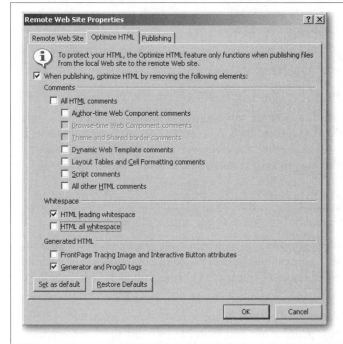

Figure 13-7:
HTML optimization options should be used only at publish time. Use them sparingly. If you publish with these options on and find that your site doesn't function correctly afterward, turn off optimization options and publish your site again.

3. To activate options on this tab, turn on the "When publishing, optimize HTML by removing the following elements:" checkbox, and then choose from the following:

Note: Most Optimize options will render many of your pages uneditable. This means that you'll never be able to copy them back to your development site. Also, letting FrontPage strip elements out of your HTML could result in your pages displaying differently than you expect.

- **All HTML comments.** Activates all the "comment" options indented beneath it. You need to turn this on to choose further options.

- **Author-time Web Component comments.** Deletes comments that go along with page elements like included content.

- **Browse-time Web Component comments.** Clears comments out of all browse-time Web components, like site search boxes and hit counters. If you're publishing with FrontPage or SharePoint services, FrontPage won't let you turn off this option.

- **Theme and Shared Border comments.** Removes all comments for themes and shared borders. If you're publishing with FrontPage or SharePoint services, FrontPage grays out this option.

- **Dynamic Web Template comments.** Removes comments from Dynamic Web Templates and their linked HTML pages. Turning on this option turns the template into a regular HTML page and breaks the connection between the template and its associated pages.

- **Layout Tables and Cell Formatting comments.** Gets rid of all comments FrontPage uses to handle layout tables.

- **Script comments.** Clears out all comments from scripts.

- **All other HTML comments.** Eliminates any comments in your code (that is all < !- - and - - > tags and their contents.) Developers use comments like this to speak with each other. However, as you read in Chapter 7 (page 121), embedded styles live within comment tags, so your page could lose these as well.

- **HTML leading whitespaces.** Removes any empty spaces that begin a line of HTML. This option is the safest and least intrusive cleanup option.

- **HTML all whitespace.** Gets rid of all multiple empty spaces in your site's code. This option turns returns and multiple spaces into one space. This can cause problems in some older browsers that can't handle very long lines of code.

- **FrontPage Tracing Image and Interactive Button attributes.** Eliminates attributes from tracing images and FrontPage interactive buttons, rendering them uneditable.

- **Generator and ProgID tags.** FrontPage plunks some <meta> tags down in the head section of every page. This option deletes them all. If you dislike these tags, you can stop FrontPage from adding them in the first place. "Authoring Modes" on page 261 shows you how.

If you click "Set as Default," on the lower-left corner of the Optimize HTML tab, FrontPage saves your optimization settings for this site.

Collaboration Tools

It's good to be the king. When you're the only one working on your Web site, you decide what goes in and what stays out. You know who to blame if you don't like how things look. Trouble is, many people don't build Web sites by themselves. They farm out the graphics work to a friend; they get a co-worker to write the "About this Site" description; and they end up composing other bits and pieces themselves.

When you bring additional authors into the mix, the whole process of creating a Web site gets more complicated. Other people can help out, but they can also cause trouble. Who knows what they'll do? They might try to open the file you're working on, for instance. Or neglect to tell you that the pages they "finished" four days ago haven't yet been approved by the Big Boss. Sheesh!

Don't fire your co-workers or banish your siblings just yet. FrontPage includes some features that help multiple Web authors work together smoothly. In this chapter, you'll learn how to assign pages to authors, classify files according to their status and topic, and protect files you're working on with FrontPage's document control feature. Also, you'll find out how task tracking can help you keep on top of jobs that you and your colleagues need to tackle.

Assigning Pages

If you've got a really large Web site that a lot of different people are working on, you need to develop a system for tracking pages. For example, imagine that your colleague, Eddie, is out sick and you're publishing updates to the site today. How do you know if his pages are complete and ready to publish?

FrontPage lets you assign pages to specific people and track their status, so you don't inadvertently publish an incomplete page. You can also group pages in categories, which helps if you want to organize pages by topic, or by a group of people, or by a department that you've assigned to edit them.

Assigning Files to Individuals

As Web site Master and Commander, one of your toughest challenges is tracking who's in charge of each page. FrontPage lets you embed this information within each file. To assign a file to an individual, start out by opening the file in FrontPage. Then select File → Properties and click the Workgroup tab (see Figure 14-1).

Tip: You can also right-click a file in the folder list and select Properties to open the dialog box shown in Figure 14-1.

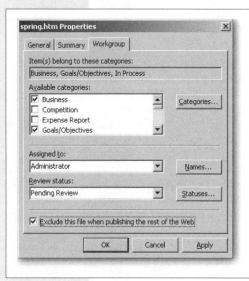

Figure 14-1:
Each page's Properties dialog box lets you assign a file to an individual, assign it to relevant categories, and track its status. The page's author can turn on the "Exclude this file when publishing the rest of the Web" checkbox until the page is ready for its debut. (Remember, in FrontPage-ese, "Web" is shorthand for "Web site.")

Within the "Assigned to" field, select a person from the drop-down list. To add a name to the list, click Names. Type in the name and click add. Then click OK.

Categories

FrontPage gives you another handy tool on the Workgroup tab to classify your files behind the scenes. You can use this feature in a couple of ways. One approach is to create categories for page *topics*. For instance, if you have a series of pages on different varieties of orchids, you could assign them all to an orchid category. You can also create categories for *departments* or *workgroups* who you've assigned to edit these files. This way, the marketing department could easily see all the pages they're responsible for by looking for files in the "marketing" category.

Assign a category to any file by opening the file's Properties dialog box and clicking the Workgroup tab (as pictured in Figure 14-1). You can assign a file to as many categories as you want. Within the Categories list, turn on the checkboxes for all those you want to use.

Categories are extremely flexible, because you can customize them to suit your site. Just click the Categories button to the right of the categories list, type in a new category, and then click Add.

TROUBLESHOOTING MOMENT

DWTs and Categories

If you created pages using a Dynamic Web Template (DWT), you may be in for a rude surprise when you try to assign categories to your Web pages. When you create a DWT, you have to manually create editable sections within your page. Subsequently, FrontPage blocks an author from changing anything else on a page created from the template. (To refresh your memory on how a DWT works, pop back to page 216.)

When you create a new DWT, FrontPage automatically includes an editable region called doctitle, so you can edit each page's title (select File → Properties to get to this field). If you're unable to add categories to a DWT's linked page (page 218), you may have inadvertently removed doctitle from the editable regions list.

To correct this problem, open your Dynamic Web Template in FrontPage. Assign the template to a category and switch to Code view. When you add a category, FrontPage adds a chunk of code to the head section that looks like this:

```
<!--[if gte mso 9]><xml>
<mso:CustomDocumentProperties>
<mso:Categories msdt:dt="string">
Business</mso:Categories>
<mso:Approval_x0020_Level msdt:
dt="string"></mso:Approval_x0020_Level>
<mso:Assigned_x0020_To msdt:dt="string"></
mso:Assigned_x0020_To>
</mso:CustomDocumentProperties>
</xml><![endif]-->
```

First, you need to wrap this chunk of code in an editable region. Do this by adding simple start and ending comments around it. Just above the first line of the preceding code passage, insert the following line:

```
<!-- #BeginEditable "doctitle" -->
```

Then, after the last line of the passage add:

```
<!-- #EndEditable -->
```

Next, you've got to get your page's title tags inside these editable region comments, too. Within the head section of your file, find the <title> tags. Select the start and ending title tags and their contents. Cut the tags (press Ctrl+X or select Edit → Cut). Place your cursor just above the "End-Editable" comment you just inserted and paste (Ctrl+V). If you inadvertently delete the title tags, or they're not there at all, just add a start and ending title tag above the "End Editable" comment with nothing between. You should end up inserting a line like this:

```
<title></title>
```

Save your changes, and you'll be able to assign categories to all pages linked to the template.

Using categories to create a table of contents

You can use categories to create a topic-based table of contents within your site. Doing so inserts a list of hyperlinks that belong to one or more categories that you specify. For example, say your site has a bunch of pages about newts and wombats.

You've got a dozen pages about different kinds of newts, and a similar number of pages about wombats.

You could then create a Newts and Wombats introductory page that, with the help of FrontPage, automatically lists links to all the pages you put in the "newt" category and then, below that, all the pages you put in the "wombat" category.

In this way, you can piece together a page that gives viewers a kind of table of contents organized by category. For this feature to work, you'll need FrontPage Server Extensions (page 251) on your Web server. You can create the table of contents if you're developing using a disk-based site (page 176), as long as you publish to a server with FPSE.

Once you've assigned pages to categories, you can create your table of contents. You'll probably want to create a special page to hold the table of contents. Also, you'll need to lay out the page with a table that includes your category headings. All FrontPage actually does is create a list of links for you. You'll insert this list beneath a heading you create for each category. In other words, it's up to you to create a page structure that makes sense, then insert one or more tables of contents (automated lists of links) into it.

After you've set up your page, place your cursor where you'd like to insert a list of links and select Insert → Web Component. The Insert Web Component dialog box appears (see Figure 14-2). From the "Component type" list on the left, choose Table of Contents and in the pane on the right, select Based on Page Category.

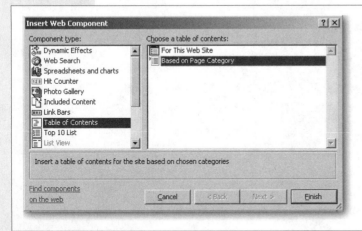

Figure 14-2:
When you select Table of Contents as your Component type, you can choose from two types of tables in the list on the right. Avoid using the first For This Web Site option. See the note below.

Note: The other option here, For This Web Site, works off your navigation diagram (page 182) and is notoriously less easy to control. If you select that option instead, you'll create a muddled table of contents full of pages you didn't want to list—like included content snippets—that won't help any of your visitors. Stay away from the navigation-based option and stick to the customizable categories-based table.

The Categories Properties dialog box appears. Turn on the checkbox for each category you want to include (you can create a list of pages belonging to one or several categories). Then choose a sort order and click OK. FrontPage inserts a model of your table of contents on the page. The list contains placeholder links that each say "Page in Category." It may not look like you're done, but you are, as shown in Figure 14-3.

Note: Whenever you add or edit categories in these pages (or new pages), run Recalculate Hyperlinks (on the Tools menu) to make sure FrontPage passes on all your updates to your table of contents.

Figure 14-3:
You create the heading and FrontPage creates the list of links (table of contents). FrontPage shows you a model with placeholders for each link (left). You won't see the actual links until you display the page in a browser (lower right). Remember also that your published site needs to be on a Web server that's got FPSE (page 251) on it.

Review Status

Review status is a great help for anyone trying to manage a large site with multiple contributors. You can create custom status labels and apply them to files in your site to track work progress. How do you know what pages the legal department needs to review? Flag them with this tool.

To apply a status to a file, select File → Properties and click the Workgroup tab (pictured in Figure 14-1). Then select the file's status from the "Review status" drop-down list.

You'll probably want to customize your status selections. FrontPage gives you a few generic status choices to start off with, but you can add ones that truly reflect the work your staff does ("Someone Check PLEASE!"). To add a status, just click the Statuses button to the right of the "Review status" box. Type in any kind of label you want and then click Add.

Workflow Reports

The beauty of document assignment reveals itself when the site manager takes a look at the big picture. Say you're in charge and want to see what files you need to review and approve today.

You'd select View → Reports → Workflow → Review Status to see a list like the one in Figure 14-4. The other reports under workflow tell you who's assigned to what pages (the Assigned To report) or let you see which pages are being held back from publishing (the Publish Status report). For details on working with FrontPage Reports, see page 242 in Chapter 12.

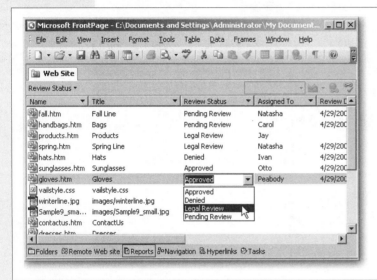

Figure 14-4:
You can edit assignments directly through this reporting screen. Click on an item to reveal a drop-down list like the one pictured here. This saves you the trouble of opening each page's Properties dialog box.

Document Control

Imagine that you open a page and make some edits. Meanwhile, at a neighboring desk, the new guy opens the same file and makes a bunch of edits at the same time. You finish first and save the file. He eventually finishes and saves the file, which replaces the copy you were working on. Poof! He overwrites your edits and obliterates your work.

You can protect yourself from the new guy. Avoid messes like this with FrontPage's document control feature.

Once you turn on document control and an author *checks out* a file, no one else can make changes to that file. Other authors see a small padlock next the file, so they know not to try.

Note: You can turn on FrontPage's document control feature if you're using a disk-based (page 176) or a server-based (page 176) site—as long as the server-based site is running FPSE; if your server has Share-Point instead, FrontPage flips on document control automatically.

Activating Document Control

Unless you're working on a server loaded with SharePoint services, you'll need to manually turn on the document check-in/check-out feature. To do so, select Tools → Site Settings. In the Site Settings dialog box that appears, turn on the "Use document check-in and check-out" checkbox. Next, you've got to specify in which of your sites (local or remote) FrontPage should apply the new checkout system:

- **Check out files from the Remote Web Site.** FrontPage grays out this option if you haven't configured a remote site (page 253). Imagine that you're collaborating on a site with your old college roommate who lives across the country. You each edit pages on your local computers and then upload your pages to the site you share on the remote Web server. That's where FrontPage mounts its virtual sentry: on the remote Web server, so that neither of you overwrite each other's changes.

- **Check out files from the Local Web Site.** Select this radio button if everyone's working on the same development server.

WORKAROUND WORKSHOP

Covert Control

Say you're a site administrator and you have a few specific files that you want to protect from others, so you tell your staff you plan to activate document control. An uproar arises, because your team members don't want to have to check documents in and out.

You can solve this problem by imposing a kind of stealth document control. To do so, activate document control in the General tab of the Site Settings dialog box, but turn off the "Prompt to checkout file when opening a page" checkbox. Then you can check out the few files you want to protect, and your staff members won't be prompted to check out documents they open. In fact, they probably won't even know document control is on. However, because they're not checking documents out, they could overwrite each other's edits just as if you'd never activated the feature at all.

Checking Documents In and Out

There's not much to checking documents in and out. If you (or the person running your site) turn on the "Prompt to checkout file when opening a page" checkbox, then FrontPage prompts you to check out any document you open. If you click Yes, a checkmark appears next to the file showing you that you've got it checked out (others see a padlock). If you click No at the prompt, FrontPage opens the file and lets you edit as usual—but won't protect the file from being opened and modified by another author at the same time. You can also right-click a document and select Check Out.

If you try to open a document that's checked out by another author, FrontPage tells you who checked it out and asks if you want to open a *read-only* copy (in which you won't be able to save any edits). Most of the time, you'll click No and wait until the document is available. If you click yes, FrontPage opens a read-only copy for you to examine. If you want, you can save the file under another file name and edit that new incarnation of the page.

To check a document back in, just right-click it (see Figure 14-5) and select Check In.

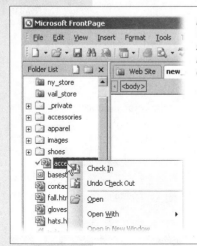

Figure 14-5:
When you right-click a document you checked out, you can check it back in by selecting Check In. Or, you can turn back time by selecting Undo Check Out. FrontPage then returns the file back to its original state prior to checkout, erasing any edits you may have made.

Tip: When you have a lot of people working on a site, how do you know who's checked out what documents? You can see a comprehensive list at a glance by running the Checkout Status report. Select View → Reports → Workflow → Checkout Status.

Assigning Tasks

Again, imagine you're in charge of a Web site that's created by a large group of people. In the course of your day, you notice that there's a missing product description on a page. Then you see that another page has a sale announcement that's out of date. But you're not responsible for making these changes (perhaps that's why you're running the site). What's the best way to let the peons know that they've got work to do?

FrontPage includes a handy feature for keeping track of all these niggling issues. It's a simple task list. The advantage is that everyone can look in one place and see what needs to be done. If you're working alone, you can also use the task list as a kind of "to do" list. See a problem but you're too busy to fix it? Just create a task.

Tasks are pretty simple: you can either assign them or work on them. Once you've added a few, you'll have a list like the one in Figure 14-6. To get to it, open your site and select View → Tasks (or click the Web Site tab in the document window and click Tasks at the bottom of the screen).

Assigning a Task

If you want to associate a task with a particular page, you need to open that page first. Then select Edit → Task → Add Task. Fill out the dialog box—you can name the task, select a person to complete it, set its priority, and type in a longer description, if necessary. Then click OK.

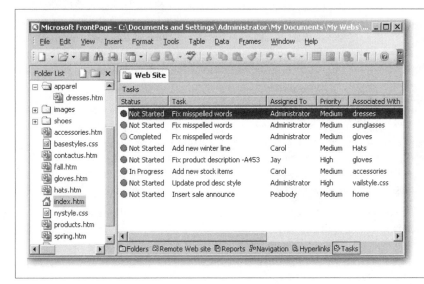

Figure 14-6:
Tasks view shows who's assigned to each task, the page or file in question, and the completion status. An author can open and execute her tasks directly from this screen. Note that FrontPage won't show completed tasks in this list. If you want to view your accomplishments, select Edit → Tasks → Show History.

Tip: The list of staff members that shows up in this dialog box is linked to the list in the Workgroup tab (page 268). Add a new person by typing in a name.

You can also assign a general task that's not associated with any one file or page—just make sure you don't have any pages open. Then create the task as explained above. Unfortunately, you can't assign a task to multiple pages or files.

WORKAROUND WORKSHOP

Tasks? Mañana.

FrontPage doesn't want to pressure you. Need to create a page? There's no rush; just give yourself a reminder.

The program gives you a chance to create tasks in the course of normal editing. Doing so lets you procrastinate on certain chores. For instance, if you select File → New and click "More page templates" in the task pane, you have an opportunity to drag your feet. Select the template you want and turn on the Just Add a Task checkbox in the Page Templates dialog box (see illustration). FrontPage creates the page in the folder you select, but won't open the new file. Instead, the program creates a task to remind you to finish making that page later. This checkbox appears on

every tab within the page template's dialog box—so you can postpone creating style sheets and other types of files as well. As you read in Chapter 12, on page 224, FrontPage lets you put off fixing your spelling errors, too. The Spelling dialog box lets you create a task for each page with misspellings.

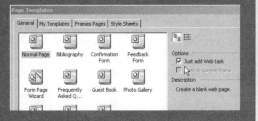

Working on a Task

To make a dent in your workload, go to Tasks view. Double-click the task you want to complete (or right-click it), and then select Start Task. FrontPage opens the page in question. Then make whatever edits are necessary. When you save the page, FrontPage asks you how much you got done. Should the program mark the task complete? If you click Yes, FrontPage changes the status of the task to Complete. If you click No, your colleagues won't think you're a shirker—FrontPage changes the status to "In Progress."

Say your boss found an error on one of your pages and created a task for you to fix it. Meanwhile, you were working away on your page and happened to resolve the problem—outside the task pane. The error is fixed, but your assignment to fix it is showing up in Task view as Not Started. If you don't execute the task via the Task list, the Task list won't update itself. But you can edit the list to reflect the true state of affairs—just right-click the task and select Mark Complete.

When it comes time to delete a task, right-click it, and then select Delete Task. You can delete only one task at a time.

Part Four:
Forms and Databases

4

Gathering Data with Forms

As you know by now, FrontPage can really help you get your message out to the world. And if you're like most Web authors, you've probably filled your pages with content and formatted them nicely for the viewing pleasure of your visitors. But what if you want to let your audience reciprocate and tell *you* a thing or two? Maybe you've wondered how to create user registration forms so you know who's visiting your site, or perhaps you'd like to create a discussion section where viewers can see messages posted by others and submit a response.

When you want to gather information from viewers, you'll need to create a *Web form:* an HTML page that includes interactive fields in which a visitor can type or make a selection. You've probably filled out thousands of forms yourself—to do things like subscribe to the PTA newsletter or access your Web-based email account.

This chapter introduces you to forms and the many ways FrontPage lets you manage them. You can create your own form manually or use a FrontPage form *template* (a ready-made form-creating tool). You'll learn how to collect the data you're receiving in a variety of formats—from email to text files, or you can even pipe the info you're gathering into a database. And you'll also learn a few form-related tricks, like how to make sure that visitors fill in certain fields and how to let them know they've successfully filled out and submitted your form.

How Forms Work

You've probably been on the visitor side of forms many times: you enter your information in boxes on a Web page. Then you click Complete My Order and your browser displays a "Thank you" page. Two weeks later, your new *Guitar Artistry of Charo* CD arrives at your door.

Now that you're going to be on the manufacturing end of forms, you'll need to know a bit more about the process through which that CD was dispatched to you. What's a form made of? And where does the information go once a visitor clicks Submit?

Pages that play host to one or more forms can look pretty complicated when you peek behind the curtain, but you're still dealing with basic HTML. A form is part of a regular Web page and consists of—surprise, surprise—a basic <form> tag. Within the <form> tag's opening and close, you'll add elements that make up your form, such as text boxes, pull-down menus, option buttons, and checkboxes.

When someone fills out and submits a form, the basic process goes something like this:

1. **A viewer fills out form fields and clicks Submit.**

2. **The data she entered travels to the Web server.**

3. **Special software on the Web server processes the data and sends it into one of the following:**

   • An email message that goes wherever you say (to the company "suggestions" mailbox or your manager's inbox, for example).

   • A file that can hold data in a variety of text formats (again, you specify which one).

   • Or, into a database.

4. **The Web server displays a "confirmation page" to the viewer, thanking her for the information she so kindly entered and letting her know the Web server has processed the data.**

You've probably been on the receiving end of a confirmation message more than a few times. The process seems pretty simple, except for step 3. If you're not a programming expert, how do you get the Web server to process information like that?

No worries. FrontPage does it for you. You just need to set your options, and then the program takes care of the rest.

Note: Forms require the presence of FrontPage Server Extensions or SharePoint on your Web server. (Chapter 13 has more about both those tools.) You can create forms if you're developing your site in a disk-based environment (page 176), but you have to upload these pages to your Web server to see how they work.

Creating a Form Manually

You can add a form to any Web page. It doesn't even have to take up the whole page. For instance, you could insert a small form with just one field at the bottom of a page. After you insert the form, you'll need to fill it with form elements—like text boxes, drop-down menus, and radio buttons.

Creating a Form

To create a form, place your cursor where you want the form to start and select Insert → Form → Form (see Figure 15-1).

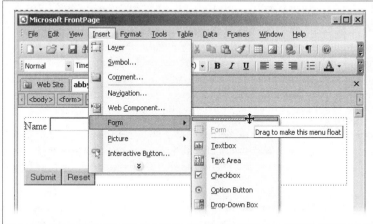

Figure 15-1:
If you'll be creating a long form, you may want to speed your work by freeing the Forms submenu from the FrontPage menu system. To do so, click the top border and drag it away from the menu. The submenu turns into a toolbar containing shortcuts to the form elements that you'll add.

FrontPage inserts a form on your page—a dotted line in the shape of a rectangle. At first, all that's in your form are two buttons: Submit and Reset. Later, a visitor will use these buttons to send you the info he's entered (Submit) or to start over again (Reset).

Tip: FrontPage supplies you with a form creation shortcut. Just insert any form element on a page (details on form elements follow in the next section), and FrontPage automatically creates a form to surround it.

The area inside the dotted lines is your work area. When you add elements to your form (which you'll do in the next section), make sure you're inserting them inside the dotted lines.

Note: If you add an element *outside* the bounds of your form, FrontPage creates another form on the page. While the program lets you include multiple forms on one page, you wouldn't want to, because a visitor can submit only one form at time (and when she does so, the page disappears from view).

If things seem a bit cramped inside your form, make some space. Place your cursor in front of the Submit button in the document window. (If you have trouble clicking in that spot with your mouse, use the arrow keys on your keyboard to get there.) Then press Enter a few times to insert some paragraph returns. This way, you'll have plenty of room above your Submit button to lay out your form.

Adding Form Fields

Inside the bounds of your new form, you'll enter *form elements* (fields that a visitor fills out) and text labels for each (so visitors know what information you're looking for). You can lay out elements of a form just as you'd lay out any Web page. For best results, insert a table (Chapter 5) in your form so you can better organize form fields and their labels. As you'll see, form elements come in all shapes and sizes. If you insert them without a table, in the regular flow of HTML text, your page can look unkempt and difficult to follow. Wrangling form elements into a table can really tidy up your page.

Each form element consists of two parts: *name* and *value.* Name is what you decide to call the field. For instance, say you've created a checkbox that a viewer can turn on if he wants more information. You could name that field "moreinfo." An element's value is the part that your site visitors provide. This can be text they enter in a text box or a checkmark they place in a checkbox.

Only when these two parts of a form element work together, does your data make sense. For instance, if a visitor turns on a checkbox, you need to know the name of it. Did they place a checkmark in the "Send me more information" or the "Never contact me again" box?

Below, you'll walk through the basic process of adding a form field, then you can read on to understand what kind of data you can collect with each type of element.

Note: Don't forget! You have to enter all form elements within the dotted line that represents the form's border.

No matter what form element you're adding, the process you'll follow is pretty much the same:

1. **Click inside a form where you'd like to place the element.**

2. **Select the form element.**

   On the Form toolbar, click the type of element you want to add, or select Insert → Form and then click the element type you want on the Form submenu. The element appears on the page.

3. **Name the element.**

   FrontPage automatically names all elements something like "T1" or "C2," which won't do you much good. Give all your page elements descriptive names that you'll recognize quickly. For instance, if you're requesting a visitor's email address, you can imagine how naming the field "email" instead of T1 will be much more helpful when you're looking over results. To name an element, right-click it, and then select Form Field Properties. Replace the text in the Name box. Names should be short, lowercase, and include no spaces or special characters.

Note: Each form element must have a unique name. If two elements have the same name, FrontPage alerts you to the problem. Correct it immediately to avoid confusing yourself and creating form validation problems (you'll learn about validation later in this chapter).

4. **Set element (form field) properties.**

   In addition to a name, each form field has other properties, which depend upon what type of element you've chosen. Details follow in the next section under each element's description.

5. **Enter a text label for the field.**

   Each field needs a corresponding label that lets a visitor know what information you want her to enter. Again, organizing fields and labels in a table will help you create a pleasing page layout that's easy to follow.

Configuring Form Fields

FrontPage offers a variety of form fields, to help you collect different types of information from your site visitors. Each element has its own purpose and properties (see Figure 15-2). To edit the properties of a form field, just double-click it. Or, right-click it and select Form Field Properties.

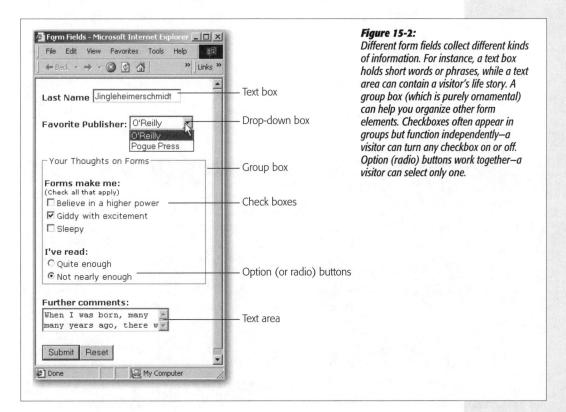

Figure 15-2:
Different form fields collect different kinds of information. For instance, a text box holds short words or phrases, while a text area can contain a visitor's life story. A group box (which is purely ornamental) can help you organize other form elements. Checkboxes often appear in groups but function independently–a visitor can turn any checkbox on or off. Option (radio) buttons work together–a visitor can select only one.

Text box

Use text boxes to collect short chunks of text, like names, email addresses, and phone numbers.

When you insert a text box, FrontPage gives you the following additional configuration options:

- **Initial value.** If you want the text box to appear with some text already in it, enter that text in this field.

- **Width in Characters** sets the size of your text box as it'll appear on the page. You can also just click a handle on the edge of the text box and drag to change its size. This figure doesn't limit the number of characters a visitor can enter; it just controls the display size of the field. To learn how to limit the number of characters a text box accepts, see "Validating Text Fields" on page 291.

- **Password field.** If you're asking for sensitive information that your visitors probably want to keep secret, then choose Yes for this option. As a result, asterisks appear instead of letters and numbers when your visitors type.

Note. Choosing Yes at the password field option affects display only. Once a visitor clicks Submit, this info travels as plain text like any other field. Therefore, this feature doesn't ensure that the information a visitor enters is secure from hackers and eavesdroppers. To truly protect information like account numbers and passwords, you've got to encrypt (scramble) it using SSL (Secure Socket Layer).

You've probably seen this in action while you've surfed the Net. Your browser usually displays a message letting you know that info you send will be encrypted. Also, a padlock icon shows up somewhere along the status bar at the bottom of the screen. When you're browsing pages on the Web, never enter sensitive information in a Web form unless your browser is displaying that little padlock. If you want this kind of security on your site, get in touch with your Web server administrator, who'll need to set this up on the server. He can also tell you what you need to do. Often you'll need to purchase an encryption certificate, but check with your host or administrator first.

GEM IN THE ROUGH

Tab Order

Most computer programs that ask you to enter data in fields feature a popular keyboard shortcut to help you move from field to field: the ever-friendly Tab key, which lets you hop from one field to the next. Most visitors expect Web forms to work the same way. If you set a tab order for your form, visitors will thank you. Doing so no only makes your page seem more professional, it also helps speed viewer entries. They'll be able to type, tab, and keep typing, without moving a hand over to the mouse.

Tab order should be intuitive. In other words, it should follow the order in which a viewer would read your form: from left to right and top to bottom. To set a tab order, just enter numbers in the tab order field for each form field's properties dialog box. Tab order goes from low to high, but they don't need to be in exact sequential order (1, 2, 3, 4, and so on). You can skip numbers if you want (3, 7, 22, for example). But always remember, the viewer's cursor moves in order from lowest to highest. (Leave this task for last, as you'll probably move form fields around until you're satisfied with the page layout.)

Text area

The text area box is for your long-winded, loquacious types. Basically this is just a very large text box. Property settings here are the same as they are for a text box, with one exception. The Number of Lines field sets the height of the text area box. You can also use this element's resize handles to change dimensions. (As with text boxes, the size of the box doesn't limit the number of characters a visitor can enter. To learn how to limit the number of characters a text area box accepts, see "Validating Text Fields" on page 291.)

Checkbox

To the simple checkbox, life's an all or nothing affair. A checkbox is either on or off. This element is great for "check all your areas of interest" type questions. A visitor can turn on one, two, all, or none—however many she wants.

If you have a checkbox or two in your form, be sure to configure the following options in the Form Field Properties dialog box:

- **Value.** This is the text you'll see (in an email, text file, or database) if a visitor turns on your checkbox. FrontPage automatically enters the text "ON" in this field, which in most cases will do quite nicely. This way when a checkbox is on you'll see the text (checkbox name)=ON.

- **Initial State.** Do you want the checkbox to appear with a checkmark already in it? This might be a way to encourage people to join your mailing list, for instance. If they neglect to uncheck it, then you've got 'em. (Actually, nobody falls for that anymore.) Whatever your strategy, if you want the checkbox turned on when a page first loads, choose Checked.

Option (or radio) button

Option buttons present your visitors with a choice. These buttons appear in groups, and a viewer can select only one. When you select or activate one option, all others turn off. You can use this field type for simple Yes or No questions, or for multiple-choice questions where you only want one answer.

Note: The rest of the world—including HTML—calls option buttons "radio buttons." Option is a good name for them, too, since a viewer can choose only one option, but you may see the old-fashioned term "radio button" as well. Perhaps those in charge of user-friendly naming at Microsoft felt that most people are now too young to remember the old radios that let you change the station by pressing a button. Press one and you were listening to a station down at the right end of the dial. Press another and you moved left, up the dial, to a different station. In other words, when you pressed a radio button—you'd selected that one *option* (radio station) only, while turning off any others that you'd previously selected.

While all other form elements require a unique name, option buttons are the exception. Because they work together, all option buttons in a group should have the same name. FrontPage takes care of this for you if you insert option buttons one right after another. Insert another element in between, and FrontPage gives the latter radio button a new unique name. (If need be, you can edit the "Group name" field (in Form Field Properties) so all the buttons in one group match each other.)

Other fields you'll configure for option buttons are:

- **Value.** Type in the name of the option here. Since FrontPage has co-opted the Name field to group your option buttons, you'll use this field to identify each individual option. When you get your results, you'll see the value for the selected option (and none of the other options). Make sure each option has its own unique value, so you can tell which one your visitor selected.

- **Initial State.** Specify, if you want, a particular button selected when the page first displays in a browser. (You can only choose one within a group.)

Drop-down box

Option buttons and checkboxes are nifty, but what if you've got a really long list of choices? Adding all those buttons to your form would take up a lot of screen real estate. If you've got a ton of options, try consolidating them in a drop-down list.

When you insert a drop-down box, it shows up empty. You've got to add choices. To do so, double-click the box to open the Drop-Down Properties dialog box (see Figure 15-3).

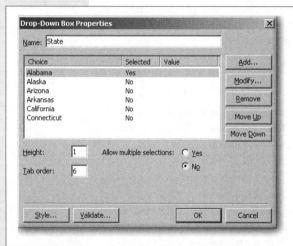

Figure 15-3:
Build your list of choices in the Drop-Down Box Properties dialog box. After you add selections, click Move Up or Move Down to position them within the list.

To add a choice, click Add. In the Add Choice dialog box that opens, type in the name for your choice. If you want the Web server to send you a result value other than the one you just typed, turn on the "Specify value" checkbox, and then type the value in the line below. Click OK, and FrontPage adds the new entry to the list.

Other configuration options in the Drop-Down Box Properties dialog box include:

- **Height.** Type how many rows of your drop-down box you want to display on the page. Most lists display only one line, but you can show viewers a few selections if you want.

- **Allow Multiple Selections.** You can let visitors select more than one option at a time, by clicking Yes here. If you activate this option, a drop-down list can serve the same purpose as a group of checkboxes.

When your list appears on a Web page, the first item in the list shows. If you'd prefer that another item in the list display instead, but don't want it at the top of the list, do the following: Highlight the choice in the Drop-Down Properties dialog box and click Modify. In the Modify Choice dialog box, under Initial state, click Selected and click OK.

Tip: You can also make your first choice, which displays on the page, be some instructional text like "Select an item below." Just enter it as the first choice and use validation settings (page 291, later in this chapter) if you want to force a visitor to choose another selection.

File upload

Suppose a form can't hold all the information you're looking for. Maybe you want visitors to send you their résumés, business plans, or pictures of their pets engaging in water sports. You don't need to make them paste any of these items in a text area box. Let them send you their files in all their glory—that's right, you can let a visitor upload an entire file to you by letting them use a form.

Note: You'll need to check with your Web server administrator to make sure the server accepts anonymous file uploads. For security reasons, many don't.

Insert a File Upload field as you would any other. Once it appears on your page, you'll see that it features a simple text field and a Browse button. FrontPage has preprogrammed this button to let a visitor browse his computer to select a file. You can't edit the button or its label.

Double-click the upload element, and FrontPage lets you select a destination folder for uploaded files. Create a special folder in your site to hold these files. If you want to keep them out of the public eye, create an *uploads* folder within your _private folder and select it. (The _private folder is off-limits to site visitors. FrontPage excludes it from searches and browsing.)

When you add a file upload element to a form, FrontPage adds a special File Upload tab to the Saving Results dialog box, which you access through the Form

Properties dialog box (see Figure 15-4). (To open it, right-click inside the form, select Form Properties, and then click Options.)

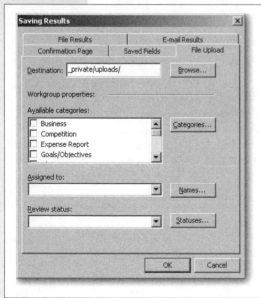

Figure 15-4:
Not only can you change the target directory for file uploads at the top of this tab, you can also assign uploaded files to an individual for review or to a category or review status. Because FrontPage lets you fold uploaded files into the program's workflow features (see Chapter 14 for details on these), you can flag and process uploaded files much more easily. Use these features to tell you when your site's received new files.

Group box

Often you'll want to group some of your form fields together, both for aesthetic reasons and to help let viewers know what you're looking for. A *group box* surrounds a bunch of elements with a border and provides a heading for them (for a picture of what the group box looks like, pop back to Figure 15-2).

When you insert a group box, it's empty. You've got to paste or insert form fields in it after you create it. Group boxes always fill the browser screen horizontally. If that's too wide for you, try inserting the group box inside a table cell.

Label

As you've read, you label your form fields using simple HTML text. All you can do is position labels next to fields to try to make it very clear which label goes with what field. While that's true, FrontPage can enhance the label setup that you created by linking a label to a field. One advantage to doing this is that a visitor won't be limited to just clicking in an element (for instance, a checkbox) to turn it on. She could click the field's label, too. More importantly, labels make your form more accessible for visitors who are viewing impaired. If an author lays out a form poorly (see Figure 15-5), screen readers can have a terrible time connecting labels with fields. This makes it really difficult for a visually impaired visitor to fill out the form correctly. If you link a field with its label, you can avoid any such confusion.

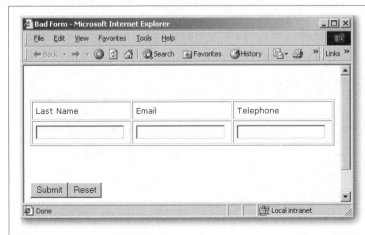

Figure 15-5:
Because screen readers read cell contents in the order in which they appear in HTML code, a form layout like this makes no sense. First, it would recite "Last Name, Email, Telephone," and then it would see three text boxes in a row. It's better to have a form field next to a label; if you link them to each other, you put the icing on the cake. Naming your fields appropriately helps a lot, too.

To link a field and its label together, you already need to have both elements in place. Select them both and select Insert → Form → Label, or click Label on the Form toolbar. FrontPage puts a dotted line around the label to let you know it's linked to its field.

Buttons

All the form fields you just read about would be nothing without a means to send the information. That's where the not-so-humble form button comes in.

Submit and Reset buttons

When you create your form, FrontPage automatically gives it two buttons: Submit and Reset.

The Submit button is the form's control center. All form activity revolves around this important hub. After a visitor fills out a form and clicks Submit, the action starts. The Submit button tells the Web browser to send the form data to the Web server.

You don't need to configure this button in any way. If you want, you can change its label (right-click the button, select Form Field Properties, and then edit the Value/Label field).

The Reset button is the visitor's "do over" option. If a visitor clicks Reset, the form returns to its original state. This button doesn't clear the form. Instead, whatever the visitor saw when he first opened that page—like empty fields and some preset options—he'll see again.

Normal button

If you want to add another kind of button to a page—perhaps one that links to more information, for instance—you can add what FrontPage calls a "Normal" button. Unlike the Submit and Reset buttons, a Normal button has no preset mission. To get a Normal button, select Insert → Form → Push Button (Figure 15-6).

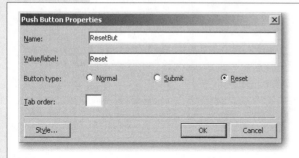

Figure 15-6:
All three types of buttons–Submit, Reset, and Normal–share this Push Button Properties dialog box (double-click any button to access Button Properties). You can change the way a button works by using this dialog box. For example, turn a Normal button into a Submit button by selecting that button type.

Advanced button

The Advanced button is a more flexible variation on the Normal button. You can type a label directly on it as soon as you create it or resize it; you can even insert an image in it.

Using a picture as a Submit button

If you want to jazz up your page, you can have a picture serve as the page's Submit button. To do so, insert a picture in your form using the Form menu (select Insert → Form → Picture or click Picture on the Form toolbar). FrontPage inserts the picture, which is automatically turned into a Submit button (because you inserted it via the Forms menu).

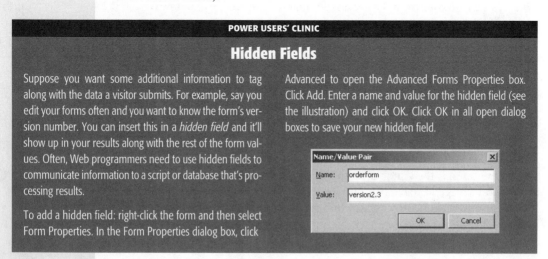

POWER USERS' CLINIC

Hidden Fields

Suppose you want some additional information to tag along with the data a visitor submits. For example, say you edit your forms often and you want to know the form's version number. You can insert this in a *hidden field* and it'll show up in your results along with the rest of the form values. Often, Web programmers need to use hidden fields to communicate information to a script or database that's processing results.

To add a hidden field: right-click the form and then select Form Properties. In the Form Properties dialog box, click

Advanced to open the Advanced Forms Properties box. Click Add. Enter a name and value for the hidden field (see the illustration) and click OK. Click OK in all open dialog boxes to save your new hidden field.

Validating Forms

Say a visitor fills out your form, but he leaves off his name and all his contact information. Those form results probably won't do you much good. If only you could force that person to give you complete and accurate information.

Well, you can. FrontPage lets you vet the data a visitor enters into a form. You can set certain parameters. For example, you might specify that a text field can't be blank, or that another must include only numeric characters. If the content entered by a visitor doesn't match the rules you set, the browser won't send the information onto the server. This process is called *form field validation*.

Note: FrontPage activates validation by inserting either JavaScript or VBScript in your Web page. Out of the box, the program is set to add JavaScript to handle this job. If you want to switch to VBScript for some reason, select Tools → Site Settings and click the Advanced tab. Then change the "Default validation script language" selection.

Accessing Validation Settings

You can validate text boxes, drop-down boxes, and option buttons. To access a field's validation settings, double-click the element to open its Form Field Properties dialog box and click Validation at the bottom. Instructions for configuring field validation for each element type follow.

Validating Text Fields

Once you've opened the Text Box Validation dialog box (see Figure 15-7), you can set all sorts of parameters for text boxes and text area boxes.

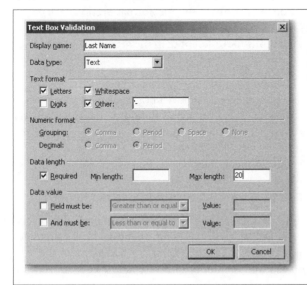

Figure 15-7:
The Text Box Validation dialog box looks complicated, but once you make a choice in the Data Type drop-down list, FrontPage activates only the relevant options—everything else is greyed out.

Selecting a data type

First, select one of the following data types from the drop-down list. (Making a choice here opens up further options.)

- **No Constraints.** This is FrontPage's automatic setting for all text fields. When you leave this selected, FrontPage won't apply any validation whatsoever.

- **Text.** The field accepts only alphanumeric characters. If you choose this data type, the following checkbox options open up in the Text format section. (You can check more than one.)

  — **Letters.** Turn on this checkbox if you want the field to accept only alphabetic characters.

  — **Digits.** Turn on this checkbox if the field should accept only numeric characters.

  — **Whitespace.** Turn on this checkbox if you'll let a visitor enter spaces, tabs, and paragraph breaks.

  — **Other.** Turn on this checkbox if you want to allow other special characters (like @, or an apostrophe, comma, or period). Then type those characters in the box next to the word "Other."

- **Integer.** The field can contain only whole numbers. If you select this option, FrontPage lets you make "Grouping" settings within the Numeric format section. Specify whether you'll let visitors format integers with a comma (5,000), period (5.000), space (5 000), or no additional characters (5000).

- **Number.** The box can contain only whole numbers or decimals. If you select this option, FrontPage lets you set both grouping (as explained in the previous entry) and decimal notation within the Numeric format section. Select the character you want visitors to enter as the decimal character—a comma or period. The decimal character must be different than the grouping character.

Entering a display name

Once you've selected options within the Data Type field (as explained above), then FrontPage lets you enter a display name. This name should match the label you gave this text field on your Web page, because FrontPage will use it in any error messages that the validation process displays to the viewer. Make it easy for your visitors to identify what they entered incorrectly.

Requiring date entry and length

If this is a text field that you don't want a visitor to leave blank, then turn on the Required checkbox in the Data Length section. Doing so automatically stipulates that the minimum length of that field will be one character and activates the Min Length field beside it (so you can up the minimum if you want). You can validate length in the following ways:

- **Min Length.** Enter the lowest number of characters the field will accept. For example, limit a Zip code field to not less than five numbers.

- **Max Length.** Enter the highest number of characters the field will accept. Use this option to avoid getting a novel in your text field.

Tip: Whenever possible, let visitors know where you've applied validation settings. For example, mark all required fields with an asterisk and put a message to this effect at the top of your page.

Setting data value

Use fields at the very bottom of this dialog box to restrict the values a visitor may enter. You'll want to use this option only with numeric values. For example, you can specify that a number be greater than 5 but less than 500.

Note: If you set the data value after you've chosen Text or No Constraints as the Data Type, data values won't be of much use. In this situation, character order rules. In other words, the letter or number that comes first sequentially is deemed less than those that come later in the alphabet. So "a" is less than "n," because "a" comes before "n" in the alphabet. Likewise, "134" is less than "2" because 1 comes before 2 sequentially.

Validating Drop-Down Boxes

If your drop-down box accepts only one choice from a visitor (this option is set within the Drop-Down Box Properties dialog box, as explained on page 286), then validation options are simple. To force the visitor to make a selection, turn on the "Data required" checkbox. If you've included a first choice that's not really an option, but just some text that says "Select an item below," and you don't want this to be a valid entry, turn on the "Disallow first choice" checkbox.

If your drop-down box accepts multiple choices, then you can set two additional options beneath the "Data required" checkbox: enter the minimum number of items a visitor can select and/or enter the maximum number she can select.

Validating Option Buttons

When it comes to option buttons, all you can do is make sure that a visitor makes a selection. Once you've accessed the Option Button Validation dialog box via the field's Properties dialog box, you can turn on the "Data required" checkbox and enter a display name. Again, make sure this name matches the general label or question that the group of Option buttons poses. This way, if this validation generates an error, a visitor knows where to make a correction.

Saving Form Results

You've got yourself a form! A visitor can open the page you created, enter the information you need, and click Submit. But then what happens?

Your form won't do you any good unless you tell FrontPage how you want to receive the information it gathers. You can save results in a text file, in an email message that you have the server send to you, or shoot the results into a database.

You set all these options within the Form Properties dialog box (see Figure 15-8). To open it, right-click inside the form, and then select Form Properties.

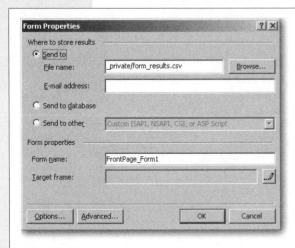

Figure 15-8:
The Form Properties dialog box lets you specify what you want to do with the data your forms have collected. Set additional details for each selection shown here by clicking Options, in the lower-left corner.

Saving Results to a File

If you want to store results in a flexible format, consider saving the results in a file. When you do so, FrontPage takes your data, creates a new file, and then plunks your data in it. The resulting file can be a simple HTML file or a more versatile text file (see the box "Data in a Text File"). Once FrontPage creates this file, it appends data gleaned from additional form submissions to the file's contents.

UP TO SPEED

Data in a Text File

Saving data in a text file is a more flexible option than saving it in an HTML file. For starters, a text file won't include any extra gobbledygook like HTML tags. If it's just data you're looking for, stick with a text file. In fact, you should use an HTML file only if you want to display the results on your site.

Many data-gathering wizards regularly use text files (with file endings like .txt or .csv) to hold data. As long as the data

in these files follows certain predictable rules (like commas appearing between each field and a paragraph return appearing between each record, for instance), a program can easily accept the text data and transform it into an Access or SQL database, or an Excel spreadsheet.

To save your data in a file, select the "Send to" radio button in the Form Properties dialog box. Next, enter a name for you file, including its location:

- If you want to store the file *within* your Web site, enter a relative URL (page 44), including a file name like *contactform_results.csv*.

- If you want to store the file *outside* your site—say, on your company's data server instead of the Web server that your site's on—enter the path. You can enter this in UNC (Universal Naming Convention) format, like *dataserver\siteresults\form_results.csv* or use a drive-letter path, like *N:\siteresults\form_results.csv*.

- If you want form results to be private, save them to a .txt or .csv file in your site's _private folder. FrontPage hides this folder from visitors, but it's not super secure. If form data is confidential or sensitive, then save results in a password-protected area in your site or in another location. (To learn how to restrict access to part of your site, see "Securing a Subsite" on page 307.)

- If you want your results to be public, save the results into an HTML file (not a text file) and store it in a file where your visitors can find it (not the _private folder, in other words).

Note: Turn on the "Include field names" checkbox. Without it, you'll see only a viewer's entry values and may have no idea what field names they belong to.

Specifying file format and type

To choose the kind of file you want to create when saving your form data, click the Options button on the lower-left corner of the Form Properties dialog box. Here you can specify a file format by selecting one of the following from the drop-down menu:

- **XML.** The server pipes data into an XML file, which uses tags to separate data elements. You can output to XML only if your Web server is running SharePoint services.

- **HTML.** The server saves data onto a Web page and applies no special formatting.

- **HTML Definition List.** As in the preceding item, data appears on a Web page, but displays in definition list style (page 41), in which field names are matched with values that a visitor has added.

- **HTML Bulleted List.** Data appears on a Web page in a regular bulleted list (page 38).

- **Formatted text within HTML.** Data appears in HTML-formatted text format (which looks like typewriter text—see page 35).

Note: Whenever you choose to output to an HTML file, FrontPage activates the "Latest results at end" checkbox below the File format field. When you send data results to a file, the Web server just appends new data at the bottom of the file, below data you've already collected. If you turn this checkbox off, the server adds new results to the top of the page. (In a text file, data always gets appended at the end of the file, no matter what.)

- **Formatted Text.** Select this if you want to output data in a text file that the server formats for easy reading.

- **Text database using comma as a separator.** Data goes in a .csv text file where values are separated by commas.

- **Text database using tab as a separator.** Data goes in a .txt text file where values are separated by tabs.

- **Text database using space as a separator.** Data goes in a .txt text file where values are separated by spaces.

Outputting to a second file

FrontPage lets you have your cake and eat it too. If you enter another file in the Optional Second File field, you can simultaneously send results to an alternate file. This means that you can gather text in a useful text format while also plunking it into an HTML file that visitors can see on your site, if you want.

Saving Results to Email

You can also have your form results delivered right to your inbox or into a mailbox that you've specially set up to receive them. If you're trying to decide whether to send results to a file or to an email, good news: it's not an either/or decision. You can do both—receive an email and output data to a file, as described above.

To start setting up an email format output, open the Form Properties dialog box (right-click the form and select Form Properties) and click Send To. You don't need to enter an email address right away. Instead, click Options, and then click the E-mail Results tab (see Figure 15-9).

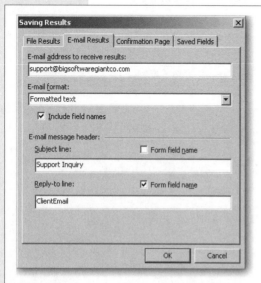

Figure 15-9:
Specify how you want to receive your email results within this dialog box. FrontPage includes options for adding a subject line (which can draw from a field on your form) and setting up an email address to which you can reply automatically (this can also be extracted from a viewer's form entry—see step 5 in the instructions for setting up email format output).

Then, follow these steps:

1. **Enter the email address to which you'll route form results.**

   Generally, this can be any address you want, but some Web hosts limit your options to email addresses within your site's domain. For example, if your domain is *www.myfabuloussite.com,* you'd only be able to send to email addresses that end in "@myfabuloussite.com"—like *joe@myfabuloussite.com.* Check with your Web hosting company, or run a quick test.

2. **Select an email format.**

   FrontPage automatically sets this field to "Formatted text," which is a good, easy-to-read option. However, this drop-down list includes all the choices that FrontPage offers for file formatting (which are listed in the previous section).

3. **Make sure the "Include field names" checkbox is turned on.**

   This way, field names will be sent with values so you know what questions visitors are responding to.

4. **Set a subject line.**

   When your email arrives, it needs to have a subject line. You have two options here:

   • **Create your own subject line.** For example, you might want to do this if you're sending support emails into your everyday mailbox. This way you'll know it's not a regular message, but a support request.

   • **Pull out a value entered by the visitor in one of your form fields and use it as the email subject line.** Say your support request form has a text box where viewers enter a brief description of their problem. If you make that field the subject line, you'll get a head start understanding what they're writing about.

5. **Set a reply-to line.**

   Here, you'll set up a recipient for any replies you make to the data results emails you receive. You can enter a specific address in this field, but that won't do you much good unless you route all your emails to a specific person for handling. On the other hand, say you want your response to go to the person who submitted the form. No problem—as long as you've had your visitor enter his email address in one of your form fields. If that's the case, turn on the "Form field name" checkbox and enter the name of that field below.

6. **Click OK.**

   The email address you entered now appears in the Form Properties dialog box as the "send to" email address.

Note: Email addresses you enter in the Form Properties dialog box end up buried within the page's regular HTML. This means that they're sitting ducks for the email address harvesters that spammers send out across the Web (see page 51 for more on keeping your email address out of the hands of spammers).

Saving Results in a Database

FrontPage makes it easy for even database know-nothings to plug information from forms into a database. In fact, the program can even create one for you, based on your form fields.

Chapter 16 covers database fundamentals. Once you know the basics, you can learn how to send your form results to a database and understand how FrontPage works with databases.

Other Output Options

You have some additional options for handling data collected in your form. If you click "Send to Other" in the Form Properties dialog box, FrontPage gives you three choices, described in the following sections.

Outputting to a custom script

The simple form handling options that FrontPage offers might not be enough for you. You may want your forms to work a little more magic. For example, if you want to send your form results to *many* email addresses or have your confirmation page total figures a visitor's entered in your form, you'll need to use a custom form-handling script. Where would you get such a script? Well, you need to write it or befriend someone who can. You can also check with your Web host to see if they offer any scripts to process form results.

A custom form-handling script steps in and does the job that FrontPage does when you output your data to a file or email. Custom scripts offer the most flexibility of all output options and are necessary for forms that handle complex data. Scripts also enable you to react to myriad visitor actions and customize result outputs to suit your needs.

To use a script to handle form results:

1. **Click "Send to other" then select "Custom ISAPI, NSAPI, CGI or ASP Script" from the drop-down menu.**

   This selection shows the types of scripts FrontPage allows. Your choices are: ISAPI (Internet Server Application Programming Interface), NSAPI (Netscape Server Application Programming Interface), CGI (Common Gateway Interface), or ASP (Active Server Pages). After you make a selection, FrontPage can tell what type of script you're using when you link to one of these file types in the next step.

2. **Click Options on the lower left. A dialog box for Custom Form Handler options displays (see Figure 15-10).**

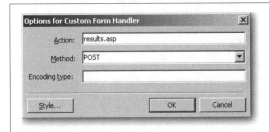

Figure 15-10:
This dialog box lets you link your form to a custom script to handle results. However, you can decorate your form from here, too. If you click Style, you can use CSS (page 115) to format fonts, borders, or shading in your form.

3. **Set the following options:**

- **Action.** Here you'll specify the URL of your script.

- **Method.** Your selection here depends upon the kind of script you're using. You've got two choices. POST is the more common and more flexible option whereby the browser first contacts the form program on the server, then sends the data to it. This method is what a browser does automatically, unless instructed otherwise. It's more secure, because all the data is passed behind the scenes. In the GET method, the browser sends data as part of the URL. Form field names and values that a visitor enters are all appended to the page's URL. For example, say a visitor types the term "platypus" in a search form. The URL that search would return looks something like: *http://wwwmysite.com/cgi-bin/search.cgi?term=platypus.* The *search.cgi* part is the special script that's handling the form. A question mark separates the main URL from the part of it that shows data. "Term" is the name of the search field. In this example, the visitor's filled out only one field, if a form has many fields, the URL can grow quite large. Since a URL can't be longer than 255 characters, you can understand how limited this method is.

- **Encoding type.** This sets some communication parameters for the form data. You can leave this blank, which means that you're sending data from ordinary form elements (no value here is the same as entering "application/x-www-form-urlencoded," but why should you tax your fingers typing that?). The only time this setting would be different is if you have an upload element (which lets users upload a file to your site) in your form. In that case, FrontPage automatically enters the phrase "multipart/form-data" for you.

4. **Save your settings.**

Click OK to save your form handler settings and then click OK in the Form Properties dialog box.

Registration form handler

If you've set up site registration (see page 306, later this chapter), FrontPage uses this selection to handle user name and password entries.

Discussion form handler

If you've set up a discussion site (see page 310, later this chapter), FrontPage uses this selection to handle all discussion entries that visitors submit.

Creating a Confirmation Page

Imagine that you're visiting your own site and you complete one of your forms. After you click the Submit button, how can you be sure that your data actually went where it was supposed to go?

Don't leave your visitors hanging in doubt. Create a page that says "Yes, the button worked, the server received your input, and someone on the World Wide Web actually cares about you." Or just a simple "Thank you for your submission." Whatever you decide to write, the screen that appears following the click of a Submit button is called the *confirmation page*.

FrontPage's Automated Confirmation Page

The confirmation page is so important that even if you don't actively set one up, FrontPage automatically creates one for you. This is a simple, unadorned page, which thanks the visitor and shows them the data they entered (see Figure 15-11).

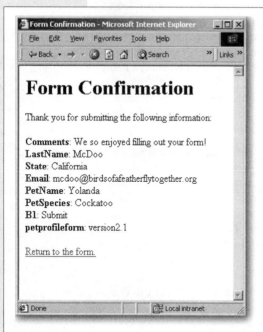

Figure 15-11:
The confirmation page that FrontPage automatically generates is spare and unattractive. Also, fields don't appear in the same order they did on your form, which may confuse some viewers. You and your visitors will be happier if you create your own custom confirmation page.

Creating a Custom Confirmation Page

If you want, you can create you own confirmation page—one that matches your site's visual style and includes your own heartwarming message. To do so:

1. **Create an HTML page as you would any other.**

   Add text to the page thanking the visitor, extolling their excellent data entry skills, or whatever you want to say.

Note: FrontPage includes a confirmation form within its Page Templates dialog box, but it's even less exciting than the completely automated one, and its field names will require some tweaking to match your form. You're better off starting from scratch.

---

2. **Insert confirmation fields.**

   If you want to display the values a visitor entered on the confirmation page, you can do so by inserting confirmation fields that draw visitors' entries from the form onto the confirmation page for them to review. To do so, place your cursor where you want the data to appear. Then select Insert → Web Component → Advanced Controls and select Confirmation field from the list of options on the right. Then type in the name of the field whose results you want to display (this text must match your field name exactly). The field name appears in brackets on your page. When a viewer sees the confirmation page, whatever value she entered in the field displays instead. You should create a label for all your fields, so these values make sense. Repeat this step for every field you plan to show.

POWER USERS' CLINIC

Custom Validation Page

When a visitor fills out a form and submits it, the server sends a confirmation page. However, when a visitor makes a mistake filling out a form, the server almost never sends a validation page. That's because validation takes place *before* form data ever reaches the server. The browser's in charge of validation. When a viewer doesn't enter information correctly and tries to submit the form, the browser doesn't send it to the server. Instead, the browser displays a pop-up message telling the viewer about the entry mistake and how to fix it. The validation page appears only if a viewer's configured his browser not to run JavaScript (very rare) and the bad data gets all the way to the server.

For those rare instances, you can create a custom validation page. You create this kind of page the same way you'd create a custom confirmation page. The one difference is, when you get to step 2 in the instructions above, don't type a field name into the Confirmation Field Properties box. Type "Validation-Error" instead (see illustration). When you click OK, FrontPage displays a message telling you that the name isn't valid. Don't be deterred! Click OK to get rid of

the prompt and FrontPage adds the field to your page anyway. (If FrontPage doesn't add the field for some reason, just type in "ValidationError" without the hyphen and click OK. Then open the page in Code view, find the "ValidationError" text, and then insert the hyphen.)

Once you've created and saved your page, open your form, right-click it, and then select Form Properties. Then click Options to open the Saving Results dialog box. Within the Confirmation tab pictured back in Figure 15-12, use the "URL of validation failure page" field to link the form to your new validation error page. You'll only be able to test the page if you disable scripts within your browser. (For example, in IE, select Tools → Internet Options, select the Security tab, click Custom Level, and disable active scripting.)

3. **Attach your custom confirmation page to the form page.**

Open the page your form is on. Right-click within the form and select Form Properties. Click Options and select the Confirmation Page tab (see Figure 15-12). In the "URL of confirmation page" field, browse to or type the relative URL path (page 44) and the file name.

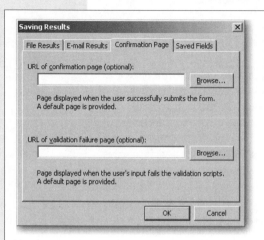

Figure 15-12:
Enter a path to a custom confirmation page. If you don't create one, FrontPage will, although you probably won't care for the results. Same goes for the Validation Failure page. FrontPage automatically creates a validation error page, but most viewers never see it (as explained in the box "Custom Validation Page").

Letting FrontPage Create Your Form

As you've read, creating forms is a lot of work. By now, you might be sorely tempted to find an easier way. Good news: FrontPage can create your form for you. In some cases, as with the Form Page Wizard, getting help from the program doesn't speed up the process much. In other instances, as with the discussion Web site, FrontPage can create a complex automated site for you easily and quickly.

As with most of FrontPage's templates and canned features, using them limits your options for modifying form elements later. Read on to learn about working with the Form Page Wizard. Maybe you're looking for a form to gather feedback, or you'd like visitors to sign a guestbook, or identify themselves before viewing your site. You'll also see how to restrict access to a subsite (page 190) and how to create a discussion board.

Form Page Wizard

For those looking for some help when creating a complex form, FrontPage offers the Form Page Wizard. Remember "wizards" from back in Chapter 10? The FrontPage page-creation tool that prompts you with questions and generates pages from your answers? Same thing goes with the Form Page Wizard.

That's all well and good, but honestly, by the time you respond to all the prompts, you could be halfway done creating your form manually with the Forms toolbar or menu.

Nonetheless, those who love a good wizard can follow the steps below for creating a form using this tool.

1. **Launch the Form Page Wizard.**

   Select File → New and click "More page templates" in the New task pane. Double-click the Form Page Wizard to launch it.

2. **Begin responding to the wizard's prompts.**

   FrontPage displays a prompt explaining how the wizard works. Click Next.

3. **Select a question type.**

   In the next dialog box, FrontPage asks you to select what type of questions you want to include on your form. Click Add to see your choices. The dialog box in Figure 15-13 displays. At top is a list of question types, which really serve as form sections. For instance, the top of your form may include "Contact Info" while the bottom half features "Ordering Info." Select a question type from the top and then click Next. (You'll have a chance to select additional question types in a minute.)

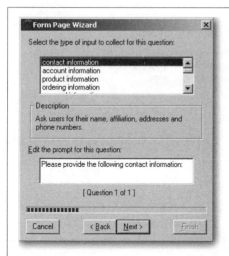

Figure 15-13:
Select a genre of questions from the list at top. In the bottom pane, FrontPage shows you what text it'll place on the page as a section header for that group of questions. You can edit this text here, or later, on the Web page itself.

4. **Add Input options.**

   Depending upon what type of question you chose in the last step, FrontPage offers you a variety of fields to add to your form (see Figure 15-14). Turn on checkboxes for all those that you want to include and then click Next.

5. **Add further question types, if you want.**

FrontPage returns you to the first wizard screen, which now features the question type you chose in step 3 (see Figure 15-15). If you want to add another question, click Add and repeat steps 3 and 4. When you've added all the regions and fields you want the form to include, click Next.

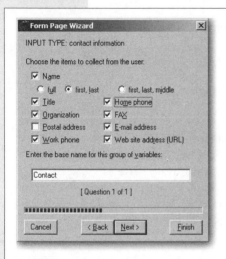

Figure 15-14:
Use this dialog box on the Form Page Wizard to select the fields you want to add to your form.

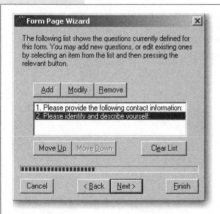

Figure 15-15:
If you've added multiple question types to your form, you can use the Move Up and Move Down buttons to rearrange the order in which these sections will appear on your page.

6. **Set presentation style.**

FrontPage then prompts you to select page layout options. You can choose to have your fields organized in normal paragraphs, or in a numbered, bulleted, or definition list (see page 37 at the end of Chapter 2 for a refresher on list types).

If you have a very long form, you may want to let FrontPage add a table of contents to the top of the page. If your form is short, don't bother.

You can also have FrontPage lay out your form in a table, which helps create a cleaner looking page. Turn on the "Use tables to align form fields" checkbox, and click Next.

7. **Select output option.**

   Here you tell FrontPage what to do with the data the form collects. You can have results appear in a Web page or be saved in a text file. (Refer back to "Saving Form Results" on page 293 for details on these options.) The last selection, "Use custom CGI script," is for those with advanced programming skills. If you don't have a custom script for saving results, you'll obviously steer clear of this choice. Select one of these options and then enter a name for the Web page or text file, if necessary. Then click Finish.

   FrontPage creates your new form page and displays it in the document window (see Figure 15-16). Look over the form and make sure it's what you expected. You can edit this page as you would any other. Change text or add validation options as you wish.

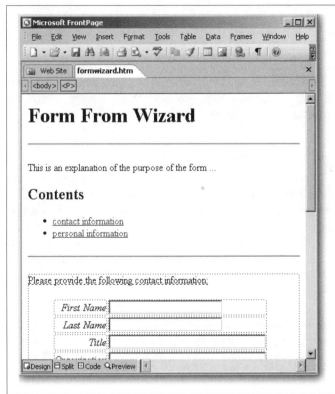

Figure 15-16:
This is the form that FrontPage creates from the wizard. The table of contents at the top includes links to each section of the form—that is, each "question type" you chose in the wizard. Make sure to replace FrontPage's boilerplate explanation text with your own.

Templates

FrontPage comes with a few canned form pages that you can use for some commonly used forms, like collecting feedback from visitors to your site or creating a guest book they can leave comments on.

To create a page using any of these form templates, select File → New. Within the New task pane, click "More page templates," and then, within the Page Templates dialog box, select one of the choices described next.

Feedback Form

This template creates a Web page with a form on it, designed to collect visitor feedback regarding things like suggestions or problems. Edit this page and configure the form as you would if you created the form from scratch. Results automatically go into a text file, but you can change this if you want. (See page 293, "Saving Form Results" earlier in this chapter.)

Guest Book

Selecting this template creates a form page containing one text area field for comments. When a visitor submits this form, results appear on the guest book page.

Note: Guest books often attract spammers who'll fill your guest log with offers for Viagra and other unwanted solicitations. So, unless you really need it, think twice about adding a guest book to your site. If you do include one, try renaming the *guestbook.htm* page to something else. This stops a lot of automated postings, but won't solve the problem entirely.

User Registration

The User Registration Form template lets you have visitors "self-register" to gain access to a subsite (page 190). In other words, you can make them fill out a user name and password of their choosing to browse any files contained in the subsite. The advantage is that you can track visitors and see where they're going within your site, because these logins will be reflected in your usage reports. However, forcing viewers to create user names and enter information may turn some people away. If you want to collect visitor information, you may as well post a form somewhere to collect it.

Note: FrontPage registration forms only work on Unix servers. If you're site is hosted on an IIS Web server, you're out of luck. Also, you must save the registration page *outside* your Web site, on the Web server. This means that you'll need to speak with your Web host (some of whom don't allow registration) or whoever is running your Web server.

To create a user registration form, you'll begin with server permissions. (*Permissions* are a set of controls on your live Web server that you use to tell the FrontPage

Server Extensions who can enter your site and what they can do there.) Next, you'll create the form itself. The steps for setting up a registration form follow.

FREQUENTLY ASKED QUESTION

Securing a Subsite

How do I create a subsite that visitors can access only by entering a special user name and password that I give them?

The user registration form that you're about to learn how to create lets visitors self-register. This means that they can type whatever they want in the registration form. In exchange for providing information, they get access to your subsite.

In contrast, creating a *secure subsite*—one that visitors can only access using the magic user name and password combination that you've approved—is a slightly different process and does not require the use of the user registration form. You can limit access to a subsite by editing your site's permissions.

To create a subsite like this, follow the steps within Phase I only. After step 5, keep your remote site open and perform the actions discussed next.

Within the Administration page, click Manage Users. Click Add a User. Enter the user name and password you want to assign and select a role for the user. (For instance, if you just want visitors to your subsite to be able to browse pages, select Browser.) Click Add User. Repeat for each user you want to add, and then close your browser.

Phase I: Creating a subsite and setting permissions

To create a subsite and set permissions, do the following:

1. **Create a subsite.**

   Open your Web site and create the subsite (page 190) to which you want to control access. The site you protect must always be a subsite. If you want to force visitors to register to enter your entire site, put it in a subsite. FrontPage needs the root folder of your Web site (the core folder that contains the *index.htm* or *default.htm* file) to house the registration form you're about to create. The form must live outside the folder to which you're restricting access—otherwise, a visitor wouldn't be able to see it or fill it out, and would therefore never get into the subsite.

2. **Publish the subsite.**

   Before you publish, click Remote Sever Properties on the upper right of the document window, select the Publishing tab, and then turn on the "Include subsites" checkbox. If you don't, FrontPage won't publish your subsite along with the rest of your site. Then publish. (Forgot how to publish? Refer back to Chapter 13.)

3. **Open the subsite on your live Web server.**

   While still connected to your live Web server, open the subsite in FrontPage. To do so, click the "Open your remote Web site in FrontPage" link within Remote Web site view (see page 260 for details) and double-click the subsite's folder. The subsite opens in a new instance of FrontPage.

---

4. **Set permissions for the subsite.**

   With the subsite open, select Tools → Server → Permissions. You may be prompted for the administrative user name and password that your Web host or IT administrator gave you. Then the Permissions Administration Web page appears (see Figure 15-17). Click Change Permissions. Within the Change Subweb Permissions page, click Use Unique Permissions. Then click Submit.

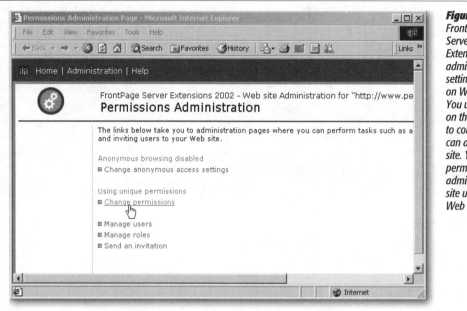

Figure 15-17:
FrontPage Server Extensions administration settings display on Web pages. You use settings on these pages to control who can access your site. You'll set permissions and administer your site using your Web browser.

5. **Turn off anonymous access for the subsite.**

   All FrontPage sites automatically allow anyone to access them without identifying themselves, which you'll have to change, of course. At the top of the page, click the Administration link, and then click Change Anonymous Access Settings. Next to the "Anonymous access is" field, click Off. Click Submit and then click OK.

Note: If you're trying to secure a subsite (with a secret user name and password) instead of creating a self-registration form, return to the box that precedes these instructions to complete your final step. (You don't need to create a registration form, so don't proceed to Phase II.)

You can close the site and end the connection to your remote Web server, if necessary.

Phase II: Creating the user registration form

To create the user registration form, do the following:

1. **Open the subsite in FrontPage.**

2. **Create the registration form.**

   Open the subsite and select File → New. Within the New task pane, click "More page templates." Then, within the Page Templates dialog box, double-click the User Registration template. The form opens in the document window.

3. **Replace boilerplate text with your subsite's name.**

   Select Edit → Replace and replace the text "name of your sub site" with the actual name of your subsite. (Refer back to page 225 for help with replacing text.)

4. **Configure registration form properties.**

   Right-click the form (anywhere inside the dotted-line rectangle) and select Form Properties.

Note: FrontPage automatically configures form results to be sent to the Registration Form Handler. Don't change this setting.

Click Options, and set the following properties on the Registration tab:

- **Web site name.** Type a slash (/) followed by the name of your subsite folder.

Note: For the field name settings that follow, FrontPage makes automatic entries that do nicely, unless you have special needs.

- **User name fields.** Type in what you'd like to call your user name field. If you're creating more than one user name field (splitting first and last name, for example), type in all field names separated by commas.

- **Password field.** Enter the name of your password field. "Password" always works quite well.

- **Password confirmation field.** It's always a good idea to make visitors type in a password twice, to make sure they haven't made errors. Type in the name of the password confirmation field.

- **Require password.** Leave this checkbox turned on to force the visitor to enter a password longer than six characters.

- **URL of registration failure page.** FrontPage creates a failure page automatically, so you can ignore this field. However, if you want to create a custom failure page, do so and enter its URL here.

Click OK, and FrontPage warns you that your new registration form must be saved in the "root Web." Click OK.

1. **Save the form page in the root Web site (parent folder to the subsite).**

   User registration forms must live in the *root Web site*. A site's root directory is the core folder where the *index.htm* or *default.htm* page lives. For example, when a visitor types in *http://yoursite.net*, the file he sees lives in your site's root folder. The path to a subsite would be something like *http://yoursite/secretfolder*. If *secretfolder* is the subsite you're protecting, the registration form must be saved in the *yoursite* root Web folder. Name the file something like *regform.htm*. (As always, include no spaces, capital letters, or special characters in the name.)

2. **Publish your root Web site.**

3. **Test your registration form on the live Web server.**

Discussion Web Site Wizard

If you want to create a discussion site, in which people can post and reply to messages, FrontPage offers you a wizard that walks you through the process. To do so:

1. **Open the site in which you'll place the discussion site.**

   A discussion site should be a subsite within an existing Web site. You can create the subsite and discussion component together, if you skip ahead to step 2. If you've already created the subsite that'll hold your discussion, open it in FrontPage.

Note: While FrontPage lets you create a discussion group within your root Web site, this is a bad idea, because every time you publish, FrontPage overwrites your discussion pages, obliterating entries by visitors. Create a special subsite to hold your discussion, and after you publish it the first time, exclude it from publishing (page 260).

---

2. **Launch the Discussion Wizard.**

   Select File → New, and in the New task pane, click "More Web site templates." If you're creating a discussion within an existing Web site, turn on the "Add to current Web site" checkbox and double-click the Discussion Web Site Wizard. If you're creating a new subsite to hold your discussion, add the new folder name at the end of your site's directory path, which appears in the "Specify location" field.

3. **Select all the components you want your discussion to include and then click Next.**

   To create a user-friendly discussion site, keep all these checkboxes turned on:

   • **Submission form** is mandatory, because this is the page visitors will use to enter their messages.

- **Table of Contents** provides an index page with a table of contents, which includes links to each message visitors post.

- **Search Form** lets visitors search all messages for special text.

- **Threaded Replies** groups messages together with related replies, which helps viewers a lot more than chronological order (which is what you'll get if you turn off this checkbox).

- **Confirmation Page** lets visitors receive a confirmation page after they've posted a message.

4. **Name the site and folder.**

   Name the discussion site (as usual, don't include capital letters, spaces, or special characters, and keep it short). Name the discussion folder. You can keep the name FrontPage has automatically entered here or type your own, but it must begin with an underscore and—you guessed it—contain no spaces, capital letters, or special characters. Click Next.

5. **Select form input fields.**

   Choose one of the three options FrontPage presents (see Figure 15-18) and click Next.

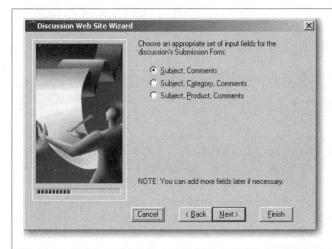

Figure 15-18:
Choose from three sets of form field groups for your page. Don't worry, you're not limited to just these fields. Once the wizard creates the form page (which always ends in _post.htm; see the file list at the end of this chapter), you can add more fields to it. Category and Product lists are drop-down lists that FrontPage populates with placeholders like Product1, Product2, and so on. You can also edit these lists through the form page.

6. **Tell FrontPage whether or not you're going to set permissions on your discussion site and then click Next.**

   See page 307 to learn how to restrict access to a subsite.

7. **Select the order in which you want to display messages and then click Next.**

8. **Tell FrontPage whether you want the Table of Contents page to be the home page for your site.**

   • If you're creating your discussion within a new site or a subsite, you should click Yes.

   • If you're creating your discussion in an existing site, clicking Yes overwrites your *index.htm* file, which is probably not what you want, so click No.

9. **Configure search form results.**

   If you elected to have a search form in your discussion site, FrontPage asks you what information you want visitors to see. Make a selection and then click Next.

10. **Select a frame option.**

   If you want to display the discussion using frames (Chapter 6), click some of the choices here, and FrontPage previews the layout on the left. Using frames lets visitors see the table of contents and messages simultaneously, but frames come with some drawbacks (see page 105). If you don't want to use frames, select No frames and click Next.

11. **Create the discussion Web site.**

   Click Finish on the last dialog box (which contains no choices).

FrontPage adds a bunch of files to your site. These file names begin with the name you gave your discussion in step 4. For example, say you created a discussion for growers to share information on kiwi fruit. If you named your discussion "kiwi," you'd find pages named:

   • **kiwi_toc.htm** (table of contents). If your discussion is part of another site, link to this page to bring visitors to the discussion. This page has all the links visitors need to search and post.

Note: If your discussion has framed pages, link to *kiwi_frm.htm* as the discussion's home page instead. With frames, you'll see additional welcome pages, too: *kiwi_welc.htm* and *kiwi_tocf.htm*.

   • **kiwi_post.htm.** The page containing the form visitors fill out to post a message. If you elect to include a Category or Product list when you create the discussion site, open this page to access those form fields. Double-click on the form field to add selections to the drop-down list.

   • **kiwi_cfrm.htm.** The confirmation page visitors receive when they add posts.

   • **kiwi_search.htm.** This lets visitors search messages within the discussion.

Working with Databases

So far, you've learned to create all kinds of Web pages using simple HTML. Maybe you've also tossed in a little CSS or JavaScript or used FrontPage's site management tools. These are all powerful features, but they're not the answer to every Web author's dreams. What if you need to show visitors loads of information—like profiles for thousands of your company's employees or details on hundreds of fly-fishing products?

You could, of course, build each of these pages by hand. But then again you could also churn your own butter or send smoke signals when you want to get in touch with friends. There's an easier way. Whenever you need to fill your Web pages with lots of similar info—employee records, product pictures, movie star marriage results—you'll probably want to store your data in a database. This chapter shows you how to set up FrontPage so that you can easily tap into these data storehouses and fill your pages with whatever info you want to retrieve. (The process works in the opposite direction too; FrontPage lets you channel form collection results *from* your Web pages *into* a database.) You'll also learn how to add a search feature to your site. As usual, you can do it all without a lick of programming knowledge.

Note: The features you'll read about in this chapter won't let viewers change or manipulate data on your site; rather, they'll only be able to view the data you've posted. The next chapter deals with interactive data access—where visitors can edit, add, and delete entries.

Letting Visitors Search Your Site

By now, your Web pages are brimming with interesting information, and you've organized your site so that visitors can find what they're looking for. Still, most savvy Web travelers these days will be on the lookout for one particularly handy navigational tool: the Web site search box. You can satisfy them by adding a gizmo that FrontPage calls the *Web Search Component,* which lets visitors enter keywords and search all the text on your site.

How a Search Works

A basic "site search" functions like this: you provide a field (a box) for visitors to enter their search term or keyword(s). A visitor types in a word or two and clicks the search form's Submit button. Then the Web server sends search results back to the visitor's browser. Results appear as a list of files (mostly Web pages, but results might also include PDFs or other types of files) in your site containing the term she entered. Each item in the list is a hyperlink that the visitor can click to open that page.

Note: If you want to use FrontPage's Web Search tool, your live Web server needs to be running FrontPage Server Extensions (page 251). If your server's loaded with SharePoint Services (page 251), you'll use FrontPage's full text search component instead. (See step 1 in the instructions that follow.) Full text search is Microsoft's "new and improved" version of the Web search, designed to deliver more accurate results.

Creating a Search Component

To add a search box to your site:

1. **Create a search box.**

   Insert a site search box in one of two ways:

   • If you want to add a search box to a page that already exists, place your cursor where you'd like to put the search box. Select Insert → Web Component. Within the Insert Web Component dialog box that appears, select Web Search from the list on the left. In the pane on the right, select Current Web and click Finish.

Note: If you have SharePoint on your server, select Full Text Search instead of Current Web.

   • If you want to dedicate an entire page to your Web site search form, select File → New and, in the New task pane, click "More page templates." Double-click the Search Page template. FrontPage creates the search page.

2. **Set Search Form Properties (Figure 16-1).**

In this step, you can configure the search buttons and text box and tell FrontPage how to format search results. If you used the Insert Web Component dialog box to create your search form, the Search Form Properties box displays. On the other hand, if you used the template, right-click inside the search form and select Search Form Properties (or, just double-click inside the form).

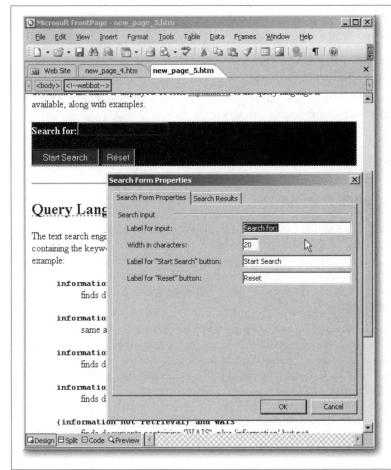

Figure 16-1:
The first tab in the Search Form Properties dialog box lets you set the form's appearance. Edit the label here for your search field and form buttons. You can also adjust the length of the search field by entering the number of characters that will be visible. As with any other form, entering a number in the "Width in characters" box doesn't change the characters a visitor can enter, just those that will display in the box.

3. **Configure search form results.**

Click the Search Results tab. Here, you'll set what results the search should return and how they'll display. You have control over the following settings:

• **Word list to search.** If you want visitors to search your entire site, leave this box set to All. If you want them to search only a subsite or subfolder, type the name of the folder here.

- **Date & Time format.** Search results automatically display the last edited date of files returned. Select the format you prefer from the date and time format lists. If you don't want any date or time to display, select None in each list.

- **Display score.** If you turn on this checkbox, FrontPage assigns and displays a search relevance score next to each page a search returns. The score shows the relevance of the file to the search criteria.

- **Display File Date.** If you don't want "last edited" dates listed next to each file the search finds, turn off this checkbox.

- **Display File Size.** If you want to let visitors know the size of each page their search returns, turn on this checkbox.

4. **Click OK and save the page containing your search form.**

5. **Publish (page 258) and test the form.**

Working with Databases

Imagine that you're running an online sock store. You'd like to show your customers all the varieties of footwear that you offer, to increase the chance of making a sale. Sure, you could create an HTML page to profile each and every kind of sock you offer. But that's a lot of work. Plus, all that information already lives in your sock database, including pictures of each style. How can you get that information onto your Web pages?

If you want your Web pages to display information from a database, you'll need to understand the building blocks that can make that magic happen. Read on to learn about database basics and *dynamic Web pages*—pages that get generated on the fly, as your visitors request them. Then find out how it's possible for these technologies to work together. After you read about what software you need, you can make sure you have all the necessary tools at your disposal. FrontPage needs extra support from the Web server to orchestrate this communications feat.

What's a Database?

Everywhere you go—from offices to shops to homes—people need to store information and do so in an organized manner, so they can retrieve it easily. Take your doctor's office, for instance. You stop in for a visit and the receptionist looks through stacks of file folders for your records, which are stored together in a manila folder.

You can think of a database as the digital equivalent of those file folder stacks. A database is made up of tables, which—like the folders in your doctor's office—group records that contain similar information. One table of a database might contain a list of products. Another table could track vendor names and contact information, and yet another might hold customer records. To see what one such table looks like, you can open the sample database that comes with FrontPage (see Figure 16-2). To locate the Northwind sample database, look in *C:\Program Files\ Microsoft Office\Office\Samples* or search your C:\ drive for the file Northwind.mdb.

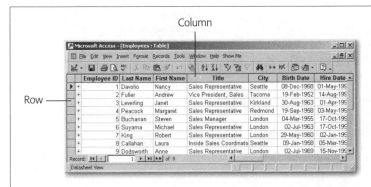

Column

Row

Figure 16-2:
This table from the Northwind sample database shows employee data. Each row contains one person's information. In other words, each row is one record. Each column stores a single type of information: Last Name, First Name, and so on. When you create a form (Chapter 15), each field corresponds to a table column.

If your database has just one table (which makes it a *flat-file* database), life will be blissfully simple. But most databases are more complex and contain many tables. Many of these tables are linked to each other by at least one field, creating what's known as a *relational* database. For example, the Northwind database includes a Products table, which lists all the products the company offers. Each product record contains information fields like Product Name, Price, and Supplier. The Supplier field is different from these other fields, because you don't just type in the supplier name, you get it from *another* table—the Suppliers table. The value in this field matches up with one record in the Suppliers table, which includes additional details like supplier location and contact information that you wouldn't want cluttering up your Products table. A simplified example of how this relationship works is illustrated in Figure 16-3.

Note: Each database table has one column called the *primary key,* which the database program auto-numbers to ensure that each record has one unique identifier. In Figure 16-3, the ArtistID and WorkID columns carry out this duty in each table.

Dynamic Web Pages

To take data directly from a database and display it on a Web page, you'll need more than plain old HTML. Sure, you need *some* HTML, so the browser knows how to display page elements, but you also need to throw in some serious scripting.

Think about the last time you shopped for books online. Say you're at your favorite bookseller's site and you enter in some search words like "Roald Dahl." The site presents you with a list of matches. Next, you enter the same search term again but add the word "Charlie" to it. You get a similar list of matches, but this time "Charlie and the Chocolate Factory" is on top.

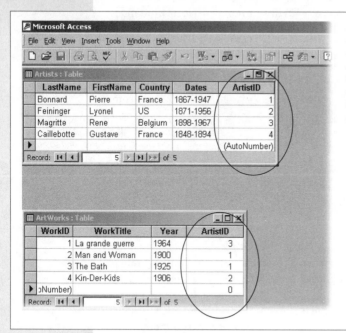

Figure 16-3:
How do you know which of the artists from the Artists table (at top) created the pieces in the ArtWorks table (at bottom)? You can solve the puzzle by matching up numbers in the ArtistID field. This kind of link between tables is a basic attribute of relational databases.

Did the site's creator anticipate your search terms and have, ready-and-waiting, two separate results pages? And what happens next when you click a link for product details? Did your bookseller create a single HTML page for each of the thousands of products on her site? No way. On a large shopping site, all the information you see when you conduct a search or click a product details link comes out of a database. It takes a special kind of Web page to take your request, use it to query (search) a database, and then produce an entirely new HTML page to display information from the database. (Now do you understand why these pages are known as dynamic Web pages?) Actually, all this activity isn't the work of the page alone; the process involves a program on the server, which works together with the dynamic Web page. These special pages come in a variety of flavors, but the most common are Microsoft's ASP (Active Server Pages).

ASP

Active Server Pages are one of the easiest and most popular building blocks you can use to create a database-driven Web site. ASP pages are *dynamic,* not *static,* like a regular HTML page. Put it another way: you use FrontPage to manually create static pages; dynamic pages get summoned into existence each time your visitors search for a word or phrase, or click a particular link.

Here's how Active Server Pages work. A browser requests an ASP page. The ASP engine on the Web server reads the ASP page and executes scripts the page contains. Then the server sends the results of that process back to the browser where it displays as an HTML page.

Note: Because scripts are processed on the Web server, out of sight, ASP provides a lot more security for your code than a regular HTML page would.

ASP.NET

ASP.NET (pronounced a-s-p dot net) is an upgrade to ASP. .NET is a more complex and cleaner variation on ASP, and it eventually will replace its predecessor. If you're deciding which technology you'd like to use, you may not have much of a choice. Some Web hosts offer only one or the other. If you're creating Web pages for a company, your Web site administrator may already have made the choice for you.

Other server-side scripting

So now you need to become an ASP programmer, right? Naw, don't worry. As you'll see, FrontPage creates your ASP or ASP.NET pages for you. However, if you want to use other scripting options like CGI (Common Gateway Interface) or PHP (Hypertext Preprocessor) to interact with your database, you'll need to be an expert or hire one.

Database Connections

So where's your database going to live? FrontPage can handle a few scenarios.

If you're working with a simple Access database that's not too big, you can store your database right inside your Web site. Other more complex databases are too large for that kind of setup. In some cases, you'll connect to a database that lives on a separate server altogether. Many databases must reside on what's known as a database server and require the assistance of an application server to act as middleman between your Web page and the data. Or your database and data-handling application can all live on one computer that's sophisticated enough to tackle all these jobs.

FrontPage can work with pretty much any kind of database. Not surprisingly, things work more smoothly if you use Microsoft Access or Microsoft SQL. If visitors are going to view your database frequently—say over a few thousand times a day—then you'll want to opt for SQL, the more robust of the two. However, if your database is small and won't experience that much traffic, Access will perform fine. If you're not a complete devotee of Microsoft products, don't worry, you can use other types of databases, too. All FrontPage needs is a way to connect with the database.

Establishing this connection is a breeze if you're linking to a simple database you've saved inside your Web site. But FrontPage can also connect to databases that live in other locations that at first might not seem compatible with FrontPage.

Thanks to a protocol called *ODBC* (Open Database Connectivity), FrontPage can connect to pretty much any kind of database you want. ODBC acts as a middleman or translator that lets a variety of programs (including FrontPage) communicate with all sorts of database types, even those made by another manufacturer like Oracle. As long as your database is ODBC-compliant, FrontPage can connect to it.

What You'll Need

You can cook up all this database magic on a disk-based site and upload everything to a Web server that's loaded with FrontPage Server Extensions. (FPSE are required for all the features covered in this chapter, except the Database Results Wizard. However, since the extensions help you publish and manage this feature, you should consider it a requirement.) However, if you're working extensively with data, you'll be much happier developing in a Web server environment. That way, you can test and manipulate the way your data displays as you work. For instance, if you develop on a disk-based site, you won't be able to preview an ASP page until you publish it. Dynamic Web pages need to live on a Web server since that's where the required server software (also called Active Server Pages) exists, making actual database-searching possible. Your Web server should have the latest version of FPSE as well as Active Server Pages (ASP) installed. (Pop back to page 176 to read about the difference between disk-based and server-based development environments.)

Tip: One easy way to create a Web server–based development environment is to install Microsoft Internet Information Services on your machine, if possible. Then download and install FPSE 2002, and you'll have all the capabilities that you need. (See page 178 for more information on turning your PC into a Web server.)

FrontPage can help you get a simple database-driven site up pretty quickly. However, if, after reading about your options, you find that your needs are more complex, you'll need to look for more assistance and maybe even hire someone to help you.

Saving Form Results to a Database

In the last chapter, you learned how to create forms and send results to a text file or email message. Now that you know a bit about databases, you're ready to save form results to a database. Say you collect visitor information (name, address, and so on) in a form on your site. If you save these results to a database, there's a lot you can do with the data. For instance, you can use your database program to sort and analyze information about your visitors. When you figure out that all the people interested in your mosquito nets live near the Okefenokee swamp, you can step up your marketing in that location. Or take your data and export it from the database into Word, where you can use the mail merge feature to automatically generate personalized letters and envelopes. Before you know it, you've mailed out hundreds of letters without breaking a sweat.

When you save results to a database, FrontPage gives you three options: you can save results to a new database that FrontPage creates for you, you can update a database that FrontPage previously created for you, or you can save results in an existing database.

Note. To save results to a database, your Web server needs to be running both FrontPage Server Extensions 2002 (the latest version) and Active Server Pages Extensions. This feature won't work on a Web server with SharePoint Services installed.

Creating a New Database with FrontPage

You can turn any HTML form into a database, if you want. FrontPage can take your field names and generate an Access database to hold your visitor's entries. It's astoundingly easy. After you've created your form, do the following:

1. **Open the Form Properties dialog box (right-click the form and select Form Properties), click "Send to database," and then click Options.**

   The Options for Saving Results to Database dialog box opens.

2. **Within the Database Results tab, click Create Database.**

   FrontPage creates an Access database with a .mdb extension.

   A prompt appears letting you know the database has been created and telling you the database name (FrontPage uses the name of the HTML file the form is in) and location (a folder FrontPage creates within your site called *fpdb*).

3. **Click OK to close the prompt and then twice more to close both open dialog boxes.**

Note: If you've created the form yourself, FrontPage then prompts you to save the page your form is on as an ASP page. You must do this for your new form results settings to work. Then click OK to close the prompt. On the other hand, if you've created the form using one of FrontPage's form templates, the program automatically saves the page as an ASP page for you.

4. **If FrontPage didn't change the file type of your Web page for you, change the file extension from .htm to .asp.**

   Within the folder list, right-click the file and select rename. Replace the file suffix, *htm*, with the letters *asp*.

5. **Save the file.**

Note: Make sure your Web server supports Active Server Pages. Ask your host or Web site administrator.

Updating a Database

FrontPage has created a nifty little database for you, but what happens if you need to add or remove a form field? Will doing so mess up your database? Nope—FrontPage is pretty flexible in this department. First, make whatever changes you want to your form. Then open Form Properties, click Options, and then click Update Database. FrontPage updates your database to match your form. Magic.

Saving Results to an Existing Database

What if you have an existing database that you want your form fields to feed into? FrontPage can help you out even though the program's fairly late (compared to its competitors) in providing this service. However, you'll have to help out with some tweaks here and there.

Note. One major limitation when you save results to a database is that FrontPage can only save form data to one table per form. If your form has fields that feed into more than one of your database's tables, forget it. In that case, you'll need to save results to a text file or single table database and then import them into your existing database somehow. Or just create separate forms for each table.

---

1. **Configure the form to send results to a database.**

   To link to a database, open the Form Properties dialog box (right-click the form and select Form Properties), select "Send to database," and then click Options.

2. **Select the database connection.**

   If you've already connected to the database, select the connection name from the "Database connection to use" list. If you need to add a connection, see the next section for detailed instructions.

3. **Match form fields to database fields.**

   Within the Options dialog box, click the Saved Fields tab. Here, match up fields in your form with fields in the database (see Figure 16-4).

4. **Click OK to close all dialog boxes and save your settings.**

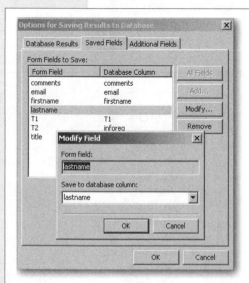

Figure 16-4:
Double-click a form field in the "Form Fields to Save" list to display this Modify Field dialog box. Select the column in the database that you want to receive the values entered in the form field. If names match between the form and the database, FrontPage makes an educated guess for you.

Adding a Database Connection

Before you can do anything with a database—like send results to it or display parts of it on a Web page, you first have to establish a connection to it.

Note. Before you connect to a database, it should reside where it belongs. In other words, if you plan to import it into your Web site, do so before connecting to it. (Instructions for importing a database follow below.) Don't connect to a database stored somewhere else on your computer's hard drive. A database must be located in your Web site, or on a network drive or Web server where your live Web site can connect to it. See step 3 within "Creating a Database Connection," next, to read about connection types.

Importing a Database

If your database is going to live inside your Web site, you have to import it before establishing a connection to it.

Note. Not all databases can reside inside your Web site. Some require more space or need to live on a database server, in which case you wouldn't import the database; instead, you'd just create a connection to it.

Select File → Import. In the Import dialog box, click Add File. Browse to and select the database file. Once it appears in the Import dialog box, click OK.

FrontPage also asks if you'd like to create a database connection for the file. This saves you the trouble of manually creating a connection (as explained in the next section). To create the database connection, type a connection name in the Name field and click Yes. FrontPage then asks if you'd like to save the database in your site's *fpdb* folder. Click Yes again.

FREQUENTLY ASKED QUESTION

fpdb folder

What's this fpdb *folder and why does FrontPage insist on saving my databases there?*

FrontPage creates this special folder specifically for storing databases. The program automatically makes the *fpdb* (FrontPage database) folder off-limits to browsers, scripts, and executable files to protect your data. That's why, when FrontPage encourages you to save your data in this folder, you should comply. In fact, if you place a database in some other folder in your site, FrontPage gets agitated and prompts you to move it each time you run a component errors report.

Creating a Database Connection

To connect to a database, follow the steps described next.

Note: If you're connecting to an ODBC data source (page 320), you must register your database within the ODBC Data Source Administrator (located in your computer's Control Panel, within Administrative Tools) before connecting to it in FrontPage. If you're making an ODBC connection, you probably have a system administrator who can do this for you.

---

1. **Initiate the database connection.**

   Click Add Connection within the form results Options dialog box. Or, select Tools → Site Settings and then click the Database tab. The Site Settings dialog box opens. Click Add to display the New Database Connection dialog box.

2. **In the Name field, type the name of this database connection.**

   You'll use this connection name each time you want to work with this database in FrontPage. This name saves you the trouble of specifying path information each time you link to the database. For best results, relate the name to the name of the database, don't use capital letters, spaces, or special characters, and don't make it longer than eight characters.

3. **Select the type of database connection you're creating.**

   Click on one of the following choices.

   - **File or folder in current Web.** This is the simplest option. If your database is small enough to store in your site, you won't need to worry about maintaining a connection to a database server.

   - **System data source on Web server.** Click this if you'll connect to the database using ODBC (page 320).

   - **Network connection to database server.** If you're connecting to a database through a simple network connection, choose this option.

   - **Custom definition.** Use this option if you're using text files—like DSN (Data Source Name) or UDL (Universal Data Link) to connect to your database.

   Note: If a user name and password are required to access the database, let FrontPage know what they are by clicking Advanced and entering them in the respective fields.

   ---

4. **Browse to the data source.**

   Depending on what type of connection you chose in the previous step, your choices differ after you click Browse.

   - If you chose to connect to a database in your Web site, click Browse and you'll see the files and folders in your site. Browse to and select the database file.

   - If you chose "System data source on Web server," click Browse, and then select the ODBC system data source name.

   - If you chose Network connection, select the type of database server, type in the server's host name, and then type in the name of the database.

   - If you chose Custom definition, click Browse to find and then select the .dsn or .udl file you'll use for the connection.

5. **Click OK five times to close all dialog boxes and save your connection.**

Note: FrontPage manages your database connections by recording them in a file called *global.asa.* Once you create a database connection, you'll see this file in your folder list. You shouldn't open or edit this file.

The Database Results Wizard

Now you know how to gather data with a Web page and save it to a database. But what if you've already got a database and your mission is to share it with the world? FrontPage can help you display parts of a database on your Web pages.

Say a group of scientists you work with have been collecting beetle profiles for years, and you're responsible for posting this information on your museum's intranet site. What with the new boll weevil collection, they're up to 11,678 specimens. Are you really going to create a Web page for each one?

Probably not. Since you're dealing with scientists (who are usually smart, rational, and efficient), they've probably stored all that beetle profile information in a database. If you get your hands on that database, you can save yourself a ton of work. FrontPage can help you create Web pages that will display whatever parts of the database you want visitors to see.

Sounds complicated, but FrontPage makes it easy with its Database Results Wizard. This tool lets you query a database for information and display whatever records you specify on a Web page.

Note: The Database Results Wizard works only on a Web server loaded with FrontPage Sever Extensions. This feature doesn't work with SharePoint.

1. **Create a new blank page.**

2. **Initiate the Database Results Wizard.**

   Select Insert → Database → Results. The Database Results Wizard displays its first dialog box, which offers the following options:

   • **FrontPage has detected that your page will display best using.** In this section, you tell FrontPage what program to use to display your database information. FrontPage pretends to take a guess here, but it actually "detects" nothing. You must select either the ASP or ASP.NET radio button. Make sure the one you choose is available on your Web server. ASP is the more common and readily available of the two.

   • **Use a sample database.** If you're testing out the capabilities of the Database Results Wizard, you can use the sample Northwind database (page 317) that comes with FrontPage. The program creates the database connection for you.

• **Use an existing database.** Select this option if you have a database whose results you'd like to display—and you've already created a connection to it in FrontPage.

• **Use a new database connection.** Click this if you need to create the connection to the database you want to display. (See the previous section for details on creating a database connection.)

Once you've made your selections, click Next.

3. **Select a data source.**

The second dialog box that the wizard presents offers you two options for selecting the data that you'll display on the Web page:

• **Record Source.** FrontPage presents the list of tables in the database you chose in the previous step. Select the table you want from the list. You can customize what parts of this table you'll show visitors in the next step, but they'll only see data from this one table. If you want to show data from multiple tables, you'll need to enter a Custom Query.

• **Custom Query.** This option lets you display any information you want by entering a SQL query string. SQL (Structured Query Language) is a programming language you can use to view and edit information in a variety of databases. If you need to draw data from multiple tables in your database, you'll need to create a custom SQL query here to do so. To enter a query, select this option and click Edit. Type or paste your query in the box provided. To use this feature, you'll need to know SQL. (Where can you learn more about SQL? Check out the "Learning More About Data and the Web" box later this chapter on page 330.)

Note: If you want to set query parameters in one table only, select it in record source and proceed onto the next step. You'll have an opportunity to set specific parameters for which records should display (see discussion of the More Options dialog box in the next step), and you won't need any knowledge of the SQL query language to do so.

After you make your selection, click Next.

4. **Edit Fields to display.**

The third screen that the wizard presents lets you select specific fields to display and set their sort order. Click Edit List to open the Displayed Fields dialog box where you can remove and order fields (see Figure 16-5).

Say you want to do more than just display the fields in the database table. If you want to set certain parameters—like employee records that display only if the department is Marketing—then you'll need to set up a query. To do so, forego Edit Fields and click More Options instead. One nice advantage to the More Options dialog box is that you can set up complex display parameters without knowing anything about how to compose SQL query statements. The More Options dialog box lets you edit the options in the list shown next.

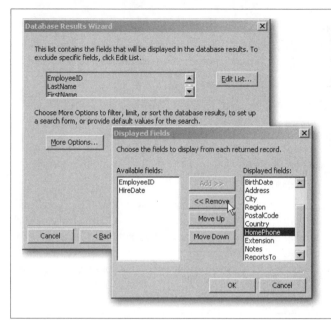

Figure 16-5:
In the Displayed Fields dialog box, FrontPage has all fields set to display (listed in the pane on the right). To remove a field from this list, select it, and then click Remove. To reorder the list, select a field and click Move Up or Move Down. The order you set here is the order in which FrontPage lists results in the table it creates for display on the Web page.

- **Criteria.** If you want to display only certain records in a table, click the Criteria button to display the Criteria dialog box. Here you can set very specific parameters for exactly what data you want to display. To do so, click Add. Within the Add Criteria dialog box that opens, select a field name, comparison, and value (see Figure 16-6). For example, if you're creating a page that lists only Managers, you might select Title in the field name, Equals from the Comparison list, and type Manager in the Value field. Use and/or settings to combine multiple criteria. If you select And, data must meet both criteria. If you select Or, data can meet either criteria.

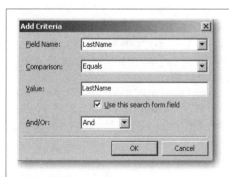

Figure 16-6:
You can also use the Add Criteria dialog box to create a search box that visitors can use to find a record. To do so, select the field. Then, turn on the "Use this search form field" checkbox. In this example, a visitor would be able to type a last name in the search field to find a specific record.

After you make choices in the Add Criteria dialog box and click OK, your parameters display in the Criteria dialog box (Figure 16-7).

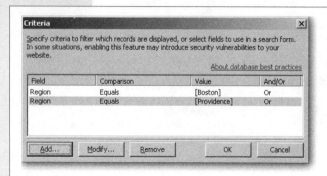

Figure 16-7:
In this example, only employees in the Boston or Providence offices will appear on the final page. To edit a criterion, select it and click Modify. To delete a criterion, select it, and then click Remove.

• **Ordering.** If you want to set a sort order for all the records that you'll display, click Ordering within the More Options dialog box. The Ordering dialog box appears (see Figure 16-8). Select the field you want to base the order on, and then click Add. FrontPage automatically makes the field sort in ascending order. To change it to descending, select the field (in the pane on the right) and click Change Sort.

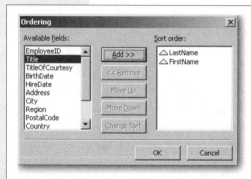

Figure 16-8:
The Ordering dialog box lets you sort records based on multiple fields. In this example, records will appear in ascending alphabetical order by last name. Where the last name is the same, they'll appear in ascending alphabetical order by first name.

Click OK to save settings in either the Criteria or Ordering dialog box, and then click OK to close the More Options dialog box. Then click Next to proceed to the next Database Results Wizard screen.

Note: If you get to the More Options dialog box to find the Criteria and Ordering buttons grayed out, this means you've entered a custom query in the previous Database Results Wizard dialog box. FrontPage grays out these choices so you don't enter parameters that conflict with the SQL query statement you entered within the Custom Query dialog box (explained back in step 3).

---

5. **Format results.**

The next wizard screen lets you set the appearance of the table or list that will appear on your Web page to display data from the database. Select one of the following from the drop-down list:

- **Table – one record per row.** FrontPage creates an HTML table to hold results. Each row is a record and each column is a field.

- **List – one field per item.** FrontPage displays each record on a separate line. (This option isn't available if you chose ASP.NET in step 2.)

- **Drop-Down list – one record per item.** This selection is for authors creating a drop-down search box. FrontPage lists the content of one of the database table's fields as items in a drop-down list. A visitor can make a selection from this drop-down list and submit it, as he would any HTML form. Specify the field that you want to display in the drop-down list (see Figure 16-9). (This option isn't available if you chose ASP.NET in step 2.) You can use this feature to create a drop-down list to filter results of a separate Data Results Wizard on the same page. (See the tutorial that follows this section on page 331 to learn how.)

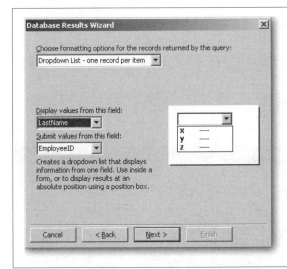

Figure 16-9:
When you're creating a drop-down list on a form, you can select one value to display (like an employee name that visitors would recognize) but another to submit (like the employee's ID number).

After you make your selections, click Next to move to the final wizard screen.

6. **Set the number of records to display per page.**

You can display all your results on one page by selecting "Display all records together." However, if you've got a large number of records, you'll want to split them up. To do so, select "Split records into groups" and enter the number of records you want to display on each page. FrontPage then creates forward and back buttons for each page and indicates to visitors how many pages of records are available.

If you turned on the "Use this search form field" checkbox in step 4, you can turn on the "Add search form" checkbox in this final wizard screen to add search capabilities to your data results.

Note: If you add a search field, no results will display on your page until a visitor enters a value in the search box and clicks submit query. Then, only records that meet the search criteria exactly will appear.

Click Finish, and FrontPage creates the page that will display your database information (see Figure 16-10).

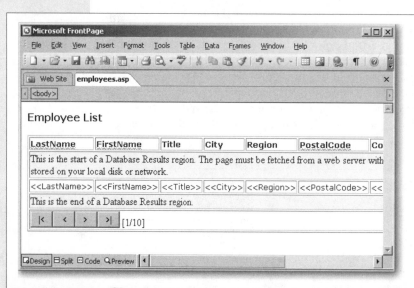

Figure 16-10:
The page you create with the Database Results Wizard displays in FrontPage without any data in it. Data appears only when a browser requests the page.

Tutorial: Filtering Database Results

After reading the steps in the last section, you know how to do a bunch of things, including how to create a search box for the data you're displaying using the Database Results Wizard. If you create this search box, a viewer can enter a value she'd like to find in a specific field within the table that appears on your site. But that option isn't particularly friendly, since you're forcing your visitors to type an exact match in the search box in order to get a result. Maybe you'd like to give your visitors a bit more help. For instance, instead of making them guess, you can provide a list of categories or options from which they can choose.

In this tutorial, you'll work with the Northwind sample database that comes with FrontPage and learn how to display a list of products that a viewer can sort by supplier.

Creating the Drop-Down Search Form

First, you'll create the drop-down list of suppliers. To do so:

1. **Create a blank page and insert a form on it.**

   Select Insert → Form → Form.

2. **Insert a Database Results Wizard *inside* the form.**

   Select Insert → Database → Results.

3. **In the first Database Results Wizard screen, select ASP and "Use a sample database." Then click Next.**

4. **Select the Suppliers table as your data source and click Next.**

5. **Edit the fields to display so only CompanyName and SupplierID display. Then click Next.**

   You'll use these two fields to create the drop-down list and to query the database. Remove all other fields by clicking Edit Fields, selecting each one, and then clicking Remove. Then click OK.

6. **In the next screen, select "Dropdown list."**

7. **In the "Display values" drop-down list, select CompanyName, and in the "Submit values" drop-down list, select SupplierID.**

   Doing so ensures that visitors see the CompanyName values, which makes sense to them, while the form submits the SupplierID number, which makes sense to the database.

8. **Click Next, then click Finish.**

Creating a Table to Display Database Results

Next, you'll create a second Database Results Wizard, which will display the drop-down list's search results.

1. **Insert a Database Results Wizard on the same page, *outside* the form you just created.**

   Select Insert → Database → Results.

2. **In the first wizard dialog box, select ASP and "Use a sample database." Then click Next.**

3. **Select the Products table as your data source and click Next.**

4. **Click More Options and click Criteria.**

5. **Click Add and select the Supplier ID field.**

6. **Turn on the "Use this search form field" checkbox.**

7. **Click OK twice to close the open dialog boxes and save your settings.**

8. **Within the More Options dialog box, click Defaults, select the SupplierID field, and then click Edit.**

9. **Enter a default value of 0 (zero) and click OK three times.**

   If you don't specify a default value, the first time your list appears, it'll contain an error message. To avoid this, just enter a value here that doesn't appear as a SupplierID value in the Suppliers table. Zero usually does the trick.

10. **Click Next, choose to display results in a table, and click Next again.**

11. **Turn off the "Add search form" checkbox and click Finish.**

12. **Save your page and test it in a browser (see Figure 16-11).**

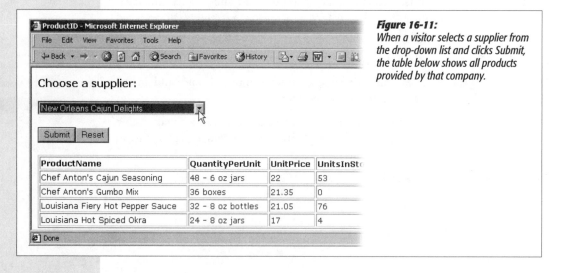

Figure 16-11:
When a visitor selects a supplier from the drop-down list and clicks Submit, the table below shows all products provided by that company.

Interacting with a Database

In the last chapter, you learned how to display portions of a database on a Web page. But what if you want to let your site viewers tap directly into your data, so that they can manipulate what they're looking at, rather than just passively view it? For example, say you've posted employee profiles for everyone in your office, but you don't have anyone's home address. Sure, you could walk around with a pen and paper jotting down names and addresses. But wouldn't it be a lot easier if everyone could just enter their *own* information right into the database? And wouldn't it be great if you could let people edit their addresses directly through their browser window, rather than having to teach them how to use the database software (not to mention installing the program on all their computers)?

FrontPage gives you this ability through its Database Interface Wizard. This wizard works kind of like the Database Results Wizard that you read about in the preceding chapter, but instead of just displaying "read-only" data to your visitors, you can let them interact with it—adding, editing, and deleting records on their own, via the Web.

This chapter teaches you how to create what is essentially a Web-based application that lets visitors work directly with a database. After you learn how to create this tool, you'll see exactly how it works within a browser.

Tip: If you want to let visitors edit or delete records, read on. However, if all you want to do is collect the info that visitors enter in a form and store the results in a database (essentially creating new records), then a simpler solution would be to create a Web form and configure it to send results to a database. (See Chapter 15 to learn how to create the form and then turn to page 320 to see how to send results to a database.)

Creating a Database Interface

How does this magic happen? As usual, FrontPage handles all the grunt work for you—but perhaps not in the way you've come to expect. A lot of the advanced features you've read about so far rely on FrontPage Server Extensions or SharePoint Services to help them work correctly.

The Database Interface Wizard works differently. FrontPage takes the choices you make in the wizard and actually writes a custom ASP or ASP.NET program to perform the tasks that you've specified. So really, when you use this wizard, you and FrontPage are working together to create an independent program your visitors can use to manipulate data.

Note: The interactive data application created by the Database Interface Wizard works only on a Web server loaded with ASP or ASP.NET (page 318). This feature won't work on a server that has SharePoint Services.

Creating a Database Interface

FrontPage makes it easy to let your site visitors get their hooks into your data. To get started, just follow these steps:

1. **Launch the Database Interface Wizard.**

   Select File → New and, within the New task pane, click "More Web site templates." Since the Database Interface Wizard is a Web site wizard, FrontPage gives you the option of creating a new site or placing the wizard within the site you already have open in FrontPage. One advantage to placing it within the open site is that you'll have access to any database connections you've already created.

   • If you want to create database interface pages within the site you have open in FrontPage, turn on the "Add to current Web site" checkbox.

   • If the interface application will be its own Web site, enter a network location path or Web address in the Location field, under Options. For instance, you may want to create this application in a subsite that you can set permissions on. (Pop back to page 190 to read about subsites.)

   Select the Database Interface Wizard and click OK, or double-click the Database Interface Wizard. The first wizard screen appears.

2. **Select the Web page technology you want to use.**

   Under "FrontPage has detected that your page will display best using," choose the ASP or ASP.NET radio button to tell FrontPage what program to use to present the database information. FrontPage pretends to take a guess here, but it actually "detects" nothing. You must select either the ASP or ASP.NET radio button. Make sure the one you choose is available on your Web server. ASP is the more common and readily available of the two, but with this wizard, using ASP.NET offers one advantage: the wizard generates the Database Editor Web page as a single Web page. The ASP method uses frames (Chapter 6) to display record information alongside the table to which it belongs. (At the end of this chapter, you'll see what the Database Editor page looks like.)

3. **Select the database connection you want to use.**

   • **Create a new Microsoft Access database within your site.** Choose this option if you want FrontPage to create a new database (which you'll design in later wizard screens). As you can tell from the name of this selection, Access is your only choice for database file format.

   • **Use an existing database connection.** Select this option to use a database connection that you already established within your Web site. After you click this option, select the connection from the drop-down list.

   • **Connect to an external database.** Select this option if you have a database that you've not yet connected to your FrontPage Web site.

   • **Use a sample database.** If you're testing out the capabilities of the Database Interface Wizard, you can use the sample Northwind database (page 317) that comes with FrontPage. The program creates the database connection for you.

   Once you've made your selections in this wizard screen, click Next.

Note: If you opted to let FrontPage create a database for you, you'll be prompted to name it. As always, keep the name short and don't include capital letters, spaces, or special characters. Then click Next. After that, skip ahead to step 4.

The wizard takes a moment to create the connection and tells you when it's finished. Click Next.

4. **Select a data source.**

   Select the table you want to display from the drop-down list. You can leave the "Specify a location for the new files" box as is. FrontPage shows you the file path where it'll place the elements that make up your interface application. The folder automatically matches the table name you choose in the field above. Click Next.

5. **Format data display.**

   The next wizard prompts you to create Web page form fields to match up with fields in your database.

Note: If FrontPage is creating an Access database for you, you'll also be able to add columns and configure their form fields.

To keep your database working correctly, you'll need to do some tweaking here. For starters, FrontPage sets all fields to appear on a page as text boxes (see Figure 17-1).

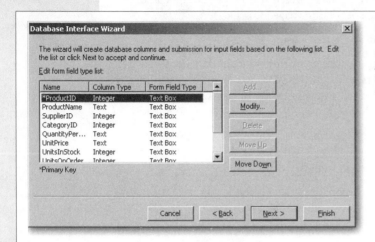

If you're going to have visitors entering records, leaving all fields set to text box will mess up your database. That's because each table in a database has a primary key (in Figure 17-1, it's the ProductID field), which your database program automatically generates to give each record a unique identifier. You don't want visitors entering text in this field, so select the primary key field (FrontPage marks it with an asterisk) and click Modify. In the Column type drop-down list, select Autonumber and click OK. When you return to the form field type list, you'll see that FrontPage changed the Column type to autonumber. This means whenever a visitor enters a new product record, the database automatically assigns an ID number. FrontPage also shows nothing in the form field type list. This means the submission form won't contain a ProductID field at all, so visitors won't even see it. (If you need a refresher on database fundamentals, pop back to page 316.)

You can modify other form fields here as well. For instance, for some fields, you may not want visitors to type in an entry. Maybe you'd like to offer values in a drop-down list instead. To do so, select the field and click Modify to access form field settings (Figure 17-2). Under "Form field input type," select Drop-Down Box, and then click OK.

When you design form fields in this wizard screen, your work is only partially done. You can set up some basic parameters here, but you'll need to edit the Web form page manually later. For example, say you want to create a drop-down list for the Title field, limiting selections to Mr, Ms, and Dr. You'd change the field format to drop-down list and, beneath that, specify that you want to provide three options. But so far, you don't have any control over what those options are. Later (after you've completed the Database Interface Wizard), you'll need to manually edit this form field within the *submission_form.asp* page that FrontPage creates for you. You remember how to edit form fields? Right-click the field, select Form Field Properties, and modify two fields: the name of each choice and the value that selecting it enters in the database. (Page 282 has more on how to configure form fields.)

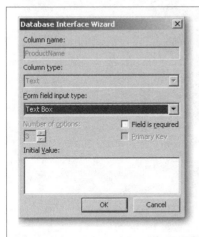

Figure 17-2:
This dialog box lets you configure how each column's form field will display on a Web page. Change the format from Text Box to Drop-Down Box or Option Button by making a selection under "Form field input type." If you select Drop-Down Box or Option Button, you can specify the number of options you'll offer. If you want to force visitors to complete a field, turn on the "Field is required" checkbox.

Once you've configured all your form fields, click Next.

6. **Select pages that you want FrontPage to create.**

   Turn on all three checkboxes and click Next.

7. **Password protect your database editor.**

   Chances are you'll want to limit access to these new pages you're creating. Otherwise, anyone would be able to access these pages and edit records in your database. If that's the kind of wild-west environment you truly want, just turn on the "Don't protect my database editor" checkbox.

   If you want to limit access to your database, you can force visitors to enter a user name and password to access the interactive pages FrontPage is about to create.

Note: User names and passwords are case-sensitive. This means a visitor must match exactly whatever text you enter here (for instance, typing capital letters wherever you did). Also, you can enter only one user name and password for all users.

FrontPage displays one final dialog box telling you what pages it's about to create and where they'll be located.

8. **Click Finish to generate the data interface pages.**

FrontPage works its magic, creating the pages and components visitors will need to interact with your database. To learn more about what you've created, read on to the next section.

Working with Multiple Tables

The steps you just followed easily create a Web application that lets visitors see and edit database records. But maybe you noticed one big drawback: FrontPage limited you to only one table. Your database probably contains multiple tables that you want to let visitors edit. If that's the case, take the steps described next.

Create a database interface as explained above, selecting your first table name. Then, within the same Web site, create another Database Interface Wizard, with one difference: in step 3, select a different table from the list. When you do so, FrontPage creates a new folder underneath the *databasename_interface* folder (*databasename* will be the actual name of your database). FrontPage names the subfolder to match the name of the table you choose. Complete the remaining steps for creating the second interface wizard. Create a new database interface like this for each table you want visitors to be able to edit.

The result will be new subfolders (within the *databasename_interface* folder) named for each table you chose. The illustration shows you how this looks within your folder list. In it, the *sample_interface* folder (named after the Sample database) contains two subfolders, Products and Employees, each of which represents a table that has an interface application attached to it.

Once you've created all these interfaces, you'll need to tie the pages together so visitors can navigate to all your new ASP pages. If your interface is its own Web site, open the *index.htm* page and create hyperlinks to all your *results_page.asp* pages. If your interface is part of a larger site, create or choose any page you wish to tie it all together with clearly labeled links. You'll find the destination ASP pages within their respective folders in the *databasename_interface* directory.

How Your Database Interface Pages Work

Now that your work is done behind the scenes, you can take your new application out for a test drive. FrontPage creates a group of Web pages that give your visitors access to your database records. You'll read about these pages below and then learn how your new feature actually works in a browser.

Web Pages FrontPage Creates

FrontPage creates three Web pages that let visitors communicate with the database:

- The **Results page** (see Figure 17-3) lists all data in the table you selected while completing the wizard.

- The **Submission Form** (that you designed in step 4 above) lets visitors add records to the database.

- The **Database Editor** lets visitors add, edit, or delete a record.

Note: If you used the Database Interface Wizard to create a new Web site, FrontPage also creates an *index.htm* (or *default.htm*) home page with links to the other three pages.

Your Pages in Action

To see how your new feature works, open the *results_page.asp* page in your browser (see Figure 17-3).

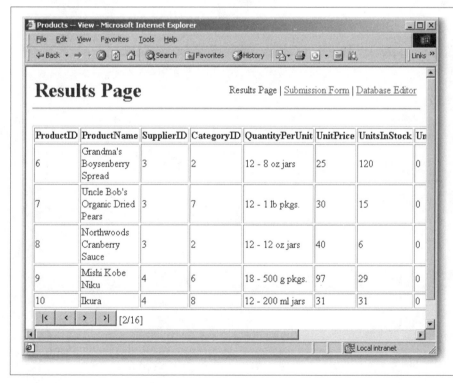

Figure 17-3:
It's not the most beautiful page ever created, but it'll get the job done. (You can tweak design elements, but don't edit page content extensively or your pages may stop working.) Hyperlinks on the upper right lead you to your interface application's other pages, where visitors can add or edit records.

Editing a record

Once you've opened your new database interface in a browser, you can play around with your data.

To edit a record:

1. Open the Database Editor.

Within the Results page, click the Database Editor link on the upper right. Enter the user name and password you set up in step 6 above and click Login. Your browser displays a list of records.

2. Open the record.

Open an item by clicking the hyperlink within the record. (In Figure 17-4, in the far left column, the Product ID value serves as the hyperlink.)

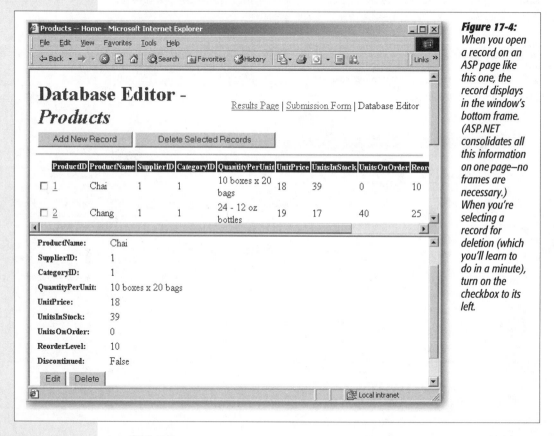

Figure 17-4:
When you open a record on an ASP page like this one, the record displays in the window's bottom frame. (ASP.NET consolidates all this information on one page—no frames are necessary.) When you're selecting a record for deletion (which you'll learn to do in a minute), turn on the checkbox to its left.

3. Click Edit.

When you click Edit (in the bottom frame, below record details), the display in the bottom frame turns into a Web form containing editable fields.

4. Make edits.

Make changes to any information you want, and then click OK. A confirmation appears to let you know that your new database interface application has updated the record.

Adding a record

Adding a new record is as simple as filling out a Web form. From within the Results page, click Submission Form. You'll be prompted to enter the user name and password you set up for the data interface feature. Enter them and click Login.

Note: You can also access the submission form from the Database Editor page. Just click Add New Record on the upper left.

The submission form opens in your browser. Complete the fields and click OK. A confirmation page displays showing you the information you entered. If you return to the Results page, you can see the record you added at the end of the list.

Deleting a record

You can delete records from within the Results page only. To do so, select the record by turning on the checkbox to its left. (You can select as many as you want.) Then click Delete Selected Records. Record details appear in the bottom frame, and the editor prompts you to confirm that you really want to delete that page. If you do, click OK.

Part Five:
FrontPage and
Microsoft Office 2003

5

Chapter 18: Integrating FrontPage with Office Programs

Integrating FrontPage with Office Programs

By now, you're a FrontPage whiz. But you probably can't say the same for everyone else who's pitching in on your Web site, whether they're your office mates or your nearest-and-dearest. If you're collaborating with a group of people, chances are they'll be sidling up to you with Microsoft Word documents, Excel spreadsheets, and meek pleas that go something like: "Hey, uh, would you mind putting this up on the Web site?"

You'd think that since all these programs—FrontPage, Word, Excel, and PowerPoint—are made by the same company, the answer would be: "Sure, no problem." But while Microsoft's Office applications do work well together, they're often not as seamless as you'd expect.

When you're transferring material into FrontPage from another Office program, there are some basic dos and don'ts, all of which you'll read about in this chapter. You'll learn about incorporating actual Word, Excel, and PowerPoint files into your site. You'll also see how to convert them into a more Web-friendly format and find out about a few other options for getting information out of Office and up on your Web site.

Importing Office Files "As Is"

One simple option is to import Office files directly into your Web site without converting them or altering them in any way. This method works best if all your visitors are using Internet Explorer and Microsoft Office.

Tip: To import a file, just drag it from Windows Explorer into your folder list. Or you can use the menu: select File → Import to open the Import dialog box, click Add File, and then Browse to and select the Office file.

If you import a Word, Excel, or PowerPoint file, how do visitors get to it? As with any Web page, you simply create a hyperlink to the file. What happens when a visitor follows that link depends on his browser and the software he has on his system:

- If a visitor's browsing with Internet Explorer (and has the Office program in question loaded on her system), your file opens up in the browser. (If that person has author rights (permission to edit files) on your server—which is unlikely—she'll be able to edit the document in Word or Excel.)

  A PowerPoint presentation opens up in the browser, and visitors can click the Page Down key to move from slide to slide. If you're worried that visitors may not have PowerPoint software or that they may not know to press Page Down to move from slide to slide, you can convert your presentation into Web pages (see page 350, later in this chapter). Doing so creates hyperlinks a viewer can follow to see each slide, but the conversion approach comes with its own problems, which you'll read about later.

Note: If you don't want visitors to be able to download and edit your PowerPoint presentation, open the presentation in PowerPoint and select File → Save As. Within the Save As Type drop-down list, select .pps (PowerPoint Slideshow) instead of the standard .ppt (PowerPoint Presentation). If you do so, visitors won't be able to edit your presentation.

- If a visitor's using a non-Microsoft browser like Netscape or Firefox, then he's presented with a dialog box that lets him open the file with the program used to create it or download it (see Figure 18-1).

Figure 18-1:
When you're using a non-Microsoft browser and you click a link to an Office file—like this Word document—you can choose to open it using Word or click the drop-down menu to select another program with which to open it. You can also download the file onto your computer.

Tip: Microsoft offers free *viewers* for each of its Office programs. The viewers let anyone who doesn't own a particular program view the files produced by that program. However, some of these viewers are pretty hefty and may take quite a while to download, which may discourage lots of visitors. You'll lose those folks who are unwilling to install additional software just to see files on your site. If you're still game, you can download these viewers from *http://office.microsoft.com/downloads/*. (In the Downloads search box that appears at the top of the page, type in "viewers" and click Go to see a list of all Office program viewers.)

Posting Files for Download

If you want visitors to download Office files, Internet Explorer may throw a wrench in your plans. As you've read, IE automatically opens Office files within the browser window.

If you want visitors to download them instead, you have two options:

- Place the file in a ZIP file (see the note below) and provide a link to it. Browsers automatically prompt a visitor to download a ZIP file. Of course, your visitors will need to know how to unzip the file.

Note: Don't know what a ZIP file is? ZIP files are compressed versions of any type of computer file, or even a group of computer files. When you zip a file, it not only takes up less space (so it's easy to email and store), it also lets you package a group of files together and send or post them as a single file. To learn more, check out *www.winzip.com*.

- Place some instructions on your page to help viewers download on their own. For example, link to a Word, Excel, or PowerPoint file and above the hyperlink, add text that says something like "To download this file, right-click the link below. Then select 'Save Target As' and browse to the folder in which you'd like to save it."

Converting Files to PDF Format

Often, the most expedient way to get your Office documents up on the Web is to convert them to PDFs (short for Portable Document Format). Converting an office file into a PDF file is like taking a snapshot of it. For example, if you turn a Word file into a PDF file, anyone who opens it will see all the fonts, alignment, spacing, and pictures appear just as the Word author originally intended, even if a viewer doesn't have Microsoft Word on her system. All she needs is Adobe Reader (which comes preinstalled on most computers or can be downloaded for free at *www.adobe.com/products/acrobat/readstep2.html*). To generate a PDF, you'll need to purchase Adobe Acrobat (the souped-up version of Reader). Once you install it, you can create PDF documents within any program that prints. (Acrobat automatically adds menu and toolbar options that make this a snap.)

Moving from Word into FrontPage

Imagine that your coworker bolts into your office asking you to post his sales report on the company intranet right away. The only problem is, he wrote the report using Word.

What should you do (aside from asking him to knock next time)? Well, you can post the Word document as is and link to it, but what if that's not good enough?

Your other options are to convert the entire document into a Web page, or you can copy the content out of Word and paste it into a blank Web page in FrontPage. There are pros and cons to each approach.

Converting Word Files into Web Pages

If you're in a real hurry, you may be tempted to use the fastest method to get your Word content Web-ready, which is the "Save as Web Page" feature on Word's menu. To save your document as a Web page, open your document in Word and select File → Save as Web Page. You can save it directly into your Web site's directory or save it somewhere else and then import it into your site. (To do so, select File → Import, click Add File, then browse to and select the new .htm file Word created.)

WORKAROUND WORKSHOP

Creating Single File Web Pages

A big drawback of Office's "Save as Web Page" option is that it often creates multiple files. So, if you named your new Web file *peoria.htm*, your Office program creates an accompanying folder called *peoria_files* to hold image and other assorted files. For the HTML file to work correctly, it needs to access the files in this folder. This complicates things a bit. For instance, if you want to email the Web page, you've got to send along that folder too, as well as explain to your hapless colleague why she needs to save both the file and the folder together.

Thankfully, in Office 2003, there's a way out of this confusion. Instead of saving your file as an HTML Web page, you can save it as an MHTML (MIME encapsulated aggregate HTML) file—which is a single file Web page. When you do so, whatever Office program you're working in consolidates all the file's information in one file—no additional folder necessary.

To create a .mht file, you just need to select this file type in the Save As dialog box. Instead of selecting "Web Page" in the "Save as type" field, select "Single File Web Page."

This method is the quickest way to turn a .doc file into an .htm file, but it's also the dirtiest. Use it only if you're in a huge hurry to post a document. The resulting files come with a lot of baggage. Word actually creates multiple files (so you can turn the HTML file back into a Word file later), which clutters up your site. Not to mention the fact that the HTML file itself is loaded with unnecessary formatting code.

In fact, FrontPage treats these files differently from regular Web pages. If you double-click one in the folder list, FrontPage opens the document's native program—be it Word or Excel—to let you edit the file (see Figure 18-2). If you want to open the file in FrontPage, right-click it, and then select Open With → FrontPage.

Figure 18-2:
FrontPage differentiates between Web pages it's created and files that other programs convert into Web Pages. Either way, the file sports the icon of the application you used to create it originally. Notice the bottom two files in this folder list, which came from Excel and Word, respectively.

Converting with drag-and-drop

There's an even better method than "Save as Web Page" that's just as fast for converting Word documents. If you drag a Word file from anywhere within Windows Explorer onto a blank page in FrontPage, you'll get a Web page that retains your Word formatting but seriously cuts out all the garbage that the Save As method can't shake. If you're in a hurry, this drag-and-drop option is the way to go. Also, the resulting file isn't one of the strange hybrid HTML files pictured in Figure 18-2. It's a bona fide Web page that FrontPage has created and treats like any other in your site.

Copying Content from Word into FrontPage

If you're looking for control over the code you feed into your Web site, another good way to get content out of Word and into FrontPage is the trusty old Copy and Paste method—but you've got to do it right.

FrontPage's paste options

Don't just paste your Word content in blindly. Use some of FrontPage's advanced paste features to help you create clean pages. When you paste, don't retain the content's original source formatting (which is what FrontPage automatically does when you paste). Instead, click the paste icon that appears and select Keep Text Only. Better yet, don't let FrontPage do anything automatically. Instead of pasting as usual (by pressing Ctrl+V or clicking the paste button on the Standard toolbar), select Edit → Paste Special and choose an HTML format for the pasted text. (FrontPage paste options are covered in detail on page 26.)

Using Notepad

Many Web authors go through an intermediary step to protect their code from the gobbledygook that comes in with formatted paragraphs from Word. They copy text *out of* Word and paste *into* Notepad, Windows's barebones text-editing program. Then, within Notepad, they select and copy the text again and paste it onto a page in FrontPage. Why the extra step? Since Notepad has no formatting features, the program automatically strips out all the frills.

Formatting pasted content

When you leave out Word's formatting, you'll need to spend some time dressing up your page so it looks good with, for example, headings differentiated from regular paragraphs. Of course, if you've applied Cascading Style Sheets to your site, this can be done with a few clicks that apply paragraph and class styles to page elements. (Flip back to Chapter 7 to read how CSS helps you format pages in your site with ease and efficiency.)

FREQUENTLY ASKED QUESTION

Word Documents with Images

I have a Word document that contains a lot of pictures. What's the best way to get it into my site?

If you still have the image files saved separately, the best thing to do is copy the text and paste it into a new Web page (or multiple Web pages) using one of the methods discussed above. Then, make sure your image files are in a Web-friendly format (see page 57). If they're not, use an image-editing program to convert them into GIFs or JPEGs. Once they're ready, import all the image files

into your site and insert or drag them onto the page where you'd like to place them.

If you no longer have copies of the image files, things are bit more challenging. In this situation, often the pictures appear when you open the HTML file in Word, but not on the Web (because they're not GIFs, JPEGs, or PNG files). Ultimately, the best way out of this fix is to save the Word file as a PDF file (page 347) and post that on your site.

PowerPoint and FrontPage

PowerPoint content doesn't convert easily into Web content. Usually the easiest and best option with PowerPoint is to save your presentation as a PPS file, import it into your site, and link to it (as explained on page 346). However, you can also convert a presentation into a series of Web pages or copy and paste parts of slides into FrontPage.

Converting a PowerPoint Presentation into a Web Page

Converting a presentation into HTML format works best if your viewers have Internet Explorer. Otherwise, the results may really disappoint you. In other browsers (or in instances where viewers have configured Internet Explorer not to show active content), a lot of elements in your converted presentation won't display properly—or at all. In those situations, you're better off posting the .pps file (page 346).

To convert a presentation into HTML format:

1. **Open the presentation you want to convert.**

2. **Initiate the conversion.**

   Select File → Save As Web Page.

3. **Select a file type to save as.**

   Within the long drop-down list to the right of "Save as type," choose either "Web Page" or "Single File Web Page" (see the box on page 348 to learn what the difference is).

4. **Name the file you're about to create.**

   In the File Name field, type in a short, descriptive name. (As always don't include capitals, spaces, or special characters.)

5. **Click Title and enter a proper page title.**

   This page title will appear in the browser's title bar. It remains the same, even as viewers move from slide to slide.

6. **Select a location.**

   Browse to the directory where you'd like to save the new HTML file. Ideally, this will be in your Web site.

7. **Click Save As or Publish (for more options).**

   If you click Save As, PowerPoint creates the new HTML version of your presentation.

   If you click Publish, you can set some additional preferences. The "Publish as Web Page" dialog box opens. Use it to tell FrontPage which slides you want to convert to HTML pages. If you want to set a special color format for hyperlinks to your slides, click "Web options."

Note: Even if you have viewers using very old browsers, leave "Microsoft Internet Explorer 4.0 or later" selected in the Publish as Web Page dialog box. Viewers who can't see special effects like an expanding outline will still see everything on your slides.

Once you've set all your preferences, click Publish. PowerPoint converts the file.

8. **Test the results in your browser.**

   Take a look at your slideshow to make sure everything works and that the HTML version of you presentation looks the way you want it to (see Figure 18-3).

Tip: If you just want to post one of your presentation's slides on your site, try saving it as an image file instead. To do so, select File → Save As and select .gif from the file format choices at the bottom of the dialog box. You can insert the GIF within a Web page or just link directly to the GIF file.

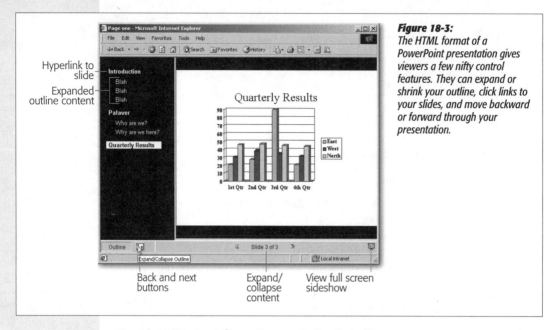

Hyperlink to slide

Expanded outline content

Back and next buttons

Expand/ collapse content

View full screen sideshow

Figure 18-3:
The HTML format of a PowerPoint presentation gives viewers a few nifty control features. They can expand or shrink your outline, click links to your slides, and move backward or forward through your presentation.

Copying Content from PowerPoint into FrontPage

Maybe you just want to get part of a slide onto a Web page. In that case, a simple copy and paste maneuver might be all that's required.

You can select the elements in PowerPoint, and then copy (Ctrl+C) and paste (Ctrl+V) them directly into FrontPage. However, one of the big problems with PowerPoint is that most of its content comes into FrontPage in VML format, which isn't compatible with the Web. (To read of the evils of VML format, take a look at page 263.)

When you paste, FrontPage automatically retains the PowerPoint-infected source formatting, which means that slide elements remain in their native VML format. In this scenario, your only option (if you want your site to remain Web-friendly) is to click the paste icon (see Figure 18-4) and select "Paste as an Image Tag."

Things will go better if you bring text and pictures in separately. In PowerPoint, select only text (not the text box that encloses it) and paste it into FrontPage without source formatting (see page 26). Likewise, select an image in PowerPoint, copy it, and then paste it into FrontPage, where it appears as a regular image tag. When you save the page, FrontPage prompts you to save the image file in your site.

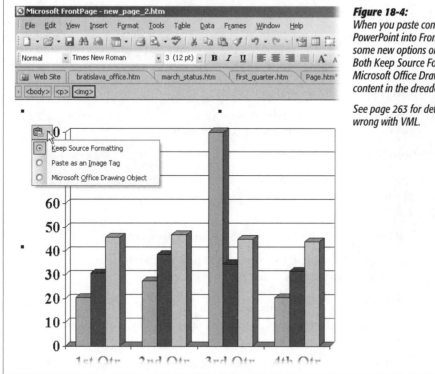

Figure 18-4:
When you paste content from PowerPoint into FrontPage, you'll see some new options on the paste icon. Both Keep Source Formatting and Microsoft Office Drawing Object pastes content in the dreaded VML format.

See page 263 for details on what's wrong with VML.

Working with Excel and FrontPage

Just as with Word, you can copy and paste content or convert Excel files to a Web page. However, when it comes to Excel, FrontPage offers some additional options. You can incorporate a spreadsheet or *pivot table* (a tool for manipulating lots of data) in your Web page and let viewers interact with it. You can even display the same data as a chart.

Copying Tables from Excel into FrontPage

One very simple solution to crossing the Excel-FrontPage divide is to select a bunch of cells in Excel, copy them (Ctrl+C), and then paste them (Ctrl+V) onto your page in FrontPage. FrontPage places them in a table, which is invisible to visitors. Of course, you can format this table any way you like. (Chapter 5 tells you all about working with tables.)

In fact, you don't even need to open your file in Excel. You can drag an Excel file onto a Web page from Windows Explorer. If you do so, FrontPage pastes spreadsheet content onto your Web page within a transparent table.

Saving an Excel Sheet as a Web Page

As with Word, you can instantly transform an Excel worksheet, part of worksheet, or an entire workbook (a collection of worksheets) into a Web page. To do so, first open the workbook in Excel.

1. **Select the data you want to convert.**

   If you want only to turn part of a worksheet into a Web page, select all the cells that make up the area. Otherwise, select nothing.

2. **Initiate the conversion.**

   Select File → Save As Web Page. In the Save As dialog box that opens, specify whether you want to convert the Entire Workbook or the selection you made in step 1.

3. **Tell Excel how much of your workbook you'd like to convert.**

   Select Entire Workbook to convert all sheets, or choose Selection: Sheet if you just want to turn the active sheet into a Web page.

4. **Select a file type to save as.**

   Within the long drop-down list to the right of "Save as type," choose either Web Page or Single File Web Page (see the box on page 348 to learn what the difference is).

5. **Name the file you're about to create.**

   Excel's automated file monikers are about as exciting as FrontPage's. In the File Name field, type in a short, descriptive name. (As always don't include capitals, spaces, or special characters.)

6. **Click Title and enter a proper title for you new Web page.**

7. **Select a location.**

   Browse to the directory (probably a folder in your Web site) where you'd like to save the new HTML file.

8. **Click Publish or Save.**

   - If you click Save, Excel creates the new HTML version of your presentation.

   - If you click Publish, you gain a few advantages. For starters, you can set additional options to configure the HTML result. For example, you can single out any one of your workbook's sheets for publishing.

     Another advantage is that the Publish option produces an HTML page that's somewhat less cluttered than the Save function does. This is important because, like its equivalent operation in Word, the "Save as Web page" method fills your pages with a lot of extraneous code. The Publish function, as its name suggests, creates a Web page truly intended for display.

After you've set your options, click Publish.

Tip: If you turn on the "Add Interactivity" checkbox when you publish, you can create a spreadsheet or pivot table Web component, which you'll read about in the next section.

After you click Save (or Publish a second time), Excel creates the Web file.

Displaying Excel Data

Maybe displaying data pulled from an Excel file isn't fancy enough for you. What if you want to provide visitors with something like a small mortgage calculator in which they can enter figures and tabulate results?

FrontPage offers a *spreadsheets and charts Web component* that lets you do just that. You can insert what's essentially a miniature version of Excel within your Web page. This component can be in spreadsheet, chart, or pivot table format, and your viewers can interact with it, using some limited Excel controls (see Figure 18-5).

Sounds great. So what's the catch? Your visitors need to be completely Microsoft-equipped in order to see the component, otherwise they'll be greeted with the not-so-friendly message shown in Figure 18-6. In other words, if you want visitors to see your spreadsheet, not only will they have to view the page with Internet Explorer (version 5.0 or later) and have Excel installed on their system, they'll also need to have Microsoft Office Web Components installed. Office Web Components are automatically installed during a default installation of Office 2003. You can also install them separately from the Office Resource Kit (for more info, visit *www.microsoft.com/office*). Because of this, you should probably use this feature only if you're sure your visitors have all this software installed—as in a corporate intranet, for example. Due to these requirements, Web developers rarely use these components for pages destined for the broader Internet.

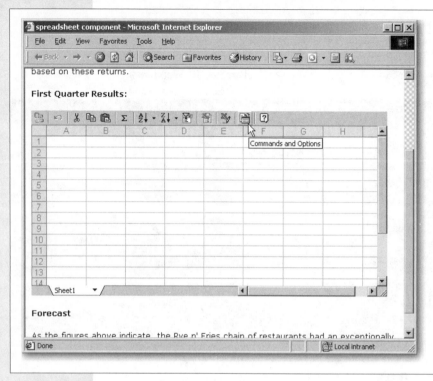

Figure 18-5:
It's a mini-Excel application right inside your Web page. Inserting a spreadsheet as an Office component creates a kind of window into your Excel spreadsheet that visitors can use to view and manipulate data. The Commands and Options button is available to authors in FrontPage, and also to visitors viewing the component in a browser—though, as you'd expect, the choices for each differ (as you'll see in a moment).

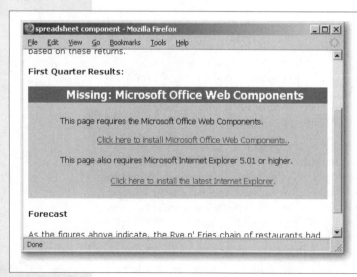

Figure 18-6:
When you try to view a spreadsheet component in a non-IE browser, your visitors will just see this big "missing" message.

Note: Spreadsheet and chart components also require the presence of FrontPage Server Extensions on your Web server.

While this is a nifty interactive feature, you'll find that its use is limited. For instance, you can't save any visitor entries to an Excel file or any kind of database. This feature is really just for on-the-fly calculations that might help your readers figure out a monthly payment or special discount. (If you want visitors to add entries to a database through your Web pages, see Chapter 17 for instructions on using the Database Interface Wizard.)

Adding a Spreadsheet Web Component

Inserting a spreadsheet component is a snap. First, open or create the page you'd like to place it on. Place your cursor where you want the component to appear. Select Insert → Web Component to open the Insert Web Component dialog box. Within the Component type list on the left, select Spreadsheets and Charts. Then, within the list that appears in the pane on the right, select Office Spreadsheet and click Finish. The spreadsheet appears on your page.

Note: If the Spreadsheets and Charts option is grayed out, select Tools → Page Options and turn on the ActiveX Controls checkbox.

Enter whatever data you want the spreadsheet to contain.

Tip: If you have an existing spreadsheet you want to display, it's actually easier to start the process in Excel. In Excel, choose File → Save as Web Page. Within the Save As dialog box that opens, click the Selection: Sheet radio button and turn on the Add Interactivity checkbox. Then click Publish (see the previous section for details on saving Excel files as Web pages).

When you do so, Excel saves the Web page as a bona fide FrontPage Web page (not a hybrid like those shown in Figure 18-2), and the program inserts the sheet as an interactive spreadsheet component within that page. You can also copy the desired cells out of Excel and then paste them inside your spreadsheet component (select cell A1, then press Ctrl+V or click the Paste button on the Standard toolbar).

Configuring the spreadsheet component

When you add a spreadsheet component, FrontPage gives both you and a visitor viewing the file through a browser some controls over spreadsheet display and behavior. As the all-powerful creator, you obviously have more options and can even limit what visitors can and can't do with your spreadsheet.

You and your visitors access these controls by clicking the "Commands and Options" button in your spreadsheet component's toolbar (pop back to Figure 18-5 to see what this looks like). When you click this button, you can set all the options you're about to read about. When site visitors click this button, the more limited dialog box shown in Figure 18-7 displays.

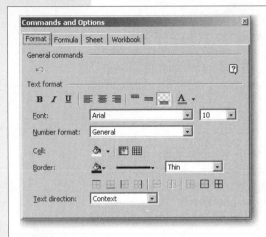

Figure 18-7:
Visitors probably won't find much use for the limited options they have in this Commands and Options dialog box. For instance, formulas can be manipulated directly on the spreadsheet.

The Commands and Options box that authors see has a few more bells and whistles (see Figure 18-8).

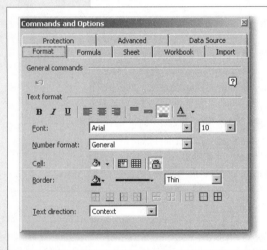

Figure 18-8:
The author's Commands and Options dialog box contains additional tabs. You'll use these tabs to decorate your Web-based spreadsheet and also to control what appears in the visitors' Commands and Options box.

To open the Commands and Options dialog box, click the Commands and Options button on the Excel toolbar at the top of the component (see Figure 18-5). The tabs in this dialog box let you do the following:

- **Set display preferences.** You probably won't need to change the component's decorative scheme, but if you want to, click the Format tab to do things like change font color and alignment, or cell background. If you want to hide grid lines, Excel's gray column headers (A, B, C, and so on), or row headers (1, 2, 3, and so on), click the Sheet tab and turn off those checkboxes.

Note: To resize the entire component, you can drag any of the eight handles (small black squares) that appear around its border when you select it.

- **Name worksheet(s).** When you insert a spreadsheet component, FrontPage actually creates three worksheets, which all compose one workbook. Click the Workbook tab within the Commands and Options dialog box to change their names. If you have only one worksheet, you can turn off the sheet selector checkbox so visitors won't switch out of it. Or select empty sheet names in the pane at bottom and click Delete to remove them.

- **Set visitor controls.** What do you want your visitors to be able to see and do? For example, you may not want to give them access to the spreadsheet toolbar. If that's the case, click the Workbook tab and turn off the toolbar checkbox. You can choose to hide scrollbars by turning off either scrollbar checkbox on this tab, too.

You can further define visitor abilities by clicking the Protection tab within the Commands and Options dialog box as explained in Figure 18-9.

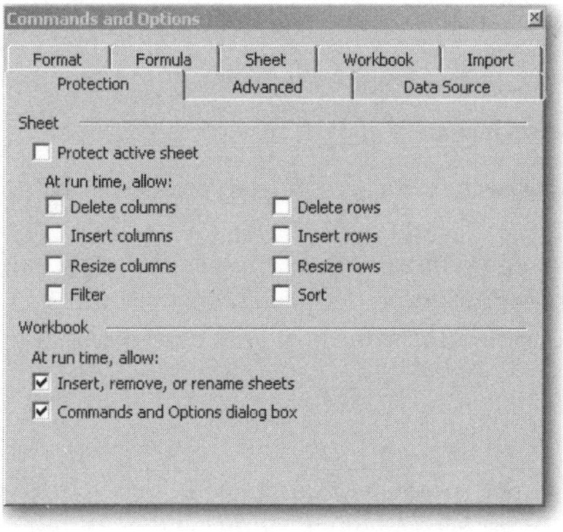

Figure 18-9:
The Protection tab lets you control visitor actions. The "Protect active sheet" checkbox acts as a master switch, which locks the spreadsheet, preventing any edits or manipulation. If you turn it on, you can then choose to allow select actions by turning on their checkboxes. The term "at run time" refers to the point at which a viewer opens the page containing the spreadsheet in a browser.

Make your spreadsheet read-only if you want, by turning on the "Protect active sheet" checkbox. Doing so prohibits visitors from entering or manipulating data in any way. You can also allow some select functions by turning on checkboxes underneath the "Protect active sheet" checkbox. For instance, you can lock the sheet from edits but allow viewers to sort information by turning on the Sort checkbox.

If you don't want viewers to have access to the Commands and Options dialog box (see Figure 18-7), turn off the "Commands and Options dialog box" checkbox at the bottom of the Protection tab. If you just want to stop visitors from creating or deleting worksheets, then turn off the "Insert, remove or rename sheets" checkbox just above that. If you do so, FrontPage removes these options from the visitor's Workbook tab within their Commands and Options dialog box.

Import data. The spreadsheet component is a simple and limited feature. You're not going to use it to display data from a database (that's what the Database Results and Database Interface Wizards are for—as explained in Chapters 16 and 17). However, you can import data if it's in the form of an HTML file, comma-separated text file (.csv), or an XML file. To do so, open the Commands and Options dialog box and click the Import tab. Select the appropriate file type, then browse to and select the file and click Open. The path and file name appear on the Import tab. Click Import Now and FrontPage populates your spreadsheet component with data from the file.

Adding an Office Chart Web Component

The spreadsheet component is great, but what if you want to present data in a graphical format that can really help visitors understand the figures? In that case, you can use the Office Chart Web component.

This works a lot like the spreadsheet component, but instead of a spreadsheet, visitors can look at a bar graph or pie chart to analyze and manipulate data.

To turn your spreadsheet into a pretty picture, do the following:

1. **Create a spreadsheet component on a page.**

   Follow the instructions in the last section for inserting a spreadsheet component. For the Chart component to work, you need to name it. To do so, right-click the edge of the spreadsheet component and then select ActiveX Control Properties. Within the ActiveX Control Properties dialog box that opens, click the Object Tag tab. Type a name within the Name box. Don't use spaces or special characters.

2. **Insert the chart.**

   Place your cursor to the right of the spreadsheet component. Select Insert → Web Component to display the Insert Web Component dialog box. Within the list on the left, select Spreadsheets and Charts. Then in the list that appears on the right, select Office Chart and click Finish. A Commands and Options dialog box displays.

3. **Select the data source.**

   You have three data options:

   • If you want to enter data manually, click "Data typed into a data sheet." Then click Data sheet and enter the information you want your chart to show.

   • If you want to display data from a database, select "Data from a database table or query," and then click Connection to browse to and connect to it.

- If you want to use the spreadsheet on your page, select the third choice, "Data from the following Web page item." Then select the spreadsheet from the list below. Next, set a range of cells. To do so, click Range and enter the range of cells that contain the data you want to show. For example, if you enter A1:F8, the chart would display cells A1 through F8. Then click OK.

4. **Choose chart type.**

Click the Type tab in the Commands and Options dialog box and select a chart style.

5. **Save settings.**

Click outside the dialog box to save your settings. A chart appears on your page.

Test your chart in a browser (see Figure 18-10).

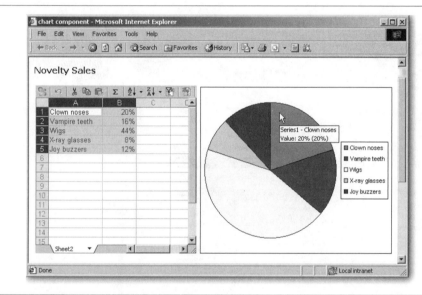

Figure 18-10:
You can use a chart to illustrate a spreadsheet you've posted. If visitors edit figures in the spreadsheet, the chart changes to reflect the new values.

Tip: If you want to let visitors change the chart type and other view options, you can give them a toolbar and a Commands and Options dialog box. To do so, right-click your chart component and then select ActiveX Control Properties. Click the Show/Hide tab and turn on the toolbar checkbox and the "Commands and Options dialog box" checkbox.

Pivot Table

Pivot tables are a way to glean essential figures when you've got lots of data. Say you've got several months worth of sales data for a bunch of different products, and you want to know which products are selling and which aren't. A pivot table helps you find the answer by quickly and easily sorting through all the info stored in your table.

Note: Unfortunately, this book can't help you with the hardest part of this process. Creating pivot tables is an advanced skill. To learn more about them (and all about Excel), take a look at *Excel: The Missing Manual.*

Since you're connecting to a pivot table you created, you already have an Excel file filled with data. So, begin by opening Excel.

Next, follow all the steps for converting an Excel file into a Web file (as explained on page 353). When you do so, add the following steps: within the initial Save As dialog box, turn on the Add Interactivity checkbox and then click Publish. A "Publish as Web Page" dialog box displays. Within the "Add interactivity with" drop-down list, select "PivotTable functionality" and click Publish.

Excel creates a Web page, which includes a pivot table Web component (see Figure 18-11).

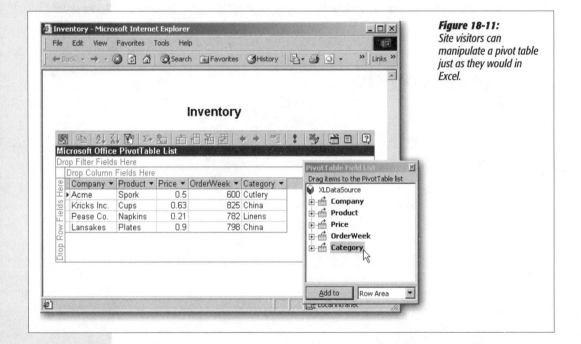

Figure 18-11:
Site visitors can manipulate a pivot table just as they would in Excel.

Part Six:
Appendix

Appendix A: FrontPage 2003, Menu by Menu

6

FrontPage 2003, Menu by Menu

When working with a powerful program like FrontPage, most people tend to home in on a handful of tools and features that they regularly use. But sometimes you need to enlist a part of the FrontPage arsenal that you're not familiar with. This appendix gives you a quick, menu-by-menu explanation of all the program's commands. Keyboard shortcuts are listed inside parentheses.

File Menu

The File menu contains basic commands that get you started with a document, help define its properties, and let you close things down when you're ready to take a break.

New

Here's where it all starts. Selecting this command opens the New task pane where you can create a new Web site or Web page (see page 8).

Open

Unfortunately, many FrontPage authors choose this command by accident when what they really mean to choose is the Open Site option (covered shortly). When you select plain old Open (Ctrl+O), FrontPage lets you open a single file—which is fine, as long as that file's not part of a Web site. Even if you're making a quick edit to one file in your site, you should always open the entire site, so FrontPage can track your changes and update your site accordingly.

Close

This menu item closes the one file that's active in the document window. If you haven't saved changes, FrontPage prompts you to do so.

Open Site

You'll use this option to open entire Web sites for editing in FrontPage (which you should always do, even if you're making a quick change to one page). Select this item and FrontPage displays the Open Site dialog box, which lets you browse to and open your site. Once a Web site folder (featuring a small globe) is active in the "Look in" field at the top of the dialog box, just click the Open button. If you're opening the same site every day, check out the Recent Sites option further down the File menu.

Note: If you're opening a site that's not on a network drive (like an HTTP site on "localhost," for example), click My Network Places on the left side of the Open Site dialog box to get to it. If you want to open a remote site in FrontPage, you won't use this command the first time you do so (you'll need to follow the instructions on page 260). After you've opened a remote site in FrontPage once, the site appears in your My Network Places list.

Close Site

Once you're done editing, choose this command to close the entire site. FrontPage prompts you to save any unsaved changes to open pages. Even if you have no other sites open, FrontPage remains active. To close the program itself, select File → Exit.

Save

Select File → Save (Ctrl+S) to save changes to the file open in the document window. If it's a new file, FrontPage opens a Save dialog box, which lets you name the file and select a location for it. If you saved the file before, FrontPage updates it.

Save As

If you want to create a new incarnation of an existing file, choose Save As to make a copy under a new name.

Save All

If you've got a lot of pages open with unsaved changes, this is a quick way to save all those changes, so you can exit the program faster. Otherwise, you'd have to save each file one by one, or wait to exit FrontPage at which point the program prompts you to save each file separately. This command saves any pending changes to all open files. (But it won't close them. To close all open pages, select Window → Close All Pages.)

File Search

Missing a file? Select File Search, and FrontPage displays a search box within the task pane, which lets you search your entire computer for HTML pages and other Microsoft Office files (see Figure A-1).

Figure A-1:
FrontPage's File Search feature opens this task pane, which lets you look for HTML and Office pages on your system from inside the FrontPage window.

The Search pane includes the following settings:

- Use the **Property** drop-down list (at the top of the pane) to tell FrontPage what you're searching for. For instance, if you want to find a file by name, select "File name." If you want to find a file that contains some specific text, select "Text or Property."

- Enter the text you're searching for in the **Value** box and click Add. FrontPage adds your search criteria to the box below the Add button. You can add multiple criteria in the same manner.

Tip: Use an asterisk in the text field as a wildcard character. To the FrontPage File Search, an asterisk means one or more of any and all characters. For example, entering "so*p" would track down "soap," "soup," and "sodapop."

- Use the **Search in** drop-down box to tell FrontPage where to search.

• Your setting in the **Results should be** drop-down list tells the program what file types you want the search to return.

Click Go to start the search. FrontPage returns a list of matching files in the Search pane. To open a file, pass your cursor over it and then click the drop-down arrow that appears. A pop-up menu displays, which lets you open the page in a browser, edit it with FrontPage (or another program), or create a new file out of it.

Publish Site

Use this command to create or update your Web site on a live Web server or to make a backup copy of it. See Chapter 13 to learn all the ins and outs of publishing.

Import

All your site's files must live and travel together within your site's core folder. Use this command to get any file you didn't create with FrontPage into your site, where it belongs. Select this option, and FrontPage opens an Import dialog box. Click Add File to browse to and select file(s) you want to include in your site.

Tip: For a quick importing shortcut, drag a file from Windows Explorer or your desktop onto your site's folder list.

Export

Select file(s) in your folder list, then select this command, and FrontPage makes a copy of the file(s) wherever you tell it to. Just browse to the desired location within the Export dialog box the program provides.

Preview in Browser

You should always test your Web pages in a browser. This command's submenu lists all the browsers that are installed on your computer. Open a page in all your browsers at once by selecting File → Preview in Browser → Preview in Multiple Browsers. (For more information on this command, see page 234.)

Page Setup

You must have a page active in the document window, or this command is grayed out. This option opens a Print Page Setup dialog box where you can set print margins and paper size.

Print Preview

Select this menu item and FrontPage shows you how your Web page will look when it prints from Design view (not from within a browser). The display appears in the document window. Use buttons at the top of the display to change your view. You can zoom in or out and view one or two pages. Click the Close button above the preview to return to Design view.

Print

This option (Ctrl+P) lets you select a printer you can use to print the Web page that's active in the document window. In the Print dialog box that opens, enter the number of copies you'd like to print and select which pages you want to print. (Long Web pages can span many written pages when you print them.)

Send

This command opens your email program and creates a new message. FrontPage inserts whatever Web page you have open in the document window as the message. If you've used FrontPage to create an email announcement in HTML format, this is a great way to distribute it.

Properties

The Properties dialog box lets you view and set information about the file that's currently open in the document window. The General tab includes a field for page title (see page 184). The Formatting tab lets you add page background and configure hyperlinks (though it's better to use CSS to format both—see Chapter 7). Use the Advanced tab to set page margins (see page 100). The Workgroup tab gives you access to collaboration tools covered in Chapter 14.

Recent Files

Use this selection as a shortcut to open any one of the last eight files you've opened in FrontPage.

Recent Sites

The submenu that this option opens lets you select any one of the last four Web sites you've opened in FrontPage.

Exit

Select this command (or press Alt+F+X) to close FrontPage. The program closes all files you have open and prompts you to save any unsaved changes.

Edit Menu

Aptly named, the Edit menu helps you with a variety of editing jobs. Use its commands to copy, paste, find, replace, or undo any tragic mistakes you've made. You'll also find a number of collaboration tools on this menu.

Undo

Turn back time with this option (Ctrl+Z). Say you just pasted a torrid diary entry onto your home page and you're having second thoughts. File → Undo saves the day and deletes everything you've just written. If you've made a series of bad edits, just select Undo again and again until your page is back where you want it. FrontPage lets you know what it's about to undo right on the File menu itself. For instance, you might see something like "Undo paste" or "Undo typing" if you've just pasted or typed some text.

Redo

If you undo an edit then change your mind, just select Redo (Ctrl+Y) to get that edit back.

Cut

If you want to delete or move some text or other page element, select it and choose Edit → Cut (Ctrl+X). FrontPage removes the selection.

Copy

If you want to duplicate a page element, select it and then choose this command (Ctrl+C). The selection stays in place, but FrontPage copies it to the Windows clipboard for pasting elsewhere.

Office Clipboard

Want to see what's on the Windows clipboard? Select this option and FrontPage opens a Clipboard task pane, which shows you all items available for pasting (see Figure A-2).

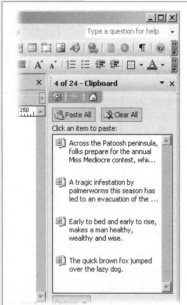

Figure A-2:
The clipboard holds up to 24 text snippets.

Paste

The Paste option inserts whatever content is active on the Windows clipboard. Place your cursor where you want to place the material and select Edit → Paste (Ctrl+V). See page 26 for more on pasting in FrontPage.

Paste Special

When you use the regular Paste option, FrontPage retains formatting from the source document, which may not be what you want. To paste text in a simpler format, use the Paste Special option instead (for details, see page 26).

Delete

This command works like the Delete key on your keyboard. If you select some content on a page and select Edit → Delete, FrontPage removes the selection. If your cursor is sitting on a page and you select this option, FrontPage deletes the character to the right of your cursor.

Select All

Often you want to select all the content in a page. Rather than clicking and dragging to select an entire page, choose Edit → Select All (Ctrl+A). If you're in Design view, FrontPage selects the <body> tags and all their contents. In other words, anything in the document's head section isn't selected. If you're in Code view, FrontPage selects the <html> tags and all their contents, including the <head> tags and everything in between.

Find

If you're looking for a word or snippet of text, select Edit → Find (Ctrl+F). FrontPage opens the Find and Replace dialog box with the Find tab active. Use it to search a page or your entire site. For details, see page 225.

Replace

Select Edit → Replace (Ctrl+H) and FrontPage opens the Find and Replace dialog box with the Replace tab open. You can use it to find a passage of text and replace it with an alternative. (For more on Find and Replace, turn to page 225)

Go To

Depending on what FrontPage view you've opened, this menu item offers different options. If you have a page open in Design view and select Edit → Go To (Ctrl+G), this selection says Go To Bookmark and opens a list of bookmarks you can jump to. If you're in Code view, this option is Go To Line and lets you enter a line number to jump to that point in your HTML code.

Go To Function

This command works correctly only when you access it on the Code View toolbar (see Figure A-3) To display the toolbar, select View → Toolbars → Code View. If you have any JavaScript functions on your page, FrontPage lists them in the drop-down list to the right of the Go To Function button. Select one, and FrontPage highlights it in Code view.

Figure A-3:
The Go To Function feature works in combination with this drop-down list of functions.

Quick Tag Editor

This command opens the Quick Tag Editor, which you can use to insert some HTML wherever your cursor is on the page. If you select an element, and then select Edit → Quick Tag Editor (Ctrl+Q), the surrounding tag opens in the editor. (To see how to use this feature, turn to page 165.)

Check Out

When you're collaborating with other authors on a Web site, you may want to implement this document control measure so you don't overwrite each other's edits. Once the site administrator has activated document control, authors can use this command to protect a document from other authors. To read all about document control, turn to page 272. (Check Out's keyboard shortcut is Ctrl+J.)

Check In

Once you check out a document, you need a way to check it back into the site. This command (Ctrl+Shift+J) ends your dominion over a checked-out file and grants other authors access to it.

Undo Check Out

Just checked out the wrong document? Regular Edit → Undo won't help you, but Undo Document Checkout can annul the relationship with one click.

Tasks

Tasks are a terrific tool for coordinating the responsibilities of large staffs or even one-person Web site operations. You can read all about them on page 274. The Tasks submenu offers the following options:

Note: If these options are grayed out, switch to Tasks view (in the document window, click the Web site tab, then click the Tasks button at the very bottom of the program window).

- **Add Task.** Select this command to create a new task. FrontPage displays the New Task dialog box. Complete it and click OK.

- **Edit Task.** Select a task in the task list to activate this option. When you select Edit → Tasks → Edit Tasks, the Task Details Dialog box opens. Make changes and click OK.

- **Start Task.** If you're actually going to tackle one of the tasks assigned to you, select this item, and FrontPage opens the page in question and initiates the task for you. (You can also right-click the task and select Start Task.)

- **Mark Complete.** If you let FrontPage initiate your task, by selecting Start Task, the program automatically marks the task complete if you tell it to. But sometimes (if you've completed the task without FrontPage's assistance, for example) you need to mark a task complete manually. To do so, select the task in the task list, then select Edit → Tasks → Mark Complete (or right-click the task and select Mark Complete).

- **Show History.** When you complete a task, FrontPage removes it from the task list. If you want to see all you've accomplished, select this command. This menu item works like an on/off switch: select it once to turn it on (you'll see a checkmark next to it) and select it again to turn it off.

Code View

This command displays a submenu of HTML code-editing aids that work in combination with FrontPage Code view. The formatting options on this submenu affect code layout only, not a Web page's appearance in a browser.

Tip: Most of these options appear on the Code View toolbar pictured in Figure A-3 (to display it, select View → Toolbars → Code View). You can also access these commands with a right-click on your document in Code view.

- **Increase Indent** (Tab). Often spacing out code in different alignments helps HTML authors know what tags are where. This option pushes the line of code in which your cursor rests farther away from the left margin of the document window.

- **Decrease Indent** (Shift+Tab). Pushes an indented line of code back toward the left edge of the document window.

- **Select Tag** (Ctrl+:). Select this item, and FrontPage highlights the entire tag surrounding your cursor.

- **Find Matching Tag** (Ctrl+;). If your cursor is in a start or end tag, FrontPage selects its mate. If your cursor is in between tags, FrontPage highlights the whole tag and all its contents.

- **Select Block** (Ctrl+'). This command works only when your cursor sits inside two curly brackets (which look like { and }). Select this option, and FrontPage highlights everything between the brackets.

- **Find Matching Brace** (Ctrl+]). If your cursor sits to the left or right of a curly bracket, this option moves your cursor to the left of its matching bracket.

- **Insert Start Tag** (Ctrl+,). Inserts an empty start tag (<>) for you to type in.

- **Insert End Tag** (Ctrl+.). Inserts an empty end tag (</>) for you to type in.

- **Insert Comment** (Ctrl+/). Inserts an empty comment tag (<-- -->) for you to type in.

- **Toggle Bookmark** (Ctrl+F2). Code view bookmarks are tools authors can use to jump around their code. This command sets or clears a bookmark on the line where your cursor sits.

- **Next Bookmark** (F2). Jumps you to the next bookmark in your code.

- **Previous Bookmark** (Shift+F2). Jumps your cursor to the closest bookmark that appears above where your cursor sits.

- **Clear Bookmarks.** Use this selection to remove all bookmarks from your code.

IntelliSense

IntelliSense helps you code HTML and other scripting languages in FrontPage. As you start to type a line of code, IntelliSense pays attention to what you're doing and offers some options to help you complete the line. For example, if you type < FrontPage displays a list of HTML tags (see Figure A-4).

If you select Edit → IntelliSense, FrontPage displays a submenu with the following options:

- **List Members.** If you type or click within a tag and select this submenu item (or press Ctrl+L), FrontPage displays its list of suggestions to complete the tag or attribute. To select a suggestion in the list, double-click it.

- **Parameter Info.** Another autocomplete feature that offers appropriate types of parameters for whatever function or attribute you're typing in Code view. To manually activate it, select this item from the IntelliSense submenu or press Ctrl+Shift+Space.

- **Complete Word.** This item completes a word you've started typing in your HTML code with FrontPage's best guess. Since traveling through the menus to get to this option won't save you much time on this front, you may want to get in the habit of pressing Ctrl+Space bar instead.

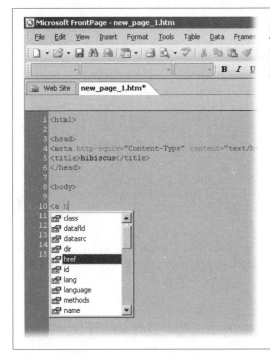

Figure A-4:
As you type code in Code view, FrontPage's IntelliSense feature displays pop-up lists like this to help you quickly find the tag you want. If this list disappears, select Edit → IntelliSense → List Members to get it back.

- **List Code Snippets** (Ctrl+Enter). This command displays a list of all the code snippets that you or FrontPage has saved for use in Code view. Double-click an entry to insert it in your code. If you want to add or edit a snippet, click "Customize list." FrontPage opens the Page Options dialog box to the Code Snippets tab where you can manage items in your snippets list. (You can also select Tools → Page Options to open the dialog box.)

View Menu

You use the View menu to tell FrontPage what parts of the program you want in sight. You can change what aspect of a Web site you see, show and hide toolbars, or open the folder list and task pane.

Page

This command fills the document window with the last page you viewed. If you have no pages open, FrontPage opens a new blank page.

Folders

Selecting View → Folders displays your site's folder structure and files in the document window. To get the same display, you can also click the Web Site tab and click the Folders view button at the bottom of the window. Chapter 10 gives you advice on how to structure your site.

Remote Web Site

This view shows your local Web site alongside your remote Web site. You can publish your entire site or selected files and configure publishing options as well. (You can also click the Web Site tab and click the Remote Site view button at the bottom of the window to get to this screen.) Chapter 13 covers the ins and outs of publishing.

Reports

Select View → Reports to see submenus listing all FrontPage's site reporting options. These reports are all covered in depth on page 242.

Navigation

Select View → Navigation (or click the Web Site tab and click the Navigation view button at the bottom of the window) to set up or view your site's navigation scheme. For details on working in Navigation view, turn to page 182.

Hyperlinks

Select View → Hyperlinks (or click the Web Site tab and click the Hyperlinks view button at the bottom of the window) to see how the pages in your site are connected via hyperlinks.

Tasks

Select View → Tasks to set up or view your site's navigation scheme. Get the same display by selecting the Web Site tab and clicking the Tasks view button at the bottom of the window. For details on working with tasks, see page 274.

Ruler and Grid

This command offers you a few options for adding design aids as background in your Web page (see Figure A-5). FrontPage's grid and ruler can help you place elements precisely. For instance, if you want all pictures to line up vertically, place them along the same grid line or at the same exact point on the ruler.

For this menu item to be active, you need to have a page open in the document window. Then you'll find the following options on this command's submenu:

- **Show Ruler.** Displays rulers on the top and left side of the document window that feature measurements in pixels (but you can change this setting—see Configure, later in this list).

- **Show Grid.** Inserts a grid behind the document window that you can use to line up any absolutely positioned elements (like layers) that you place on your page.

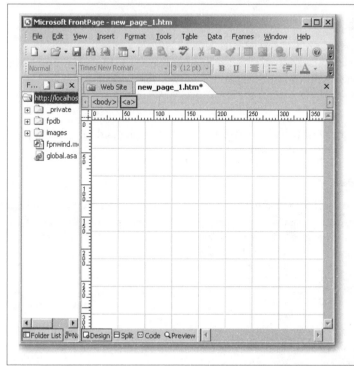

Figure A-5:
When you turn on both the ruler and grid, a page looks like this in Design view.

- **Snap to Grid.** If you turn on this option by selecting it, FrontPage forces you to place absolutely positioned items along the invisible "snapping grid"—an invisible set of lines that elements must line up with. (To learn how to adjust the dimensions of this grid see Configure, later.)

- **Set Origin from Selection.** If you select an item on the page and then choose this submenu item, FrontPage recalibrates your rulers to set the location of zero-by-zero (which is normally the top-left corner of your Web page) to the upper-left corner of the element you chose. Adjusting the origin point won't change how your page displays in a browser. Instead, you can use this feature to do things like measure the distance between objects quickly, without the need to do any math.

- **Reset Origin.** If you've changed your origin point using the previous menu item, select this to set it back to the upper-left corner of the page.

- **Configure.** This command opens the Page Options dialog box with the Ruler and Grid tab active. Here you can change ruler measurement from pixels to inches or centimeters; or make the squares on your grid smaller or larger by reducing or increasing the spacing number, or do the same with the "snapping grid" to give yourself more or less leeway in placing elements (the higher the number, the wider apart lines in the grid are, which gives you less placement leeway). You can also change the line style and color. Click OK to save changes.

Tracing Image

If you want to insert a grayed-out picture behind your page to aid in page design, select View → Tracing Image → Configure and browse to the file you want to use. (See page 104 to learn how to work with a tracing image.)

Folder List

Select View → Folder List (Alt+F1) to display your site's files and folders in a pane on the left side of the FrontPage workspace.

Navigation Pane

Select this item to display the Navigation view in a vertical pane on the left side of the FrontPage workspace (see Figure A-6). The advantage is you can have the Navigation view open while you work in the document window.

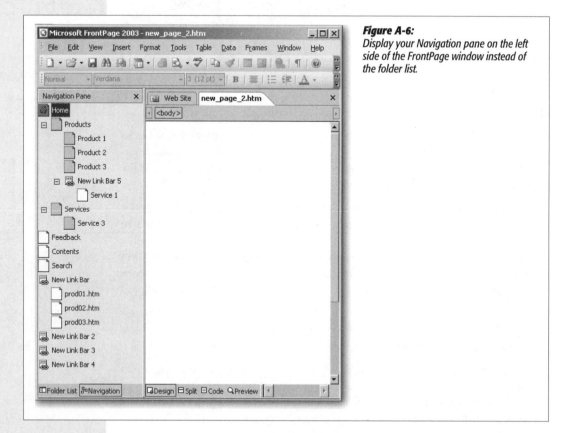

Figure A-6:
Display your Navigation pane on the left side of the FrontPage window instead of the folder list.

Reveal Tags

This command is an on/off switch, which inserts yellow markers showing where HTML tags fall within Design view (also try the keyboard shortcut Ctrl+/).

Quick Tag Selector

Choose this option to display the Quick Tag Selector toolbar (see page 6).

Task Pane

Select View → Task Pane (Ctrl+F1) to display the task pane on the right side of the FrontPage workspace. The pane contains shortcuts to menu items and specialized workspaces for various features covered throughout this book (see page 6).

Toolbars

This item reveals a submenu of FrontPage toolbars. Select one to open it. Any toolbar with a checkmark to its left is already displayed in the program window. To remove one, select it from the submenu to remove its checkmark.

Page Size

If you're designing for a particular screen resolution, you can set your design environment up so it reflects those dimensions. Select View → Page Size and select a monitor resolution size. If you don't see the one you want, select Modify Page Sizes at the bottom of the submenu.

Refresh

Select View → Refresh (or press F5) to refresh the view of your Web site. Why would you want to do this? Say you have your site open in FrontPage and you open Excel, and then use Excel's File → Save As option to save a file in your Web site's folder. You won't see that file in FrontPage until you refresh your view.

Insert Menu

The Insert menu lets you add a variety of elements to your pages—from a simple line break to interactive database components.

Break

This option opens a dialog box that lets you insert a variety of line breaks (see page 22).

Horizontal Line

Select this item and FrontPage adds a simple horizontal line wherever your cursor sits. Horizontal lines help break a page into sections.

Layer

This command places a 100×100 pixel layer in the upper-right corner of the Web page that's active in the document window. You can move and resize the layer. Read all about layers in Chapter 8.

Inline Frame

Inserts an inline frame wherever you placed your cursor before selecting this option. Read about inline frames on page 113.

Date and Time

Often viewers will want to know when the page they're reading was last updated. Let them know by selecting this item and completing the dialog box that follows.

Symbol

If you want to add a special character that doesn't appear on your keyboard, select this menu item. (For details on inserting symbols, see page 24.)

Comment

This command lets you insert an HTML comment in your code. Comments appear in Design view in purple text. Comments don't show up in browsers, so they're often used by developers to communicate with one another.

Navigation

This option opens the Insert Web Component dialog box with Link Bars already selected. See page 201 to read all about using link bars to help visitors navigate your site.

Page Banner

Use this option to add a page banner to display a page's title at the top of your page (see page 205).

Web Component

This command displays the Insert Web Component dialog box (see Figure A-7). You can read about using this dialog box to create features like link bars (see page 201) and included content (see page 206).

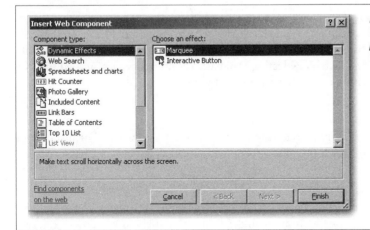

Figure A-7:
The Web Component dialog box provides one-stop shopping for all your Web component needs.

Some other options here include:

- **Hit Counter** tracks how many times a page has been visited (requires FrontPage Server Extensions on your Web server). If you want to gather valuable information about who's visiting your site, check out the Usage Reports covered on page 245.

- **Top 10 List** lets you display some information on site usage to your viewers. Show them the top 10 visited pages in your site or the top 10 search strings visitors have entered.

- **MSN Components** aren't terribly useful. They add an MSN search engine box (you're better off inserting one from Google instead—visit *www.google.com/services/websearch.html*) or an MSN Money Central Web site stock quote search box.

- **MSNBC Components** add a feature to your site that pulls a headline image from the MSNBC site and places it on your page. No, Microsoft doesn't pay you for the advertising, and when a visitor clicks the graphic, he's taken away from your site.

Database

This command leads to a submenu featuring the following choices:

- **DataView** and **Web Part.** These are two options that rely upon SharePoint Services. Since SharePoint features don't require FrontPage and can be edited directly through a browser, this book covers them only cursorily. (For more information on how SharePoint handles data, check out *Essential SharePoint* by Jeff Webb [O'Reilly], *Advanced SharePoint Services Solutions* by Scott P. Hillier [Apress], and *Windows SharePoint Services Inside Out* by Jim Buyens [Microsoft Press].)

- **Results.** Use this command to create a Database Results Wizard (see page 325).

- **Column Value.** When you've created a table using the Database Results Wizard (see page 325), you can click in a cell and use this command to add another column to the display. Otherwise, you need to take the long way around by right-clicking the results table, selecting Database Results Properties, and editing the column list within the wizard screens that follow.

Form

Create a new Web form by selecting Insert → Form → Form. The Form submenu also includes commands for adding form fields. Read all about it in Chapter 15.

Picture

This menu item lets you browse to find a picture file to add to your Web page. You can also drag a picture file from the folder list (or anywhere in Windows Explorer) directly onto your Web page to insert it. Chapter 4 covers working with images in FrontPage.

Interactive Button

This command displays the Interactive Buttons dialog box, which lets you add a button that animates when a cursor passes over it. Read more about interactive buttons on page 146.

File

This option lets you browse to and select a file to insert directly within your Web page. You can accomplish the same thing by dragging files onto your page from within the folder list or Windows Explorer.

Bookmark

Select Insert → Bookmark (or press Ctrl+G) to insert a bookmark hyperlink destination. Bookmarks let you hyperlink to specific places within a Web page (see page 54).

Hyperlink

This command (Ctrl+K) opens the Hyperlink dialog box. Use it to tie all the pages of your site together. Chapter 3 covers hyperlink particulars.

Format Menu

Options on the Format menu help you decorate and lay out pages, or animate site elements. You can use them just to prettify a word or to add complex interactivity to your site.

Note: When it comes to many items on the Format menu (namely Font, Paragraph, Borders and Shading, and Position), you're better off using the equivalent controls within the Styles dialog box–applying styles with Cascading Style Sheets, in other words. Formatting your Web pages with CSS saves you a lot of work in the long run. Chapter 7 tells you all about it.

Font

Select this item to display FrontPage's Font dialog box (see page 27).

Paragraph

This command lets you adjust paragraph alignment and spacing with the Paragraph dialog box. For details on formatting paragraphs, see page 32.

Bullets and Numbering

This option opens the Bullets and Numbering dialog box. Turn to page 38 to learn about creating bulleted and numbered lists.

Borders and Shading

Give a paragraph a colored background or a border. To learn about the Borders and Shading dialog box, see page 123.

Position

If you select an item on the page, and then choose this option, FrontPage opens the Position dialog box, which you can read about on page 124.

Behaviors

This command opens the Behaviors task pane, where you can add interactivity to your pages by creating behaviors that respond to viewer actions. To see what kinds of effects you can create, turn to page 151.

Layers

Select this option to open the Layers task pane, which lets you create layers. What are layers and why would you want to use them? Chapter 8 explains it all for you.

Theme

Selecting Format → Theme opens the Theme task pane, where you can view FrontPage's themes and apply one to your page(s). See page 192.

Style

This command opens the Style dialog box, which lets you create formatting styles that you can apply to various page elements. Chapter 7 tells you everything you need to know about styles and explains how to work with this dialog box.

Style Sheet Links

If you want to attach Web pages to an external style sheet, select them in the folder list, then select Format → Style Sheet Links. See page 125.

Shared Borders

As you can read about in Chapter 11, you're better off avoiding shared borders. Should you choose to ignore this sage advice, select Format → Shared Borders to add them to your pages.

Page Transition

If you want to add one of the animated page transitions discussed on page 147, open the page and select Format → Page Transition.

Background

Select Format → Background to open the Page Properties dialog box to the Formatting tab where you can set page background color or choose a picture to use instead.

Dynamic Web Template

This command reveals a submenu that lets you manage all tasks involving Dynamic Web Templates. To learn about creating and managing Web pages with this valuable tool, turn to page 216.

Remove Formatting

If you want to remove any decorative formatting from your text, select the text, then select Format → Remove Formatting (or press Ctrl+Shift+Z). FrontPage returns the selected passage to the program's no-frills Normal style.

Properties

Depending upon what page element you select before choosing this menu option (you can also press Alt+Enter), FrontPage displays the Properties dialog box for that item. For example, if you select an image, the Image Properties dialog box opens.

Tools Menu

The Tools menu offers a variety of site management features that let you do everything from check spelling to set site access permissions.

Spelling

Select Tools → Spelling (or press F7) to check spelling on a page or across your entire site. See page 222.

Thesaurus

Grasping for just the right word? Select the word that's not quite right, then choose this option (Shift+F7) to open FrontPage's Thesaurus, which presents alternatives for you to choose from.

Set Language

Use this command to set the language used by the speller and the thesaurus.

Accessibility

Select Tools → Accessibility (or press F8) to open FrontPage's Accessibility Checker (covered on page 231).

Browser Compatibility

This command launches FrontPage's Browser Compatibility checker, which you can read about on page 240.

Auto Thumbnail

Use this option to create thumbnail images. Select a picture, and then select Tools → Auto Thumbnail (or press Ctrl+T) to make it into a thumbnail. Read about thumbnails on page 73.

Recalculate Hyperlinks

When you select this item, FrontPage cleans house. The program not only checks all hyperlinks in your site, it also checks other functional elements, like form handlers and Web components, to make sure that everything is working as it should.

Optimize HTML

This command opens the Optimize HTML dialog box, but (as you can read about on page 241) you should use the Optimize HTML command only when you publish. "Optimize at publish" settings are in a different location, within Remote Web site view (see page 263).

Server

This option is grayed out if you're working in a disk-based site. To see it, you'll need to connect to and open your remote site. Use this command to access FrontPage Server Extension permissions pages, where you can set access rights to your site. For example, you can force visitors to enter a user name and password to access a subsite (see page 307). If you develop on a Web server, you'll also see this command. However, you should set permissions only on your live Web site—permissions won't publish with the rest of your site.

Packages

This command lets you import or export a *Web package.* Packages require the presence of SharePoint services on your Web Server. See page 180.

Save Web Part To

If you're working on a server that has SharePoint Services, you can use this command to save a Web part as a file. Web parts are SharePoint site components that display data. They can also be manipulated directly through a browser. (For more information on how SharePoint handles data, take a look at *Essential SharePoint* by Jeff Webb [O'Reilly], *Advanced SharePoint Services Solutions* by Scott P. Hillier [Apress], and *Windows SharePoint Services Inside Out* by Jim Buyens [Microsoft Press].)

Macro

If you know how to program in VBA (Visual Basic for Applications), you can create macros that help you edit Web pages faster. Select Tools → Macro → Visual Basic Editor to create a macro. Select Tools → Macro → Macros to access a list of macros you created.

The third option on the Macro submenu, "Microsoft Script Editor," opens your page in an entirely new program—the Microsoft Script Editor (see Figure A-8), which helps you create and edit scripts. If you don't have the Script Editor installed (it's not part of the automatic installation), FrontPage prompts you to install it. You can use this program to edit your site's HTML, JavaScript, or VBScript. (To learn more about the Script Editor, visit *http://www.microsoftfrontpage.com/content/ARTICLES/HighendScriptinFP02.html.*) If you love to code, or are just getting started as a coder, this is a handy tool.

Add-ins

This command displays the "Add-ins" dialog box. Use it to add, view, or modify add-in programs that extend the way FrontPage works, like the Spam Spoiler mentioned on page 51.

Customize

Most authors are relatively happy with the layout of FrontPage's workspace just the way it is. If you're not, you can customize it using this command. Selecting

Tools → Customize displays the Customize dialog box where you can modify menus and toolbars. Rearrange menu items by dragging them to the position you want.

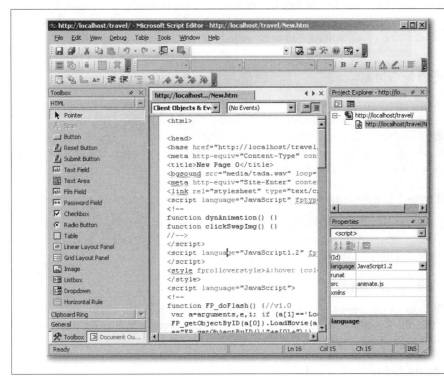

Figure A-8:
Microsoft's Script Editor gives you myriad coding shortcuts and task panes. For example, if you drag an item from the element list on the left onto your page, the editor inserts most of the tag. You just need to finish it (by typing in the path and name of an image file, for example).

Site Settings

This command opens the Site Settings dialog box, which contains general information about your site. You can impose document control (see page 272), create a database connection (see page 323), change link bar navigation labels (see page 202), and even rename your site (only if it's a subsite).

Tip: To see all the files and folders in your site—even those managed by FrontPage—click the Advanced tab within the Site Settings dialog box and turn on the "Show hidden files and folders" checkbox.

Options

Select Tools → Options to configure FrontPage settings. The Options dialog box that displays lets you tell FrontPage what to display when the program starts. On the Configure Editors tab, tell FrontPage which programs you want to use to open certain file types. You can also set Reporting options (see page 242) and customize FTP or ASP.NET settings.

Page Options

This command opens a complex dialog box teeming with tabs. You'll find the Authoring tab here (see page 237 and page 261), as well as the Thumbnail tab (see page 73). You can set IntelliSense preferences, Ruler and grid settings, add code snippets, configure HTML code format (even tell FrontPage what colors code elements should be), and adjust other behind the scenes editing preferences.

Table Menu

Many selections on the Table menu are grayed out if you don't have your cursor in a table or if you haven't selected at least a portion of a table. This menu lets you create tables and adjust their layout and formatting. You can speed your work by accessing these same options via the Tables toolbar (to open the toolbar, select View → Toolbars → Tables).

Layout Tables and Cells

This command opens the Layout Tables and Cells task pane. *Layout* tables allow pixel-precise design, so they differ from traditional HTML tables. Turn to page 96 to learn all about them.

Cell Formatting

You must have your cursor in a *layout* cell (not an ordinary cell) within a layout table for FrontPage to activate this menu item. Selecting it displays the Cell Formatting task pane. Read all about layout tables on page 96.

Draw Table

This option turns your cursor into a pencil so you can draw a table on your page. The pencil remains active until you select the Draw Table command again. See page 88.

Insert

Select Table → Insert → Table, and FrontPage displays the Insert Table dialog box covered in detail on page 84. If you've place your cursor within an existing table, you use this option to insert columns, rows, cells, or a caption.

Delete Cells

If you select a table cell or a few cells, this command deletes them.

Select

When you select this menu item, FrontPage displays a submenu that lets you select a table or parts of a table. The area that FrontPage selects depends on the location of your cursor. The program selects the table, column, row, or cell in which your cursor sits.

Merge Cells

To turn two or more cells into one big cell, select them and then choose this option. Find details on merging and splitting cells on page 95.

Split Cells

The opposite of the previous menu item, this command divides whatever cell your cursor sits in into two cells.

Split Table

This option splits a table into two tables, at the point where your cursor rests within the table.

Table AutoFormat

Select Table → Table Autoformat to get help from FrontPage with table formatting. Choose from the program's preset decorative schemes. See page 92 for more.

Distribute Rows Evenly

When you're resizing or filling your table with content, row and column sizes change automatically. If you want to make rows a uniform height, select cells that span those rows, and then select Table → Distribute Rows Evenly. All rows take on the height of the tallest row.

Distribute Columns Evenly

This command is the same as the previous item but evens out column widths. To make columns a uniform width, select cells that span those columns, and then select Table → Distribute Columns Evenly. All columns take on the width of the widest column.

AutoFit to Contents

This command eliminates extra space within columns and shrinks them so they're only wide enough to contain their contents.

Convert

Use this command to convert text into a table or table into text. To learn how, turn to page 98.

Fill

This option lets you copy content from one cell into adjacent cell(s), without the hassle of cutting and pasting (see Figure A-9). To use it, click in the cell that you want to duplicate. Drag across the cell(s) that you want to fill with content (these must be to the right or below the cell in question) and select Table → Fill. Within the submenu that appears, click either Right or Down, whichever direction you'd like to fill cells. You can also select a column or row and duplicate it in the same manner.

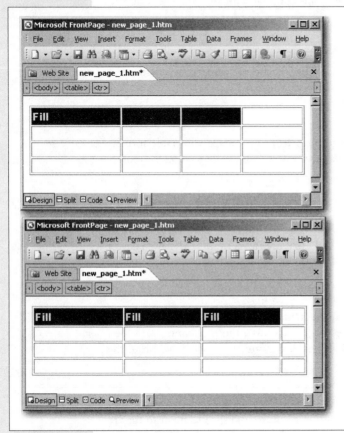

Figure A-9:
Select a cell you want to duplicate, along with the empty target cells (top). After you select Table → Fill, the target cells display the same content as the initial cell (bottom). Cell formatting copies over too.

Table Properties

This option opens a submenu that lets you access Table Properties, Cell Properties, or Caption Properties. As with other items on the table menu, the Properties dialog box that opens belongs to the table or cell that your cursor rests in.

Data Menu

The items on this menu are grayed out unless you're working on a server featuring Windows SharePoint Services. Because SharePoint sites can be edited and configured through a browser without help from FrontPage, this book covers them only cursorily. For more information on how SharePoint works, check out these books: *Essential SharePoint* by Jeff Webb (O'Reilly), *Advanced SharePoint Services Solutions* by Scott P. Hillier (Apress), and *Windows SharePoint Services Inside Out* by Jim Buyens (Microsoft Press).

Frames Menu

The Frames menu offers commands to help you configure framed Web pages. To find out what these are and how to use them, see Chapter 6. If you're not working with frames, FrontPage grays out these options.

Split Frame

This command is the only way to add a new frame to a frameset. Place your cursor in a frame and select Frames → Split Frame. FrontPage creates two frames where there was previously one.

Delete Frame

Select this option, and FrontPage removes whatever frame your cursor sits in.

Open Page in New Window

If you're editing pages within a frameset, you can use this command to open one of them all by itself in the document window. Doing so lets you see more of the page as you edit.

Save Page

If you're editing framed pages within the frameset and you use FrontPage's regular Save feature (Ctrl+S), FrontPage saves the frameset, not the page you've edited. With your cursor still in the page, select Frames → Save Page to save a framed page instead of the frameset.

Save Page As

Again, when you're editing pages through the frameset page, place your cursor on a page and select this option to save the page as a new page. This command is a handy way to create new framed pages to display in the same frame. See the box on page 112.

Frame Properties

Select this option to access the properties of the frame you're working in. The Frame Properties dialog box that appears lets you resize the frame, rename it, or change the initial page. See "Modifying Frames" on page 109.

Window Menu

The Window menu's main function is to help you switch between open documents, though clicking tabs within the document window is faster and easier. You can also use this menu to open a page or a site in a new instance of FrontPage (see Figure A-10).

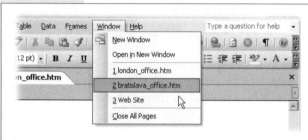

Figure A-10:
The Window menu displays all open documents. Select one to display it in the document window.

New Window

This command opens your Web site in a new instance of FrontPage. There's no real reason to use this command, since it's easy to switch between different views of your site and pages within a single instance of FrontPage.

Open in New Window

This option opens the Web page (along with the site) you have open in a new instance of FrontPage. This means you can edit in two screens at once if you want to. Changes you make in one window are reflected immediately in the other window.

Close All Pages

If you have a lot of pages open, this command is a great shortcut to close them all at once rather than one by one. After you select this option, FrontPage prompts you to save changes in unsaved pages.

Tip: If you want to save all your changes, use another similar menu item in combination with Close All Pages to make a fast exit. First, select File → Save All. Then select Window → Close All Pages.

Help Menu

You'll find a modicum of help here on this menu, along with a lot of URL hyperlinks to Microsoft Web sites and information about your installation of FrontPage.

Microsoft Office FrontPage Help

This command displays the Help task pane, where you can search for (often terse and incomplete) answers to your FrontPage questions. Many of these options also link to URLs on the Microsoft Web site, where you can get further assistance and downloads. Obviously, you'll need to be connected to the Internet for those menu items to work correctly.

Show the Office Assistant

If you're looking for relatively useless companionship, this is the option for you. Select it and you'll see Clippit, the Microsoft Office assistant, who'll hang out in the upper right of your screen, pretend to tap on your monitor glass, and occasionally offer an annoying suggestion. Click once on the assistant and you can enter a question for the Help system (though you may as well enter it in the Help task pane, accessed via the previous menu item).

Microsoft Office Online

This command launches your system's main browser and opens Microsoft's Office Online Web site where you can read about Office and FrontPage.

Microsoft FrontPage Developer Resources

This option launches your system's browser and opens Microsoft's Web Developer Resources Web page.

Contact Us

Select Help → Contact Us to display a window containing Microsoft's support Web site URL and telephone numbers.

Check for Updates

If you select this option, your browser displays Microsoft's Downloads page, which includes a feature that can scan your computer and provide the appropriate FrontPage bug-fixing downloads.

Detect and Repair

FrontPage relies on many files to function correctly. If another function (or wayward colleague) has compromised or deleted one of these files, Detect and Repair can get FrontPage back on its feet. To repair your FrontPage installation, this process may prompt you to insert your FrontPage or Microsoft Office installation CD.

Activate Product

In a bid to fight software piracy, Microsoft has added a new step to its software installation procedures. In addition to installing your copy of FrontPage, you've got to activate it over the phone or on the Web, so Microsoft can verify your product key isn't being installed on a thousand computers when you bought only one license. If you install FrontPage but don't activate it, the program works fine during a short grace period, after which you can't access essential features, and work on your Web site grinds to a halt.

Customer Feedback Options

This command opens the Service Options dialog box. Here you can choose to participate in (or excuse yourself from) Microsoft's Customer Experience Improvement Program, whereby Microsoft tracks your actions and errors. The company uses this information to improve their software products. If it's all too "big brother" for you, just click "No, I don't wish to participate." Use the "online content" link on the left side of this dialog box to control options that let FrontPage connect to Microsoft support sites when you're using the program's Help features.

About Microsoft Office FrontPage

If somebody asks you "What version of FrontPage are you using?" and you don't know the answer, you can select this menu option. It displays the About Microsoft Office FrontPage dialog box, which shows the exact program version along with licensing information.

Index

Colophon

Mary Brady was the production editor, and Linley Dolby was the copyeditor for *FrontPage 2003: The Missing Manual*. Mary Brady proofread the book. Genevieve d'Entremont and Claire Cloutier provided quality control. Johnna VanHoose Dinse wrote the index.

Ellie Volckhausen designed the cover of this book, based on a series design by David Freedman. Karen Montgomery produced the cover layout with Adobe InDesign CS using Adobe's Minion and Gill Sans fonts.

David Futato designed the interior layout, based on a series design by Phil Simpson. This book was converted by Keith Fahlgren to FrameMaker 5.5.6 with a format conversion tool created by Erik Ray, Jason McIntosh, Neil Walls, and Mike Sierra that uses Perl and XML technologies. The text font is Adobe Minion; the heading font is Adobe Formata Condensed; and the code font is LucasFont's TheSans Mono Condensed. The illustrations that appear in the book were produced by Robert Romano, Jessamyn Read, and Lesley Borash using Macromedia FreeHand MX and Adobe Photoshop CS.

Better than e-books

Buy *FrontPage 2003: The Missing Manual* and access the digital edition FREE on Safari for 45 days.

Go to www.oreilly.com/go/safarienabled
and type in coupon code KUAU-J94B-VZNA-44BA-7C25

Search thousands of top tech books

Download whole chapters

Cut and Paste code examples

Find answers fast

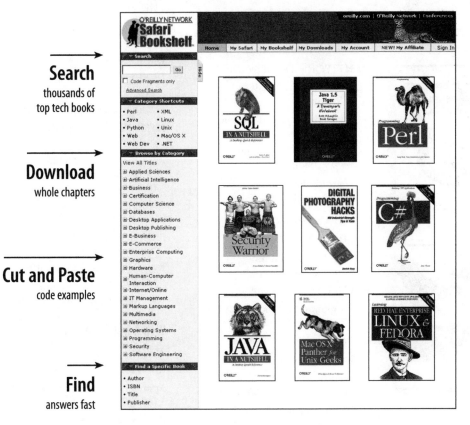

Search Safari! The premier electronic reference library for programmers and IT professionals.

Related Titles from O'Reilly

Web Programming

ActionScript Cookbook

ActionScript for Flash MX: The Definitive Guide, *2nd Edition*

Dynamic HTML: The Definitive Reference, *2nd Edition*

Flash Hacks

Essential PHP Security

Google Hacks, *2nd Edition*

Google Pocket Guide

HTTP: The Definitive Guide

JavaScript & DHTML Cookbook

JavaScript Pocket Reference, *2nd Edition*

JavaScript: The Definitive Guide, *4th Edition*

Learning PHP 5

PayPal Hacks

PHP Cookbook

PHP in a Nutshell

PHP Pocket Reference, *2nd Edition*

PHPUnit Pocket Guide

Programming ColdFusion MX, *2nd Edition*

Programming PHP

Upgrading to PHP 5

Web Database Applications with PHP and MySQL, *2nd Edition*

Webmaster in a Nutshell, *3rd Edition*

Web Authoring and Design

Cascading Style Sheets: The Definitive Guide, *2nd Edition*

CSS Cookbook

CSS Pocket Reference, *2nd Edition*

Dreamweaver MX 2004: The Missing Manual, *2nd Edition*

Essential ActionScript 2.0

Flash Out of the Box

Head First HTML & CSS

HTML & XHTML: The Definitive Guide, *5th Edition*

HTML Pocket Reference, *2nd Edition*

Information Architecture for the World Wide Web, *2nd Edition*

Learning Web Design, *2nd Edition*

Programming Flash Communication Server

Web Design in a Nutshell, *3rd Edition*

Web Site Measurement Hacks

Web Administration

Apache Cookbook

Apache Pocket Reference

Apache: The Definitive Guide, *3rd Edition*

Perl for Web Site Management

Squid: The Definitive Guide

Web Performance Tuning, *2nd Edition*

Keep in touch with O'Reilly

Download examples from our books

To find example files from a book, go to: *www.oreilly.com/catalog* select the book, and follow the "Examples" link.

Register your O'Reilly books

Register your book at *register.oreilly.com* Why register your books? Once you've registered your O'Reilly books you can:

- Win O'Reilly books, T-shirts or discount coupons in our monthly drawing.
- Get special offers available only to registered O'Reilly customers.
- Get catalogs announcing new books (US and UK only).
- Get email notification of new editions of the O'Reilly books you own.

Join our email lists

Sign up to get topic-specific email announcements of new books and conferences, special offers, and O'Reilly Network technology newsletters at:

elists.oreilly.com

It's easy to customize your free elists subscription so you'll get exactly the O'Reilly news you want.

Get the latest news, tips, and tools

www.oreilly.com

- "Top 100 Sites on the Web"—PC Magazine
- CIO Magazine's Web Business 50 Awards

Our web site contains a library of comprehensive product information (including book excerpts and tables of contents), downloadable software, background articles, interviews with technology leaders, links to relevant sites, book cover art, and more.

Work for O'Reilly

Check out our web site for current employment opportunities:

jobs.oreilly.com

Contact us

O'Reilly Media, Inc.
1005 Gravenstein Hwy North
Sebastopol, CA 95472 USA
Tel: 707-827-7000 or 800-998-9938
　　　 (6am to 5pm PST)
Fax: 707-829-0104

Contact us by email

For answers to problems regarding your order or our products: **order@oreilly.com**

To request a copy of our latest catalog: **catalog@oreilly.com**

For book content technical questions or corrections: **booktech@oreilly.com**

For educational, library, government, and corporate sales: **corporate@oreilly.com**

To submit new book proposals to our editors and product managers: **proposals@oreilly.com**

For information about our international distributors or translation queries: **international@oreilly.com**

For information about academic use of O'Reilly books: **adoption@oreilly.com** or visit: *academic.oreilly.com*

For a list of our distributors outside of North America check out: *international.oreilly.com/distributors.html*

Order a book online

www.oreilly.com/order_new